Arnold B. Come is emeritus professor of systematic theology and president of the San Francisco Theological Seminary.

D0075098

KIERKEGAARD AS THEOLOGIAN
Recovering My Self

In his later writings Søren Kierkegaard sought to "get further forward in the direction of discovering the Christianity of the New Testament" to resolve his own spiritual crisis. *Kierkegaard as Theologian* explores his deliberately Christian writings, from *Upbuilding Discourses in Various Spirits* (1846) to *For Self-Examination* (1851).

Arnold Come's appraisal of Kierkegaard's struggle to understand how authentic theologizing relates to the spiritual struggles of personal faith leads him to a discussion of the three basic foci of Kierkegaard's theologizing: the self as gift, that is, a creation "out of nothing" from God; the self as failure, which brings on a state of despair; and the self redeemed by God's love and healing compassion.

Come probes some of the problematic aspects of Kierkegaard's theology. He addresses the question of theodicy: do God's high intentions and demands for human achievement of selfhood and spirituality justify the unspeakable sufferings entailed in human failures to fulfil those demands? He also explores the puzzling relation between Kierkegaard's seeming assignment of exclusivity to the Christian understanding and experiences of both sin and salvation and his assumption of the capacity of humans to recognize the need to turn to the eternal that is immanent in every human consciousness – so-called Religiousness A.

ARNOLD COME is professor emeritus of systematic theology and president of the San Francisco Theological Seminary.

McGill-Queen's Studies in the History of Ideas

KIERKEGAARD AS THEOLOGIAN
Recovering My Self

Arnold B. Come

McGill-Queen's University Press
Montreal & Kingston · London · Buffalo

© McGill-Queen's University Press 1997
ISBN 0-7735-1023-0
Legal deposit fourth quarter 1997
Bibliothèque nationale du Québec

Printed in Canada on acid-free paper

McGill-Queen's University Press acknowledges the support
received for its publishing program from the
Canada Council's Block Grants program.

Canadian Cataloguing in Publication Data

Come, Arnold B. (Arnold Bruce), 1918–
Kierkegaard as theologian: recovering my self
(McGill-Queen's studies in the history of ideas: 24)
Includes bibliographical references and index.
ISBN 0-7735-1023-0
1. Kierkegaard, Søren, 1813–1855.   2. Self (Philosophy).
3. Christianity – Philosophy.   4. Theodicy.
I. Title.   II. Series.
B4378.C5C65 1997   230'.01   C97-900472-1

This book was typeset by Typo Litho Composition Inc.
in 10/12 Baskerville.

Dedicated to
Maude McAllister Come
My Mother in the Faith
and
Otto A. Piper
My Father in the Faith

Contents

Preface

For those who are reading this volume without benefit of the previous one on *Kierkegaard as Humanist*, I offer both a word of warning and a word of encouragement. The two volumes were originally conceived of as one continuous treatment of Kierkegaard's concept of the self. But as the first two topics of a five point outline consumed five hundred pages for their explication, a break had to be made. And Kierkegaard himself suggested one in his distinction between "the human self" and "the theological self" (KW 19:79). But since he rigorously observes his basic thesis that "a system of existence cannot be given" (KW 12.1:109), it is impossible to divide his thinking and writing neatly under these two topics. So the reader of this volume will find frequent reference to materials in the first volume, and most of what this second volume offers about the topic of human failure and despair is obviously relevant for a comprehension of the purely humanist self.

So, ideally, the two volumes should be read as one. And it is important to do so if one is interested to see if and how Kierkegaard's theology goes beyond, adds to, and perhaps at certain points transforms his purely humanist understanding of the self. One early reader of the manuscript of volume one commented that if one grants much of the capacity of Christian loving to humanity in general, one has to wonder what is left that is essential and unique to a Christian view of self. This question has haunted me throughout the writing of this present volume. And I have tried to be honest in seeking an answer and in being faithful to what Kierkegaard actually says himself. I would couch my own answer somewhat differently from where Kierkegaard ended up on this issue, and I have suggested a critique of his position at a number of points along the way and especially in the concluding chapter.

Nevertheless, I would encourage readers of this present volume to take it on its own, as a serious effort to explore what is essential and distinctive in the Christian experience and vision of ultimate truth for every human being – of course, from Kierkegaard's own peculiar perspective. If one is a *seeker* of what he calls "the way" to God and to one's "eternal blessedness," then one may find this volume to be a helpful aid. If one is already at some stage of being a *follower* of this way, then I invite her or him to use this account of Kierkegaard as Christian theologian to challenge, to test, and perhaps to enlighten and strengthen one's own understanding of and commitment to the truth of that "way" that alone is the life of ultimate "eternal blessedness."

As in volume one, here too my main aim is to let Kierkegaard speak for himself, and hence not to drown or muffle his voice and vision in debate with other philosophers/theologians, or in discussion of his views with other interpreters of Kierkegaard. As in volume one, there are a few exceptions here also; for example: with Louis Mackey in chapter 1, with Karl Barth in chapter 2, with Freud in chapter 3, and with C.S. Evans, M.J. Ferreira, D.J. Gouwens and E.F. Mooney in chapter 4, and with Paul Sponheim in the Postlude. I should also note that the title, "Kierkegaard as Theologian," has been used before, namely, by Louis Dupré (but not with my subtitle, of course). But in his original Dutch publication it was called *Kierkegaard's Theologie.* The latter title is a more accurate indication of the book's contents. In fact, it might even be called "A Kierkegaardian Theology," since Dupré is also defining his own position vis-à-vis Kierkegaard, and enters into complicated discussions of Kierkegaard's positions in relation to those of both medieval and modern Catholicism (his own religious orientation) and to those of Luther and orthodox Lutheranism. Dupré's book, written in the early 1950s, is still well worth reading, and I note several basic agreements between his interpretation and mine (as well as several disparities).

Now allow me to make a couple of personal notes.

The dedication to Otto Piper may mystify most. Who is he? During my years of study at Princeton Theological Seminary (1939–46), there were few voices among the faculty that stimulated me with new and exciting insights. The two notable ones that did, however, were both exiles from Hitler's Europe: Joseph Hromadka from Czechoslovakia and Otto Piper from Germany. It was Otto Piper who led me into the hidden interior depths of the Biblical literature as the locale of the self-revelation of God. And he did it with that same baffling and irritating indirection that puts off so many readers of Kierkegaard. In other words, he did not assume the power to give or impart the faith directly and immediately. He hung the truth out there in the "middle distance" between us and forced me to reach out and *appropriate* it for my self. I had been baptized and confirmed in the faith by the church. I was raised in the faith, with total indirection and unconsciousness, by my Scotch-Irish Presbyterian mother, Maude Fanny McAllister-Come. But I had grown up under the preaching of a social-gospel minister, and I had attended a totally secular land-grant college, with majors in history and English literature. So I arrived at theological seminary still fighting the insistent notion that I was "called" to the ministry, and the Christian faith was for me still largely an intellectual matter. But with the help of Otto Piper, I had made the "leap" *into* faith by the time I finished my doctoral studies.

During those years, however, another strange voice spoke to me. I was introduced to the person and the thought of Søren Kierkegaard by a brief reference in a lecture by the seminary president, another European from Scotland, John Mackay. Years later, when coming to teach in another theological seminary (on the West Coast), I began to offer a seminar on Kierkegaard, and did so yearly for twenty-five years. But it has only been in retirement that I have had the time and the sense of leisure to explore the depth and complexity of his thoughts at length. Now with this publication I come to the end of that fourteen-year odyssey under the Kierkegaardian firmament. And, although I now turn to other projects, everything I do will bear the stamp of and will be intimately informed by the mind and spirit of Søren Aabye Kierkegaard.

I have had significant companions during this long journey. And I do not wish to come to its close without having recalled their helpfulness and memorialized their names in this only appropriate place. At the very beginning, in the autumn of 1982 and within the hallowed precincts of Cambridge University, Paul Sponheim was kind enough to go over the first embryonic outline of my project and to share with me the wisdom of his own experience with and enthusiasm for the mind and spirit of Kierkegaard. A few years later, on my first serious visit to Copenhagen, my friend, the Rev. Bent Hansen, introduced me to several members of the Kierkegaard establishment. And so on this trip and succeeding ones, Niels Jørgen Cappelørn, Paul Muller, Julia Watkin, and Poul Lübcke showed great generosity in sharing their time and insights for the benefit of my studies. On that first occasion, Howard Hong appeared in the Kierkegaard Library, reviewed my emerging outline, and made many helpful suggestions. Then back home in North America, I early on visited Montreal and became acquainted with the work of Alastair McKinnon, who soon became my running correspondent and telephone companion concerning numerous problems of research, and was instrumental in introducing the manuscript of my first volume to the editor of McGill-Queen's University Press. And in my own neighborhood (the San Francisco Bay area), I must mention my friend, Malcolm McAfee, who was the first one to insist on reading the messy draft of volume one and proceed to encourage me with good insights and great enthusiasm.

I must also express my profound gratitude for the confidant and unfailing support of the editor of these volumes. I was quite overwhelmed by the quick judgment of Philip Cercone, executive director of McGill-Queen's, that my treatment of *Kierkegaard as Humanist* was eminently worthy of being included in the Press's distinguished *Studies in the History of Ideas* – even though he put it through a rather long and arduous (and very beneficial) process of critique and revision. And several years later, I was even more grateful for his enthusiastic acceptance of *Kierkegaard as Theologian*. At the work-a-day level of seeing the manuscripts through their final preparation and production at McGill-Queen's, I wish to express my appreciation for the cheerful and expert help of Joan McGilvray as coordinating editor, and for the very precise and detailed work of Judy Williams and Carol Sippy as copy-editors. I also wish to thank Roy Carlisle, my editorial consultant, for all his encouragement and expert advice throughout the whole process.

In connection with the appearance of this volume, as with the first, it is with profound warmth of spirit and heartfelt gratitude that I record here the names of those dear friends, and former colleagues on the Board of Trustees of San Francisco Theological Seminary, who affirm the value of my many years of work on Kierkegaard by supporting the publication of scholarly works by McGill-Queen's University Press. As with the first volume, Jim Johnson, Dorothy and Leslie Dobbins, and Jane and James Bryson again participated with alacrity and enthusiasm, and they were joined this time by Jane Newhall with an especially generous gift.

Finally, there are the totally inexpressible feelings of gratitude I have toward members of my own immediate family. My beloved wife, Elizabeth McClure Come, has been not only my cheerful companion along this lengthy journey but also the inspiration for some of the deeper insights in my study of the human self – for which I have given evidence in the text itself of *Kierkegaard as Humanist* (pp. 170–72). My son Bruce Come, while earning his living as a computer programmer, is a covert student of history and an amateur but insightful analyzer of human motivations, and he was always ready to listen and to evaluate as I tried out my latest ideas about the human self. And my son Lee McClure Come, who is a composer of new and important music, along with his wife, Suzanne Kaufman, who is a creative photographer, have always been willing to read a page or two of manuscript and then enter into a spirited critique and debate.

Arnold B. Come
San Francisco Theological Seminary, San Anselmo, California
Graduate Theological Union, Berkeley, California

Note on Notes

References to S.K.'s collected works include (in this order): (a) page number(s) in the older English translation; (b) in parenthesis, the volume and page number(s) for the same reference in *Kierkegaard's Writings* if published (Howard V. Hong and Edna H. Hong, editors, Princeton University Press, publisher); in volumes of KW that appear after the publication of this book, references may be found by using the page reference of the first edition of SV [item (d) below] which are marked in the margins of the volumes of KW; (c) the volume and page number(s) for the same reference in the third edition of *Søren Kierkegaard: Samlede Værker* (abbreviated as SV), edited by Peter P. Rhode and published by Glydendal, Copenhagen, 1962; (d) in parenthesis, the volume and page number(s) for the same reference in the first edition of *Samlede Værker*, edited by A.B. Drachmann, J.L. Heiberg and H.O. Lange and published in Copenhagen 1901–1906.

References to *Søren Kierkegaards Papirer* include (in this order): (a) the entry number (1–6969) for the English translation as (and if) contained in Søren *Kierkegaard's Journals and Papers* (abbreviated *Journals*), vols. 1-7, edited and translated by Howard V. Hong and Edna H. Hong (Bloomington: Indiana University Press, 1967–78); (b) the standard reference to the same item in the Second Enlarged Edition of *Papirer*, edited by Niels Thulstrup and published in Copenhagen by Glydendal, 1968, consisting of twenty-two volumes or part-volumes of papers, plus three volumes of index compiled by Niels Jørgen Cappelørn. Roman numerals designate the volume; superscript Arabic numbers designate a part-volume; "A" designates an entry in Kierkegaard's personal diary or journal, "B" designates either an early draft of a passage in a published work or a draft of an unpublished work, and "C" designates notes from lectures or readings, or miscellaneous comments of Kierkegaard on various topics. The final Arabic number is the number assigned to each item by the editors (in chronological order within each group – A, B, or C).

KIERKEGAARD AS THEOLOGIAN

Recovering My Self

Kierkegaard: A Peculiar Kind of Theologian

Louis Mackey contends that "Kierkegaard is not a philosopher and theologian who puts up poetic advertisements to recommend his product. ... [H]e is a poet whose orientation is primarily philosophical and theological."[1] He insists that, in this interpretation, he is simply taking Kierkegaard "quite literally and quite simply when he described himself as 'a peculiar [*egen*] kind of poet and thinker who ... would read the fundamental document [*Urskrift*] of the individual, human existence-relationship, the old, well-known, handed down from the fathers.'"[2]

It is the contention of this present study that Kierkegaard is primarily a theologian (of a very peculiar kind) who indeed is also a poet, but that his being a poet is precisely in the service of his being a theologian. As Sylvia Walsh puts it, "Kierkegaard was a religious and philosophical thinker who possessed a touch of the poet."[3] Kierkegaard's linguistic

1. Louis Mackey, *Kierkegaard: A Kind of Poet*, pp. 259, ix.

2. Ibid., p. xi. This is a quotation from the Foreword to *Two Discourses at the Communion on Fridays*, sv 17:27 (12:267), written in December 1849. The first phrase of the quotation is picked up by Kierkegaard from a journal entry of the previous year (6227; IX A 213), and the latter phrase is, as Kierkegaard indicates, a quotation from the concluding sentences of *Concluding Unscientific Postscript*, that is, from "A First and Last Declaration" appended to *Postscript.*

3. Sylvia Walsh, *Living Poetically: Kierkegaard's Existential Aesthetics*, p. 1. At last someone has given us a thorough and expert overview of and guide to this much neglected subject. Her first seven chapters are a masterful summary of every facet of this important aspect of Kierkegaard's thought and life. Then chapter 8 and the Epilogue relate all of it succinctly to Kierkegaard's major religious/theological positions and to several recent currents of thought. By the time it was available, the present volume faced a deadline and could not take account of it in a thorough way. But it will be referred to at a few points in what follows.

theory is too complicated even to summarize here, but a few of his comments on his being a poet must be looked at in order to clarify in what
sense he is a theologian.

First, it must be noted that when Kierkegaard says he is a poet, he almost always adds, "and thinker [*Tænker*]." This term is his equivalent for
"theologian." Just as he writes "discourses" and not "sermons" because
he is "without authority" of ordination, so he uses "thinker" to indicate
that he is "a theologian but not appointed."[4] And he sees the two functions (poet and thinker) as distinct and interactive. So he says, "I cannot
repeat enough what I so frequently have said: I am a poet but of a quite
peculiar (*egen*) kind, because the dialectical is the determinate-nature of
my very being, and as a rule dialectic is precisely what is alien to the
poet."[5] And what dialectic does he have in mind? Mackey says, "his dialectic is a dialectic of images ... rather than a dialectic of concepts in the
abstract."[6] Actually, it is neither. Kierkegaard's dialectic is the dialectic
that is inherent in existing as a human being: the tension between being
finite and being infinite, between being temporal and yet oriented toward the eternal, between being possibility and becoming actuality. And
this given dialectic of universal human nature is qualitatively intensified
for him when it is apprehended from the perspective of the dialectic
(paradox) of the presence of the eternal in time. Of course, in analyzing
and depicting this dialectic of existence, he uses both the dialectic of
images and the dialectic of concepts because he is both a poet and a
thinker.

So the "peculiar" character of his being a poet lies in the requirement
of his being also, and primarily, a thinker for the task of explicating the
essentially "Christian." He says, "If I had not been brought up strictly
in Christianity, ... I would have become a poet. ... But I do not want to
be a poet [as described in *Either/Or*]. ... What is it to be a poet? It is to
have one's own personal life, one's actuality, in categories completely
different from those of one's poetical production." Later the same year
(1849), while reflecting on the prodigious writings of the previous year
as "the most valuable I have produced," Kierkegaard says that he must
accept one humiliation as an author, namely,

4. *Journals*, 667; x¹ A 136. Admittedly, this is only an indirect reference to himself, but
he clearly is thinking about what *he* would say, and what impact it would have, if he were to
preach in the church which he attended.

5. Ibid., 6227; IX A 213.

6. Louis Mackey, 1971, p. xii.

I may not venture myself to express in actuality that which I present and according to the criteria I set forth, as if I myself were the ideal. Here I am obliged to admit to being predominantly a poet and thinker. ... It is now clear to me ... how God has led me to this task: to illuminate Christianity, to depict the ideal of [what it means to be] a Christian. ... I have ventured much farther out than a poet usually does. This too was necessary in order to accomplish the task: Christianity, the ideal for being a Christian. ... So all my enthusiastic discourse about the ideal of being a Christian will resound with the sigh: Alas, I am not that, I am only a Christian poet and thinker.[7]

Kierkegaard repeats these ideas later in the same year but with a significant modification. In the writings of "the most intensive, the richest time I have experienced" (1848), he says, "I understood myself to be what I must call a poet of the religious." And, "that I am a 'poet' expresses that I do not confuse myself with the ideality." But he adds the qualification: "not however that my very own life should express the opposite – no, I strive continually." Thus, "My task was to cast the uniquely-Christian into reflection, not poetically to idealize (for the essentially-Christian, after all, is itself the ideal) but with poetic fervor to present the total ideality according to its most ideal norm – always ending with: I am not that, but I *strive*. If the latter does not prove correct and is not true about *me*, then everything is cast in intellectual form and falls short"[8] (emphasis added). In other words, when Kierkegaard repeatedly says, "I am not that," he does not mean (as so often asserted) that he is not a Christian in any sense. Rather, he means that he has not attained the ideal. Yet, as every other Christian who deserves the name, he is *striving*.[9]

7. *Journals*, 6300, 6391; x[1] a 11, 281. Also cf. 6718; x[3] a 789; in this late entry of 1851 he says, "I am a poet. But long before I became a poet I was intended for [the life of] religious individuality. And the event whereby I became a poet was an ethical break or a teleological suspension of the ethical. And both of these things make me want to be something more than 'the poet'." And in his second "note" on "The Individual" appended to his *Point of View*, he traces how he moved beyond being a poet into the ethical/religious category. He concludes, "This movement from 'the poet' to religious existence is fundamentally the movement in my entire work as an author, considered as a whole." *The Point of View for My Work as an Author*, pp. 131f.; sv 18:164; (13:605f.).

8. *Journals*, 6511; x[2] a 106.

9. So from 1848 onward, Kierkegaard increasingly emphasizes that there is a radical distinction between the poetic/reflective illumination of what is essentially Christian and, on the other hand, the *striving* to enact and to become the ideal in actuality, within the conditions of the concrete "situation." So in a journal entry of that year (about his projected "New Discourses on the Lilies and the Birds") he says, "In these discourses there will be a

The point, however, in which we are interested is this: he is clear that his calling and task as an author (which he has received through God's governance) is not to be a "witness to the truth" through trying to be and to enact in his life the Christian ideal. His task as an author – which has consumed his whole life's energies – is to be precisely "a poet and a thinker." In our previous study of Kierkegaard as Humanist (at the end of chapter 1) it was clearly recognized that he does consciously operate as a poet, that all of Kierkegaard's thinking about the self is "subjective reflection" and finds expression always in figures and images. Or as Louis Mackey puts it so well, "His writing, even the most ostensibly theoretical, is not syllogistic but figural." So we also agree with Mackey that Kierkegaard's aim as thinker is not to produce a system of ideas nor to capture the truth in rationally coherent concepts. Rather, he resorts to the "indirect communication" of metaphors and analogies which, in Mackey's words, "challenge the will to the ethical activity of realization."[10] His aim is spiritual edification (upbuilding). In other words, "figural" language creates space and time (a gap) in which the hearer must make up one's own mind and appropriate the truth in and for action.

---

development of the conflict between poetry and Christianity, how in a certain sense Christianity in comparison with poetry ... is prose. ... Of course the lilies and the birds, that is, the sketching of nature, will this time have an even more poetic tone and richness of color, simply to indicate that the poetic must be put aside" (*Journals*, 1942; VIII[1] A 643). And when he comes to write those discourses the following year (1849) he comments (in the opening pages) on how a purely poetic interpretation of Jesus' words totally misses the point. "The poet," he says, "cannot come to an understanding with the Gospel. For at bottom the poet's life is despair of being able to become the thing he wishes. ... The poet is the child of eternity, but he lacks the seriousness of eternity." *(Christian Discourses*, pp. 319f.; SV 14:132f.;[11:11f.].) After his sense of personal forgiveness and transformation during Easter week of 1848, he feels this contradiction very personally: "I now am in faith, in the deepest sense. ... As poet and thinker I have presented everything in the medium of imagination. *Now* life draws nearer to me, or I draw nearer to myself, come to myself. – For God all things are possible. This thought is now in the deepest sense my watchword" (*Journals*, 6135; VIII[1] A 650; emphasis added). And in journals entries from 1848 to 1854 he explores "the infinite difference which exists between understanding something in possibility and understanding the same in actuality" (3345, 3346; X[2] A 114, 202). And he makes this point especially by emphasizing repeatedly the crucial significance of "the situation": "It is situation, especially catastrophe, which discloses to what degree a person's protestations are the truth within him, are [his personal] character" (see *Journals*, 4314, X[2] A 608; 4326, X[1] A 417; 4354, XI[1] A 558; 4623, 4626, IX A 349, 407; 4933, 4934, X[3] A 470, 471).

10. Louis Mackey, 1971, pp. 259, 289.

Nevertheless, Kierkegaard distinguishes between his work as thinker and as poet. The conceptual content of his thoughts possesses for him a substantive importance which alone imparts ultimate significance to his passionate concern for its poetic expression and thus for the mode (the "how") of its subjective appropriation by an other. As we have seen (in note 9 above), he insists that it is only the Gospel that imparts true meaning ("seriousness") to the "poetic" words of Jesus about how we must become like the lilies and birds. Likewise, in a postscript to his discourse entitled "Has a Human-being the Right to Let Himself Be Put to Death for the Truth?" (attributed to H.H.), he makes this point even more directly. He says that the piece is indeed a "poetic experiment – but, be it observed, by a thinker," and so he does not give any details about the author's life. "Just because *qua* poet I have plenary poetic power, I will in this respect say nothing, lest by talking in a novelistic fashion I might perhaps say something which would divert attention from the essential thing, the thought-content."[11]

In fact, in this critical year (1848), he even began to see that "the maieutic [*det Maieutiske*]" used in "indirect communication" has its limits for a Christian.[12] So even though a poetic maieutic must be used in every human relationship where one person tries to help another person to grasp the eternal truth of the spirit, yet Kierkegaard becomes more deeply convinced that his being a "thinker" (as well as "a poet") plays an important, even an indispensable, role in the fulfillment of his "task," namely, "to illuminate Christianity, to depict the ideal of [what it means to be] a Christian." Just after asserting that Christians must finally be witnesses by proclaiming the revelation in Christ, he says, "But on the other hand, reason [*Forstand*], reflection is also a gift of God" which one

11. For a translation see, *The Present Age and Two Minor Ethico-Religious Treatises*, translated by Alexander Dru and Walter Lowrie, pp. 134f.; SV 15:48; (11:91).

12. In a series of journal entries he comes to see that the decision finally to publish *The Crisis and a Crisis in the Life of an Actress* served to convince him that in the future "it will be indefensible to use [indirect communication] ... lest the awakening effect end by being confusing. The thing to do now is ... to step forth definitely and directly in character, as one who has wanted and wants to serve the cause of Christianity." (*Journals*, 6231; IX A 218; see also 6209, 6211, 6212, 6213; IX A 175, 178, 179, 180) So he says, "The communication of the essentially-Christian must end finally in 'witnessing.' The maieutic cannot be the final form, because, Christianly understood, the truth does not lie in the subject ... but in a revelation which must be proclaimed. ... The one who uses the maieutic must become a witness." And he protests that he himself has already participated in witnessing because "all my upbuilding discourses are in fact in the form of direct communication." (Ibid., 1957, 6234; IX A 221, 222)

must use. "And if one uses it in fear and trembling not for one's own advantage but to serve the truth, ... believing that it still is God who determines the issue in its eternal significance, ... is this not fear of God and serving God the way a person of reflection can."[13] And he insists, "I am a thinker, a prodigiously passionate thinker," who must submit to being considered mad by the populace "simply to be allowed to think. Otherwise I must disguise it [i.e., being a thinker], I must clink glasses and chat in every gathering [in order to be] loved and honored by all those who do not think."[14]

Perhaps the clearest example of Kierkegaard's own defense of his use of reason and reflection, of the formation of concepts and even definitions, in his commitment to the task of illuminating and depicting the essentially Christian, is to be found in his journal entry entitled, "Report about The Sickness unto Death."[15] He says, "This book has one difficulty; it is too dialectical and stringent in order to use properly the rhetorical [i.e., the poetic], the awakening, the gripping." He admits that the title is "lyrical" and suggests a book of discourses. And he gives an outline of the topics that he would have used if he had written it in the form of discourses. But, he says, "The fact is that before I really can begin using the rhetorical, I always must have the dialectical thoroughly fluent, must have gone through it many times. That was not the case here." Furthermore, he concludes, "The task is much too great for a rhetorical treatment, since in that case every single figure would have to be depicted poetically. The algebra of the dialectical works better."[16] And in the text of *Sickness* he points out a specific example of what he means by "algebra" as a general definition in place of a figurative depiction. He has defined sin as: "before God in despair not to will to be oneself, or before God in despair to will to be oneself." Then he says, "The definition embraces every imaginable and every actual form of sin. ... As a definition it is algebra; for me to begin to describe particular sins in this little book would be out of place. ... The main point here is simply that the definition, like a net, embraces all forms."[17]

13. Ibid., 6234; IX A 222, which directly follows 1957; IX A 221, in the *Papirer*.
14. *Papirer*, IX A 161 (not in Hong's English edition).
15. *Journals*, 6136, 6137; VIII¹ A 651, 652.
16. The word translated "algebra" is *Bogstavregning* which literally means "literal-workingout," that is (in this case), the literal working-out that is characteristic of dialectical thinking. But it also connotes an abstract formula that covers all specific cases.
17. *Sickness*, pp. 212f.; (KW 19:81f.); SV 15:135f.; (11:193f.).

In other words, Kierkegaard highly valued and was greatly excited by his discovery of ideas and concepts which "define" what Christianity is all about. And he was particularly thrilled with what had come to him in the writing of *Sickness*, even before it was published. "Here I am allowed to present Christianity once again and in such a way that a whole development can be based on it. ... All the papers [in *Sickness* and *Practice in Christianity*] contain such a rich abundance of ideas that again and again I cannot praise God enough. ... I am convinced that it will serve for the inward deepening [*Inderliggjørelse*: interiorization, intensification] of Christianity." And again he says that in *Sickness* "it was granted to me to illuminate Christianity on a scale greater than I had ever dreamed possible; crucial categories are directly disclosed there."[18] So Mackey misses Kierkegaard's point when he says, "Whatever philosophy or theology there is in Kierkegaard is sacramentally transmitted 'in, with, and under' the poetry."[19] Kierkegaard is insisting that the very "ideas" and "categories" that were discovered or came to light in *Sickness* will be effective for the "illumination" and "inward deepening" of Christian faith, and that they will accomplish this in their form of algebraic definitions without being submitted to a "rhetorical treatment" by being "depicted poetically."

So, although his categories, ideas, and concepts are "figural" (see at note 10 above) in the sense that they are not themselves the truth (in their abstract generalized form) but point to the truth (in living human existence), nevertheless, they help to specify the content of the truth in a way that pure poetry never can. When Kierkegaard says that he is a *passionate* thinker, we suggest that he has in mind this peculiar role of concepts serving as "figures." As figures (images), concepts (categories, ideas) participate in the shaping, deepening, securing of faith, because the concepts define and clarify ("illumine") some condition or event in the life of a unique particular self in (faith) relationship with God. In this role the concepts acquire passion and seriousness and thereby help in the emergence of conviction and courage in the self for the task of acting and living in accord with one's new understanding. And note, this new insight requires the interplay among all the active elements: the concept, the self-conscious deciding self, and the situation which calls for action. Thus a concept loses its abstractness, disinterestedness, and universality, leaving room and setting the stage for the free leap of decision by the

18. *Journals*, 6238, IX A 227; 6361, X[1] A 147. These are entries of 1848 and 1849, and they indicate that *Sickness* had not yet been published.

19. Louis Mackey, 1971, p. ix.

conscious responsible self. If Mackey wishes to call this figural function of concepts "poetry," he may. But this is not what Kierkegaard means by "poetic depiction," because the concepts function in an illuminating way in their form of "the algebra of the dialectical."

THE DISTINCTIVENESS OF THEOLOGY

With this line of thought Kierkegaard must have confronted the central question about the discipline that is called "theology." What is the relationship between, on the one hand, the figurative language of the rhetorical/poetic with its unique comprehension of and power to communicate the truth, and on the other hand, the definitional language of the dialectical/conceptual with its particular kind of comprehension and formulation of the truth? How does the first-order expressive language (and its content) of the "poet of the religious" relate to the second-order reflective language (and its content) of the "passionate thinker?" Does each require and is each dependent on the other? Can religious (Christian) faith get along quite well with just *one* of the two, and exclude the other? Is one really primary and the other secondary? Is it true that faith can exist without theology, but that theology cannot exist without faith? Is theology, then, nothing more than *fides quærens intellectum* (Anselm), producing an "understanding of faith" which serves only as a secondary and non-essential pursuit for the amusement of the intellectually curious, or for the use of authoritarians to root out and persecute heretics? Or can the rational, conceptual, definitional reflection of theology also broaden, deepen, heighten and thereby enrich, strengthen, and actually secure faith itself, and therefore be seen as integral to and a function of faith? Or to pose the issue from a different perspective and in more recent conceptuality, is faith simply and essentially a language event, or is faith a relational state (between God and the individual) which involves and employs and calls into play all dimensions of human being (sensual, emotive, intuitive, rational, volitional, active, personal, social)? If the latter, then does not language (in both its poetic and conceptual forms) comprise an integral factor or dimension of the dynamic of that relational state? Kierkegaard is certainly aware of the basic issues at stake in these questions. How then does he answer them? Paul Sponheim says that "one lacks the material for a solid affirmative answer."[20] Let us see what we can find.

20. Paul Sponheim, *Kierkegaard on Christ and Christian Coherence*, p. 244.

Kierkegaard was clear about a fundamental difference between philosophy and theology (dogmatics) from early on, while still in university. Philosophy has as its basis "the purely human view of the world, the *human* standpoint," whereas "Christian dogmatics, it seems to me, must grow out of Christ's activity, ... because Christ did not establish any doctrine; he acted." So, "from a purely human point of view the secret of all knowledge is to concentrate upon what is given in immediacy; in faith we assume something that is not given and that can never be deduced from the preceding consciousness." Hence he argues that "universal human existence does not explain Christianity, ... but Christianity explains the world."[21] This conviction developed with his own personal growth in faith until it received its definitive statement at the beginning of part 2 of *The Sickness unto Death*. There he says, "The previously considered gradation in the consciousness of the self is within the determinant: the *human self*, or the self whose criterion is the human. But this self takes on a new quality or qualification by being a self directly before God. This self is no longer the merely human self but is what I, hoping not to be misunderstood, would call the *theological self*, the self directly before God. And what infinite reality [*Realitet*] the self gains by being conscious of existing before God, by becoming a human self whose criterion is God!"[22] (emphasis added) So Kierkegaard undertakes the role of theologian in order to define a human self "theologically." We have seen the "peculiar" sense in which Kierkegaard is a poet. What then is the peculiar sense in which he is a theologian?

Kierkegaard warns that he does not want to be "misunderstood" (*misforstaaet*) in this role because he had a very negative view of the theology and the theologians of his day. This view finds expression in the hyperboles of the last years of his life. In May of 1854 he says, "In all Christendom today there is not one single ... clergyman, professor, teacher ... who does not avail himself of the counterfeit expansion of Christianity. ... It is nothing but a perfidious and hypocritical or scatterbrained and stupid adulteration." And a few weeks before he died, he is recounting once more that "to be a Christian ... is suffering from beginning to end," which means "to get rid of this world." Then he confides to his journal that he knows that the day will come when these thoughts (his) will be

---

21. *Journals*, 3253, II A 77; 412, I A 27; 1100, III A 39; 3276, II A 517.

22. *The Sickness unto Death*, p. 210; (KW 19:79); SV 15:133; (11:191). For the sentence about "infinite reality," Lowrie (in his translation) weakly conflates the Danish to read, "What an infinite reality this self acquires by being before God!" (Lowrie, 1954)

"declared to be the loftiest of wisdom," and by whom? By "assistant professors – those animal-creatures. ... If any class of men deserves to be
called animals in comparison with the rest of us, it is professors and
preachers."[23]

Why this negative view? He puts it very simply (in both *Postscript* and
Practice in Christianity) by pointing out that there were no theological
professors when Christianity came into the world. Now, he says, they
have taken over and control Christianity by "explaining" it, that is, by
turning faith into reasonable ideas, thus eliminating the paradox and
"smuggling Christianity out of the world" by removing the possibility of
offense.[24] The result is that theology has been turned into philosophy
and hence "in our time it is necessary for the theologian to be a philosopher."[25] So imagine the apostle Paul being examined in theology by a
theological professor: "of course he is rejected."[26]

Kierkegaard's primary objection to theology which has become "speculative philosophy" or a "scholarly science" is this: it turns Christianity
into a set of doctrines, and faith becomes belief in certain concepts or
ideas. His objections to this view of faith, and to the correlative nature
and role of theology, appear in his earliest journal entries and are ech-
oed and developed throughout his writings to the very end. In the midst
of his university days (October 17, 1835), he tells his journal that "*philosophy and Christianity can never be united*, for I am going to hold fast to
what is most essential in Christianity – namely, redemption. ... The
yawning abyss is *here* where Christianity posits human cognition as defec-
tive on account of sin, which is rectified in Christianity. ... To be sure the
philosopher can arrive at the idea of human sin, but it does not follow
that he knows that the human being needs redemption, ... which ...
must be left to God."[27] And thirteen years later at the pinnacle of his
specifically Christian authorship, Kierkegaard repeats this same point
in *Sickness*. "Through a curious misunderstanding, a so-called speculative dogmatics, which was involved with philosophy in a dubious way,
thought it could *comprehend* [*begribe*] this stipulation that sin is a position.

23. *Journals*, 3336, XI¹ A 156; 1940, XI² A 434.
24. See *Postscript*, p. 198; (KW 12.1:220f.); SV 9:184; (7:185); *Practice*, p. 104; SV 16:103;
(12:97). See entries under "faith" in the index of *Kierkegaard as Humanist.*
25. *Forord*, SV 5:238f.; (5:53f.). Kierkegaard attributes the quotation to "philosophy's
priest," by whom he means J.L. Heiberg, who had written an article entitled "A Speculative
Theology Is an Inescapable Requirement."
26. *Journals*, 3195; X¹ A 401.
27. Ibid., 3245; I A 94.

But if this is true, then sin is a negation. ... I steadfastly hold to the Christian teaching that sin is a position – yet not as if it could be comprehended, but as a paradox that must be believed."[28]

This objection to "speculative dogmatics," however, is made even more specifically in *Postscript* where Climacus is enlarging his interpretation of what he had laid out in *Fragments*. He is agreeing that it is possible and even desirable that an investigation be made as to what Christianity is so as to clarify what its essential principles or determinants are. But, he protests, this must not be done in a "learned" or "partisan" manner "under the presupposition that Christianity is a philosophical doctrine." This procedure would be in error because it assumes that as "a phase [*Moment*] within speculative thought" Christianity can be transformed into "a doctrine to be understood [*forstaae*]." On the contrary, "Christianity is not a doctrine, but expresses an existence-contradiction and is an existence-communication. ... Existence and existing are precisely the opposite of speculation. ... It is one thing to have a philosophical doctrine which is meant to be comprehended [*begribes*] and speculatively understood [*forstaaes*], quite another thing to have a doctrine which is meant to be realized in existence." In the latter case, "understanding" the doctrine consists in "understanding that the task is to exist in it, understanding how difficult it is to exist in it, what a tremendous existence-task this doctrine sets for the learner. ... To speculate upon it is a misunderstanding." So Kierkegaard prefers "to call Christianity an existence-communication," because to call it a "doctrine" immediately gives the impression that it is "a philosophical doctrine which demands to be understood."[29] The latter trend means that "dogmatics as a whole is a misunderstanding, especially as it now has turned out." Therefore, "A new science must be introduced: a Christian rhetoric." This new "Christian eloquence will be ... concerned only with *improbability*, with showing that it [Christianity] is improbable, in order that one can then *believe* it."[30]

Thus Kierkegaard is not recommending that we do away with all theology (in the sense of the formulation of doctrines or concepts for the

---

28. *Sickness*, pp. 227, 229; (KW 19:97f.); SV 15:149f.; (11:207ff.). For those unfamiliar with the distinction between Kierkegaard's first and second (Christian) authorships, see *Kierkegaard as Humanist*, pp. 191–200 and, in this present volume, the section entitled "Kierkegaard's Own Personal 'Being in Faith'" at the end of this chapter.

29. *Postscript*, pp. 331, 336–339; (KW 12.1:370–301, 377–379); SV 10:67, 73–76; (7:321, 326–29).

30. *Journals*, 627, 628; VI A 17, 19.

illumination of what it means to be a Christian), but this theologizing
must be done in such a way that it is clear that the doctrinal concepts are
not the substance and content of faith. Kierkegaard insists that this point
was clear in what he often calls "the older dogmatics." He speaks fondly
of "those old theological works by an authentic spiritual guide" in contrast to the "theological knowledge" of doctors of theology of his day with
their "pious bosh on Sundays" and their "dissertation nonsense" at the
university.[31] Throughout *The Concept of Angst* he speaks positively of dogmatics in contrast with Hegelian philosophy which confuses ethics and
dogmatics and identifies innocence with immediacy. And in response to
Schelling's explorations of God's "moods," he comments, "How strange
everything becomes when metaphysics and dogmatics are distorted by
treating dogmatics metaphysically and metaphysics dogmatically."[32] And
the same view carries over into *Sickness* where he speaks of the "later [or
speculative] dogmatics" which has lost "understanding" and "sensitivity"
for the idea of sin as "before God," in contrast with the "older [or ortho-
dox] dogmatics" which always contended that sin was a "position" rather
than a "negation," indeed, a position "before God."[33]

THE OBJECTIVE SOURCE OF THEOLOGY

So how does one develop a dogmatics that is not metaphysics?[34] How
does this new "Christian rhetoric" (which is an "existence-communication") come into being so that it is qualitatively different from philosophy? From our study of Kierkegaard as Humanist, it should be
abundantly clear that he did not disdain philosophy as such. Rather, he
stood in awe of a figure such as Socrates who could come to so profound
a comprehension of human existence on the basis of "the merely human self" that he considered Socrates to be but one step away from the
uniquely Christian theological understanding. He came to be stimu-

31. Ibid., 4778; VIII[1] A 433.

32. *The Concept of Angst*, pp. 11, 32, 53n.; (KW 8:12, 35, 59n.); SV 6:111, 130, 151n.;
(4:284, 307, 329f.n.). Also throughout the Introduction and several places in the main
text.

33. *Sickness*, pp. 211, 227f.; (KW 19:80, 96f.); SV 15:133f., 148f.; (11:192, 207f.).

34. Here we leave aside the question of whether there is such a thing as a Christian
(theological) philosophy. But in the next three chapters we will occasionally ask whether
Kierkegaard's so-called theology is indeed a qualitative step beyond his humanist philosophy, or whether his purported philosophy is so infused and informed by his Christian faith
as to be a clandestine theology.

lated by and to borrow from Aristotle in innumerable ways. He openly acknowledged the startling clarifications and illuminations that came to him from reading Trendelenburg. And, although he was filled with horror at the System produced by Hegel and the Hegelians, the simple fact is that he learned as much from Hegel as he rejected, so much so that his own corpus of writings (as they stand) would have been impossible and inconceivable without Hegel as his teacher and his foil. What then, for Kierkegaard, are the unique source, methodology, and content that distinguish theological thinking and understanding from philosophy? A full answer and its exposition will come only in the next three chapters, but a preliminary treatment of the issues is required to clarify if, and in what sense, Kierkegaard's writings are theological.

On the question of the source or ground of Christian thinking and understanding (theology), Kierkegaard accepted the basic thesis of the traditional Christian doctrine of a special revelation of God in the Judeo-Christian religious experience, centered and fulfilled in the incarnation, in the historical event of the appearance of the God-man, Jesus as the Christ.[35] Of course, he develops his own particular interpretation of each of the key terms in this doctrine, and some of his basic perspectives found expression in early journal entries while he was still

35. He had been reading and hearing lectures on dogmatics throughout his university days, long before he actually enrolled in the Pastoral Seminary in the fall of 1840. A good account of these studies is to be found in the numerous entries on H.N. Clausen, H.L. Martensen and P.K. Marheineke in Niels Thulstrup's *Kierkegaard's Relation to Hegel* (1980). Kierkegaard took or obtained extensive notes on Martensen's "Lectures concerning 'Speculative Dogmatics'" during the year 1838–39, and in them we find a very careful account of the incarnation in fairly traditional terms: "The Christian idea of God's appearance is contained in the dogma of the incarnation or the doctrine of God's real *historical* becoming-human in Christ. In this becoming-human the dualism between God and creation is factually canceled, since divine nature has thus united with human nature, so that God is revealed not simply *by means of* or *in* but *as* the historical personality. The dogma of incarnation thus excludes the heathen consideration of revelation." And later: "Since the dogmatic [factor] in Christendom is inseparable from the historical, whose midpoint is the fact of the incarnation, there must exist concerning this fact an infallible historical and religious testimony, without which no historical church would be possible. This infallible and original testimony concerning Christ is preserved in the holy Scripture. In the dogma of its inspiration it is asserted that this testimony is not simply from the human but singularly from the Spirit." (*Papirer*, XIII, pp. 28, 40) He found a less conventional (Hegelian) and more sophisticated interpretation in the writings of the German theologian, Marheineke, and when in Berlin 1841–42, he took extensive notes of his lectures, including twenty-three pages on Christology (*Papirer*, XIII, pp. 219–242; see especially pp. 224f., 228 on incarnation). In seeking a resolution to the contrasts between the views of Martensen and Marheineke, Kierkegaard found his own particular insights and formulations.

in university. We have heard him say that "Christian dogmatics ... must grow out of Christ's activity," and he goes on to say that through this activity "his nature was also given; Christ's relationship to God, human nature, human state *was conditioned by his activity.*"[36] In other words, what is revealed in the coming of God in human form is not a concept or doctrine to be grasped with the mind and accepted as true; rather, revelation occurs as an event in which I am involved in my total being in an activity in the life of Jesus as the Christ. As Kierkegaard says in this same entry, "Christ *did not teach* that there was redemption for human beings, but *he redeemed human beings.*" Redemption is not an idea, it is an event, and only in and through participation in this event is an understanding of God and human nature "given" (revealed).

Kierkegaard makes this point explicitly in a couple of other entries a few years later. "Revelation," he says, "contains not only something which human beings have not given themselves, but something which has never occurred to the mind of any human being even as a wish, an ideal, or anything else."[37] So the "assurance of forgiveness of sins" is neither "given" nor "comes about (*fremgaar*)" by "being deduced from a preceding consciousness," that is, "by way of an internal consequence." Rather, "consciousness of the forgiveness of sin is linked to an external event, Christ's full appearance, which indeed is not external to us in the sense of being foreign to us or of no concern to us, but external as *historical.*"[38] So the source of (Christian) theology is qualitatively different from general or universal human experience and knowledge that are "given in immediacy," that is, are open to be explored by any human being at every time and place. Theology is indeed "internal" to us as something subjectively appropriated, but this process of appropriation is dependent on a relationship to something that is not only "external" to us but that is further delimited as a unique particular event in space and time, and so is "historical."

The importance of this point about the source of theology cannot be exaggerated for the understanding of Kierkegaard's total conceptuality. The implied epistemology is fundamental to and pervasive of his characterization of truth and being, as they come to be known both philosophically and theologically (and, he would add, scientifically). Throughout his writings and journals he increasingly emphasizes the role of the em-

---

36. *Journals*, 412; I A 27.
37. Ibid., 3276; II A 517.
38. Ibid., 1100; III A 39.

pirical and the contingent (*Tilfældighed*) in all experience, the indispensable and crucial function of specific enactment in the concrete
"situation" for the realization and the understanding of the spiritual, intentional, free self.[39] After the completion of his major works (1849), he
declares that there is a qualitative difference between understanding
something in possibility and imagination and understanding the same
thing in action and actuality.[40] And twenty years after saying that "Christian dogmatics ... must grow out Christ's activity, and ... Christ did not
establish any doctrine; ... he acted," he further confides to his journal,
"The Christian thesis goes not: *intelligere ut credam*, nor *credere ut intelligam*.
No, it goes: *Act* according to the commands and orders of Christ; *do* the
Father's will – and you will become a believing-one" (emphasis added).[41]
The interplay of one's inner essential self with the brute facts of one's en-
tire finitude (including one's own body and the contingent conditions

39. Ibid., 4314, x^4 A 608; 4326, x^1 A 417; 4354, xi^1 A 558; 4623, 4626, IX A 439, 407; 4933, 4934, x^3 A 470, 471.

40. Ibid., 3345, 3346, x^2 A 114, 202; 4326, x^1 A 417; 4933, x^3 A 470.

41. Ibid., 3023; xi^1 A 339 (1854). This emphasis on "act" in the "situation" in entries from the years 1834 and 1854 is an excellent illustration of what Kierkegaard meant when he praised Trendelenburg for providing him with "the apparatus for what I had thought out years before" and thereby making everything "much more lucid and clear to me" (*Journals*, 5977, viii^2 C 1; 5978, viii^1 A 18). In my monograph, *Trendelenburg's Influence on Kierkegaard's Modal Categories* (Inter Editions, Montreal, 1991), in a section entitled "On the Empirical," I compare Kierkegaard and Trendelenburg on the role of act in finite conditions of existence. Since then, I have run across and read a book by Gershon George Rosenstock, *F.A. Trendelenburg: Forerunner to John Dewey*. His first two chapters (100 pages) provide an excellent account of Trendelenburg's work and thought. He makes a convincing case that Trendelenburg's Aristotelian organismic system was a creative anticipation of twentieth-century philosophic naturalism, and more particularly, that his "Naturalistic Epistemology" can be accurately described in twentieth-century pragmatic terms as operationalism or functionalism: we learn and define what a thing is from the way it functions or operates in the finite, contingent, factual sphere, and no thing exists in and of itself but only in dependence on and as conditioned by the relations in which it stands to all other things. In his section on "A Naturalistic Epistemology" Rosenstock gives many revealing quotations from Trendelenburg's major work, *Logische Untersuchungen* (with the German original in endnotes), and they contain many interesting parallels to Kierkegaard's language. For example, behind Kierkegaard's language about act and situation (quoted above at note 36), it is easy to imagine his taking note of Trendelenburg's words, "A thing can only be completely understood in the way in which it comes into being (*selbst ensteht*)," and "What a thing does is judged from its concept," or as Rosenstock interprets these words, "The nature of a substance must be understood in terms of its manifest determinable operations." (Rosenstock, pp. 89f., and for the German, pp. 155f.) But as I argue in the section in my monograph, Kierkegaard comes to a different view of human self (spirit), its identity, its psychology, and most importantly, its freedom and responsibility (the leap).

and situation in which one is called to act) is the mode of being in which one becomes oneself and reveals oneself, to oneself and to others. (We will see how this epistemology works itself out in Kierkegaard's Christology; see entries under "Christology" in index.)

This perspective on the source of theology is picked up by Kierkegaard, and given its formal position and statement for the total authorship, in *Postscript*'s fundamental distinction between religiousness A and religiousness B. In A one "finds the God-relationship within oneself," in B one "relates to something outside oneself." So "in immanence [religiousness A] God is neither a something, but is all and infinitely all, nor outside the individual, because upbuilding consists precisely in the fact that [God] is in the individual." On the other hand, "the paradoxical-upbuilding [religiousness B] corresponds to the determinant of God-in-time as an individual human being, because when such is the case, the individual relates to a something outside himself."[42]

And this objective character of the source of theology carries with it an objectivity in content. "Religiousness A is the dialectic of interiorization [*Inderliggjørelse*]; it is the relationship to an eternal blessedness which is not conditioned by something [else], but is the dialectical interiorization of the relationship, and so is conditioned only by the interiorization, which is dialectical." In contrast, religiousness B operates by the "paradoxical dialectic" in face of the "absurdity" of the eternal-within-time. So "religiousness B ... has conditions in such a way that the conditions are not [merely] the dialectical deepening of the interiorization, but are a definite something which more closely determines [defines, identifies] the eternal blessedness, not because it defines more closely the individual's appropriation of it, but more closely defines the eternal blessedness itself (whereas in A the only closer definition is the closer definition of interiorization)."[43] We will come to a specification of this closer definition of eternal blessedness a little later (under topic of "Subjective Transformation of Self").

This interpretation of the source of theology was then given a restatement (by Kierkegaard) in more traditional Christian terms at the very beginning of his second (theological) authorship. While writing *Upbuilding Discourses in Various Spirits* (in 1846) and *Works of Love* (in 1847), he

---

42. *Postscript*, p. 498; (KW 12.1:561); SV 10:229f.; (7:489).

43. Ibid., p. 494; SV 10:225; (7:485). For a fulsome exposition of religiousness A see my previous volume on *Kierkegaard as Humanist*, chapter 6, the section entitled, "The Leap as Transition from the Ethical to the Religious."

was also composing his (largely) unpublished work *The Book on Adler*.[44] The work has been generally ignored, in spite of Walter Lowrie's judgment that "it reveals his intimate thoughts so clearly"; in fact, he says, "Nothing but his *Journals* reveal him more clearly."[45] In it we find some remarkably direct statements on both the source and the methodology of Christian theology. That he was conscious of entering into direct debate with the doctrinal positions of the church of his day is evidenced in his first preface to the work, where he says, "Essentially this book can be read only by theologians," and they should see that Adler "is used to throw light upon the age and to defend dogmatic concepts."[46]

The central dogmatic concept on which Kierkegaard concentrates is that of revelation. His extensive (225–page) analysis of the case of Adler is basically motivated not by his desire to attack the church (at this time) but by his own personal need to clarify the grounds and the meaning of his sense of being called by God as an *extraordinarius* to produce a wholly new (post *Postscript*) authorship which would explore and expound the sphere of religiousness B, that is, the peculiarly Christian faith experience. So in

---

44. It is generally assumed that the major reason Kierkegaard did not publish this work at the time it was written was that it contained a clear and vicious "attack" on the theology and the church of his day, an attack which he was not ready to make publicly, an attack he was sure to make later and which would end his life. In his several prefaces to this work, Kierkegaard made clear that his primary intent was to take Adler simply as "a phenomenon" and so proposed that he might call the book *The Religious Confusion of the Present Age*. In that preface he states explicitly, "The whole book is essentially an ethical investigation of the concept of revelation; ... about the confusion from which the concept of revelation suffers in our confused age" (see Walter Lowrie's essay on the prefaces in the preface to *On Authority and Revelation: The Book on Adler*. For quotation, see *Papirer*, VIII² 27, p. 76). He also expressed reluctance to attack Adler himself openly, because he felt that the latter had been badly treated by the church when it ridiculed him and deposed him from its ministry. So in the last section of the book, he says that Adler is an "epigram of Christendom of our day" in the sense that "as a pagan [i.e., a Hegelian philosopher] he became a Christian priest, and just when he had come somewhat nearer to being a Christian, he was deposed" (*On Authority and Revelation*, p. 178; *Papirer*, VII² B 235, p. 218f.).

A.P. Adler was a country pastor in Denmark who published a book of sermons in 1843, and in the preface claimed to base his sermons on a direct "revelation." Kierkegaard, in a letter to his brother Peter on June 29, 1843, takes note of the book of sermons and comments that Adler "is a phenomenon worth paying attention to" (see KW 25:156, Letter 83). In 1846 Adler published four more books which Kierkegaard immediately bought (July 12) and studied assiduously for some months before starting to write about them. He used this experience as an occasion to clarify his own views of revelation and his own sense of having an "extraordinary" calling from God. (see Lowrie's preface to *On Authority*, pp. ixff.)

45. Preface to *On Authority and Revelation* (1955), p. vii.

46. Ibid., p.xv; *Papirer* VII² B 269, 270.

the opening pages he notes, "By his fact-of-revelation, by his new doctrine, by standing under the direct outpouring of the Spirit, Magister Adler might easily become aware of being placed as a particular or peculiar individual [*særlig Enkelt*] altogether outside the universal, altogether *extra ordinem* as *extraordinarius*."[47]

Kierkegaard first seeks to establish the essential character of what properly can claim to be a revelation in the Biblical-Christian sense. He puts it simply: revelation is a paradoxical event, and it cannot be proved or made plausible by factual or rational evidence and argument. "This paradoxical fact (offence of the understanding, object of faith) does not become more true after eighteen hundred years than it was the day it happened. The [fact] that the eternal once came into existence in time is not a truth which must be tested in time, not something which must be *tested by human beings*, but is the paradox *by which human beings must be tested.* ... And the paradox itself did not last throughout many years; it existed when Christ lived, and since that time it exists only each time someone [either] is offended or in truth believes." Encounter with this paradox requires each individual to make "a qualitative essential decision."[48] In a footnote Kierkegaard refers his readers to the fuller treatment of this theme in *Fragments* and *Postscript*.[49]

But now in *The Book on Adler* he addresses his argument directly to those who claim to be Christians, rather than to those who are interested in religion in general. He specifically takes to task the Biblical exegesis and Christian dogmatics of his day for submitting to the method of speculative (Hegelian) philosophy and thus seeking to comprehend and explain revelation, reducing revelation to a set of "plausible" doctrines or concepts and thereby abolishing the paradoxical. Rather, he recommends that they "go through their curriculum in the situation of contemporaneity [with Jesus as the Christ]."[50] So he also takes Adler to task when the latter (under pressure from church leaders) backs off from his original claim to have talked with Jesus and received a revelation, and now adopts the position that he preaches only what is in the Bible. Adler says that by his quoting "words of the Scripture as proof-texts, it must be evident to what Gospel and to what revelations I hold and have taught others to hold." But, Kierkegaard says, "One must immediately ask Adler

---

47. Ibid., pp. 20f.; VII² B 235, pp. 31f.

48. Ibid., pp. 57f.; VII² B 235, pp. 75f.

49. On revelation, see particularly *Postscript*, pp. 191f., 219f.; (KW 12.1:213f., 245f.); SV 9:178f., 204f.; (7:179f., 206f.).

50. *On Authority and Revelation*, pp. 64, 102; *Papirer* VII² B 235, pp. 85, 136.

how he comes to use the words of Scripture as evidence."[51] In other words, the basic issue is that of authority. What is the particular source, and therefore the peculiar authority of what Christianity calls "revelation"?

Kierkegaard gets at this issue in *The Book on Adler* by expositing "the difference between a genius and an apostle" (which he rewrote as a separate essay under that title, with all references to Adler excised, but did not publish until May of 1849). We are not persuaded, he says, that the apostle Paul speaks with divine authority because of the beauty of his metaphors, the power of his analogies, or the logic of his arguments. We do not have independent criteria by which we can judge the form and content of his doctrines to be eternally true (divine). No miracle of healing, even the raising of the dead, can be taken as undeniable proof. The words of Scripture acquire their true authority only when we are convinced that "it is God himself or our Lord Jesus Christ who speaks." This means that "authority is a specific quality which comes from-another-place and qualitatively validates itself." This place is "the sphere of the paradoxical-religious and of faith," in which all approaches and methods of immanence are shattered and absolute transcendence asserts itself.[52] The point he seeks to make is that to encounter divine authority (the authority of God or the eternal) is qualitatively different from our encounter with every other kind of authority. Therefore, the concept formation (theology) which derives from, or takes place in relationship to, this authority has a different status and function than all other concept formation (philosophy, science, technology). And the mode or methodology by or in which this authority asserts itself and becomes operative in the minds and hearts and lives of human beings is qualitatively different from the methodology of every other kind of authority. It is difficult (Kierkegaard would say impossible) to characterize this authority as the objective source of theology without getting involved with the methodology (what he calls the "way" [*Maade*]) in which it comes to be known and acknowledged (i.e., faith). But at least a tentative look at some of the terms or concepts which Kierkegaard uses to refer to this authority will help to clarify what he calls the "objective" source of theology.

51. Ibid., pp. 76–80; B 235, pp. 104–110; the first quotation is from p. 78; p. 105; the second quotation is omitted from the translation and is from B 235, p. 108.

52. Ibid., pp. 107–111; B 235, pp. 140–144. The quotations are from pp. 108, 110, 111; B 235 pp. 141, 143, 144.

In *The Book on Adler* he uses just once a key Christological term and then provides a formula to interpret it, both of which are to have growing significance for him throughout the rest of his writings. The term is God-humanbeing (*Gud-Menneske*)[53], and he applies it strictly and exclusively to the particular individual, Jesus. He had heard it expounded and explained at length in lectures and readings on theology during both his university days and his first trip to Berlin. Now when he comes to use it for himself he strongly rejects the interpretation of D.F. Strauss (in *Das Leben Jesu*) which he had come to know both in readings and lectures.[54] According to Strauss (he read in Schaller) "the actuality [of the

53. Although it is awkward, we will use "humanbeing" instead of the usual "man" because, as we will now see, Kierkegaard strongly rejects the notion of Jesus Christ as the unity of two generalized impersonal "natures," that is, of "the divine" and "the human." Rather, Jesus is a unique individual human being in and with whom the living God has come to dwell in a unique but not clearly definable unity. Furthermore, the Danish *Menneske* is the term for that humanity which is held as common by both man (male) and woman (female); in contrast to English, Danish conveniently has the term *Mand* to indicate the male human being. But Kierkegaard never speaks of the *Gud-Mand*, although he slips once (in *Practice in Christianity*) and speaks of Christ as "true God and [true] man (*Mand*)," but then twice corrects himself later in the same work when he refers to Christ as "true human-being (*Menneske*)" (*Practice*, pp. 160, 181, 197; SV 16:155, 174, 189; [12:149, 169, 186]). The Augsburg Confession (in Danish) could not be the source of this one use of *Mand*, because when it asserts that "there is one Christ, true God and true man" (from the Definition of Chalcedon adopted by the fourth ecumenical council in 451 A.D.), it uses *Menneske*. But it is interesting to note that a number of Christmas hymns (in Danish), which Kierkegaard must have heard and sung, use *Mand* when they paraphrase the Chalcedonian formula. For example, in the hymn "From Heaven There Came an Angel Clear," the third stanza says, "Because one has become God and man / So now he your brother is" (originally composed by Luther but rewritten by Grundtvig in 1837). And in "Lo, How the Rose Lies Blooming," we hear, "In truth man and God / He helped us out of pain of sin." And in other hymns, Grundtvig often used the term *Frelsermand* (Savior-man). This usage in hymns may explain why Kierkegaard slips once and uses *Mand*, but I think that he self-consciously corrects that usage, and (I hope) deliberately uses *Menneske* to stress that Jesus Christ was an individual human-being like all the rest of us, males *and* females. It should also be noted that the translation of *Menneske* as "human-being" instead of "man" preserves the distinction Greek makes between ανθρωπος (human-being) and ανηρ (man), which is important for interpretation of Paul's central Christological statement that Jesus Christ was "born in the likeness of human-beings (ὁμοιωματι ανθρωπων)" (Phil 2:7) (and in the Danish translation of this passage *Mennesker* is used for ανθρωπων).

54. Kierkegaard apparently did not read Strauss' own book, but in 1838 he read and took copious notes from Julius Schaller's *Der historische Christus und die Philosophie* in which Schaller summarizes and critiques Strauss's position, but in the end Schaller's Hegelianism put Kierkegaard off (see Niels Thulstrup, *Kierkegaard's Relation to Hegel*, pp. 157–163; for his notes, see *Papirer* XIII, II C 54, pp. 157–172, and especially pp. 167–169 on Strauss). In 1842–43 Kierkegaard heard the lectures of Philip Marheineke in Berlin and again heard a

God-man] in no way exists in the particular historical person; but in the nature of humankind. The essential Christian doctrine is that all human beings now participate in the God-humanity of the particular person (Christ)."[55] Kierkegaard replies (in *The Book on Adler*) with a formula for which he became famous (through Karl Barth), "*Between God and the human-being there is an eternal essential qualitative difference*, which no one ... can allow to vanish in the blasphemous assertion that ... in eternity the difference must vanish in the essential equality, so that God and the human-being become equals." And this means that "Christ as the God-humanbeing is in possession of the specific quality of authority which no eternity can compromise or place Christ on the same level as essential human equality."[56]

Hegelian critique of Strauss's views (see his notes in *Papirer* XIII, III c 26, pp. 197–252, especially pp. 227–229 on "Christ is the Middlepoint of World-history" and on his view of Strauss).

55. This is Schaller's summary of Strauss' position as found in Kierkegaard's notes, *Papirer* XIII, II c 54, p. 168.

56. *On Authority and Revelation*, pp. 112, 114; *Papirer* VII^2 B 235, pp. 145, 147. This formula is picked up and reformulated about a year and a half later in the more familiar passage in *Sickness* where he says, "God and human-being are two qualities, between which there is an infinite qualitative difference [or literally, difference-of-quality: *en uendelig Qvalitets-Forskjel*]. ... In paganism the human-being made God [a] human-being (Human-being-God); in Christianity God makes himself human-being (God-humanbeing)." (p. 257; [KW 19:126]; SV 15:175; [11:235]) The language of *Sickness* seems to reflect more the perspective of the two-nature doctrine. But just after using the formula a second time he says, "Out of love, God becomes human-being. [God] says: Here you see what it is to be [a] human-being; but he adds: Take care, for I am also God. ... As human-being [God] takes the form of a lowly servant. ... He says, ... The Father and I are one, and yet I am this particular (*enkelte*), insignificant human-being, poor, forsaken, surrendered to humanity's violence." (pp. 258f.; [KW 19:127f.]; SV 15:176f.; [11:237]) Furthermore, Kierkegaard consistently uses here the singular, personal "human-being" (*Menneske*) rather than the collective, impersonal "humanity" (conveyed in the Danish by the plural, *Menneskene*) which was readily available to him. In the same passage (p. 259; [KW 19:128]; SV 15:177; [11:238]) he uses the collective when he says, "Without a bodyguard and servants to prepare the way for him and make humanity (*Menneskene*) aware of who it was who was coming, Christ walked on the earth in the form of a lowly servant." And just a few pages previously he says, "Sin, however common it is to all, does not gather humanity together in a common idea, into an association, ... instead, it splits humanity up into single individuals." (p. 251; [KW 19:120]; SV 15:170; [11:230]) Kierkegaard also continues to use the formula God-humanbeing in *Practice* (see pp. 131, 139; [KW XX:131, 140]; SV 16:128, 135; [12:123, 130]). In the second passage Kierkegaard also speaks of "The yawning abyss between the single individual (*Enkelte*) and the God-humanbeing, over which only faith reaches."

The point Kierkegaard is making through the assertion of the "qualita-tive difference" between God and the human being (and therefore be-tween Jesus as the God-humanbeing and every other human being) is that Jesus' authority (in what he said/did, in the entirety of his life) is not any kind of *human* authority, not that of the greatest genius or the most powerful king or the supreme general. As human, Jesus indeed does share in "the essential human equality," and as such he is strictly an *individual* (*enkelte*) human being, suffering and being tempted and tried like every other human being. In coming to act and be revealed in time, in human existence, God (the eternal) does not appropriate impersonal, generalized, abstract "human nature"; God relates to (unites with) the complete humanity of a unique individual human being. So, although Jesus is an ordinary human being, his authority is not his own but issues from a source that is "qualitatively different." It is important to stress that Kierkegaard holds to this view of Jesus as the Christ throughout the entirety of the second (theological) authorship. Only so (he believes) can the *divine* authority of Jesus' life (as God-humanbeing) assert and maintain itself. Only so does Christian revelation manifest itself in the sit-uation of the absolute paradox and the methodology of faith for its ap-propriation, and thus makes the "possibility of offense" inevitable and inescapable.

A few examples of this view of Jesus' humanity should serve to estab-lish this position. While he was completing *The Book on Adler*, Kierkeg-aard was also writing *Works of Love*. He is arguing that the need for loving companionship is grounded as an essential component in every human being. And then offers this as evidence:

Even he who was one with the Father, and in the communion of love with the Father and the Spirit, he who loved the whole race, our Lord Jesus Christ, even he felt the human need to love and to be loved by an individual human being. Truly he is the God-humanbeing and thus eternally different from every human-being, but he nevertheless was also a true human-being and tested in everything human. The fact that he experienced this [need] is precisely the sign that it is inherent in the human-being. He was an actual human-being and therefore could participate in everything human, ... participate in a purely hu-man way.[57]

---

57. *Works of Love*, p. 154; (KW 16:155); SV 12:150f.; (9:148).

A year later Kierkegaard makes his point in the very direct language of *Practice in Christianity*.[58] In Part 2 entitled "Blessed Is the One Who Is Not Offended at Me," the term God-humanbeing appears on almost every page. And in the introductory "brief summary" of the essay, he provides an explicit definition. He says that the "situation" which is inherent to the phenomenon "God-humanbeing" is this: "a particular (*enkelt*) human being who is standing beside you is the God-humanbeing." This means that "the God-humanbeing is not a unity of God and humanbeing [humanity as such]; such terminology is a profound optical illusion. The God-humanbeing is the unity of God and a particular (*enkelt*) humanbeing. That the human race is or is supposed to be in kinship with God is ancient paganism; but that a particular human-being is God is Christianity, and this particular human-being is the God-humanbeing."[59] The first kind of unity (of God and human nature in general) Kierkegaard consistently labels a "fantastic speculation" which he rejects (as we have seen) in the formulations put forth by Strauss and the Hegelian theologians of his day. But he must also have had in mind all the theologians who, from Cyril and the so-called Alexandrian theologians (perhaps Apollinarian) on down to our present day, have insisted that Christ had only the one nature of the "son" of God who appropriated a naturally impersonal (anhypostatic) human nature which remains distinct from but subjugated to the will of the divine logos.[60] In *Practice* Kierkegaard is vociferous in his critique of this kind of "unity" of God and the human.

How then does one become aware of and attentive to the other kind of unity (of God and a particular human being), so that one meets the unique authority of God in and with the totally human person Jesus? Without raising yet the nature of the *method* by which the divine authority of Jesus gets established in the heart and mind of another human person, we must ask: through what *medium* does the *objectivity* of this authority (which is the source of theology) establish itself? The absolute

---

58. Originally he conceived of each part as a separate book. Then he considered publishing them together in one volume along with *Sickness*. But the very direct language of *Practice* made this book the opening volley of his "attack" on Christendom, and in 1849 he was not quite ready for that. So he published *Sickness* that year and put off publication of *Practice* until September of 1850. (See comments of Howard and Edna Hong on these matters in the introduction to their new translation of the latter work: *Kierkegaard's Writings*, vol. xx, pp. xiii-xvii.)

59. *Practice in Christianity*, pp. 84; (KW 20:81f.); SV 16:86; (12:79).

60. I of course realize that there are several interpretations of Cyril's own position, but I have only in mind the *type* of Christology described, which is often attributed to Cyril and to which, I believe, Karl Barth comes very close.

centrality of this question asserted itself for Kierkegaard in his struggle to clarify Adler's claim of having received a revelation. But how is it that the great apostle of subjectivity as truth (*Postscript*) becomes so concerned with the objectivity of the source of absolute (Christian) truth?

In *The Book on Adler* itself Kierkegaard reminds us that this matter has been dealt with by Johannes Climacus in *Concluding Postscript*, and says, "I refer readers to the distinction [made there] between religiousness A and B, or to that which has the dialectical merely in the first place, and that which has the dialectical in the second place."[61] And there in *Postscript* (as we have seen above) he explains that in the dialectic of the second place (of religiousness B, Christianity) is "the qualitative dialectic of the absolute paradox" in which "the upbuilding [factor or power] is something outside the individual [*Individ*], [so] the individual does not find upbuilding by finding the God-relationship in oneself, but relates to something outside of oneself in order to find upbuilding." Therefore, "[t]he paradoxical-upbuilding corresponds to this definitive-circumstance [*Bestemmelse*]: God in time as particular [*enkelt*] human-being."[62]

He reformulates this view of the objective historical dimension (in the Christian experience of God) in much less abstract, more personal terms in *The Book on Adler.* The case of Adler intrigued him because Adler had become totally converted to the Hegelian view of Christianity, had even written scholarly books in Hegelian theology, while becoming the pastor for a small rural church. But in this setting, he became aware of the irrelevance of such a theology to the lives and minds of simple farmers. As he read the Bible and prepared his sermons, he heard a different voice, even the voice of the living Christ, and was so seized and startled that he could describe and explain it to himself in no other way than as having received a "revelation." Kierkegaard analyzes this event thus: "By a qualitative leap [*Spring*] Magister Adler was transported out of the fantastic medium of philosophy, particularly Hegelian philosophy (of pure thinking and pure being), and into the sphere of religious inwardness [intensity]; ... by a qualitative leap out of the objectivity of abstract thinking, Magister Adler comes to himself, because all religiousness consists in sub-

61. *Papirer*, VII² B 235, p. 200n. This footnote is omitted from Lowrie's translation. The sentence in the text (for which this is a note) is also omitted and, although not relevant to our present concern, is interesting: "The historical [factor] is simply the fact that a man has been shaken, that by this shaking he will not become somebody other, but awakens and becomes his self."

62. *Postscript*, p. 498; (KW 12.1:561); SV 10:229f.; (7:489f.).

jectivity, in inwardness, in coming to oneself" (and a little later he adds "emotion" and "trembling" to this definition of religiousness).[63]

How, then, is this analysis of religiousness a step beyond type A in *Postscript*? Where is the element of Christian objectivity? Kierkegaard is very aware of this lack, and he traces Adler's failure to defend his position properly (against the attacks of the church officials) and his reversion to his Hegelian position precisely to this lack.

It was greatly to Adler's credit, he says, that he was obviously "grasped, shaken in his inmost being, that thus his inwardness came into existence, or that he came into existence according to his inwardness." But it should be noted that "in regard to all inwardness which reflects on the purely human [*Menneskelige*], the merely human [*Humane*] (*thus in regard to all inwardness in the sphere of immanence*), the fact of being grasped, of being shaken is to be taken in the sense of shaking a man until he awakens. ... If this emotion expresses itself, breaks out into words, then the transposition occurs in feeling and imagination within such concepts and definition-of-concepts which every human being can be said to discover in his using them. The transposition is not limited by specific qualitative concepts which have an historical validity outside the individual and higher than every human individual," not limited therefore by a "paradoxical historical validity."[64]

With Christianity it is qualitatively different, because "to be thus grasped [in the immanent sense] is a very indefinite expression for something so concrete as a Christian awakening, and yet one dare say nothing more of Magister Adler. To be shaken (pretty much in the sense that one speaks of shaking a person to make him wake up) is the more universal foundation for all religiousness; this shaking, this emotion, this coming into existence of subjectivity in the intensity of inward turbulence the pious heathen and pious Jew has in common with a Christian. Upon this common basis of the more universal emotion, the qualitative difference must be erected and make itself felt, because the more universal emotion refers only to something abstract: being grasped by something higher, something eternal, an idea. One does not become a Christian by religiously being grasped by something higher; and not every outpouring of religious emotion is a Christian outpouring." The

63. *On Authority and Revelation*, pp. 150, 155; *Papirer* VII² B 235, pp. 185, 190. Lowrie omits some of this from his translation (1955).

64. Ibid., pp. 163f.; *Papirer* pp. 199f.

qualitative difference is just this: "a Christian religious awakening ... *oc-curs in the sphere of transcendence.*"[65]

If, then, "not every outpouring of religious emotion is a Christian out-pouring," how does one know if the "emotion" and "being shaken" in one's own "religious awakening" (or that of another, such as Adler) is truly Christian, know whether or not it occurs in transcendence? Where had Adler gone wrong? What did he lack? Kierkegaard's answer, in his analysis of Adler's failure to understand revelation properly, may come as a surprise to those who conceive of him as the prophet of subjectivity as the only truth. "Emotion which is Christian," he says, "is controlled by the definition-of-concepts [*Begrebs-Bestemmelser*], and when the emotion is transposed or expressed in words in order to be communicated, this transposition must constantly occur within the definition-of-concepts." He immediately acknowledges (as noted above) that the religious emo-tion of simple human inwardness (immanence) also gets expressed in words and uses concepts and definitions, but then goes on to argue that "Christian emotion" is "of a specific qualitative sort," and therefore "in order to be able to express oneself Christianly, there is required (be-yond emotion's universal language of the heart) skill and schooling in the Christian definition-of-concepts." Just as the Christian emotion is specific and qualitatively unique, so the language for its expression in concepts "is specifically, qualitatively concrete." So, he concludes, "For a Christian awakening there is required, on the one hand, the Christian emotion, and on the other hand, firmness and definiteness of concep-tual-language [*Begrebs-Sprogets*]."[66]

In other words, even though Christian faith is essentially subjective, in-ward, personal, private, incommunicable, unprovable (even to oneself), yet it is not autonomous, independent, or self-contained. Rather, in faith's origin, formation and coming-into-existence, in its upbuilding, maintenance, and maturation, there is necessarily and integrally in-volved the play and participation of what Kierkegaard calls "Christian conceptual-definitions" (*christelige Begrebs-Bestemmelser*) and their "Chris-tian conceptual-language" (*christelige Begrebs-Sprog*). One must be "skilled" and "schooled" in these definitions in order that one may have a "qualita-tively unshakable criterion by which one can test whether one's emotion is a Christian religious awakening." And "if one wishes to express one's emotion, one [must] have ... qualitative direction from the qualitatively

65. Ibid., pp. 163f.; *Papirer*, pp. 199–201.
66. Ibid., pp. 163–165; *Papirer*, pp. 200–202.

definite conceptual-language."[67] This is precisely what Adler lacked. "His misfortune is just this, that the Christian conceptual-language is not sufficiently and thoroughly familiar to him, that he does not have it under his control."[68]

In other words, the *medium* through which is asserted the unique objective authority (of the divine "qualitative difference" and "transcendence" which is present in the peculiar unity of God and a particular human being, Jesus) is a unique, particular set of conceptual definitions expressed in a unique, particular conceptual language. These definitions, in this language, are what define, for Kierkegaard, the proper milieu, the peculiar character and focal concern of Christian theology (dogmatics). He recognized that other religions may have their own dogmatics, but with a difference. He says, "A Mohammedan dogmatics (*sit venia verbo*) would be a development out of Mohammed's teaching, but a Christian dogmatics is a development out of Christ's activity [*Virksomhed*]."[69] Just *how* these concepts and language emerge from "Christ's activity" and what *content* that activity gives them we will explore in what follows. But it just may be that Kierkegaard's use of the term "conceptual-definitions" (*Begrebs-Bestemmelser*) is the best clue we have to his view of the role played by thought, concepts, theology, and their language in the event of Christian faith.

The term (in its singular or plural, hyphenated or unhyphenated forms, and variously translated) appears incidentally in a few early works (*The Concept of Irony*; *Philosophical Fragments*; *Concept of Angst*).[70] But it receives a clear and technical formulation in Chapter 4 of *The Book on Adler,* where it is used repeatedly in conjunction with "conceptual-language" and occasionally takes the form of "Christian conceptual-

67. For the phrases, "Christian conceptual-definitions" and "Christian conceptual language," see ibid., pp. 164, 165; *Papirer*, pp. 201, 202. For the quotations, see *Papirer*, VII² B 235, p. 202. This particular sentence is omitted from Lowrie's translation (1955), although a similar one is contained in a section drawn (by Lowrie) from a later addition by Kierkegaard (*On Authority*, pp. 165–166; *Papirer*, VII² B 266, p. 304).

68. Ibid., p. 165; *Papirer*, VII² B 235, p. 202.

69. *Journals*, 412; I A 27. The Latin phrase, "the word being permitted," obviously suggests some doubt as to whether any other religion should be permitted the attribution of having a "dogmatics" since the term emerges in a peculiar way in the history of Christian thought.

70. *The Concept of Irony*, pp. 147, 274; (KW 2:117, 257); SV 1:158, 272; (13:203, 331); *Philosophical Fragments*, p. 49; (KW 7:40); SV 6:40; (4:207); *The Concept of Angst*, p. 119; (KW 8:133); SV 6:216; (4:400).

formation" (*christelig Begrebs-Dannelse*). Let us summarize once more
what he says there.

Kierkegaard's concern is how an authentically Christian "awakening"
occurs so that it is a decisive and qualitative step beyond even the most
profound subjectivity of a purely immanent and human awareness of fallibility and of the need for the divine. (We will ask later: an awakening from
what and to what?) It appeared to Kierkegaard that Adler certainly had an
awakening as he sought to preach the Bible to his humble parishioners;
he seemed to have been "grasped and shaken in his inmost being"
by God; but this "emotion" proved to be unstable and deficient. A truly
Christian "emotion" is "of a specific qualitative sort." This quality of
course derives ultimately from being involved in "the activity of Christ" (as
the God-humanbeing), and most of Kierkegaard's contemporaries considered themselves to be Christians because they had been baptized and
confirmed in the faith within the communion of the Christian church.
They even used a vague indefinite Christian terminology to talk about
themselves. But Kierkegaard regarded most contemporary Christians as
merely nominal or "geographical" Christians, and hence their Christian
language was not "bound up with decisive thought."[71] He saw that something more rigorous was involved in one's being seized by the truly Christian passion. "The emotion which is Christian is controlled [*controlleret,*
that is: examined, checked, controlled] by conceptual-definitions [*Begrebs-
Bestemmelser*];" it must be "limited [*limiteret*] by specific qualitative concepts
[*Begreber*] which have an historical validity that ... is higher than every
individual human-being, ... a paradoxical historical validity." For "the
Christian emotion" one must be "skilled and schooled in the Christian
conceptual-definitions."[72]

---

71. *On Authority,* p. 166; *Papirer,* VII² B 266:21, p. 304.

72. Ibid., pp. 163–165; *Papirer,* VII² B 235, pp. 200–201. It should be noted that in both
instances quoted, Kierkegaard deliberately hyphenates the term *Begrebs-Bestemmelser* and
capitalizes the second part as a separate word, thus distinguishing the compound term
from the word *Begrebsbestemmelse,* which in (our) contemporary Danish means simply "definition," and thus indicating that both words of the composite term should be called to
mind (definition-of-concepts, or more accurately, conceptual-definitions). This meaning is
clearly indicated in the other quotation where he parallels "controlled by conceptual-
definitions" with "limited by specific qualitative concepts [*Begreber*]," and is also clearly indicated when he frequently uses *Begrebs-Sprog* (conceptual-language) as a parallel in these
same pages. And this double-worded meaning is then certainly intended by Kierkegaard even
when he lapses into use of the unhyphenated term, for example, when he says that it would
seem that Adler, trained as a priest, was "in possession of the schooling-in-concepts [*Begrebs-
Skole*] which is necessary in order, with assurance, to be able to express his emotion within

At what point in one's "becoming a Christian" does this schooling and acquisition of this skill come? What shape does the "qualitative direction from the qualitatively definite conceptual-language" take? Are the relationships among "emotion" and "concept" and "language" sequential, that is, does one precede the other and does one cause or produce the other? In our contemporary computer language, is the physical/mental/spiritual process, in which the emotion and the concept interrelate, "digital"? That is to say, are there direct equivalencies between the terms of the conceptual definitions and the total psychic/spiritual event (in which there occurs awareness of meanings, ethical valuations, ultimate commitments, intentional choices and decisions, etc.)? And, therefore, can the meanings, values, commitments, and decisions be skimmed off and reduced to or totally caught in the conceptual/linguistic definitions which themselves then become "the truth"? Or is the process "analog," in which the multiple levels (dimensions) of human, individual existence (neural, physical, emotional, sexual, conceptual, linguistic, self-conscious, personal/subjective, valuational, decisional, religious, active, social, political, economic, etc.) interplay simultaneously, or occur in overlapping patterns, so that each plays a constituent role and so that the "language" (numbers, words, formulae) used to express or to control the process is recognized as abstract, symbolic, and "unreal," and hence the resulting dominant and unifying religious consciousness includes all dimensions, and the person feels responsible for that result, even though some of the interactions may occur at a more or less unconscious level and remain uninterpretable in any available language?

Kierkegaard's analysis of the role played by the "Christian conceptual definitions" in the emergence of the faith-relationship with God clearly describes the process as "analog." He is aware of both subjective and objective aspects (or problems) in his analysis. Let us look at them in that order.

---

the Christian qualitative conceptual-definitions [*Begrebsbestemmelser*]" ibid., p. 166; *Papirer*, p. 203; (Lowrie [1955] does not translate the concluding phrase). So we will use the double-worded phrase also to translate its use below in *Practice in Christianity*, even though Howard and Edna Hong translate *Begrebsbestemmelse* simply as "definition" in their new translation [KW, Vol. 20; see the title of part 2 and its usage on p. 205; SV 16:192; (12:189)]. It is interesting to note that they translate the phrase *en Begrebs-Bestemmelse* as "the definition of a concept" in their new translation of *Philosophical Fragments* [KW, Vol. 7:40; SV 6:40; (4:207)], and that Reidar Thomte translates *Begrebsbestemmelse* as "conceptual determination" in the new translation of *The Concept of Angst* [KW, Vol. 8:133; SV 6:216; (4:400)].

Again, in considering the subjective side of this event of being "controlled" by conceptual-definitions, we verge into our next topic, the methodology of Kierkegaard's theology (that is, The Subjective Source of Theology). But it must be touched on in order to get the correct perspective on how Kierkegaard regarded the role of objectively formulated concepts. The basic point is that he never allowed the subjective and the objective to collapse into each other or for one to be absorbed into the other. He regards Adler's fundamental failure to have been the misidentification of his own inner dialogue with himself as a dialogue with something objective to him, that is, as a "revelation" from God. This occurred, he says, because Adler remained essentially a Hegelian, and "the Hegelian philosophy cannot make room for the qualitative concept of revelation in its system." Rather, "it has volatilized it so far that at last it becomes a determinant of subjectivity, or a determinant in the simple identity of subject-object."

In contrast, in Christian faith revelation has an objective dimension that cannot be absorbed and therefore "designates a breach with the Hegelian philosophy of identity and the immanent process." Revelation has "a transcendent point-of-origin [*Udgangspunkt*] which stands qualitatively immovably firm" so that "immanence [subjectivity] in all eternity cannot assimilate this point-of-origin." And this "sphere of transcendence" does not reside unseen up in the air or in hidden subconscious depths. Its presence is very concrete, in the God-humanbeing, in the historical Jesus as the Christ. "The Christian [reality] exists before any Christian exists, it must exist in order for anyone to be able to become a Christian. ... It maintains its objective-subsistence [*Bestaaen*] apart from all believers, while at the same time it is the inwardness of the believer. In short, there is no identity between the subjective and the objective." So "even if no one had perceived that God had been revealed in human form in Christ, yet [God] had been revealed." And, as we have heard, Adler falls victim to this confusion of the subjective with the objective because he "has not been schooled earlier in the Christian definition of the concept."[73]

Nevertheless, while Kierkegaard here stresses the objective, transpersonal dimension in the revelational event and insists that schooling in the received "Christian conceptual definitions" is necessary for our clear awareness of this objective presence of God, he is just as insistent that

73. *On Authority*, pp. 168–70; *Papirer*, VII² B 235, pp. 205–207 (some of which is omitted from the translation), and B 266:23, p. 305 (which is included in the translation).

these concepts, with their definitions in specific language and terminology, do not comprise the *content* of revelation, nor are they themselves the "object" of faith. We will specify this content and object in the next section of this chapter but must note here that no matter what crucial significance Kierkegaard attaches to these concepts, he still insists (here in *Adler*) that it is not "the content and form of the doctrine" that is the final grounds of Christ's divine authority but the power of his life and spirit to "grasp" and "shake" a person "emotionally" to the core of one's being. "Is authority the profundity of the doctrine, its superiority, its cleverness? Not at all. ... Authority is a specific quality which comes from another place." In the "paradox-religious sphere" there is a "dialectic of authority" which is indicated by the fact that "all thinking ceases ... in the sphere of the paradox-religious and of faith."[74]

So here Kierkegaard assumes what he had stated specifically in *Postscript*, that "Christianity is ... not a task for thinking, as if Christianity were a doctrine rather than an existence-communication." In other words, Christianity is "the paradoxical transformation of [human] existence through the relation to an historical [fact]."[75] He anticipates here the same point he makes three years later in *Practice in Christianity*, where he picks up the language of *The Book on Adler* concerning "conceptual definitions." "Christ is the truth," he says, "in the sense that to *be* the truth is the only true explanation of what truth is. ... This means that truth in the sense that Christ is the truth is not a sum of sentences, not a conceptual-definition [*Begrebsbestemmelse*] etc., but a life. The being of truth is not the direct reduplication of being in terms of thinking, which gives only thought-being. ... No, the being of truth is the reduplication [of truth] within yourself, within me, within him. ... And, therefore, Christianly understood, truth is obviously not to know [*vide*] the truth but to be the truth."[76]

So the subjective problem of the role that Christian conceptual definitions play in the emergence of faith (see p. 31 above) can be summarized as follows. On the one hand, Kierkegaard assumes that the concepts, expressed in their own particular language, are *there* in one's environment *before* the faith event in which one is confronted and challenged with the claim of a divine revelation, whose objectivity can never be totally absorbed and assimilated into one's own subjectivity. On the

74. Ibid., pp. 109–111; *Papirer*, pp. 142–144.
75. *Postscript.* pp. 496f., 515; (KW 12.1:559, 581); SV 10:228, 248; (7:488, 507).
76. *Practice in Christianity*, pp. 200f.; (KW 20:205); SV 16:192f.; (12:189).

other hand, there is no way of knowing and proving beforehand that the concepts point to and express a revelation whose authority is from "God" and therefore transcends every kind of human authority. This assurance or trust (faith) comes only as the conceptual definitions play a part in the remolding and transformation of one's own subjective selfhood in accord with the hidden divine being and act of the Christ, in such a way that the concepts now define who and what I am in my very being. Hence there is an unending, never completed or perfected interplay of objective conceptual definitions and subjective spiritual event. On the one hand, the objective definitions can never actually contain and impart the subjective event, and yet, on the other hand, the subjective event can never become totally self-sufficient and independent of the objective definitions. Hence it is always possible – as Kierkegaard believed to prevail in his day – that people will talk and think about themselves in vaguely correct Christian terminology and yet totally lack the spiritual reality of the words. On the other hand, Kierkegaard seems also to imply that a truly spiritual transformation (after the likeness of Christ and by the power of the spirit of Christ) requires, somewhere in one's environment, the mediation, the shaping and control of these conceptual definitions, expressed in their particular Christian language.

Such a conclusion leaves us with a truly serious objective problem about these definitions. Who or what is the source and the provider of these normative definitions expressed in a normative conceptual language? Where did they come from and how are they preserved? Adler had received the same theological education as Kierkegaard in the same years, and they both received the degree of Magister Artium (then the equivalent of the Ph.D.). But as we have seen, Kierkegaard condemned the dogmatics and theological education of his day as seriously flawed because the dominant interpretation of the Christian tradition was thoroughly Hegelian. Adler was at first totally persuaded of the truth of Hegelian theology and philosophy and wrote learned books on the subject. But Kierkegaard was drawn to "those old theological works by an authentic spiritual guide," and was "nauseated" by what passed as "theological knowledge" on the part of those who earned a *summa cum laude* in theology and by the "pious bosh on Sunday" that he heard from the pulpits. And it is no secret as to the source of his grounding in traditional Christian faith: "As a child I was strictly and seriously brought up in Christianity." And this original piety of his father remained the norm for him: "I have never broken with Christianity," rather "I have ... firmly determined to devote all [my powers] to defend it, ... to present it in its true form."[77]

Kierkegaard never specifies which "old theological works" he honors. He comments favorably on Luther often, and even Calvin occasionally, but also takes serious exception to both of them, and even says, "Luther altered New Testament Christianity. ... He reduced Christianity."[78] He read the early church fathers and especially admired much of Augustine but totally rejected his view of election (predestination); there is also an occasional quotation from a medieval theologian. For him the only unquestionable, normative source for theology remains the Bible, or more particularly "New Testament Christianity."

This emphasis on the ultimate authority of the New Testament, as opposed to the theologians of his day, was apparently formed early in Kierkegaard's intellectual development. In the midst of his university studies, in one of his earliest entries in his journal, he says, "It appears to me that on the whole the great mass of interpreters more damage than benefit the understanding of the New Testament."[79] But he does little to develop this point until after he had completed his writings. Then, as he turns in 1850 to his so-called "attack on Christendom," his journals contain constantly recurring assertions of this theme.[80]

---

77. *The Point of View*, pp. 76f.; SV 18:127; (13:564f.). Kierkegaard's reflections about his early training in Christianity by his father are, of course, always tinged with regret and serious reservations. These he summarizes in the concluding chapter of *Postscript*. It is especially notable that perhaps the most powerful image of Christian faith he carried forward from these early days (throughout the rest of his life) was that of the crucifixion of Christ and its mystery. See the two agonizing accounts of how his father slipped a picture of the crucifixion into a stack of other pictures in order to lead the child to ask about its meaning: (1) *Two Minor Ethical-Religious Essays*, in the introduction to "Has a Man the Right to Let Himself Be Put to Death for the Truth?"; pp. 81–85 in Walter Lowrie's translation of the essay in *The Present Age and Two Minor Ethico-Religious Treatises* (1949); SV 15:17–19; (11:59–61); (2) *Practice in Christianity*, pp. 174–179; (KW 20:174–179); SV 16:168–172; (12:162–167). In the former essay, the author says, "This picture followed him through life, ... and he never escaped the picture." And, "[h]e lived on year after year. He conversed only with himself, and God, and this picture." Also, compare these accounts with Kierkegaard's childhood memory of being told that " 'the crowds' spit upon Christ" (*Journals*, 6389, X¹ A 272). Also, read the second chapter in Lowrie's biography, *Kierkegaard*, on "Home and School."

78. *Journals*, 2551, XI¹ A 297.

79. Ibid., 202, I A 54.

80. See Niels J. Cappelørn's listings for *Det nye Testamente* (under *Testamente*) in his index to *Papirer*, Vol. XVI, or Hong's listings under "New Testament" in his index to *Søren Kierkegaard's Journals and Papers*.

He insists that teachers in the Christian nation ought not be required to take an oath to conform with the creeds and confessions of the church, because "good Lord, Christianity is no 'doctrine.'" Rather, they should have to swear to "act according to the New Testament." Unfortunately, he says, it does not occur to a single professor of theology "to take the New Testament and read it directly and simply, and before God ask himself the question: Does my life in any manner, even the remotest, resemble Christ's life, so that I dare call myself a follower?" He calls again and again for a return to the older view held in the church, that the Bible is not just another book to be understood by means of scientific philology and scholarly exegesis, but that the Bible is "Holy Scripture, the word of God," that "there is a clearly revealed word of God" and "we have nothing else to go by but the New Testament."[81]

It should be noted, however, that what Kierkegaard means by the "word of God" is not identical with the words of Scripture. "The Holy Scriptures are the highway signs: Christ is the way." "God has given us his word, ... Christ is the word." So he derides the use of commentaries and the scientific critical and exegetical methods of interpretation as the foolproof means of determining what God is saying in the Scriptures (even though he owned and quoted from a four-volume set of Calvin's commentaries). He says these tools too often get in the way of actually listening for God's own word and provide the excuse for not reading the Bible, since it seems so difficult, and even the experts disagree as to what it means. His recommendation: simply "take the New Testament for yourself – lock your door, talk with God, pray – and then do what it says simply and plainly in the New Testament, do it in actuality by expressing it existentially [*existentielt*] – this is Christianity." Ignore the scholars who pretend that "the New Testament is the word of God, but ... forget that God still exists," as they get involved in debates as to which letters Paul really wrote and whether Paul ever lived at all. Simply be unabashedly "primitive, alone with God."[82]

81. *Journals*, 2870, x³ A 33; 3568, x² A 633; 207, VIII¹ A 20; 4781, x² A 548; 6677, x³ A 435.

82. Ibid., 208, VIII¹ A 50; 214, x⁴ A 433; 3014, x¹ A 396. This theme of: "taking the Bible, shut your door," and being "*alone* with God's word," so that one listens to it "as if God himself speaks to me," as if "[i]t is talking to me; I am the one it is speaking about" – this theme is picked up by Kierkegaard and developed at length in his very late little work, *For Self-Examination*, specifically pp. 23–40; (KW 21:25–37); SV 17:68–79; (12:315–325). He is especially cynical about those who take with them "ten dictionaries and twenty-five commentaries" so that one can read the Bible "as calmly and coolly as you read newspaper ad-

The Christocentric emphasis in these passages on Christ as "the way" and "the word," on modeling one's life on that of Christ and becoming his "follower," bring us into the area of the methodology of Kierkegaard's theology. But they also clearly establish the New Testament, and within it the historical life of Jesus as "God with us," as the objective source of Christian theology. Yet, this emphasis on the authority of the Bible, in one's private, immediate encounter with it, did not mean that Kierkegaard had forgotten or rejected the intermediate but integral role played by "conceptual definitions" of dogmatics in the emergence of Christian faith.

About a year before his death, six years after finishing *Practice in Christianity*, he writes a commentary on his *Øiebliksstriden 1854–55* (The Struggle of the Moment) in which he reminisces about his whole life's "task."[83] Here again we hear that, in contrast to Luther's ninety-five theses, Kierkegaard has "one thesis: Christianity, the Christianity of the New Testament, does not exist at all." Indeed, the Protestantism of his day, especially in Denmark, has become "the very opposite of what the New Testament understands to be Christianity." Not in the sense that it is full of "dissoluteness and wild debauchery, by no means; no, it is sunken in inanity, in trivial philistinism, ... into this flat mediocrity and spiritlessness, ... which in secularized mediocrity has blabbered Christianity down into something meaningless, into being spiritless impotence, suffocated in illusion." And what does he propose to do about it? He believes that he has been "consecrated and dedicated by the highest approval of divine governance to become a vexing 'gadfly,' a quickening whip on all this spiritlessness." He is thus called to "work for an awakening." And so he begins his attack on the Christendom of his day and especially of Denmark through his articles in *Fædrelandet* (*The Fatherland*) and the publication of *Øieblikket* (*The Moment*). As a result, he accepts his destiny under governance that he will "become a martyr to grinning mockery."

---

vertising," especially when you discover from them that "there are several variations, and perhaps a new manuscript has just been found, ... and perhaps there are five interpreters with one opinion and seven with another and three who are wavering or have no opinion." Then you agree that you will surely do what the Bible says but only when "the discrepancies are ironed out and the interpreters agree fairly well. ... What a tragic misuse of scholarship, that it is made so easy for people to deceive themselves." (pp. 33f.; KW 21:32)

83. Ibid., 6943, XI³ B 53.

But this fate, "voluntarily" chosen, marks only the very end of his life. It is not how he sees his major and lifelong contribution to the Christianity of his day and, as he clearly foresees it, to Christianity for generations to come. In the paper we are looking at, he says, "I understand it as my very particular task assigned by governance, for which I was selected very early and was educated very slowly, and which I now for the very first time fully embrace ... – I understand it as my task to undertake a complete revision of all the Christian ideas [or conceptions: *Forestillinger*], to extricate [literally: peel out of] the Christian ideas from the illusions in which we have enveloped them, and thereby, with all the power the Almighty has granted me, ... to effect an awakening." Or a little later in stronger language, he defines his task not as a "revision" but as "stripping the Christian ideas [*Forestillinger*] and concepts [*Begreber*] of [all] costumes and disguises of illusions." So his task is not just to "revise" the current Hegelian reinterpretation of Christianity, which he regards as quite beyond redemption. He views the whole (Hegelian) System as a mad delusion and a total misrepresentation of Christianity. So his task is a redefinition of the Christian concepts by stripping away the illusions and rediscovering the original, dependable "conceptual definitions" in which he had been nurtured. (And the radicalness of his redefinition will really come to light only as we get a clarification [in chapters 3 and 4 below] of his understanding of sin, faith, and love, that is, of human failure, God's forgiveness, and the new life in Christ.)[84]

So our question about the source and the preserver of these normative definitions intrudes again but now in a very personal way for

84. The quotations are from the same note or paper as in the endnote 83. We will deal later (mainly in the concluding chapter) with the fact that in this single paper Kierkegaard presents his "task" as twofold. The major one is what he has been doing his entire adult life: writing his voluminous works and journals in the seclusion of his study. The other one: drawing the implications of his writings for the current condition of Christianity and the church in the established religion of Denmark, and doing so in direct, abrasive language that cannot be misunderstood or variously interpreted or ignored – as had happened to all of his writings but especially to his second or Christian authorship, even to *Practice in Christianity*, which in a way anticipates his attack on Christendom in the last few years of his life. Many twentieth century readers of Kierkegaard, both secular and religious, have managed to find great stimulation in his major works, picking and choosing those (and those particular themes) that suit their own purposes. But no one has spent much energy in drawing their implications for the churches (largely disestablished) in this century as Kierkegaard did in his "attack" literature of his last few years. And the question remains as to whether his attack implied a total denial of the (Christian) legitimacy of any institutional form of Christianity. We will address this question briefly now and more fully later on in chapter 5.

Kierkegaard: for whom is he called (by governance) to redefine the basic, essential concepts that help form authentic Christian faith? Four years before the note referred to in the last two paragraphs (no. 6943), he had confided to his journals (of 1850) that Christians face an absolute choice, a radical either/or: either you stand with "the established [church]" or with "the single-individual [*den Enkelte*], unconditionally the single-individual," and just as important: with "nothing in between," that is, with no "parties, sects, etc." Or as he puts it a little later, "the human's interest is that there be a religious establishment. ... God's interest is that there be no religious establishment." Well, Kierkegaard asks, how can these two positions be harmonized? He replies that since hardly any human being "manages to be unconditionally the single-individual," the only recourse is to acknowledge that "an established [church] is for the sake of our human frailty," and that this means that everyone in it accepts a reduced version of "what it is in the most rigorous sense to be a Christian."[85]

Did Kierkegaard himself accept this accommodation to human frailty? One widely held interpretation is that he did not, as evidenced, they say, when he finally said, "Love of God is hatred of the world" (*Practice in Christianity*), and in its more extreme form, "New Testament Christianity consists of loving God in hatred of humans, in hatred of self, and thereby in hatred of other human beings, hating father, mother, one's own child, wife, etc.," so that if a man really loves a woman, Christianity would demand "hating oneself and the loved one, to let her go in order to love God" (*The Moment*, no. 5, July 27, 1855).[86] From these extreme,

---

85. *Journals*, 6705, 1415; x³ A 647, 658. In a journal entry of two years earlier he makes the point even more clearly when he says, "the real meaning of religious sociality (*Socialitet*)" is this: "when the ideality of the God-relationship has become too strong for the unique-individual (*den Enkelte*), ... he must have another human-being to discuss it with. From this we see that sociality is not the highest but is really a concession to human weakness. ... The idea ... of sociality is then a middle term between God and the single individual" (Ibid., 1377, IX A 315). And a year earlier yet, in *Works of Love*, Kierkegaard recognizes the need for this sociality even on the part of Christ's disciples: "Christ ... succeeded in forming a band of disciples whose qualification was to stick together in a willingness to be scourged, persecuted, mocked, crucified, beheaded, and whose qualification also was not mutual flattery, but on the contrary a mutual helping of each other to humility before God." So he thinks it might help to bring about "a beneficial awakening" if someone would advertise that "he proposed to form such a society [*Forening*] of love" (*Works of Love*, p. 126; (KW 16:122); SV 12:122; (9:118).

86. *Practice*, p. 218; (KW 20:224); SV 16:209; (12:205); *Attack upon Christendom*, p. 163; SV 19:177; (14:196f.).

deliberately hyperbolic statements, Mark C. Taylor concludes that Kierkegaard's vision of the fulfilled, unified self "breaks down, leaving spirit fragmented. ... Historical existence becomes a period of exile – the self an estranged wanderer. Rather than presenting the realization of authentic selfhood, this form of life is the desperate expression of self-alienated spirit." And Josiah Thompson asserts that Kierkegaard concludes that "man must suffer his estrangement from God in guilt, despair, and uncertainty, and ultimately this estrangement is not to be overcome." Indeed, "[a]t the core of Kierkegaard's vision of Christianity lies a fascination with the horrific. For according to him, it is in a paroxysm of terror that one confronts the essential truth of Christianity." So in his final works "Christianity's poet articulates a vision of Christianity as the ultimate *horror religiosus*."[87] Neither Taylor nor Thompson seem to have any comprehension of what Kierkegaard means by "hatred" of self and others (i.e., rejection of humanity which lives merely at the sensate and social levels, rejection of any attachment which deters one from self-sacrificial love of others, rejection of all dependence on human intellect which deflects one's dependence on God's grace, etc.).

In the concluding chapter, we will deal more fully with Kierkegaard's view of corporate Christianity and Christian history. But here it must be briefly but clearly affirmed, against the extravagant misreadings of Kierkegaard as illustrated by those of Taylor and Thompson, that Kierkegaard also had a positive view of – even a devotion to – the Christian church as the carrier and proclaimer of the Christian tradition. In other words, his radical condemnation of the established Christianity of his day, expressed theologically but calmly in *Practice in Christianity* and proclaimed bluntly and vociferously in the articles of his last year of life, was conceived by him as the work of a "gadfly," as a "corrective" which would lead, he hoped, to an "awakening" and hence to "reform" within the church.

There are several expressions of hope in his journals that Bishop Mynster would read his *Practice in Christianity*, see the light, and openly confess that the church had lost its way. More than once he expresses anxiety for fear that Anti-Climacus has stated the case of pure and authentic Christianity too strongly and will discourage sincere Christians from trying more seriously to conform their lives to the "pattern" of Christ's life. Again and again he declares that Christianity is a dialectical

---

87. Mark C. Taylor, *Journeys to Selfhood*, p. 275; Josiah Thompson, *Kierkegaard*, pp. 200ff. Their views are dealt with more fully in *Kierkegaard as Humanist*; see index.

unity of "rigorousness" (*Strenghed*) and "mildness" (*Mildhed*), but in times of confusion, "first, the rigorousness of the ideal, then mildness." His own nature, he says, is "a synthesis of rigorousness and gentleness," but he is so predominantly gentle that he must hide it, lest he "preach human-beings into a [sense of] security."[88]

This concern for Christianity and the church is expressed clearly in *The Book on Adler.* Kierkegaard is analyzing whether Adler can rightly be considered to be an *extraordinarius* because of his sense of having received a revelation. He exposits the "dialectical relationship among a) the *universal* [i.e., the established corporate church], b) the *individual,* and c) the *special individual,* that is, the extraordinary-one." In order to be the latter, one must "bring a new point-of-departure ... in relation to the fundamental presupposition of the established [church]" and by "placing oneself directly under God must work to transform [*omskabe*] the established [church];" he must "be willing to make *sacrifices ... for his own sake* and *for the sake of the universal.*"[89] He concludes that Adler does not fit this definition of an extraordinary-one, but in a journal entry (made just as he was finishing *The Book on Adler*), he claims "before God's judgment seat" that there is probably no one "in the kingdom suitable to be that except me." In fact, he argues that it is now clear that he is not suited to be either a state teacher of religion or a clergyman, but rather that it is his "calling" and "task" to fulfill the function of an extraordinary-one because his "whole *habitus* [intelligence, talents, skills, mental constitution] was designed for this," and "I will bear a huge responsibility if I refuse a task like that." He is to fulfill this task through "my position as author," and he clearly understands that this (new) authorship is to be addressed to the established church "in the literary, social, and political situation." He understands that this will bring him into confrontation with Bishop Mynster who "has never been out in 70,000 fathoms of water" (the condition of radical faith) but "has always clung to the established order and now has completely accommodated to it." This he knows will bring "insult and ridicule, ... going headlong toward certain ruin," but he will "trust in God" because "for God all things are possible."[90]

88. *Journals,* 6275, IX A 413; 6535, X² A 204; 6710, X³ A 716; see also 4893, X¹ A 625; 6590, X² A 525.

89. *On Authority and Revelation,* pp. 34f., 38; *Papirer,* VII² B 235, pp. 40f., 45.

90. *Journals,* 5961, VII¹ A 221.

Four years later, he expresses his sense of responsibility to and concern for the established church very explicitly in "A Supplement" (*Følgeblad*) to his *My Activity as a Writer.* He says, "In regard to an 'establishment' – since my concern had been 'the unique-person' [*den Enkelte*] with polemical aim at the numerical, the crowd, etc. – I have always done precisely the opposite of attacking [it]. I have never been in or with the 'opposition' which wants to get rid of 'government,' but [I] have provided what one might call a 'corrective'. ... In so far as the church establishment understands itself, it will in the same degree understand also the last book, *Practice in Christianity,* as an attempt ideally to find a point-of-strength for an establishment."[91] And he maintains this view to the end of his life, as is clear from a journal entry made shortly before he began his overt "attack" in December of 1854. Here, as we have heard, he defines his calling and task as author more exactly, namely to strip Christian ideas and concepts of the illusions in which they have been encased (by Hegelian theologians), and his goal and purpose is to "work toward an awakening."

An awakening of whom? And how? Clearly: an awakening of individual Christians within the church. And in order to do this, he believes that these individuals must be impacted by the "extricated" and "revised" Christian concepts through the "proclamation of Christianity" which in the church of his day was being done, he says, in a style so "artistically perfect and secularly sagacious" that the whole generation had been lulled into "a kind of aesthetic spell." So "the whole proclamation of Christianity used today must be done over completely." It is precisely this task that he has in mind when he says, "I consider it my responsibility to the established [church] – thus manifesting how I acknowledge an established [church] as an authority [*Instants*] – to express my view and opinion of the established [church] as definitely and candidly as possible" (even, he adds, if this means "enabling the established [church] ... to take measures against me with the powers and authority it has").[92]

---

91. *The Point of View for My Work as an Author,* p. 156; sv 18:75f.; (13:507).

92. *Journals,* 6943, xi³ B 53. In a journal entry of 1851, Kierkegaard comments on "the definition of 'church' in the Augsburg Confession, that it is the communion (*Samfund*) of saints where the word is rightly taught and the sacraments rightly administered." He says the Confession got it right "on the two points of doctrine and sacraments," but it ignores the basic requirement that there be a *communion* of saints "which is the determinant in the direction of the existential (*Existentielle*)," and hence all the right doctrine and right sacraments in the world will not do any good (Ibid., 600, x⁴ A 246). What he means by this existential determinant was indicated in an entry of 1849 where he says, "Nowadays the

So it is clear that in spite of his central concern to protect the single, unique individual from being swallowed up in the mass or crowd and to place the highest demands upon the individual to find his or her own personal relationship with the eternal God, yet Kierkegaard asserts that even Christ recognized that human frailty requires that some form of a "society of love" be formed for "mutual helping of each other to humility before God" (see note 85 above on sociality). And he sees the institutional church, in spite of its constant failure and compromises in regard to the true Christian faith and its need for continual reform, as the best hope for providing this help. In spite of the fact that he could not even bring himself, in the last year or so of his life, to attend official worship,[93] yet he never proposed to form a new church but vociferously opposed the move of his contemporary, N.F.S. Grundtvig, to form new and free congregations (called The Danish People's Church [*Den danske Folkekirke*]) based on fellowship in the sacraments of baptism and communion and without any actual doctrinal unity or government.[94]

So Kierkegaard claims to have an "objective" historical event of revelation (in the life of the God-humanbeing, Jesus as the Christ) as the *source* and ground of his role as theologian, and he claims that this event continues to assert its divine authority through the norm of "New Testament Christianity" as this textual testimony is used as the basis of the church's proclamation. He further claims that there is a set of "conceptual

---

preaching almost always fails ... to occasion the listener to *apply* what he has heard, to get him to *begin*, to *pledge* himself at that very moment to a very specific task" (emphasis added). This, he says, should also happen every time one goes to communion. But today "pastors are like a person who stands on dry land and gives swimming lessons – he dares not let it become decisive," and so would be "anxious and afraid if one of the listeners took it seriously and sprang into the water" (Ibid., 668, x^1 A 185). What Kierkegaard means by the *communion* of saints will be developed in the last chapter of this work, using the material in *Practice in Christianity* about the "congregation" (*Menighed*) as "having no place in time but only in eternity," and in his later comments on this theme in "The Accounting" in *My Activity as an Author*, plus an addition in a later note on "The Accounting" (*Practice*, pp. 217ff.; [KW 20:223]; SV 16:208; [12:204f.]; *My Activity as an Author*, p. 149; SV 18:68; [13:498f.]; *Journals*, 595, x^5 B 245).

93. *Journals*, 6943, xi^3 B 53. But did he not continue to attend "communion on Fridays"?

94. See the short book by Poul Dam, *Nikolaj Frederik Severin Grundtvig*, pp. 60–65. There is also extensive material about Grundtvig in Bruce H. Kirmmse's *Kierkegaard in Golden Age Denmark*. For Kierkegaard's critique, see the listings under Grundtvig's name in either Cappelørn's index to *Papirer* or the Hongs's index to *Journals and Papers*.

definitions" of that testimony that the Christian church has formulated
and has passed along down through the ages, and he claims that it is his
divinely appointed calling and life's task to help free the current formulations and proclamation from their Hegelian corruption and to bring
them back into conformity with the New Testament testimony. In other
words, Kierkegaard clearly conceived of the central, decisive role of his
life's work in the fairly traditional terms of a Christian *theologian*. But the
title of this chapter indicates that he was (is) a "peculiar kind" of theologian. For an indication of his peculiarity we turn to the methodology
and content of his theology (see pp. 14ff above). These will be treated
only briefly here because they will comprise the major substance of the
later chapters of this study on sin, faith and love.

THE SUBJECTIVE SOURCE OF THEOLOGY

The central point of Kierkegaard's theological methodology is this:
there is both an objective source and a subjective source of Christian
theological formulation, and neither one works without the other. We
have given a lengthy summary of the main aspects of the objectivity of
that source, and have had to touch on its subjective dimension and quality from time to time (especially at notes 74–76 above). Simply put, the
subjectivity involved in theological formation consists in my personal becoming a Christian in the faith-relationship with God as God encounters
humans in the life and being of Jesus as the Christ. If I do not stand and
live in that relationship, I cannot be a Christian theologian. I can know
in infinite detail every doctrinal formulation in the history of the Christian church, all the disputes involved, and the positions of every party in
the debates. I can be adept at recounting the interrelationships among
all the various doctrines, manipulate them as a system of interrelated
ideas in a creative way, become an excellent teacher of all this knowledge to others, and yet – I can be totally lacking in the one resource that
is necessary for me to critique and to reformulate Christian "conceptual
definitions," (and thus fail to be a Christian theologian) because I personally do not stand and live in that faith-relationship with God in Jesus
as the Christ. I lack Christian faith as, what Kierkegaard calls, an "existential" element in my being.

In theory, this view of Christian theology is widely held, but Kierkegaard's "peculiarity" is that he insists that most theologians, most preachers and teachers of the Christian tradition and community, forget and
neglect to call into play this absolute requirement of Christian concep-

tual definition. They teach all about God but forget that God is a living reality who must be dealt with personally if one is to speak of God knowingly. They do not know how to wait in silence for the living God to speak and to reach out and grasp them "spiritually" at the core and depth of their beings as persons, as self-conscious, free, responsible selves, and to do this at the "objective" place where this God promises to meet them, namely, in the "word" of the New Testament and in the "sacrament" of the Lord's table.[95] Kierkegaard is peculiar among theologians not only in his insistence on this point theoretically but in his following it in practice. As we have argued elsewhere, Kierkegaard's method is phenomenological in the sense that he constantly thinks and writes out of his own experience, that is, out of his own personal involvement with the subject matter before him.[96] He does not reason and write toward a conclusion that he knows before hand. He follows the leading of his inquiry down into the depths and out into the far reaches of his own life in all of its inner and outer complexities – all as enlightened by the blazing truth that has come to him in and through the life of Jesus as the Christ. Kierkegaard certainly is not unique in his demand that existential faith play an integral role in theological formulation. But no other Christian thinker has matched the depth and complexity of his analysis of how this "subjectivity" comes into being and operates in the process of one's becoming a self and, especially, in becoming a Christian self. And among those who agree with him on the centrality of the role of subjectivity, no one matches his intransigent, uncompromising faithfulness to and application of this principle. In this sense, he is a "peculiar" theologian.

As noted, this methodology of faith will be explored at length in chapter 4, but let us provide just a suggestion of it here. As we have seen, faith, for Kierkegaard, is not rational belief in or comprehension of a set of ideas or doctrines. Rather, faith is being in a certain *relationship* with God, and that means a relationship with God-in-Christ because, for him, God is present with us in Jesus as the Christ, the God-humanbeing. In *Practice in Christianity* Kierkegaard works this position out as follows.

95. See *Journals*, 1494, x[5] A 103; he is saying that one needs to have grace even to go to "the objective, the sacraments and the word."

96. See chapter 1 of my previous volume, *Kierkegaard as Humanist*, and for a more extensive treatment, my article, "Kierkegaard's Method: Does He Have One?" in *Kierkegaardiana*, XIV, 1988.

Christ is the truth in the sense that *being* [*at være*] the truth is the only true explanation of what truth is. ... Therefore, Christianly understood, truth is obviously not knowing [*at vide*] the truth but being the truth. ... For knowing the truth is something that, entirely of itself, ensues from being the truth, not the other way around. ... Christ would never have known the truth if he had not been it, and no one knows more of the truth than what one is of the truth. Indeed, one cannot really know the truth. ... The truth, if it is there, is a being, a *life*. Therefore, it says, 'This is eternal life, to know [*kjende*] the only true God and the one whom [God] sent,' the truth. That is, only then do I in truth know the truth, when it becomes a life in me. ... Therefore one sees what a monstrous mistake it is ... to didacticize [*docere*] Christianity; and how altered Christianity has become through this continual didacticizing is seen in this, that now all the expressions are formed according to the view that truth is cognition [or knowledge: *Erkjendelse*], [so] now one speaks continually about comprehending [*begribe*], speculating, contemplating, etc., whereas in original Christianity all the expressions are formed according to the view that truth is being.[97]

Closely connected with this exposition of what truth is and how one acquires it, one always finds references to three other topics in the authorship: that in Jesus as the Christ one meets God (truth) in the form of absolute paradox, and that the condition of paradox always confronts one with the possibility of offense, and that whether one takes offense or believes is voluntary (the leap). The distinction between the method of reason and abstract speculation on the one hand, and that of faith on the other, comes to Kierkegaard early in life, then receives its first formal and full statement in *Philosophical Fragments,* and continues to be a central concern throughout both the first authorship (up through *Postscript)* and the second (Christian) authorship to the end of his days. It permeates all of the overtly Christian works and is a constant theme throughout the journals. So the methodology of theological formulation, as essentially involving faith, is complex and will require detailed analysis under the topic of faith (see chapter 4 below).

97. *Practice,* pp. 200–202; (κw 20:205f.); sv 16:192–194; (12:189f.). Kierkegaard was a great admirer of Pascal, and in a late journal entry of 1850 he shows how he found the above ideas in Pascal: "Pascal declares that knowledge (*Erkjendelse*) of the divine stands in inverse relation to knowledge of the human. In regards to the human, one must first know and then love; in regards to the divine, one must first love and then know. By this Pascal means that knowledge of the divine is essentially a transformation of the person; one must become a different (*andet*) human-being in order to know the divine."(*Journals,* 3109, x³ A 609)

Kierkegaard is a peculiar kind of theologian, however, in a second way. Knowing the truth by being the truth in faith is not just a change in one's relationship with God and in one's subjective self-understanding. We have also heard that "I only know the truth [in Jesus as the Christ] when it becomes a life in me." And this new life in me means "a transformation of the person; one must become a different human-being in order to know the divine." And for Kierkegaard, this new life and new person includes one's ethical life, that is, includes all one's active relationships with "neighbor," and "neighbor" is every human being one meets, without exception.[98] So being in faith *is* a life of love (and as we shall see, Christian love makes demands that not even the highest of human love knows about). So theological formation of "conceptual definitions" requires not only the methodology of faith but also the *enactment in life* of a specific *content* that characterizes faith. In other words, faith *includes* the "works of love," and only in those acts or works does one really and finally come "to know the divine," know the truth. So "faith" and "love" are two different descriptions of the same phenomenon, are two sides of a single coin. This is an emphasis that runs throughout, and receives increasing emphasis in, the authorship: one comes truly to know (*kjende*) and understand (*forstaa*) the truth not in anticipatory "imagination" (*Phantasie*) but only in "actuality" (*Virkelighed*). In other words, there is a reciprocal interplay, a circular movement, between knowing and doing, between believing and obeying, between imagining in possibility and becoming in actuality. Indeed, authentically human and free doing, obeying, and becoming must be formed and informed by knowing, believing, and imagining, but, equally so, authentic knowing, believing, and imagining are finally filled with content and meaning only from actual, concrete doing, becoming, and obeying.

This emphasis is truly rare in the whole history of Christian thinking, and Kierkegaard's coming to it as an absolute conviction and as a controlling principle of his reformation of Christian "conceptual definitions" makes him a very peculiar kind of theologian indeed. Perhaps the most eloquent statement of this principle ever formulated is found in the ecstatic closing words of Albert Schweitzer's *The Quest of the Historical Jesus*:

98. See my exposition of Kierkegaard's view of love in my previous volume on *Kierkegaard as Humanist*, chapter 7, sections on "The Object of Love" and "Love's Triad." The notion that the religious life includes the ethical is of course part of his concept of the stages or spheres of life, namely, that each successive stage catches up and brings forward the previous stage(s) as operative and integral to the new stage.

He comes to us as one unknown, without a name, as of old, by the lakeside, he came to those human-beings who knew him not. He speaks to us the same word: 'Follow thou me!' and sets us to the tasks which he has to fulfill for our time. He commands. And to those who obey him, whether they be wise or simple, he will reveal himself in the toils, the conflicts, the sufferings which they shall pass through in his fellowship, and, as an ineffable mystery, they shall learn in their own experience who he is.

Kierkegaard would greatly approve such words as "obey ... toils ... conflicts ... sufferings." And in his last major work, *Practice in Christianity,* he spells out how one comes to know Jesus as the Christ by obeying him, using as his key concepts: Christ as our "prototype" or "pattern" (*Forbillede*), and a disciple as "following" and "follower" of Christ (*efterfølge* and *Efterfølger,* which may also be translated as "imitating" and "imitator").[99]

With this emphasis on the cruciality of learning from doing, as applied to the crucial Christian event of becoming a Christian, Kierkegaard is engaged in his central task in life, namely, in the reformulation of one of the essential "conceptual definitions" of the Christian theological tradition. Somewhere early in that tradition there emerged a formulation that continued to play a significant role right up through the major Reformation theologies, namely, the distinction between the doctrine of the person of Christ and the doctrine of the work of Christ. It was assumed that the issue of the person of Christ (incarnation, God/man) must be clarified and definitively decided *first,* and if that could be accomplished, then resolution of all the questions about the work of Christ (salvation) would easily follow. This basic distinction assumes that "revelation of God in Jesus Christ" means that we disciples *first* come to know "who he is," namely, that the "person" of Jesus is the "person" of God (two natures but one person). And therefore, and only then, in the *second* place (ontologically and chronologically) do we experience Christ's redeeming work of reconciliation and sanctification, both as objective, cosmic event and as subjective experience of God's grace. So

99. Both the Latin version and a Danish translation of *The Imitation of Christ* by Thomas à Kempis were in Kierkegaard's library, and that he read it is attested to by the fact that he quotes it occasionally throughout the journals. The Danish title is *Om Christi Efterfølgelse.* For the listings in his library, see *Auktionsprotokol over Søren Kierkegaards Bogsamling,* no. 272–274 in the section on *Hovedsamling.* It should be noted that the Danish word, *Indøvelse,* which does mean "practice," carries the connotation of "putting-into-operation," seriously trying it out.

incarnation is the first and primary truth, and redemption is the second-ary and derivative truth.

Kierkegaard maintains that both the New Testament evidence and his (my) subjective experience of becoming a Christian contradict this tradi-tional formulation. Finally, Kierkegaard argues, it is my own personal, in-dividual experience of the power of Christ's life to transform my own entire existence that "reveals" that God is in and with Jesus as the Christ. And moreover, God comes in such a way in the individual human life of Jesus that I am left, alone, *either* to be offended and to fall away into dark-ness and death, *or* to believe and to be set free into light and life eternal. The rest of this present study will comprise an exploration of how Kier-kegaard depicts the myriad of details and complexities of the "truth" of this Christian perspective on human existence; in other words, an explo-ration of the *content* of the process in which "the transformation of the person" takes place in coming into faith, the process in which I "become another human-being" in imitation of Christ. The primary "conceptual definitions" by which Kierkegaard depicts this content are: the human being as a creation of God (My Self: A Gift), the human being's fall into sin and despair (My Self: A Failure), becoming a Christian through the forgiveness of sin and entering the life of faith/love (My Self: In Need of the Eternal) – as we shall see in the next three chapters.

There is, however, one futhur, nagging question before we can pro-ceed to these main topics of our exploration: did Kierkegaard himself think and speak and write out of faith? If "Christ is the truth" and if "no one knows more of the truth than what one is of the truth" (see text at note 97 above), then Kierkegaard can, on his own terms, speak only of those dimensions of Christian faith that are operative in his own being. It is common to interpret the pseudonyms as signifying that Kierke-gaard himself disclaimed all pretence of being a Christian himself. So Josiah Thompson argues that Kierkegaard knew he never became more than a poet because he saw that humanity's "estrangement from God in guilt, despair, and uncertainty ... ultimately ... is not to be overcome." And Mark Taylor claims that "Kierkegaard confesses his own inability to make the final movement of faith."[100]

The evidence from Kierkegaard's own most personal entries in the journals clearly and strongly puts the lie to such an interpretation. This false conclusion usually comes from those who read early and late in the total writings and neglect the central, normative Christian authorship

100. Thompson, 1974, pp. 202, 200; Taylor, 1980, p. 259n.

from *Upbuilding Discourses in Various Spirits* (1846) through *Practice in Christianity* (1848).[101] The issue of how one comes to faith is of central interest to Kierkegaard; indeed, he several times says that the unifying concern of his entire authorship is, "How to become a Christian within Christendom." And, as with every other topic to which he gives serious attention, this one grows out his own self-concern.

Very early on he was aware of his contradictory feelings of attraction/ defiance, of adoration/resentment, toward his father for his smothering of the child Søren with his (the father's) own experience of Christian religiousness. Søren's early years at university were filled with attempts to break the hold of that childhood nurturing, not only intellectually but also in life-style. This story need not be repeated here because it has been frequently told.[102] But we must look at the solid evidence of his

101. In a personal conversation, I raised this point with Josiah Thompson and he blandly admitted this neglect, saying, "Those works simply did not interest me." My critique of this position is supported by Bruce Kirmmse in his truly impressive work, *Kierkegaard in Golden Age Denmark*, where he notes that "The seven major pseudonymous works [published] from February 1843 to February 1846 [*Either/Or* to *Postscript*] have generally attracted most of the attention which scholars have given to SK," and that the works that followed "have usually not been accorded the same quantity and quality of attention" (p. 263), whereas he uses the latter works as normative, as I do.

102. For example, in Walter Lowrie's *Kierkegaard*, chapters 2 and 4. But I agree strongly with Bruce Kirmmse's warning that we should avoid "the psychological reductionism" of "the psychologizing biographer." And he points out that Walter Lowrie's biographies of SK "lean heavily on the ingenious but unproven work of P.A. Heiberg ... and Frithiof Brandt's clever but discredited historical sleuthing," and that therefore their influence on interpretation of Kierkegaard in the English-speaking world has been "unfortunate." He lists several more recent biographical studies which he judges to be dependable, all written in Danish and so not accessible for most English-readers. He also proposes that Kierkegaard's personal life – "including such matters as his relationship to his father, his possible youthful visit to a bordello, and his broken engagement to Regine Olsen" – remains an "insoluble riddle" and should not intrude "in the understanding of his works." (see *Kierkegaard in Golden Age Denmark*, note 1 on pp. 509f.) I would modify this latter conclusion by insisting that the biographical materials used should be limited to Kierkegaard's own reflections on such matters, and, even more importantly, by insisting that Kierkegaard used his own experiences simply as points of departure for his exploration and characterization of what he calls "the universally human." In other words, his works do not finally describe simply his own limited human experience but transcend it in order to describe your and my humanity. For example, a friend asked me why I was so interested in Kierkegaard, when obviously his life-view was so distorted by the aberrations of his own life. My reply was: Kierkegaard used his own profound illnesses as the occasion to discover the universal illnesses of humankind and used his own awakening Christian faith as grounds for projecting authentic health. Hence we do not explain his concepts of despair and love/faith in the terms of his illness, rather we seek to explain the illness of and cure for all of us in the terms of his concepts. In this

move into faith which can be found in his own testimony in the journals. Toward the end of his sixth year at university, he mused on the pattern of his rebellion: "May it not seem right to do as that ancient sect (see Church History) did – go through all the vices simply to have experience of life." But a year later he expresses his equally profound sense of allure and captivation: "I think that if I ever do become an earnest Christian my deepest shame will be that I did not become one before, that I had to try everything else first." And a few months later, ambivalence: "If Christ is to come and live in me, it will have to be according to the Gospel for the day [Jo 20:19] given in the almanac: Christ enters through closed doors."[103]

But the doors began to open. Just a month before he wrote these words, Kierkegaard had been shocked out of his complacency (on March 13, 1838) by the death of his favorite professor and mentor, Poul Martin Møller, who had repeatedly warned him of the fatal dangers of his pattern of life and thought. And shortly after this entry (perhaps on his 25th birthday on May 5), his father seems to have made some dramatic move to effect reconciliation with his estranged son.[104] In any case, during this period something radical happened to Kierkegaard so that (on May 19, 1838) he cries out, "There is an *indescribable joy* that glows all through us

---

light, it is not only possible but requisite to use Kierkegaard's reflections on his own psychological difficulties, and on his own "way" of seeking spiritual healing and health, in order to come to a better understanding of his conceptual formulations.

And, I would add, if Kirmmse is correct in his warnings against "psychological reductionism" in the explanation of Kierkegaard's writings, it is also correct to warn against "sociological reductionism." Kirmmse never loses sight of Kierkegaard's central concern for the particular, unique, individual human-being, but his quite valid interest in Kierkegaard's concern for the social/political setting of individual life does lead him at times very close to "explaining" Kierkegaard sociologically. After all, Kierkegaard labeled two of his most significant works (*Concept of Anxiety* and *The Sickness unto Death*) as "psychological" studies, whereas he never uses the designation of "sociological." Be that as it may, I do want to say that all Kierkegaard readers and scholars are deeply in the debt of Prof. Kirmmse and a growing number of others who are showing that Kierkegaard had a profound interest in and understanding of the social and political dimensions of being authentically human. We look will look more closely at this interest in chapter 5 and will see that the study of the topic is far from arriving at firm conclusions.

103. *Journals*, 4391, I A 282; 5280, II A 202 (Dec. 8, 1837); 5313, II A 730.

104. Walter Lowrie, on the suggestion of Emanuel Hirsch, proposes that such a meeting took place on that date because in Denmark a man attained his legal majority on his 25th birthday (in *Kierkegaard*, pp. 182–184). He even speculates that the father confessed to Søren his weaknesses and sins, and that in this way Søren came to see that his "crazy bringing-up" by his father was prompted by the loving desire to protect his son from the father's

just as inexplicably as the apostle's exclamation breaks forth for no apparent reason: 'Rejoice, and again I say, Rejoice.' – Not a joy over this or that, but the soul's full outcry ... – a heavenly refrain which, as it were, suddenly interrupts our other singing, a joy which cools and refreshes like a breath of air, a breeze from the trade winds which blow from the grove of Mamre to the everlasting mansions."[105]

To call this event his "first conversion" (Lowrie) may be an exaggeration, but two months later he is obviously going through a spiritual struggle. "It takes some time," he says, "before one really settles down and feels at home (knows where everything has its place) in the divine economy. One gropes around amid a multiplicity of moods, does not even know how one should pray; Christ does not take any definite configuration in us – we do not know what the cooperation of the Spirit means, etc." And a few days later he tells his journal in a very sober tone, "I am going to work toward a far more inward relation to Christianity, because up until now I have in a way been standing completely outside of it while fighting for its truth; like Simon of Cyrene (Lk 23:26), I have carried Christ's cross in a purely external way."[106]

The realization of this resolve (to a certain degree), however, was slow in coming. According to Kierkegaard himself, all of the pseudony-

---

own weakness and sin. Only so can Lowrie understand the fervor of Kierkegaard's first prayer entered in the journals (July 9, 1838) in which he thanks God, "Father in heaven, for having kept an earthly father present for a time here on earth, where I so greatly need him; with your help I hope that he will have greater joy in being my father the second time than he had the first time" (*Journals*, 5328, II A 231). But our confidence that a radical change took place in Kierkegaard's psyche about this time need not depend on such speculations. A month later his father died. And from then on, in numerous places in his journals and writings, Kierkegaard expresses his great devotion and indebtedness to and his love of his father. Lowrie gives some of these (in his book *Kierkegaard*, pp. 182–184).

105. *Journals*, 5324, II A 228 (dated 10:30 A.M. May 19, 1838). A little exegesis is called for. Immediately following the words quoted from the apostle (Phil. 4:4), Paul writes, "The Lord is at hand. Have no anxiety about anything. ... And the peace of God, which passes all understanding, will keep your hearts and your minds in Christ Jesus." And the reference to the "grove of Mamre" is from Genesis 18:1 where we read, "The Lord appeared to [Abraham] by the oaks of Mamre, as he sat at the door of his tent in the heat of the day." And Abraham "bowed himself to the earth and said, 'My Lord, if I have found favor in your sight, do not pass by your servant." Kierkegaard does not pick his words casually, and every image he uses carries a poetic, symbolic meaning.

106. Ibid., 4405, 5329; II A 756, 232.

mous works of the next seven years (through *Postscript*) were not written by a Christian, even though all of them were written in explanation
and defense of Christianity. Climacus "said he was not a Christian."[107]
In fact, as author of *Postscript*, Climacus contends that even the discourses published by Magister Kierkegaard (up to that time) are not
"upbuilding" in a Christian sense because "they use only ethical categories of immanence, not the doubly reflected religious categories in the
paradox" (that is, they use the categories of religiousness A rather
than those of religiousness B or Christianity).[108] And it is quite possible that Kierkegaard would have followed his intention of finishing his
writing career with that great work by the non-Christian Climacus, if it
had not been for the *Corsair* affair (beginning in January 1846) and its
repercussions in Copenhagen society's treatment of Kierkegaard. But
Kierkegaard plumbs the psychological/spiritual significance of this
apparently petty annoyance and comes to a profoundly disturbing
awareness of his own spiritual shallowness and concomitantly to an
overpowering sense of the call, the demand, of divine providence
that he begin a whole new authorship in which he would explore
Christian faith to its depths, especially Christianity as a call for sacrificial suffering.[109]

The first production of this new Christian authorship consisted of
three sets of discourses entitled, *Upbuilding Discourses in Various Spirits*,
written from May to November of that fateful year (1846) of the *Corsair*
affair. Kierkegaard is quite conscious of the fact that they mark, within
themselves, the transition through the three stages (aesthetic, ethical,
religious) and, within the religious, from the perspective of religiousness A to that of religiousness B (Christianity). In a journal entry shortly
after they were completed and before they were published, he says that
part 1 (on purity of heart) is essentially "ethical-ironic and thereby upbuilding, Socratic;" part 2 (on the lilies and birds) is "humorous," and
the three subsections "are related to one another aesthetically, ethically,
religiously" (clearly religiousness A which asserts the priority of God's

107. Ibid., 6431, X¹ A 510. Here Kierkegaard is contrasting Climacus with Anticlimacus
who is "a Christian to an extraordinary degree."

108. *Postscript*, p. 229; (KW 12.1:256); SV 9:214; (7:216). Climacus even claims to have
talked with Magister Kierkegaard on this matter, and that they agreed.

109. See my account of this event in Kierkegaard's life in my previous volume, *Kierkegaard as Humanist*, chapter 5, the section entitled, "The Change in the Concept of Necessity
after *Postscript*."

kingdom over worldly things);[110] but in part 3 (on "The Gospel of Suffering") the transition is clearly to Christian faith, starting off with an appeal to those who "belong to the Lord Jesus Christ" and who are "followers" of Christ as their "pattern" or example. And in the year following (1847) he produces two more books of discourses which openly advertise themselves as Christian, namely, *Works of Love*, subtitled "Christian Reflections," and *Christian Discourses*.

Behind the confident bravura of these writings, however, the journals reveal a soul struggling in agony to make it all real and actual for itself. In his determination to remain in the insecurity of being an author in the service of God, he prays, "God, give me your blessing and assistance, and above all spiritual assurance ... against the doubts that arise within me." Now, he says, "I must once again steer into the open sea, live in grace and out of grace, utterly in God's power." It is now "impossible for me to forget that [God's] eye sees me. Having been looked at by God, I ... have to look at God." And having finished *Works of Love*, "From now on the thrust should be into the specifically Christian. ... 'The forgiveness of sins' must be emphasized. ... [I]t must be established again as a paradox before anything can be done." And this emphasis on forgiveness was not just conceptual but very existential for him.

I now feel a demand to come to myself in a deeper sense by coming closer to God in an understanding of myself. I must ... be renewed inwardly. ... I must get hold of my melancholy. ... It is clear that my work [as an author] has helped others and that God has sanctioned it. ... But now God wants something else. Something is stirring within me which indicates a metamorphosis. ... I will be still, ... to think through the idea of my melancholy together with God. In this way my melancholy may be lifted and the specifically-Christian [*det Christelige*] may come closer to me. ... Now, by faith that God has forgotten in forgiveness whatever guilt I have, I must learn to forget it myself, ... not in any distance from it, but in God, ... and in that way learn myself to dare to forget it in forgiveness (Aug. 16, 1847).[111]

110. *Journals*, 5975, 5970; VIII[1] A 15, 1. For clarification on the distinction between irony and humor, see Climacus' discussion that opens with the statement: "There are three spheres of existence: the aesthetic, the ethical, and the religious. Two boundary zones correspond to these three: irony, constituting the boundary between the aesthetic and the ethical; humor, as the boundary that separates the ethical and the religious." And he is in the midst of describing the "essential expression" of religiousness A (*Postscript*, pp. 448–454; (KW 12.1:501–508); SV 10:179–185; [7:436–442]).

111. *Journals*, 5962, VII[1] A 222; 6012, 6037, 6043, VIII[1] A 158, 229, 250.

This passionate concern and determination apparently bore fruit.[112] By the following Easter (April 23, 1848), just as he was finishing *The Sickness unto Death* and beginning *Practice in Christianity,* he cries out, "My whole being is transformed. My hiddenness and enclosing-reserve [*Indesluttethed*] are broken – I may speak. Great God, grant me grace! ... Maundy Thursday and Good Friday have become true holy days for me." But, of course, the struggle goes on. A few days later he confesses in anguish, "No, no, my enclosing-reserve still cannot be broken. ... I do believe in the forgiveness of sins," and yet "I cannot come to such heights of faith, I cannot yet win such cheerful confidence of faith that I can believe that painful memory away. But in faith I protect myself against despair." And three weeks later, "It is wonderful how God's love overwhelms me still. ... Now (since Easter, although with intermissions) a hope has awakened in my soul that it may still be God's will to lift this elementary misery of my being. That is, I now am in faith in the deepest sense. ... I draw nearer to myself, come to myself. For God all things are possible. This thought is now in the deepest sense my watchword and has gained a meaning for me which I had never envisioned."[113]

This sense of being "in faith" continues to deepen and gain confidence over the succeeding years. He comes to see all his troubles and suffering as signs of the love of God. "At all times there is a world of help possible, because for God all things are possible; ... how blessed that [God] is also love, that for the loved one all things are possible. ... If sin wins a temporary victory over me, at all times for the honest penitent there is a world of help in the reconciliation [*Forsoning*] for all our sins with him our savior and reconciler." And again, "However much I suffer, ... when my soul is weary, ... [God] grants me the ability to rest in the concise thought that [God] is love, that Christ died for me as well. ... Christianity seems inimical to humankind, but that is because the natural human-being is lazy and weak and sensate, and Christianity is the absolute. ... If a person will cling to God, ... then Christianity is in fact love." After finishing *Sickness* and the first two parts of *Practice in*

112. In the third part of *Christian Discourses* entitled, "Thoughts That Wound from Behind – for Upbuilding" (written at the end of 1847), Kierkegaard frames a confession of faith for a hypothetical "individual" who (Lowrie suggests) is probably Kierkegaard himself. This individual confesses, "With an eternal decision I have secured my life by believing on him [Christ] – if he is a delusion, my life is lost. But this is not so, [for] I *believe*. ... I do not live by any 'if.' ... I ventured out so far (that is what venturing means), now I believe" (p. 244; SV 13:225; (10:238).

113. *Journals*, 6133, 6135; VIII[1] A 645, 650.

Christianity, he reflects, "I have been educated by this writing, have developed more and more religiously. ... It is my opinion that here [in these works] I am allowed to present Christianity once again and in such a way that a whole development can be based on it. ... It will serve for the intensified-interiorization [*Inderliggjørelse*] of Christianity; ... the more rigorous it is, the more grace becomes manifest as grace and not a sort of human sympathy."[114]

Who can doubt that these most intensely personal confidings to one's journal express as profound a sense of being and living within Christian faith as has been possessed by most Christians. And dozens of such entries continue to the end of the journal (even though the late ones are tinged with growing bitterness and "life-weariness" [*livslede*], untypical of Kierkegaard's earlier sparkle and confidence). And, of course, Kierkegaard repeatedly asserts that he is only an "ordinary Christian" who makes no claim to being the ideal example of his absolute statement of the ideal. Yet he knows that his God-given task is the unrelenting depiction and ever sharper restatement of that ideal as revealed to him in the paradoxical life of Jesus as the Christ, the God-humanbeing. So in his short unpublished work of 1849, *Armed Neutrality or My Position as a Christian Author in Christendom*, he says he wants to prevent "any sort of impression that I am a Christian to any extraordinary degree, a remarkable kind of Christian." Yet he wants to do this in such a way that "it cannot mean that I want to leave undecided the question of whether or not I myself am a Christian, am pursuing it, fighting for it, praying about it, and hoping before God that I am that."[115]

In this, his life-long task, Kierkegaard is clearly what we today would call a Christian theologian, even though a lay theologian without the church's authority or appointment. And just as he claimed that "the distinction between clergy and laity is unchristian" in regard to marriage,[116] he clearly was convinced that God had ordained (called) him

---

114. Ibid., 6229, 6237, 6238; IX A 216, 226, 227.

115. *Armed Neutrality and An Open Letter*, p. 33; *Papirer* X⁵ B 107, p. 288.

116. *Journals*, 2621, XI¹ A 313. Of course, at this point in his life (July 1854) Kierkegaard is arguing that neither clergy or laity, that is, no Christian should be married, that all marriage is unchristian. This is an example of the uncharacteristic bitterness and life-weariness that overwhelmed him as he neared the end of his life, as his task of reforming the church seemed hopeless, as most of his friends and family deserted him, as all hope of reconciliation with Regine was lost, as his health failed and his money was almost gone. In earlier days as he began his Christian authorship with *Works of Love*, he did not believe that love of God meant rejection, even hatred, of friendship and personal love between two human beings. Rather he argued that love of God and neighbor should "penetrate (*gennemtrænge*,

to the task of recovering the basic, essential Christian "conceptual definitions" (doctrines) from both their subversion to the bourgeois social, political, and economic forms of Danish life, and their corruption by an illusionary Hegelian redefinition – which subversion and corruption had been accomplished by those very clergy and theologians who had been ordained with the church's authority and appointment. We have tried to show, in a preliminary way, how he was a very "peculiar" theologian in certain emphases within his theology. We will now proceed to explore them.

---

diffuse) every relationship," should "transform human-love and friendship" (*Works of Love*, p. 117; (KW 16:112); SV 12:112; (9:109). So in a journal entry of the same time (1847), he is arguing that "the majority of people live far too securely in life and therefore get to know God so little." He is thinking of the things he does not now and never will have ("permanent positions" and "the comfort of wife and children"), and yet he says, "I shall never disparage this happiness" (*Journals*, 5962, VII¹ A 222).

2

My Self: A Gift

In the opening two pages of *The Sickness unto Death*, Kierkegaard provides a summary statement of the five basic elements in his understanding of the human being as spirit, as self: the self is a relation; the self is a relation, which relates to itself; the self (as such a relation) is established by an Other; the self fails to relate to itself and to the Other, and ends in despair; despair is rooted out (healed) when the self rests transparently in the Power that established it. The first two elements have been exposited at length (in our earlier volume entitled, *Kierkegaard as Humanist*) under the topics of: "My Self: A Synthesis of Two" and "My Self: A Task."

We come now to Kierkegaard's third assumption about the self: "Such a relation, which relates to itself, a self, must either have established itself or have been established by an other." In the following paragraph, he draws a key inference: "If the relation, which relates to itself, is established by an other, then the relation is indeed the [positive] third, but this relation, the third, is yet again a relation [that] relates to that which established the entire relation." His own assumption is clear: the self did not "establish itself"; rather, "The human self is such a derived, established relation, a relation, which relates to itself and in relating to itself relates to an other."[1]

THE GIFT AND GIVENNESS

In other words, my self (as inherent potentiality) is a "gift" from an other, and (throughout *Sickness*) Kierkegaard unabashedly calls the Power (that

---

1. *Sickness*, p. 146; (KW 19:14f.); SV 15:73; (11:127f.). A preliminary comment on these words is provided in my earlier volume, *My Self: An Interpretation of Kierkegaard as Humanist*, pp. 11–13.

is, the Power that established the self) "God." Precisely what he has in mind by the word "established" (*sat*, from *sætte*) he had already stated clearly in *Works of Love*:

To have unique-distinctive-individuality [*Eiendommelighed*] is to believe in the unique-individuality of every other [person]; because unique-individuality is not mine, but is the gift of God, by which [God] gives me being, and [God] indeed gives all things, and gives all things being. This is precisely the inscrutable richness of goodness in the goodness of God, that [God], the *almighty*, yet gives in such a way that the receiver obtains unique-individuality, that [God] who creates out of nothing, yet creates unique-individuality, so that the creation standing opposite to [God] does not become nothing, although it is taken from nothing and is nothing, yet becomes unique-individuality.[2]

In this same passage Kierkegaard expresses and reveals one of the central themes of his understanding of the self (and it runs throughout all of his writings), namely: in order for the human self to become itself, it must stand in a certain relationship to its "source and origin," it must have the courage to be itself *"before God."* Hence, in this passage (as we have noted before) there are subtle overlappings between Kierkegaard's perspective as humanist and his perspective as theologian.[3] On the one hand, Kierkegaard avers that every human being that has ever lived is constructed with the potentiality and the task of becoming a unique individual person or self by relating subjectively, immanently to "the eternal."[4] On the other hand (as will be explicated below), Kierkegaard gives to the knowledge of God as "my creator" uniquely Christian origins and characteristics. At the beginning of the above passage from *Works of Love*, he says, "Christ ... came into the world to become the prototype [*Forbillede*], in order to draw human-beings unto himself that they might become like him." But in his *Christian Discourses* (which he began to write just as he finished *Works of Love*) he says, "What then is the lowly Christian, who is himself before God? She is *human-being* [*Menneske*]. Insofar as she is human-being, she is in a certain sense like the bird, which is what it is. ... But at the same time she is *Christian*. ... As *human-being*

2. *Works of Love*, p. 253; (KW 16:171–2); SV 12:261; (9:259). *Eiendommelighed* is one of those words to which Kierkegaard gives a special meaning and which he uses to indicate what he means by being a "self." Literally, *Eiendom* means "property," and so in Kierkegaard's usage it means "that property or distinctive quality which belongs to me alone."
3. See *Kierkegaard as Humanist*, pp. 445–450.
4. This perspective is analyzed in detail in Chapters 4, 5, and 6 of *Kierkegaard as Humanist*.

she was created in *God's image* [*Billede*], but as *Christian* she has *God* for prototype [*Forbillede*]."[5]

So Kierkegaard is assuming that every human being is "created in God's image," but the human being is not aware of it in those terms. Rather, in the terms of religiousness A (a potentiality of every human being), it takes the form of awareness of the task set by eternity's demand (subjectively, immanently) that every human being become a self.[6] In the Christian experience of and relationship with the eternal (religiousness B), the believer comes to know God as "my creator," that is, as the Giver of my being as a unique-individual. This means that I have being over against and objective to God, and I now have the task to model my life on the prototype of God's own being as manifested in Jesus as the Christ. But now a profound problem confronts me: awareness of my self as gift compels me to ask, "Who and what is the Giver?" In traditional theological language: what is Kierkegaard's doctrine of God? And how are his leading concepts derived phenomenologically[7] from the Christian faith-relationship with God in Jesus Christ?

A first answer to these questions is that Kierkegaard does not have or seek a "doctrine" of God. As we have seen (in chapter 1), for him Christian faith does not have doctrines as its object, nor does it seek a system of concepts as its mode of expression. Rather, faith is a dynamic relationship of believing trust, and it finds expression in living and action. And yet "Christian conceptual definitions" play an integral role in the formation of faith and in the direction of action (see above pp. 28–33). So it is not surprising that nowhere in the authorship do we find Kierkegaard providing an extended and summary statement concerning the nature of God. Rather, we find isolated statements and brief expositions about the nature of God scattered throughout the writings and journals, sometimes referring to God as experienced within religiousness A, sometimes within religiousness B, or a combination of the two. And these state-

5. *Works of Love*, p. 247; (KW 16:264); SV 12:254; (9:252); *Christian Discourses*, p. 44; SV 13:45; (10:46). In the latter quotation "prototype" means a pattern or model which one should follow and imitate. This concept will later be traced in Kierkegaard's writings and explicated.

6. See *Postscript*'s exposition of the difference between religiousness A and B, pp. 493–519; (KW 12.1:555–586); SV 10:224–252; (7:485–511). For my own exposition, see the section entitled "The Leap as Transition from Ethical to Religious" in chapter 6 of *Kierkegaard as Humanist*.

7. It is my thesis that Kierkegaard's "method" is phenomenological and analogical. For a statement of this thesis see *Kierkegaard as Humanist*, Chapter 1, the section on "Kierkegaard's Method." Or for a fuller statement see my article, "Kierkegaard's Method: Does He Have One?" in *Kierkegaardiana*, Vol. XIV (1988), pp. 14–28.

ments use poetic images and analogies on the one hand, as well as abstract "conceptual definitions" on the other.

It is difficult to know where or how to begin a summary of these analogies and concepts. Clarification of what it means for God to "create out of nothing" emerges only from the event of reconciliation with God in the Christian faith-relationship. But this event consists essentially in the experience of forgiveness of sin, which assumes the prior event of human failure (sin) and the "fall" into despair. This failure, however, consists essentially in a break (disrelation) in the original, established relationship of creator/creature. So we are involved in a circular process of clarification with no single best point of beginning. Hence beginning (as we are) with the character of God as creator, we must anticipate something of the event of faith. And we may also anticipate that Kierkegaard brings to each of these terms of traditional Christian theology his own unique perspective and gives to each a profoundly subjective and intriguing meaning.

What is it, then, in the emergence of the faith-relationship with God (as known in Jesus as the Christ), that is the source and ground for the Christian consciousness and conviction that "unique-individuality is not mine, but is the gift of God, by which [God] gives me being, ... and gives all things being," and how does this source serve as a clue as to what it means to say that God "creates out of nothing?" Kierkegaard's clearest description of this source and ground is probably found at the beginning of the third discourse in *Practice in Christianity*, entitled "From on High He Will Draw All unto Himself."

He begins the discourse by insisting that we must "become very clear about the precise meaning of the thought *to draw to itself.*" He spells out his answer in four dense paragraphs (which should be read in their entirety) that combine many elements of his whole complex understanding of God.[8]

His first point is that the meaning of this "drawing" (of human beings by Christ into the redeeming relationship of faith) "depends upon the nature of what is to be drawn." His answer: it is a being that "is in itself a self," and whose "continuing-existence" (*Bestaaen*, objective subsistence) as a self must not be "lost" in the process. Therefore,

when that which is to be drawn is in itself a self, then truly to draw to itself means *first* to help it truly to become itself in order *then* to draw it to itself, or it means

---

8. *Practice in Christianity*, pp. 159f.; (KW 20:159f.); SV 16:155f.; (12:149f.). This reference covers the quotations in the next three paragraphs.

in and through drawing it to itself to help it become itself. – Therefore, truly to draw to itself means something twofold: first to make the self, which is to be drawn to itself, to be itself, in order then to draw it to itself (emphasis added).

In other words, if God is to draw a human being into a truly redeeming faith-relationship (with God), God must do so in such a way that the human being is helped and enabled to be and become one's own authentic self and in such a way that, in the process, one never loses one's identity as a self "in one's self," distinct from the being of God. But this statement leaves us with a profound ambiguity. Does God (in Christ) merely "help" the self to become itself or does God "make" the self become itself? In order to answer this question, Kierkegaard asks another: "And what is it to be a self?"

Here in the midst of his last major work, he proposes, in a few sentences, to answer a question that has haunted his writings from the beginning and whose answer received its definitive formulation at the beginning of *Sickness*.[9] Here (in *Practice*) he says very simply that the self is a "duplexity [*Dobbelthed*]" and a "reduplication [*Fordoblelse*]" (the latter being a much more technical abstract term, which we will make much of below). The first term refers to the fact that the human-being "is in itself a self" and yet must "become itself." The second term indicates the nature of the event in which the given potential self *becomes* itself. "Reduplication" simply means that "a self ... is freedom." Therefore, for God (in Christ) to "draw to himself means to posit a choice," because "a self can truly draw another [self] to itself only through a choice." And Kierkegaard repeats this point even more strongly: "Therefore, Christ wants first and foremost to help every human being to become itself ... by repenting. ... He wants to draw the human-being to himself, but in order truly to draw her/him to himself he wants to draw the human being only as a free being to himself, that is, through a choice."

In other words, at the very heart and depth of the most profound and radically transforming relationship that a human being can have with God as the giver and creator of human being and life, God gives or creates ("helps" and "makes") in such a way that God calls into play the definitive quality of being "a self in itself," namely, freedom, choice. As we have heard (in *Works of Love*), even though God is "almighty," yet God "gives in such a way that the receiver obtains unique-individuality, ... so

9. See the section entitled " 'My Self' as the Unifying Focus" in chapter 1 of my *Kierkegaard as Humanist*.

that the creation standing opposite to God does not become nothing, although it is taken out of nothing." This means that the phrase "creates out of nothing" has reference strictly and only to the emergence of each and every human being as an utterly and permanently unique psyche/spirit, one who has never existed before ("out of nothing") and will never be repeated again. And at the core of the being of such a psyche/spirit, there is built in the divine demand: choose, freely. Choose what? Choose, freely, to accept or to reject *becoming* one's unique potential self with compassionate help from one's creator, the help that comes in the loving relationship of faith (or the faithful relationship of love).

The nature of the negative act of rejection will be spelled out in detail in the next chapter, "My Self: A Failure," that is, my self as sinner. But here we are being told that the structure of freedom at the core of human selfhood exists for the positive act of becoming one's self by accepting God's help, as that help comes to us gracefully through God's "drawing" us into the faith relationship. And the happy successful outcome of this "drawing" awaits and depends on the free and joyful acquiescence of the human heart (spirit/self), because (as we hear in the poetic analogy of *Philosophical Fragments*) the omnipotent love of God "desires to be equal with the beloved," even though this character of God's love opens up the negative possibility that the beloved (every human being) will lose confidence and be offended and so fail to respond in love. And this thought of Climacus is repeated and expanded by Anti-Climacus in *Sickness.* Even "in the infinite love of [God's] merciful grace, [God] nevertheless makes one condition: ... [God] cannot remove the possibility of offense. What a rare act of love, what unfathomable grief of love, that even God cannot remove the possibility."[10] And Anti-Climacus picks up this concept and develops it at length in the second discourse of *Practice in Christianity* which opens by saying that "despite his love, [Jesus Christ] out of love cannot make impossible whether or not you will be offended at him; ... he who omnipotently can do all things and yet ... impotently ... must leave it up to you yourself whether you will be offended or not."[11] And when (in the next chapter of this present study) we come to analyze the event of the human being's failure (sin), it will prove to be very important to note the fact that this negative possibility of human freedom has been established by God (and no other) in

10. *Philosophical Fragments*, pp. 4of.; (KW 7:32); SV 6:33f.; (4:200); *Sickness*, p. 257; (KW 19:126); SV 15:175; (11:235).

11. *Practice in Christianity*, p. 80; (KW 20:76); SV 16:82; (12:74f.).

the very act of "creating" the human being free, with choice. And there we will have to ask in what sense God remains omnipotent in the face of human failure, especially in face of Kierkegaard's assertion that this failure is universal.

The point here, however, is that, in spite of our failure, God's love pursues us and confronts us and offers us the help we need to achieve the task which we have failed to fulfill: the task of becoming our authentic selves in the image of God, of modeling our lives after the prototype that has appeared in Jesus as the Christ. Again, we will have to wait until chapter 4 on faith/love to spell out fully and precisely the form and content of this help ("repentance" and "forgiveness"). But here, in a preliminary way, we hear Kierkegaard trying to discern and to depict a puzzling double-dialectic: on the one hand, the omnipotent God offers help to the failed, impotent human being and yet must wait impotently to see if the recipient will freely and willingly accept the gift; on the other hand, the free and self-contained ("is in itself a self") self stands aware that it is impotent to achieve the actualization of the self's infinite potential unless and until it gladly and humbly accepts the gift of God's help. And the most amazing thing about this human awareness is that this "gift" assumes the startling form of: something out of nothing, life out of death, and that is the nature and meaning of "creation."

Kierkegaard contends that there is an anticipation of this awareness even in religiousness A (open to humanity as such). It comes when one has the sense of having reached the dead end of human capacities (reason, ethical striving, physical control) to affirm the infinite dignity and worth of the human self and to set the self free to accomplish its infinite potentialities. Then, as one turns to the inward depths of one's own subjectivity, one comes to a halting spot, before an enormous chasm. In fear and trembling, one enters a place of silence and assumes a posture of listening; one gasps for air like a fish out of water and knows that the silence is the death of all one's own possibilities. Then one hears a voice that is not one's own, a voice from "the eternal," affirming and encouraging and enabling the one who has lost the way. And a new life is given.[12] This rather vague and formless experience, however, is given definite shape and content in the Christian experience of repentance and forgiveness. And Kierkegaard argues that its primary character is that of

12. For the sources of this exposition, see the section entitled "The Breach in Religiousness A" in chapter 6 of *Kierkegaard as Humanist*; for a fuller exposition, see also the section, "The Nature of Confession" in chapter 4 below.

"resurrection," that is, life out of death, not physically up out of the grave, but spiritually, at the depth of one's selfhood.

His clearest and most forthright statement of this quality of Christian faith comes at the end of the authorship in *For Self-Examination*. Kierkegaard moves from "looking at oneself ... in the mirror of the word" (part 1), to imitation of Christ as "the way" (of suffering and death) (part 2), to the Spirit who "gives life" (part 3). But in part 3 he warns, "This life-giving in the Spirit is not a *direct* heightening of the natural life in a human-being in *immediate* continuation from and connection with it. ... No, it is a new life, literally a new life – because ... death goes in between, dying to, and a life on the other side of death." What death? dying to what? "You must first die to every merely earthly hope, to every merely human confidence; you must die to your selfishness, or to the world."[13] And the apostles had indeed died in this way, but even after the resurrection and ascension of Christ, they still had no life. "Then came the Spirit who gives life." But when and how does the Spirit come? By bringing "the gifts of the Spirit." And the first gift is *faith*, "faith in the strictest sense of the word – only after death has come in between." "This faith is stronger than the whole world; it has the power of eternity; it is the Spirit's gift from God, it is your victory over the world."[14]

So now we have found Kierkegaard's answer to the question (with which we started) as to what it is in the Christian faith-relationship with God that reveals to us that we are "created out of nothing." It is precisely the experience of God's power to give us a *new* life (after our "death" in the alienation and despair of sin) that leads to our belief-ful conviction (understanding) that our original being (life), with the built-in potentiality of selfhood, was also a gift or creation from the hands of the same God. In the language of *Sickness*, "Such a relation, which relates to itself, must either have established itself or have been established by an Other. ... The human-being's self is such a derived, established self, a relation which relates to itself, and in relating to itself relates to an Other."[15]

THE GIVER: GOD

We are investigating, however, not Kierkegaard's basic anthropology but his theology proper, that is, his understanding of the nature of "God" as

13. *For Self-Examination*, p. 89f.; (KW 21:76f.); SV 17:114f.; (12:360f.).
14. Ibid., p. 96; (KW 21:81f.); SV 17:118f.; (12:365).
15. *Sickness*, p. 146; (KW 19:13); SV 15:73; (11:127f.).

such. And first we must ask whether Kierkegaard believed that we come to know anything about the being of God as such. If he had followed his philosophical mentor, F. Adolf Trendelenburg, he would have answered in the negative. In the last two chapters (in the first edition) of his major work, *Logische Untersuchungen,* Trendelenburg attempts to show that philosophy goes beyond the capacity of the sciences by seeking to discover and to portray a unity of all human experience. And in the final chapter he argues that this unity is rooted in and derived from an Absolute whose nature is best indicated as "*Das Ubetingte*" (the chapter's title). He avers that what the philosophers call "the unconditioned" is designated "God" in religion, and he agrees with Kant that the unconditioned is essentially unknowable. There are, of course, analogies of God in the universe, such as rationality and purposiveness. So just as one can "comprehend a poem without knowing the poet," so one may see the world as "an image [*Bild*] of God" or even as "the body of God." "But the image remains an image."[16]

Kierkegaard is interested in and fascinated with the concept of the unconditioned (or unconditional) throughout his writings, but in almost every instance the unconditional consists of a quality of an ethical demand in human relationships, or a quality of the demands one becomes aware of in relating to the infinite or to God. And in this sense, the unconditional is a characteristic of religiousness A as much as of religiousness B.[17] Only in some late journal entries (of the 1850s) does Kierkegaard come close to characterizing God-as-such as the Unconditioned and hence describes faith as an unconditional relationship with God. And characterizing God as the Unconditioned is one way in which he specifies "an infinite qualitative difference" (his words) between the being and nature of God, on the one hand, and that of every human being and the whole created universe, on the other hand. But it does not follow (for Kierkegaard) that God is unknowable. Rather, as we have seen above, it is precisely as God asserts and manifests *presence* with us and *likeness* to us, in the act of "drawing" us into that presence in Jesus as the Christ, that we come to *know* and (in a sense) understand the profound qualitative otherness of God. Through reconciliation in forgive-

16. Friedrich Adolf Trendelenburg, *Logische Untersuchungen* (Third Edition), pp. 473, 509. For a discussion of this point see Gershon George Rosenstock, *F.A. Trendelenburg: Forerunner to John Dewey*, pp. 15f., where he contends that, for Trendelenburg, God remains unknowable behind the image.

17. For my summary of this point, see the section entitled, "Kierkegaard's Conception of the Unconditional" in chapter 6 of *Kierkegaard as Humanist.*

ness, in the new life given us in the spirit, we come to the ineffable awareness of the reality of one who is creator, not creature, of one unconditioned by our essential spatiality and temporality, hence infinite and eternal. As will become clear later in chapter 4 on faith/love, God as the Unconditioned comes to dwell with us, to become known in love and worship – yet, without in the least diminishing, let alone erasing, the "infinite qualitative difference."

This phrase, however, does not tell us just what the difference is; it does not tell us what God's *being* is like, except by negation or, at best, in general terms. As noted in the previous chapter (at note 56), Kierkegaard's first formulation of this phrase came in *The Book on Adler* where he asserted (against D.F. Strauss) that "between God and the human-being there is an eternal essential qualitative difference." But the only way he describes this difference is to say that Jesus as the God-human-being does not relate to other humans "in the relationship of [one] human-being to [another] human-being, as human-being, he relates not in a quantitative difference (as a genius, etc.)." Rather, "he relates ... by his paradoxical specific quality: the divine authority."[18] And in the same year (1846) he says in his journals that between God as subject and the human being as subject "there always remains an infinite qualitative difference."[19]

In the previous year (in *Postscript*) he anticipated this concept by asserting an "absolute difference" between God and the human-bring, and he provides a general notion of what he means by it. He says that this difference is the ground of the absolute paradox experienced in Christian faith, in that a human being who has the nature of being an "existing" individual (i.e., in time and space, finite and temporal) must relate to God who is infinite and eternal.[20] This difference is "absolute" and therefore a human being must relate to God "absolutely" as one's "absolute telos." This relationship takes the essential form of worship as one is filled with a sense of the "sublimity" of God "because the *qualities* are absolutely different" (emphasis added).[21] However, except for the general terms of infinite and eternal, he does not tell us what these qualities are. And he does not really add anything when later he tells us that even the equality of love between God and the human-being must take

18. *On Authority and Revelation* (Walter Lowrie's translation of *The Book on Adler*, Princeton University Press, 1955), p. 112; *Papirer*, VII² B 235, p. 145.

19. *Journals*, 1349; VII¹ A 201.

20. *Postscript*, p. 1(KW 12.1:217); SV 9:181; (7:182).

21. Ibid., p. 369; (KW 12.1:412); SV 10:103f.; (7:357f.).

the form of the humility of lowliness in the human being.[22] We must never forget, he warns, "the qualitative difference" between "what comes from God and what comes from the human-being."[23] Here is the first instance of where he speaks of a "qualitative" difference.

It is when Kierkegaard comes to write *The Sickness unto Death* that the "infinite qualitative difference" becomes a regulative concept for him. And all four of the key passages occur in the uniquely and decisively *Christian* part 2 of this normative work in the whole Kierkegaardian corpus.

First, it should be noted that there is a significant switch in terminology (in all four passages): Kierkegaard speaks of a "difference of quality" (*Qvalitets-Forskjellen*) rather than a "qualitative difference."[24] In this way he picks up the point Climacus made in *Postscript* (note 21 above) that Christian worship of God issues from a recognition of God's sublimity (or majesty), that is, from an awareness that "the qualities [of God and the human] are absolutely different." Here in *Sickness* he puts it bluntly: "God and human-being are two qualities, between which there is an infinite difference of quality."[25] The problem of the relationship between quantity and quality had been of a matter of interest and serious attention for him from university days onward.[26] In *Fear and Trembling* (1843) he begins to explore "the movement of infinity" as a "leap" which "is carried out through passion [*Lidenskab*]" and never by reflection, and in a background note for this book he asks, "Can a transition take place

22. Ibid., p. 439; (KW 12.1:492); SV 10:170f.; (7:427).

23. Ibid., p. 514; (KW 12.1:580); SV 10:246; (7:580).

24. The four passages are in *Sickness*, pp. 230, 248, 252, 257; (KW 19:99, 117, 121, 126); SV 15:151, 167, 171, 175; (11:210, 227, 231, 235). The new Hong translation (KW 19) does not reflect this change but continues to use the adjectival form as found in *The Book on Adler* and in the five journal entries of the year 1849 where Kierkegaard refers to the qualitative difference. But I believe that the switch to the noun was deliberate by Kierkegaard. He had the adjective handily available if he wanted to use it. In a journal entry of 1850 he uses both forms. He is contrasting our knowledge of the human and of the divine and comments: "This is a difference of quality, and it makes it impossible to be otherwise; the qualitative heterogeneity between God and human-being must manifest precisely this state of affairs." (*Journals*, 3646; X³ A 23)

25. *Sickness*, p. 257; (KW 19:126); SV 15:175; (11:235).

26. The terms appear in *Irony* [pp. 219, 271; (KW 2:194, 254); SV 1:222, 269; (13:275, 328)] and in notes he made while reading Tennemann's *Geschichte der Philosophie* in 1842 (*Journals*, 5572; IV C 2; cf. 258; IV C 47). And in his philosophical notes of 1843 he muses about the relation of being and quality (Ibid., 1598–1600; IV C 66–68) and notes Leibniz's observation that "there are great difficulties involved in the inference of quality from quantity" (Ibid., 2367; IV C 37).

from a quantitative determinant to a qualitative one except by a leap?"[27] The very next year he answers this question unreservedly in *The Concept of Angst* (while considering how the first sin came into being): "It is a superstition when it is maintained in logic that through a continued quantification a new quality is brought forth. ... The new quality appears with the first, the leap. ... Thus sin comes into the world ... by a leap; but this leap also posits the quality."[28]

This language about quantity and quality means that the "infinite difference" between the quality that is God and the quality that is human-being cannot be bridged (let alone erased) strictly and exclusively from the human side. As we have attempted to show in a previous volume on *Kierkegaard as Humanist*, Kierkegaard puts a rather positive construction on the capabilities of universal human nature for exploration and implementation of the religious dimension of human consciousness – more so than many Christian theologians. He believes that at the depth (or height) of human subjectivity, every human is capable of an awareness of a structure or dynamic that is "other" than human being, that must be called infinite and eternal, that even manifests itself as "all-things-are-possible." But before this Other the human self must stop and wait in silence and impotence, waiting to "hear" or sense affirmation and encouragement from the eternal, from beyond one's self. And in this moment the human self is also aware that the eternal makes an inescapable and inexorable demand: to believe, to choose, to love – and to risk all.

Kierkegaard makes clear, however, even in *Postscript*, that in religiousness A this Other remains largely undefined. Only when the Other (God, the eternal) takes the initiative to enter our temporality in the figure of Jesus does the character of God become clear through God's act of "qualifying [*bestemmer*] more specifically the eternal blessedness."[29] And throughout the entire second authorship that followed *Postscript*, Kierkegaard explores ever more profoundly the "infinite difference of quality" that separates the human-being from this God.

What is it, then, that comes to be known (seen, understood) about God's own *being* at the depth/height of the Christian faith-relationship with God? Does Kierkegaard succeed in "qualifying more specifically" not only what God demands of human beings but also the very own and

27. *Fear and Trembling*, p. 53; (KW 6:42); SV 5:40; (3:93); *Journals*, 261; IV C 12, 87.
28. *The Concept of Anxiety*, pp. 27–29; (KW 8:30, 32); SV 6:126, 127; (4:302–04).
29. *Postscript*, p. 494; (KW 12.1, 556); SV 10:225; (7:485).

unique character of the One who makes these demands? Does the Christian experience of life as a "gift" enclose a revelation of the "Giver"? He speaks more and more about the "majesty" of God and (especially in late journal entries) associates that majesty closely with God as "the unconditioned" and as "being-in-and-for-itself."[30] But does he provide specific definition, or at least clarifying content, of these terms?

As was stated at the beginning of this chapter, Kierkegaard's statements about the nature of God are expressed in both poetic images/analogies and abstract conceptual-definitions. In the late journal entries where he explores the unconditioned, he calls into play two concepts and two analogies in an attempt to clarify the content of the "infinite difference of quality." The two concepts are: "being-in-and-for-itself" (*Iogforsigværende*) and "reduplication" (*Fordoblelse*). The two analogies are: "infinite subjectivity" (*uendelig Subjektivitet*) and "personhood" (*Personlighed*). When we have clarified what each of these four terms say about God and how they interrelate and modify each other, we will then have to reinterpret them in the light of two other terms that are ultimately and pervasively regulative for Kierkegaard: the concept that God is "all-things-are-possible," and the analogy that God is "love." And let us remember that all six of these terms form a cluster for the clarification of Kierkegaard's declaration with which we began this chapter: "unique-individuality is not mine, but is the gift of God, by which [God] gives me being, ... gives all-things being, ... creates out of nothing, yet creates unique-individuality, so that creation standing opposite to [God] does not become nothing."

There is an urgent question that Kierkegaard's explication of these terms forces upon us: do they describe the structural being of God, or describe the dynamic action of God, or both? Do some describe one and some the other, or do they comprise an undifferentiated cluster? Is there an ultimate and irreducible polarity in God, or is God a polarity within a homogeneous unity? An answer to this question must wait upon the explication (which follows).

GOD AS BEING-IN-AND-FOR-ITSELF

In his journals of the last three years of his life, Kierkegaard uses the concept of being-in-and-for-itself as a key weapon in his attack upon the

---

30. See especially *Journals,* 1436, 2079, 1447, 1449; (XI² A 6, 124, 130, 133). Alastair McKinnon has provided me with a study that shows that the association of these three words in these and other entries is statistically very significant.

church. He believes that Christianity of his day is fatally flawed because most of its adherents have faith in God only "up to a point." Therefore, "Christianity is without God," because "what help is it to have something called God that is only a name, because after all God is surely uncondi-tioned being [*ubetingede Væren*]," and "the unconditioned" (*det Ubetingede*) is "the being-in-and-for-itself" (*det Iogforsigværende*). Kierkegaard chal-lenges Christianity of his day: "Show me if you can ... a single person living who has the remotest impression of such a being or who could en-tertain the thought of wanting to relate himself to such a being."[31]

What does it mean that God is "being" that is in-and-for-itself? This compound word came into Kierkegaard's vocabulary during his univer-sity studies and was used in the writing of his dissertation, *The Concept of Irony*, and he clearly derived it from Hegel.[32] But Hegel's usage is irrele-

31. *Journals*, 4918; XI² A 205. This entry was made in December 1854. In what follows we will be using material from three entries made in August and September of 1852 (from Volume X⁴ of *Papirer*) and from three others made in October and November of 1854 (from Volume XI²). It would be interesting to speculate as to why Kierkegaard did not use this concept of God in his public attack on the church in these last three years of his life. Probably he thought it not wise to use abstract philosophical language (especially of Hege-lian origin) but to stick to his main thesis that the church of his day had deserted and be-trayed the Christian faith of the New Testament and to use primarily Biblical language in support of his thesis.

32. The full compound term appears half a dozen times in the appendix to part 1, en-titled "Hegel's Conception of Socrates" [see *The Concept of Irony*, in either the translation by Lee M. Capel (Indiana University Press) or that by Howard and Edna Hong (in *Kierkegaard's Writings* Vol. 2, Princeton University Press) [pp. 246, 248, 254f.; (KW 2:226, 228, 236); SV 1: 248, 250, 255; (13:304, 306, 311)]. Kierkegaard also uses (as a variation of this term) "in and for itself" (sometimes *i og for sig*, sometimes *i og for sig selv*). This latter phrase occurs throughout the writings but usually means simply "as such" or "essentially." But in *The Con-cept of Irony* he is clearly using the term or phrase as he has derived it from Hegel, in part from university lectures, but decisively from Hegel's *Lectures on the History of Philosophy*. Kierkegaard is discussing "in what sense is Socrates the founder of morality," and he quotes Hegel as saying, "Socrates expresses essence [*Wesen*] as the universal I, *as the good*, the con-sciousness resting in itself; the good as such, free from existent reality, free from [using the *von* in Michelet 1842 edition of the *Vorlesungen* instead of the *gegen* in K.'s 1836 edition] the relation of consciousness to existent reality." Then Kierkegaard goes on to say that this means that "Socrates has arrived at being-in-and-for-itself [*Iogforsigværende*] as the being-in-and-for-itself for thought" [ibid., p. 246; (226); 248; (304)]. This compound term is not in the paragraph he quotes from Hegel but is in the very next paragraph, where Hegel says that Socrates adopts Anaxagoras' belief that self-conscious "thought, understanding is the ruling *self-determining universal*," and that, for Socrates, "this substance, existing-in-and-for-itself [*anundfürsichseiende*] and self-maintaining [*sich Erhaltende*], has become determined as the goal, and more closely as the true, the good." (See C.L. Michelet's edition, Berlin, 1842, Vol. II, p. 40; E.S. Haldane's translation, London, 1892, Vol. I, p. 385.) Two pages

vant because, typically, Kierkegaard develops his own unique meaning in his second (Christian) authorship.[33] We find a form of the concept in the first products of that authorship, namely, *Works of Love* and *Christian Discourses*, and in *Works* it is related to reduplication. Then, as the litera-

---

later (in *Irony*) Kierkegaard again attributes the concept of being-in-and-for-itself to Socrates and makes the point that for Socrates it means that "the individual would no longer act out of fear of the law but with a conscious knowledge of why he acted" [ibid., pp. 248f; (228); 250; (306)].

In fact, earlier in *Irony*, Kierkegaard argues that the essential idea of being-in-and-for-itself was first formulated by Socrates, as reported in Plato's *Phædo* (75, 78, 79). Socrates is distinguishing compounds (ξυνθετα) from non-compounds, the former being things that appear to be equal, beautiful, good, just, holy, and the latter being the essences of beauty, goodness, justice, holiness *as such*; the former being subject to change, the latter being unchanging, indissoluble, without variation. So Kierkegaard says that each of the latter realities is "in and for itself" (*i og for sig*), and quotes Socrates as saying that these realities "we designate, in our questions as well as our answers, as that which is [*det, det er*]" [*Phædo*, 75 D; *Irony*, p. 106; (KW 2:70f.); SV 1:122; (13:163f.)]. Plato's Greek for "that which is" is το αυτο δ' εστι, literally "it is itself." But Kierkegaard says it means that which is "in and for itself" (i og for sig), or those things which "always presuppose themselves." And a few pages later [pp. 108f.; (KW 2:72f.); SV 1:124; (13:165)] he uses this language to interpret a passage in the *Phædo* that is even closer in its language. He does not quote but paraphrases Socrates: "The uncompounded is that which always behaves [forholder sig] in the same way. Does that essence [Væsen], he asks (78 D), to which we ... attribute genuine being [Væren] always behave in the same way or sometimes one thing and sometimes another? This in-and-for-itself equality, beauty and everything that has genuine being – can it ever undergo any kind of change? 'These things are always themselves the same, are formless and cannot be seen' (79 A)." Plato's own language in 78 D is very interesting as Kierkegaard's claimed source for the meaning of his phrase "in and for itself." After asking whether equality itself or beauty itself can ever change, Socrates asks, "[O]r is each of them always what it is [δ' εστι], being of one kind [μονοειδες] itself for itself [αυτο καθ' αυτο]?" So it would seem that when Kierkegaard, in *The Concept of Irony*, speaks of being which is in-and-for-itself, he is describing an entity which is not qualified in its essential being by any participation in spatial/temporal dimensions. And we shall see that the kernel of this idea remains in Kierkegaard's application of this language to the being of God in his late journal entries.

So it is clear that Kierkegaard derived this compound term from Hegel and that Hegel used it in the context of his interpretation of Socrates. In his translation of *Irony*, Lee Capel argues (p. 403f., note 31) that Kierkegaard depends on Hegel's interpretation in great detail and yet arrives at a different picture in totality, but this issue is not relevant to Kierkegaard's final use of the concept.

33. In Kierkegaard's only early usage of the term, he is clearly talking about Hegel's concept of the necessity that is inherent in the concept of the absolute in pure thinking, and then comments, "It is otherwise with the good. The good is because I will it, and otherwise it is not at all. ... The good is the being-in-and-for-itself [*I-og-for-sig-Værende*], posited by the being-in-and-for-itself, and this is freedom." [See *Either/Or*, 2:228; (KW 4:224); SV 3:208; (2:201).] So even here he is distancing his usage from that Hegel.

ture of the "attack" on the church takes shape, Kierkegaard drops this
(Hegelian) philosophical language and uses it only in very late journal
entries for his own clarification (see note 31 above). For the sake of clarity and brevity, we will conflate these sources.

In *Christian Discourses* Kierkegaard says, "There is only one who knows
[*kjender*] himself, who in and for himself [*i og for sig selv*] knows [*veed*]
what he himself is: that is God. ... The human-being who is not before
[*for*] God is not himself, which one can be only by being in the One who
is in and for himself." In the next paragraph he carefully explains that
to be "before" an other means simply being "in relationship to others."
Hence God "knows what he himself is" because God is simply and directly "in and related to himself."[34] In *Works of Love* he gives one explanation of what it means for God to be "in and related to" himself, in a
way that is qualitatively different from human being (existence).

The temporal [the human] has three times [past, present, future], and therefore actually never exists wholly, nor wholly in any one of them; the eternal *is*. A
temporal object can have many different qualities [*Egenskaber*]; it can in a certain sense be said to have them simultaneously, insofar as it is what it is in these
specific qualities. But a temporal object never has reduplication [*Fordoblelse*] in
itself [*i sig selv*]; as the temporal vanishes into time, it *is* really only in [its] qualities. On the other hand, if the eternal is in a human-being, then this eternal is
reduplicated in her in such a way that every instant it is in her, it is in her in a
twofold way: in an outward direction and in an inward direction back into itself,
but in such a way that these [two] are one and the same; because otherwise
there is no reduplication. [Then there follows this key statement:] The eternal *is*
not merely in its qualities, rather is in its qualities within itself [*i sig selv*]. It does
not merely *have* qualities, but is in itself as simultaneously [*idet*] it has qualities.
(Emphasis added in last two sentences.)[35]

34. *Christian Discourses*, pp. 42–43; SV 13:43–44; (10:45).
35. *Works of Love*, p. 261; (KW 16:280); SV 12:269; (9:267). Kierkegaard goes on to say,
"So it is with love" – but we will use this point later. It should be noted that by translating
Fordoblelse as "reduplication" I am breaking with the Hongs' consistent use of "redoubling"
and their reservation of "reduplication" for Kierkegaard's Danish word *Reduplication*. After
careful study of the occurrences of both Danish words throughout both the works and the
journals, it seems to me that no rigorous distinction between Kierkegaard's uses of the two
Danish words can be made. And in English, to "redouble" means literally to make twice as
great or, broadly, to intensify. This is not at all Kierkegaard's meaning. In Danish *fordoble* can
mean to "redouble" but also to "reduplicate." From his usage, Kierkegaard clearly intends
the meaning of "reduplication," or more simply, of "repetition." The general notion is developed by him in the context of his theory of communication. He argues that in the realm

In other words, within the eternal (God) there is a dialectic between its being "in and related to itself" and its being "in its qualities," but in such a way that the one form of being is never without the other. And this dialectic comprises the dynamic of reduplication within God's own eternal being.

The only explicit development of these concepts, as applicable to God's own being, comes in the late journal entries (of 1852 and 1854).[36] In them Kierkegaard describes more specifically and directly than anywhere in his published works precisely how God is "qualitatively different" from

---

of subjectivity or spirituality only indirect communication is effective, as distinguished from the direct communication that is desirable and possible in objective communication of facts and abstract concepts. Communication is "indirect" when the communicator leaves a gap, leaves space and time for the recipient to "appropriate" (*tilegne sig*) (to reduplicate) by and for him/herself the communication, as one's own inner insight and conviction. This usage of reduplication can be traced throughout Kierkegaard's works by using the indices of the Hong KW series and the index of the Hongs' translation of *Kierkegaard's Journals and Papers* (looking under both "redoubling" and "reduplication"). Often in the journals the point is also made that in Christian faith there must be a reduplication of thought or insight in one's existence, in act. So in a late journal entry of 1850 he can say that "direct relationship is really not Christianity. The essentially Christian is the rigorousness of reduplication" (*Journals*, 518; x³ A 100). But in *The Book on Adler* Kierkegaard generalizes the concept of reduplication when he says, "In the case of spirit, nothing can be conquered in some accidental or external way but only in the essential way; but the essential way is nothing more nor less than reduplication [*Redupplikation*] of the victory; that is to say, in the world of the spirit the form is the reduplication of the contents [or: substance, subject matter]." Or as he summarizes it, "The *mode of acquisition* and the *possession* are one and the same." And his prime example is the way or mode in which God was present in Christ (lowliness), and the way or mode in which Christ conquered the world: by being crucified (*On Authority and Revelation*, pp. 42n–43n; *Papirer*, VII² B 235, pp. 50n–51n). And this definition was immediately followed by the passage in *Works of Love* (just quoted) in which Kierkegaard says that the eternal is reduplicated in a human-being, and in such a way that there is double movement of the eternal, both outward and inward. How this reduplication takes place, what form it takes in the conscious experience of the human-being, we will explore in the next chapter on faith/love. But just now, in a few pages, we will see that Kierkegaard also explains how God "relates objectively to [God's] own subjectivity" as only a reduplication [*Fordoblelse*] of [God's] subjectivity, and that the eternal distinction (in God) between right and wrong is "a reduplication [*Fordoblelse*]." And when we come to the explication of the Christian experience of faith/love, one of the key passages will be from *Practice in Christianity* in which Kierkegaard says, "And what is it to be a self? It is to be a reduplication [*Fordoblelse*]. ... A self is a reduplication, is freedom" [p. 159; (KW 20:159); SV 16:155; (12:149)].

36. Nine entries will be referred to: *Journals*, 6793, 536, 4901, 4902; (x⁴ A 474, 581, 613, 636); 2570, 4571, 2079, 1449, 4918; (xi² A 54, 97, 124, 133, 205). The entries will be identified in the following text by inserting the item numbers from the Hong translation.

all other kinds of being, precisely how God is "unconditioned" and "eternal" in contrast to the relativity and temporality of human existence.

GOD AS INFINITE SUBJECTIVITY

He makes his main point by saying (in no. 2570) that "God is pure subjectivity, sheer unmitigated subjectivity, and intrinsically [*en Væren*] has no trace at all of the objective as such [*i sig*], since everything with such objectivity comes thereby within the realm of relativities." This means that "God is infinite majesty in such a way that nothing in and for itself [*i og for sig*] can concern [or engage] [God] but only insofar as it pleases [God's] majesty ... Whether something concerns [God] does not derive from the object but from [God's] pleasure – [God] is infinite subjectivity." For Kierkegaard, this is a startling and unprecedented attribution to the nature of God, that is, to speak of God's "subjectivity," which is his definitive and most carefully worked-out anthropological concept. In applying it to God, he obviously has in mind his detailed exposition of human subjectivity in *Postscript* because here in his journals he also contrasts subjectivity with "objectivity."

In *Postscript* he delineates several main features of subjectivity which are relevant to our present discussion of God's nature.[37] Subjectivity is essentially a turning inward to the infinite and eternal core of one's being, in order to make decisions (actions) freely as dictated by that being, without consideration of or determination by external, temporal, relative, and contingent circumstances. But this attentiveness to one's essential being presumes *consciousness* of this inner "self" or "spirit." But consciousness presumes reflection, and reflection is awakened and initiated by giving attention to a *distinction* within the immediacy and unity of being. For the human-being this is the distinction (and conflict) between one's finitude and one's infinitude, between what one is and what one dreams of becoming (between one's necessity and one's possibility).

Obviously, for God there is no conflict of this kind because there is no trace of the objective in God, no awakening from a dreaming immediacy in God. Does Kierkegaard assume some other kind of distinction and differentiation within the pure, unmitigated, unconditioned being-in-and-for-itself which God is? What can that differentiation be without

---

37. See my extensive summary of this topic in my volume on *Kierkegaard as Humanist*, Chapter 3, the sections on "Reflection: the First Step toward Self-consciousness" and "Consciousness of My Self."

the contrast of objectivity? But if there is no such differentiation how can God be subjectivity with and through self-consciousness?

In another journal entry (no. 4571, a month later than the previous one), he qualifies his insistence that God's subjectivity is "pure," "sheer," and "unmitigated." He repeats that "God is infinite subjectivity" and "does not have an objective-element in [God's] being ... because that would limit [*begrændse*] [God] and set [God] down into the realm-of-relativities [*Relativiteterne*]" (the clause beginning with "because" is omitted from the Hong translation). Then he adds this startling and mystifying qualification: "but [God] relates objectively to [God's] own subjectivity." What can "objectively" mean if there is nothing objective in God? To explain, he uses what he admits is "an infinitely faint analogy" (Socrates), and then resorts to one of his favorite concepts (reduplication).

When most people face the risk of losing their lives, he says, they avoid the danger by dissociating themselves from the person they really are, pretending not to be that person who is being condemned, and taking the guise of "a third person" who is not one's true "I." On the contrary, when Socrates is in danger and is condemned to death, "he relates objectively to his own personhood [*Personlighed*]," and dissociates himself from his sentence to death as if it were happening to a "third party." "He is subjectivity raised to the second degree; his relationship is one of objectivity just as a true poet would relate to his poetic production; with this objectivity he relates to his own subjectivity." (Note: he uses subjectivity and personhood as synonyms, which we will explore below in reference to God's "personhood.")

The key to the use of Socrates as an analogy of God is in the use of the poet as an analogy of Socrates. Kierkegaard is recalling a journal entry (of five years before) where he says that to be a poet "is to have one's own personal life, one's actuality, in completely different categories than those of one's poetical production, to relate to the ideal only in imagination."[38] Thus Socrates regards inner subjectivity to be the realm of truth, his authentic "actuality," the only valid object of his conscious, free, ultimate commitment; concomitantly, he regards the social/political realm that is condemning him to death as untruth, unreal, a place of illusionary shadows not to be taken seriously.

Thus, Kierkegaard proposes, Socrates' attitude and behavior is a faint analogy of how God acts (always, absolutely, unconditionally) out of passionate attention (only, purely, sheerly) to what *God* is (being-in-and-for-

38. *Journals*, 6300; x¹ A 11. See the discussion of this point above in chapter 1, at note 7.

itself). This is what it means to say that God is *infinite* subjectivity and that God relates *objectively* to God's subjectivity. So we have heard Kierkegaard say that God acts only out of a sense of what concerns and pleases God (no. 2570). And he spells this out again and again by insisting that God never acts out of "intentions" or to accomplish a goal or a "cause" because this would imply that God has "a relationship to an environment, a relationship to the other and therefore has, must have, intentions. Only that which infinitely, subjectively has its subjectivity infinitely in its power as subjectivity, only that has no intentions" (no. 1449 but see also no. 4901, 4902, 4571).

GOD AS REDUPLICATION

Nevertheless, to relate to subjectivity "objectively" also carries the sense of conscious attention to what one's subjectivity is in contrast to what it is not. Does Kierkegaard then perceive a distinction within God's subjectivity? Yes, in a very subtle way. After saying (no. 4571) that God "relates objectively to [God's] own subjectivity," he adds, "[Y]et this is again only a reduplication [*Fordoblelse*] of [God's] subjectivity." The word "only" [*kun*] stresses the point that nothing objective, in the sense of something foreign to God's subjectivity, is involved in God's relating objectively to subjectivity. Nevertheless, Kierkegaard is drawing a line or distinction, setting a distance, between the fundamental, infinite subjectivity that God *is* and God's act of "relating objectively" to that subjectivity. This act, by God, in no way changes that fundamental subjectivity that God *is*, because "in [God's] being subjective there is no imperfection at all that should be taken away, nor is there anything lacking that should be added, as is the case of human subjectivity." Yet the notion of reduplication in Kierkegaard's writings always carries the sense of drawing an essential distinction and difference within a unity.

A prime example is found in the extended quotation from *Works of Love* above (at note 35). When the eternal (God) reduplicates itself in a human-being, this involves the eternal (Kierkegaard maintains) in a constant and simultaneous twofold orientation (a kind of motion!): in an outward direction into the human-being and in an inward direction "back into itself." These two states or moments in God's being God are, of course, "one and the same"; they comprise an act of simple reduplication in that nothing is "taken away nor ... added" in God's essential being or subjectivity (unlike human subjectivity). Nevertheless, this state of the eternal's being in a human-being in a twofold way is clearly an *act* of God, an act taken totally on God's initiative, not on that of the human-being. And an act that involves two "directions" (*Retning*) clearly is some kind of *motion.* And even though it does not involve an externally motivated intention or purpose or cause, it is more than a dialectical movement of thought. It is a motion of God's *willing* to express and to embody what is "pleasing" to God alone, that is, a motion or act that takes into consideration only what is consonant with God's own eternal being.

This movement in two directions clearly draws the line of distinction and differentiation within God that serves as the ground for reflection and self-consciousness, which in turn lend meaning to the attribution of subjectivity to God and to the notion that God relates objectively to that subjectivity. But the fact that the Eternal always and essentially moves "in an inward direction back into itself" means that God never resides as such in, nor becomes identical with, that to which he moves "in an outward direction." In other words (as already suggested), God's reduplication also draws a line of distinction between what God subjectively is and is not. This line is one of the chief indicators of what Kierkegaard means by the "infinite qualitative distinction" between God and the whole of "creation" (including human-beings) and also what he means by God's transcendence and sovereignty (more on sovereignty later).

It is crucial to note that this line of distinction (between what God is and is not) is not only *ontological* (a matter of independent, transcendent being-in-and-for-itself) but also *ethical.* This point was also explored and explicated by Kierkegaard in his discourse, *Thoughts Which Wound From Behind* (finally included in his *Christian Discourses* after much hesitation[39]).

In this discourse he is commenting on some words of Paul (as reported by Luke), "The resurrection of the dead is at hand, of the righteous and of the unrighteous" (Acts 24:15, Kierkegaard's version). In Kierkegaard's usual convoluted (but also phenomenological) fashion, he traces the distinction between righteous and unrighteous back into the eternal being of God. And the language of his conclusion is so important that a lengthy quotation is called for:

The imperfection of this earthly life is precisely that it cannot manifest this difference between righteous and unrighteous. ... But the truth and perfection of eternal life is to manifest eternally the difference between right and wrong with

---

39. See *Journals,* 6111, 6112, 6113, 6118, 6125; VIII[1] A 559, 560, 561, 576, 602. We can take the point made in this discourse as central to his own thought because he wrote it just as he began to write *The Sickness unto Death.*

the stringency of eternity. ... Because what is the eternal? It is the difference between right and wrong. Everything else is transitory: heaven and earth shall pass
away; every other distinction vanishes. ... But the distinction between right and
wrong remains eternally, as he remains, the eternal, who fixed this distinction
from eternity, ... and it remains *unto eternity* as he, the eternal, remains, he who
rolls up the heavens like a garment changes everything, but never himself – and
therefore never [changes] this distinction within eternity. ... But how can the
eternal be [*være*] a distinction? Is not being a distinction a far too imperfect
[form of] being to be constituted as [*til at kunne være*] the eternal? Well now, the
eternal is certainly not the distinction, the eternal is righteousness. But the very
being of righteousness has this perfection, that it has within it a reduplication
[*Fordoblelse*]; this reduplication, which it has within itself, is the distinction between right and wrong. A being which has no distinction at all within it is a very
imperfect being. ... The eternal, righteousness, has the distinction within itself,
the distinction between right and wrong.[40]

Here Kierkegaard again uses the concept of reduplication as an essential characteristic or capacity of the eternal (God), of being-in-and-for-
itself. But now it serves as the ground not just of God as "infinite subjectivity" and hence not just of God as reflective, self-conscious, active, willing being. Rather, the pure, undifferentiated being of the eternal is here
described as righteousness, and the functioning of reduplication in pure
righteousness is to draw a *negative* distinction or differentiation: unrighteousness. It must be stressed that this negative distinction does not occur in the reduplication by which God gives being to a being which is
capable of subjectivity like God but which is unlike God in being finite
and temporal. This giving of being is a creative act of bringing good
(righteousness) into being, in the "image" of God along side of God. But
the functioning of reduplication also serves God's perfection in regard
to God's goodness (righteousness) in an act of negation: it draws an
absolute, unchanging, eternal, inescapable distinction between God as
goodness-in-and-for-itself and every other alternative as not-good, not-
right, and (as Karl Barth argues) as non-being.

40. *Christian Discourses*, pp. 214–216; SV 13:196–197; (10:207–209). I have not tried to
correct Kierkegaard's gender prejudice in this case because, on the one hand, it is essential
to retain the personal pronoun [*han*] which he clearly uses to indicate that the eternal is
personal in nature – which point we will soon demonstrate, and, on the other hand, in this
passage it would be too awkward and diverting to use he/she. God, as eternal being-in-and-
for-itself, is surely neither male or female, nor some androgynous mixture – even though
the biblical Hebrews and Kierkegaard preferred to think of God as masculine.

It is important to note that the implications which Kierkegaard draws from this eternal distinction within God's eternal being are not couched in abstract, objective, impersonal concepts, but in ethical, spiritual (subjective), personal terms. Resurrection or immortality (one's "eternal blessedness" in life with God), he says, "is not a life indefinitely prolonged" but involves judgment (discernment, distinction), namely, "the eternal separation of the righteous and the unrighteous." So for Kierkegaard immortality is not something future beyond physical death but is something demanded of the believer here and now. The problem is that most people have turned immortality from being "a task for action" into a question as to whether it exists (beyond the grave). "There must be no question about immortality, whether it is, but ... whether I live as my immortality requires me to live, ... [the question] about my immense responsibility in the fact that I *am* immortal" (emphasis added). In this earthly life it appears that the unrighteous succeed and vanquish all before them, while the righteous suffer and fail. But the eternal will not be mocked, ultimately it judges, because "immortality is the judgment."[41]

One could make the speculative point that only the eternal (God) is being-in-and-for-itself and everything else is only derivative and dependent being; therefore, whatever else tries to exist on its own and by itself experiences non-being, annihilation. Karl Barth thinks along these lines in his creative and intriguing interpretation of the demonic as *das Nichtige*. He contends that whatever form of existence seeks to go its own way apart from God experiences the hard inescapable fact that the very being of God negates that possibility (*das Nichtige* should not be translated as "nothingness" but as "that which God has negated"). So the demonic does not "exist" as an independent being because only God and God's good creation has being.[42] Kierkegaard recognizes this implication by saying that "when one negates [*nægter*] God, one does God no harm but annihilates [*tilintetgjør*] oneself."[43]

GOD AS PERSONHOOD

Kierkegaard, however, never (to the knowledge of this author) spells out these implications in a purely conceptual way but sticks to his phenome-

41. Ibid., pp. 212–213; SV 13:194–195; (10:206–207).

42. See my brief exposition of Barth's concept and for references to his development of it in his *Kirchliche Dogmatik* in *An Introduction to Barth's Dogmatics for Preachers*, pp. 217–221.

43. *Journals*, 1349; VII[1] A 201 (d. 1846).

nology of Christian faith in its ethical and interpersonal character. In later chapters we will see how he does the latter in his treatment of human failure (sin) and the self's rebirth (faith/love). But at this point it is important to bring into play the second analogy (as proposed above in the text that follows note 30) which Kierkegaard uses to explicate the "infinite qualitative difference" between God who is being-in-and-for-itself and human-beings to whom God gives being: the analogy of personhood. As noted above, he uses personhood as a synonym for subjectivity in one journal entry (no. 4571), and in *Postscript* subjectivity is always qualified as being not only passionate and interested but also as "personal." But using the substantive (personhood) as an essential characteristic of God provides an additional perspective on the complexity of and "distinction" within God's being that we have been attempting to explicate in terms of subjectivity and reduplication.

The idea of God's being "personal" had probably been familiar to Kierkegaard since his childhood (from his father's pietism). We find an early entry in his journals (1837, while still in university) in which he comments on the name of God given to Moses: "I am who I am" (Ex 3:14). He says, "In these words ... the personal eternal consciousness has already taken precedence and therefore does not develop a fatalism as does the cold 'unity' [as in Mohammedanism]." And in extensive notes of H.L. Martensen's lectures on "Speculative Dogmatics" (1838–1839, probably secured by Kierkegaard from another student), we find a section about "God's absolute personhood in which idea God is known not simply as absolute *substance* but as infinite, free *subject*," which means that God is self-consciousness, self-determination, intelligence, and will.[44]

---

44. Ibid., 2734, 2737; II A 86, 89. The Martensen notes are in *Papirer*, II C 26–27, § 5, the contents of which are found in Volume XIII of Thulstrup's Second Edition, pp. 11–13. In his *Kierkegaard's Relation to Hegel* (pp. 115, 133), Thulstrup confuses these lectures with Martensen lectures on "The History of Newer Philosophy from Kant to Hegel." Strange as it may seem, it is hard not to believe that Kierkegaard, a year before he died, reread these notes. Simply compare the vocabulary and ideas of these two pages from Martensen with those of Kierkegaard's two journals entries no. 4571 & 1449 (XI² A 97 & 133). For example, Martensen says, "Freedom is absolute independence [or, sovereignty] and infinite self-determination: that which has itself *in its power*. ... Only that is free which has itself completely [or, perfectly] *in its power*. ... Spinoza thought of substance essentially as power, but not as that which has itself *in its power*." Kierkegaard says (in no. 1449), "Only that which infinitely subjectively has its subjectivity infinitely *in its power* as subjectivity, only that has no intentions." (emphasis added) In Danish the phrase is exactly the same: *i sin Magt*. It is interesting to note also that the term *Eiendommelighed*, which Kierkegaard used almost exclu-

Nevertheless, Kierkegaard was very reluctant, indeed refused, to speak of God as being personal as such until the very end of his life. He never explains this reluctance directly, but again in late journal entries we find a couple of clues. First, he mentions the long-standing attempt to set aside the mystery of the trinity by conceptualizing the personhood of God, and how the Hegelians claim to have resolved it. They simply assert that God's personhood is identical with God's being triune in the sense of "the old logical trinity" of thesis-antithesis-synthesis.[45] Kierkegaard wants nothing to do with this kind of personhood.

Even worse for Kierkegaard is the fact that professors and preachers prattle on about God's being personal and claim to be able to prove it as a simple fact. Hence they "make the congregation happy" because the members can assume that God is personal (i.e., friendly) to each of them. Kierkegaard agrees that God is indeed personal, indeed is "personhood" (*Personlighed*), but God is such for *us* only by grace and in faith. And in this relationship God's personhood proves to be a "jolting and soul-stirring" burden for human beings to bear.[46] Why? For several reasons.

1) *Definition of Personhood* First of all, "personhood is not a sum of propositions, nor is it something *immediately* accessible; personhood consists of a curving inwardly into oneself, a *clausum* [enclosed place], an αδυτον [sanctuary], a μυστηριον [secret]; personhood consists of this 'in there,' ... the in-there to which oneself (as personhood) must be related

---

sively in *Works of Love* for the uniqueness of each individual self, is also found in this section of Martensen's notes. *Works of Love* was written seven years before the above journals entry. Does this mean that Kierkegaard reviewed these notes on and off throughout his career, or that his mind retained all kinds of bits and pieces that it thought might be useful later on? Was Kierkegaard even conscious of his borrowing from Martensen?

45. Ibid., 1615; x² A 431. Kierkegaard found an interpretation of Hegel's treatment of God's personhood in his copy of the extensive notes of Schelling's lectures on "Philosophy as Revelation" in Berlin 1841–1842 – which lectures he attended only briefly. See Thulstrup's second edition of the *Papirer*, Vol. XIII, p. 275. Of course, later he read many of the works of the Danish Hegelians. Indeed, he was aware that his professor, H.L. Martensen, was largely sympathetic with Hegel, even though drawing some distinctions. Kierkegaard must certainly have found Martensen's interpretation of the Trinity as too speculative and as illustrating the attempt to conceptualize the personhood of God. So Martensen says that the idea of the Trinity consists in the idea of the absolute personhood of God which "is completed through an eternal immanent genesis and process;" so "the Christian logic conceives of God not only as *cause* of the world but also as ground, God as immanent in the world." For the latter, see the same set of lectures mentioned in note 44, but in §14, pp. 26–28 of Vol. XIII.

46. Ibid., 1452; XI² A 175.

believingly. Between personhood and personhood no other relationship is possible" (emphasis added).[47] Kierkegaard agrees with Pascal that God is "hidden" (for the person without faith) more profoundly in the "humanness" of the Incarnation than God is hidden in nature. Hence Johannes Climacus is also correct in maintaining that "a revelation, the fact that it is a revelation, is known by its opposite, that it is a mystery. ... There is nothing of the direct."[48] So a personal relationship, even with oneself let alone with God, is not easy or cozy and reassuring.

Indeed, the character and impact of this hidden indirect presence of God (in the faith-relationship) is profoundly disturbing. When the eternal reduplicates itself in a human being, this presence does not produce an automatic and easy fulfillment of the natural potentiality of the individual human being. Rather, the first result is that the individual shrinks from this person-to-person relationship because one is forced first of all to look at oneself as unique individual person: "one is so illuminated that one cannot hide from oneself – yes, illuminated as if one were transparent. ... [P]ersonhood could be called transparency." And we do not like what we see; so "we shrink from being revealed."[49] Why? As noted above (see at notes 40 and 41), the eternal brings with it "the distinction within itself, the distinction between right and wrong." And the presence of this distinction in its eternal purity forces upon human awareness the element of "judgment," that is, discernment between righteousness and unrighteousness. This awareness in turn poses the inescapable question of "whether I live as my immortality requires me to live, ... [the question] about my immense responsibility in the fact that I am immortal." If one is honest and courageous at this point, the inevitable answer is: No, I do not so live.

This disturbing awareness brings the ultimate (eternal) crisis and decision in the human spirit. Will one face one's "immense responsibility" or turn away from it? Will one accept God's love and grace in order to "become [one's potential] personhood" in a faith-relationship with God as personhood, or will one shrink from it, will one (in the language of *Sickness*) be "offended"? Kierkegaard repeatedly asserts that "a human-being's salvation lies in becoming personhood,"[50] and

47. Ibid., 180; XI¹ A 237.

48. Ibid., 3110; X³ A 626. For Climacus' treatment, see *Postscript*, p. 220; (KW 12.1:245); SV 9:205; (7:206–207).

49. *Journals*, a blend of 3223 and 3224; XI¹ A 393 and XI² A 107.

50. Ibid., 4224, 3225, 3228; XI² A 107, 177, 402.

that this salvation comes in the faith/love relationship with God. He agrees (again) with Pascal that "the human: one must first know and then love; the divine: one must first love and then know." This means that "knowledge of the divine is essentially a transformation of [one's] personhood; one must become an other human-being in order to know the divine."[51] In other words, in this crisis-moment of confrontation, I must learn and accept the fact that God's judgment *is* God's love because only by coming to see transparently that I dwell in untruth, in unrighteousness, in non-being can I be transformed into the authentic being of goodness and so become my authentic personhood. In this transformation by the graceful love of God I come truly to know and understand who God is, what being-in-and-for-itself really is – even though this knowing and understanding is intuitive, indirect insight into the being of an other, an insight caught in the interplay of analogies and concepts, and tested and "proved" in belief-ful risky actions.

In still other language: in the event of the transformation (salvation, fulfillment) of my personhood I come to know God as creator, to know what it means to say that my very being is a "gift" from God, both in its origin and now in its renewal. So we have come full circle (but at a different level) to the point at which this chapter began: first, that I (like every human being) have the potentiality of coming to know that my self, my unique-individuality "is not mine but is the gift of God;" but secondly, that as Christian I know God's act of giving as God's act of creating a second time. "As *human-being* one was created in *God's image*, but as *Christian* one has *God* as *prototype*" (note 5 above).

2) *Implications for the Preceding Three Sections* Now, however, we have seen that Kierkegaard claims that coming to know God through God's presence as prototype (in Jesus as the Christ) provides a vision and a knowing of several significant complexities in the very being of God: being-in-and-for-itself, reduplication, infinite subjectivity (including relating objectively to subjectivity), and finally personhood. And it is God as personhood that gives the other three their special content and meaning, namely: that God's majestic, infinite difference of quality, that God's unique transcendence in being-in-and-for-itself, that God's hidden inner complexity in reduplication, subjectivity, and objective self-consciousness – all and every

51. Ibid., 3109; x³ A 609.

one of these qualities[52] of God's essential being always operate as modified by the fact that God is also and essentially personal, that God is personhood as such. That is to say: God eternally lives and acts self-consciously with caring and careful concern. This is very close if not identical with saying that "God is love" or "loving goodness."

Kierkegaard even avers that "Christianity is precisely the personal [*det Personlige*] and entered into the world for this very reason: to install personhood in order to put an end to all abstractions, ambiguities, hoaxes, impersonhood, in which, according to Christianity, evil has its very abode."[53] Five years before, at the consummation of his second (Christian) authorship, he had made this strong declaration of the crucial importance of this element of "the personal" in human existence:

From the religious point of view, to achieve "actuality" ["*Virkelighed*"] means [that] ... what the believer does ... [is] promptly and directly to set her/his personal God-relationship into actuality ... by saying: In this matter I have deliberated with God and am acting out of confidence in God. ... This is how actuality is achieved, this is how God can become present, this is how the spell is broken, this is how illusions are blasted, and God is able to communicate [*communicere*] with actuality.[54]

Again, it must be emphasized that in this "personal God-relationship," God as personhood is not "immediately accessible" because personhood is a "secret sanctuary," a being "in there." Hence the relationship between any two personal beings is always a *faith* relationship, and that means it is "indirect" and a "mystery" (see notes 47 and 48 above). This character of interpersonal relationships has, for Kierkegaard, a very profound grounding in and implication for the Christian understanding of God, and so also for the understanding of the human self as created in the image of God. In *Postscript* he puts it succinctly: "Not even God

52. Here we are using Kierkegaard's own term, *Egenskaber* (see at note 35 above), in the sense of an essential character, an inherent feature or property. As noted above, Kierkegaard says that the eternal does not "have" qualities (in the sense of added attributes that may change) but "is in itself as simultaneously it has qualities." So he makes a distinction between God's being and God's qualities but insists that God's being and qualities are each other at the same time, and hence are equally "eternal."

53. *Journals*, 3223; XI[1] A 393 (d. 1854).

54. Ibid., 3655; X[2] A 197 (d. 1849); strangely the Hong translation omits the word "personal."

relates directly to a derived spirit (and this is the wondrousness of creation: not to produce something that is nothing in relation to the Creator, but to produce something that is something …); even less can one human-being relate in this way to another *in truth*. … With regard to the essential truth, a direct relationship between spirit and spirit is unthinkable. If such a relationship is assumed, it actually means that one party has ceased to be spirit."[55] In other words, in the hiddenness and indirectness of God's presence in the Incarnation and in the faith-relationship, God is not being difficult and self-protective of God's own holy, infinite being, but just the opposite. God is present and is giving divine help in a way that honors, affirms, and protects the infinite dignity and worth (holiness, sacredness) of the unique personhood of each individual human being. In this holy personhood, the human being is in the image of God.

Kierkegaard develops and intensifies this point two years later in *Works of Love*. He says again that "the inscrutable richness of the goodness of God" is manifest in the fact that although God is omnipotent, God creates a human being as unique-individuality [*Eiendommelighed*] "so that creation standing opposite to [God] does not become nothing, although it is taken from nothing and is nothing, yet becomes unique-individuality." This requires the human being to acknowledge that "to have unique-individuality is to believe in the unique-individuality of every other [human being]; because unique-individuality is not mine, but it is the gift of God, by which God gives being [*at være*] to me … and gives being to all."[56] Therefore human beings must transcend ordinary preferential love because it is really nothing but self-love which denies selfhood to the beloved and simply seeks to absorb the other into itself: "At the peak of [such] love and friendship, the two actually become one self, one I," but then "neither of them has attained the spiritual qualification 'self'." One must learn to love everyone as "neighbor" unconditionally, spiritually, because "love to one's neighbor is love between two eternal essences [*Væsener*], each for itself qualified as spirit. … Only in love to one's neighbor is the self, which loves, purely spiritually determined as spirit, and one's neighbor [is] purely spiritually determined."[57]

55. *Postscript*, pp. 220–221; (KW 12.1:246–247); SV 9:206; (7:207–208). Note that the context of this passage was still quoted by Kierkegaard favorably in an 1850 journal entry (see at note 48 above).

56. *Works of Love*, p. 253; (KW 16:271–272); SV 12:261; (9:259).

57. Ibid., pp. 68–69; (KW 16:56–57); SV 12:60–61; (9:58–59). For an exposition of these passages see my *Kierkegaard as Humanist*, chapter 7, at notes 27–29.

Thus we see that the permanent "indirectness" and "mystery" of the faith-relationship with God is matched (in a sense, identical) with the "inscrutability" of the love-relationship in which God, out of "goodness," gives each and every human being one's own inviolable unique-individual-identity or being, that is, selfhood or personhood – distinct and free even in its relationship to the personhood of God, the Giver and Creator of all being.

3) *Conflict with Recent Ideas of God* The critical role that the notion of personhood plays in Kierkegaard's understanding of divine nature and of human nature sets him and his position at variance with some of the strongest intellectual/philosophical and religious currents of the last one hundred years. These currents of thought have often extended their attack to call into question (or forcefully reject) the entire western tradition of the universal dignity and worth of every individual human being. Some have conceived of truth strictly in the non-humanistic terms of an ultimate mathematical vision of natural universals. Others have proposed that ultimate human reality lodges in macro-social movements of history and have restricted the significance of human action either to heroic individuals or to elite groups who serve as the media of social forces or the implementers of social goals. Even for some who are still interested in the possibilities of Biblical-Christian theology, the role and destiny of the individual and the personal are seen as ultimately absorbed into some transcending, transpersonal unity of either a socio/ historical, a nature-mystical, or a metaphysical character. Let us look briefly at a few arbitrarily-chosen, very different but equally informative examples. First, two philosophers, then, two theologians.

Alfred North Whitehead has inspired one the most influential of twentieth century interpretations of Christian thought, namely, process theology, but he is also an important source for a broader, less specific "theology in process modes of thought."[58] It would be out of place here to attempt a summary of relevant ideas from Whitehead's major works. But it is to the point to note that in his late, more general work, *Adventures of Ideas*, he did relate his view of reality specifically to Christian theology.[59] He says that in order to avoid "noxious superstitions" and their

58. I owe this very helpful distinction to my colleague, Benjamin A. Reist. By the latter he means any Christian theology which remains primarily informed by the Biblical-Christian tradition, but which finds some of Whitehead's concepts helpful in interpreting that tradition in the post-modern scientific world. See Reist's *Processive Revelation*; e.g., see pp. 25, 52–3, 121, 134, 187–8.

59. A.N. Whitehead, *Adventures of Ideas*. See chapter 10, "The New Reformation."

"wild emotions," Christianity must control emotions by "a civilized criticism of the metaphysical intuitions" it had developed.[60] In a typically Anglican viewpoint, Whitehead finds this task seriously attempted especially by the theologians of Alexandria and Antioch, who "have the distinction of being the only thinkers who in a fundamental metaphysical doctrine have improved upon Plato."[61] He gives them good marks for the following. (1) They explicated the Trinity as asserting that "a multiplicity in the nature of God, each component unqualifiedly Divine, involves a doctrine of mutual immanence in the divine nature." (2) On the person of Christ, "these theologians rejected ... an association of the human individual with a divine individual, involving responsive imitations in the human individual. They decided for the direct immanence of God in the one person of Christ." (3) In their doctrine of the third person of the Trinity, "they also decided for some sort of direct immanence of God in the World generally." Thus they laid the ground for "a metaphysical discovery," namely, "a rational account of the role of the persuasive agency of God." Nevertheless, the theologians of the church generally did not follow up on these leads in order to develop a general metaphysic. Hence they ended with a monarchical view of God, the absolute sovereign who is complete within himself and untouched by the world.[62]

Whitehead says that if the church had followed up on the leads of the Alexandrian/Antiochian theologians, it could have developed an adequate metaphysic with the following elements: (1) The plurality of individuals is consistent with the unity of the universe. (2) The World requires union with God, and God requires union with the World. (3) The Ideals in God's nature are persuasive elements in creative advance in the World. (4) The derivations of the persuasive elements from God are not grounded upon the accidents of will (Plato) but are grounded upon "the necessities of the nature of God and of the nature of the World."[63]

The implications of this viewpoint for the question of the personal identity of God and of human beings are not clear, and this is recognized in the book, *Christ in a Pluralistic Age*, by John Cobb, perhaps the leading first-generation formulator of a Whiteheadian process theology.

60. Ibid., p. 207.
61. Ibid., pp. 214–215.
62. Ibid., pp. 216–217.
63. Ibid., p. 215.

He believes that he can identify Whitehead's vision of the Consequent Nature of God with the New Testament vision of the Kingdom of Heaven ("the possible future world that is envisioned and which, through the envisionment, is already effectively present"). But, Cobb notes, "It is objected that even if the Kingdom preserves the perished world in its immediacy, what are retained are individual events and not persons. But this is not Whitehead's intention." He quotes *Process and Reality* and concludes that "Whitehead means that persons as persons inhabit the Kingdom."

Cobb then quickly adds, "Yet these persons are not to be conceived as closed within themselves," which he interprets by approvingly quoting Lewis Ford and Marjorie Sochocki: "There can be no clearly defined 'border' of the personality; ... [the] center of personality ... extends and flows to others in the giving and receiving which is the Harmony of God. ... [T]he greater intensity of feeling made possible by the complex structure of personality ... may now be put at the disposal of its ultimate purpose – the enrichment of the whole. In the process the narrow confines of the self have been lost." Cobb then concludes that "those who can conceive of no fulfillment that is not that of the personally identical individual will find Whitehead's vision of hope unsatisfactory. But it is doubtful that an eternal self-identity can be truly envisioned as fulfillment. What is reasonably required is the participation in the redemption of the human actuality, not that this be conceived in the categories of individualism."[64]

It could be argued that this interpretation of Whitehead by Cobb *et alia* is a reductionist simplification and is achieved by ignoring many unresolved conundrums (contradictions?) in Whitehead's writings. When these interpreters speak of the loss of self-identity in the enrichment of the whole, one wonders what they make of Whitehead's subjectivist principle as meaning "that the whole universe consists of elements disclosed in the analysis of the experiences of subjects," and "that apart from the experiences of subjects there is nothing, nothing, nothing, bare nothingness."[65]

In any case, it is clear that Kierkegaard has a very different view of the role and importance of the individual self than Whitehead and his

---

64. John B. Cobb, Jr., *Christ in a Pluralistic Age*, pp. 243, 247–248. I have not explored this issue in more recent writings in process theology.

65. A.N. Whitehead, *Process and Reality* (Corrected edition by David Ray Griffin and Donald W. Shelburne published by Macmillan), pp. 166–167.

interpreters. In his "analysis of the experiences of subjects," Kierkegaard
specifically finds "eternal self-identity," with absolute "border[s] of personality" though never "clearly defined" nor nor finally set. And the fulfillment comes as the individual makes its way through "the accidents of
will" precisely by means of "responsive imitations" of the Ideals of God's
nature, that is, by means of ethical (loving) acts toward others. For him,
if personhood finds its "ultimate purpose" in being lost in the "enrichment of the whole," then "truth" has been defined in terms of abstract,
objective, conceptual universals, and the subjectivist principle has been
dissolved. For Kierkegaard, the truth of individual subjectivity remains
ever "higher" than the truth of the objective whole.

Kierkegaard agrees with process thought that all being is essentially
relational. He defines the human self as "a relationship, which relates to
itself," and in so doing "relates to an other." Indeed, to succeed in the
interior act of relating to itself, the relationship must simultaneously be
caught up in the act of relating to the other. Authentically relating to an
other is called "loving." Since "God is love," then God too is essentially
involved in the process of relating to an other, even though in a qualitatively different way ("creating"). But for Kierkegaard, relationality
assumes the inviolability of the terms (elements, components) of the relationship. There is no sublation or absorption of the subjective terms
(selves) in some ultimate synthesis called the "whole" or "human actuality" or "Divine Spirit." If the "enrichment of the whole" means the loss
of "borders" which define individual "self-identity," then the whole is an
empty hole composed only of the plus signs of the equation with no
terms or components to be related. We will see later that, for Kierkegaard, love of the other aims precisely and only at the affirmation and fulfillment of the unique, individual self of the other. And this is true in
human relationships just because God's love toward humans has that
character.

Kierkegaard insists that for Christian faith the human individual is
"higher" than the human race. Human self-conscious individuals are not
elements to be blended together in some divine sauce. It is not the whole
that is tasty. The God-given value of human beings consists precisely
in their unique, unpredictable, unfathomable eccentricity as individuals.
Authentic community of individuals consists precisely in the acceptance
and enjoyment and encouragement of each other in their individual
uniqueness as definitive of their humanity. It is precisely the mixing and
blending of individuals into social, political, ethnic, religious, or any mass
unity for "the enrichment of the whole" that leads to the dangerous,

destructive, horrifying, demonic loss of authentic humanity. The more profoundly human beings are related in the communion of Christian love, the more they become aware of the inexhaustible and inexplicable depths of the unique otherness of each other. As Kierkegaard says,

> If one posits only the development of the generation or the race or at least posits it as the highest, how does one explain the divine squandering that uses up the endless host of individuals of one generation after the other in order to set the world-historical development in motion? ... Why does not God make haste if that is all he wants? ... And if that is all he wants, how horrible, tyrannically to squander myriads of human lives. ... If, however, becoming subjective is the highest task assigned to a human-being, then everything turns out beautifully. ... There is no squandering, because ... the task of becoming subjective is assigned to every [human-being].[66]

In Jürgen Habermas we find a philosopher/social scientist who undertakes to defend the "human dignity" of the individual and who asserts the continuing reality of a structure that deserves to be called "God." Nevertheless, he sees the individual as essentially defined socially and understands the God-structure ("the concept of a *Logos*") in strictly impersonal terms. He claims to find support for his position in "the re-politicization of the biblical inheritance observable in contemporary theological discussion (Pannenberg, Moltmann, Solle, Metz), which goes together with a leveling of this-worldly/other-worldly dichotomy." This trend, he says, "does not mean atheism in the sense of the liquidation without a trace of the idea of God – although the idea of a *personal* God would hardly seem to be salvageable with consistency from this critical mass of thought."[67]

Kierkegaard would respond to Habermas by (perhaps) quoting a dictum of H.L. Martensen (in spite of the latter's Hegelianism): "If God were not personal, then the personhood of the human-being would be an unsolved and insoluble contradiction."[68] From Kierkegaard's perspective,

66. *Postscript*, pp. 141–142; (KW 12.1:158–59); SV 9:132; (7:130–131).

67. See Habermas's *Legitimation Crisis*, p. 121. The original German text was published in 1973, and hence in the quotation "contemporary theological discussion" refers to the 1960s. During that period there was much talk about the "secularization of the Gospel" which would have encouraged Habermas's point of view. But much has happened in Christian theology since then toward a re-emphasis of the personal nature of God and Christian piety – some of which would make Kierkegaard very nervous.

68. Kierkegaard's *Papirer*, II C 26–27, § 5, in Volume XIII, p. 11.

Habermas faces disillusionment if he thinks he can, with his concept of
God, firmly establish what he calls the "old European human dignity" and
the "unity of the person." In other words, Habermas faces an impossible
task if he thinks he can (in his language) accomplish "the legitimation of
orders of authority and basic norms" with a "world-maintaining interpre-
tive system" which has no other "God" than "a communicative structure
that forces men, on the pain of a loss of their humanity, ... to encounter
one another *indirectly*, that is, across an objective something that they
themselves are not."[69] For Kierkegaard, humanity's dignity consists precisely in being unique, individual persons, and one can believe *indirectly* in
that dignity only if one also believes (indirectly) that the "objective something" (the "Logos") is also personal.

Paul Tillich provides us with a profound and, for our present concerns, a more challenging statement of the issues from a theological/
philosophical perspective. He certainly had read and learned much
from both Kierkegaard and Martin Buber (although typically never
gives them credit). He writes with greater clarity and coherence than either one – which of course is both his strength and, from their point of
view, his weakness because he exalts the conceptual and metaphysical
above the complexity and indefinability of personal subjectivity.

Kierkegaard would certainly agree with Tillich when he says that
" 'personal God' does not mean that God is *a* person" (that is, like I am a
person). Rather, it means that God "carries within himself the ontological power of personality. He is not a person, but he is not less than personal." There is much that Kierkegaard would find congenial in Tillich's
entire section, "God as Living," especially his view of the Trinity and
Spirit.[70] But just as Tillich was finishing volume 1 of his *Systematic Theology*, he was also giving the Terry Lectures at Yale and then the Richard
Lectures at the University of Virginia. In these he expresses his views less
guardedly and probably reveals his own mind more clearly.

In the former (*The Courage to Be*) he speaks about "the God above the
God of theism," that is, the God above the God of the Jewish-Christian
tradition which emphasizes "the divine-human encounter" and "the
person-to-person relationship with God." He insists that this tradition is
also aware of "a transpersonal presence of the divine," and hence in
prayer you speak "to somebody to whom you cannot speak because he is
not 'somebody,' " and hence you are made "a part of that which is not a

69. *Legitimation Crisis*, pp. 143, 118, 121.
70. Paul Tillich, *Systematic Theology: Volume I*, pp. 241–252; see p. 245 for the quotation.

part but is the ground of the whole," and hence "absolute faith" consists in "acceptance of being accepted" even though "there is nobody and nothing that accepts;" rather, one "accepts his acceptance by the power of being-itself in which he participates." He insists that this power of being does not swallow the individual selves but "acts through the power of the individual selves."[71] But in the Richard Lectures it becomes even clearer that the "power" of the individual to "accept being accepted" may not be "swallowed" but certainly is purely passive under "the power of being-itself," and that the divine power is no longer relating in a "person-to-person relationship" to the individual self of the human being.

Even the title, *Biblical Religion and the Search for Ultimate Reality*, betrays the hidden conviction that Ultimate Reality is better understood by the Philosopher of Athens than by the Rabbi of Galilee. Philosophy, prior to all the deliverances of religion, explores "the question of being, ... what it means to *be*." It seeks to understand "being-as-such" which "has neither static nor dynamic implications. It precedes any specific qualification." Tillich provides a powerful and sympathetic account of Biblical-Christian faith that resolves the very human and continuing problems of doubt and sin. But his most convincing passion is associated with the problem of cognition. Of course, the philosopher's existence is involved in his quest for ultimate reality, but "the existential element does not swallow the theoretical." The philosopher "wants to *know*; he wants to know what being means, what its structures are, and how one can penetrate its mystery." So "faith includes the ontological question, whether the question is asked or not." Indeed, "only against the background of the universal Logos is the incarnate Logos a meaningful concept," and "the ontological question of being creates not a conflict but a necessary basis for any theoretical dealing with the biblical concept of the personal God."[72]

How then does Tillich's theory finally perceive the personal God? In spite of his protests to the contrary, his Ultimate Reality swallows up, or in Hegel's term, sublates the personal character of both God and the human being. "The Word of God is God's creative self-manifestation and not a conversation between two beings; ... it is God manifesting himself to himself." He claims that divine activity does not "destroy the

---

71. Paul Tillich, *The Courage to Be*, in sequence of quotations: pp. 183, 187, 177, 176, 188.

72. Paul Tillich, *Biblical Religion and the Quest for Ultimate Reality*, in sequence of quotations: pp. 6, 16, 20, 59, 75, 83.

divine-human reciprocity," and yet "this can be understood only through the ontological polarity of freedom and destiny and through a distinction between the levels of being, namely, between the ground of being, which *transcends* all polarities, and finite being, which is subject to them" (emphasis added). How then does this theory understand prayer, the most profoundly reciprocal, interpersonal moment in the God-relationship of Christian faith? "In every true prayer God is both he to whom we pray and he who prays through us. ... [T]he ontological structure which makes God an object of us as subjects is infinitely transcended. God stands in the divine-human reciprocity, but only as he who transcends it and comprises both sides of the reciprocity."[73]

Kierkegaard would reply: the essence of Christian faith has been lost. Neither God nor the human-being is any longer personal. No authentic reciprocity remains. One does not pray to a "ground of being." In prayer God is never an "object" and we the "subjects;" rather, God is always the infinite, transcendent "I" in relationship to whom alone do we become a "thou," an authentic self (person). And the prayer-relationship is one of faith, not of theoretical understanding. And faith means that the human-being remains free, free even to take offense. Only so is the human-being authentically spirit (self, person); only so is God authentically Spirit (personhood). It is precisely in this relationship that God is and remains sovereign in love. And in his closing words, Tillich finally admits that Ultimate Reality for him is "impersonal." He says, "Religious experience ... exhibits a deep feeling for the tension between the personal and the nonpersonal element in the encounter between God and man. The Old as well as the New Testament has the astonishing power to speak of the presence of the divine in such a way that the I-thou character of the relation never darkens the transpersonal power and mystery of the divine."[74]

As opposed to Tillich, Kierkegaard does not search for an "ultimate reality" that is "above" and beyond the personal God who is self-revealing to us in a faith/love relationship through Jesus Christ. The only sure ground and source of our *belief* in our own infinite dignity and worth as unique, individual persons is God's own self-revealing to us as infinite, eternal personhood in whose image we have been created and re-created. The inscrutable mystery of God's infinite sovereignty, of God's eternal qualitative difference as being-in-and-for-itself, of God's holy transcendence in self-reduplication and in relating objectively to subjectivity

73. Ibid., pp. 78, 80, 81.
74. Ibid., pp. 83–84.

– all of this ineffable mystery lodges not *behind* and *above* but precisely *in* the complex event through which this eternal and infinite structure of essential being becomes a present dynamic *within* the temporal/finite and psycho/socio/biological realm of human existence, namely, in the event of Jesus as the Christ of God.

In other words, Tillich claims that being-as-such transcends the polarity of the ontological elements (individuality and universality, dynamics and form, freedom and destiny), but his characterization of Ultimate Reality is clearly on the side of conceptual universals, structural form, and all-determining destiny. Kierkegaard, on the other hand, (in answer to a question raised on p. 70 above) asserts a dialectic *within* the ultimate unity of God, namely, the dialectic between being-in-and-for-itself and subjectivity, and therefore he sees God's personhood as lodging in the dialectic and as expressing (perhaps achieving?) itself in perpetual reduplication. So these basic theological qualities cannot be ascribed to either dynamics or form; rather, they modify each other in a way that defines God's essential being as dynamic-form. In God there is no being-as-such that transcends these qualities.

For Kierkegaard, therefore, the philosopher's quest for knowing the meaning and structures of being by means of conceptual universals is delusionary. The universal Logos does not provide the meaning of the incarnate Logos. A grasp of the ontological question is not the clue to the meaning of God's personhood. God as ultimate reality is not grasped and caught in the abstract concepts of philosophical speculation. Rather, conceptual definitions and metaphorical analogies interplay with each other in the human attempt to describe and to point to the reality of a living event, that is, of a living relationship that occurs and develops on an initiative from beyond human existence in general and human individuality in particular. And the most adequate and most profound description, whether in concepts and/or in analogies, remains only an approximation that helps to stimulate and to enhance that relationship, but never captures that relationship in itself and hence never replaces or serves as a substitute for that relationship. For the Christian, Kierkegaard says, the most adequate and most profound description of our relationship to God emerges from our being encountered by and united with the initiative that comes from God in Jesus as the Christ, because in faith-union with Christ, the human being "has her/his self directly before [*lige over for*] God."[75]

75. *Sickness*, p. 211; (KW 19:81); SV 15:134; (11:192–3).

In this relationship there is a kind of knowing or understanding. But, Kierkegaard avers, there are (at least) two kinds of understanding (*Forstaaen*) and hence two kinds of knowledge (*Viden*). In the language of *Postscript*, there is objective knowledge and understanding of the world, generally called science or common sense, and then there is subjective knowledge of a personal, ethical, and religious character. The latter is the kind of knowing that comes as a fundamental recognition or perception (*Erkjendelse*) that one is confronted with the truth, even though this truth seems to be contrary to what can be comprehended (*begribe*) by direct sense or by reason (*Fornuft*). Kierkegaard bewails the fact that the human race is so rapidly amassing such vast knowledge of the first kind that it feels it does not need the second kind. So "someone is able to understand (*fortaa*) the whole truth about how mean and sordid the world is ... and then the next moment not recognize (*kjende*) what he has understood, for almost at once he himself goes out and participates in the very same meanness and sordidness, is honored for it, and accepts the honor."[76]

In this section of *Sickness* dealing with the Christian definition and knowledge of sin, Kierkegaard states his own view baldly. He asks, "Can any human-being comprehend [*begribe*] what is uniquely Christian [*dette Christelige*]? By no means, precisely because it is the uniquely Christian and therefore involves offense. It must be believed [*troe*]. To comprehend is the scope [capacity] of the human-being in relation to the human, but to believe is the human-being's relation to the divine." So he specifically rejects all "speculation" which claims that it can grasp (*begribe*) Christian truth through rational comprehension. "All Christianity turns on this, that it *must* be believed and not comprehended, that *either* it must be believed *or* one must be offended by it." He praises Socratic ignorance as equivalent with the Biblical principle that "the fear of the Lord is the beginning of wisdom," because Socrates was thereby "keeping watch so that the deep gulf of qualitative difference ... was maintained between God and human-being, so that God and human-being did not merge in some way ... into one."[77]

76. Ibid., pp. 221–223; (KW 19:90–92); SV 15:142–145; (11:202–203).

77. Ibid., pp. 226, 229, 230; (KW 19:95, 98, 99); SV 15:147, 150, 151; (11:206, 209, 210). The entire section (part 2, chapter 2), "The Socratic Definition of Sin," should be read in order to see how Kierkegaard works out the relationships among understanding, believing, and revelation. In this section, he uses four terms (in both verbal and noun forms) that are similar, related, and even overlapping in meaning. This similarity and overlapping also characterizes their English equivalents. Yet it seems to me that Kierkegaard

To conclude our Kierkegaardian critique of Tillich, then, it is clear that absolute faith is not "acceptance of being accepted" even though "there is nobody and nothing that accepts" (or as Tillich puts it in his sermon on acceptance, "without knowing the someone or something that accepts"). For Kierkegaard, "to believe is the human-being's relationship to the divine," a relationship in which God comes near and in a very personal way affirms my being as person. In this event I do know (in the sense of recognizing and acknowledging) and understand (as passionate acceptance) God's love. I gladly acknowledge and accept that I am being met and affirmed by the very creator and giver of my being as spirit/self/person, as one capable either of loving and worshiping God in return, or of being offended and turning away into darkness and death. So the mystery of God lies not in God's being some unknown and unknowable "God above God," some "transpersonal presence of the divine."

Rather, the mystery is: why God is what God is, namely, the ultimate mystery that puts an end to all our inquiries. That is to say, the God who is revealed and hence "known" cannot be described and so explained in any other terms than those that emerge from that relationship of love which God alone establishes. *This* God is absolute and unconditioned. In Christian faith, there is no such thing as a "God above [this] God" who can be explained as a transcendent unity of "ontological elements" that "constitute the basic ontological structure."[78] When one is met and loved by the creator of all, then one has no more "whys" to ask: why did God create me? why does God love me? I acknowledge and gladly

---

makes some basic distinctions among them, which distinctions I have been trying to make in the last several paragraphs. The basic term is *forstaa*, meaning to understand in a general and neutral sense; so we have heard Kierkegaard say that there are different kinds of understanding. The term *vide* means to know in the basic sense of being aware of and having information about something in an objective sense, and hence is used in the compound *Videnskab* to mean science or scholarship. The other two terms are more elusive in their meanings. The term *erkjende* (in current orthography the j is dropped) means to apprehend (as distinct from to comprehend) in the sense of to perceive, recognize, acknowledge, or come to a cognition of something, but in a subjective rather than an objective sense. Finally, the term *begribe* means to comprehend in the sense of grasping something with the understanding so as to be able to give it conceptual definition – at least, that is the sense Kierkegaard gives it in this section of his writings. I think it is unfortunate that neither Lowrie nor the Hongs are consistent in making these distinctions in their translations of these terms in this section, because these are precisely the distinctions that Kierkegaard is trying to make.

78. Tillich, *Systematic Theology*, Vol. 1, pp. 164–165, 244.

accept that I have come to know (like Isaiah) "the everlasting God, the Creator of the ends of the earth" whose "understanding is unsearchable" (Is 40:28). And I must cry out (with Paul), "O the depth of the riches and wisdom and knowledge of God! How unsearchable are [God's] judgments and inscrutable [God's] ways!" (Ro 11:33) This God is personal from beginning to end, from top to bottom, even (or precisely) when this "God is no respecter of persons" but accepts "any one who fears God and does what is right," and "sends rain on the just and the unjust" (Acts 10:34–35; Mt 5:45). So even when Kierkegaard uses ontological language and describes God as being-in-and-for-itself, he is doing so because of some personal quality of God's love as manifested in the Judeo-Christian revelation of God, that is, in one's faith-relationship with God-in-Jesus-Christ.

4) *Comparison with Karl Barth* The second theologian for our consideration on the issue of the personal nature of God is Karl Barth. On the main point of this issue Barth supports Kierkegaard's position. In the very first chapter of volume 1 of *Church Dogmatics* Barth clearly and vigorously affirms that God is personal, and in the second chapter that God is person only in the ultimate unity of the Trinity. In discussing the personal nature of the Word of God, he speaks of God's "person-nature [*Personsein*] as distinguished from all thingness [*Dingsein*] or factuality [*Sachesein*]." Then he defines *Personsein* as "being subject, not simply in the logical sense but also in the ethical sense, being free subject, ... able to *be in charge of* its own existence [*Dasein*] and essence [*Sosein*], ... also able to *choose* new possibilities of existence and essence." And he asserts that to "personalize" God in this sense is not "a case of anthropomorphism" because "[i]t is not problematic whether God is person, but it is problematic whether we are that. ... God is actual person, actual free subject."[79]

For Barth, furthermore, God's personhood (*Persönlichkeit*) is not just one of Tillich's ontological elements that is transcended in God's ultimate being-as-such. Rather, God is person or subject in the ultimate, eternal, perfect unity of God's three-in-oneness (*Dreieinigkeit*). "The name of Father, Son, and Spirit means that God is the one God in threefold repetition." Therefore, it is "to the one single essence of God ... that there belongs what we today call the 'personhood' [*Persönlichkeit*] of

---

79. Karl Barth, *Church Dogmatics*, 1–1:138–139 (using the new translation of the 2nd edition of 1–1, 1975); *Die Kirchliche Dogmatik*, 1–1:143 (1–1 means volume 1, part 1). In all the following references to this work in the notes, the title will be indicated simply by the initials CD for the English version and KD for the German, and will omit the author's name.

God." Indeed, " 'Person' in the sense of the church's doctrine of the Trinity has nothing directly to do with 'personhood'."[80] Hence neither the Father nor the Son nor the Spirit is person (in our contemporary sense) "as such ... but as identical with the one God," that is, when "brought into relationship to the personhood [*Personalität*] of God."[81]

So Barth argues that it is hopeless to try to explain the doctrine of the Trinity in terms of three "persons," and proposes that instead of "person" we use "mode-of-being" (*Seinsweise*). Thus "the statement: 'God is one in three modes-of-being, Father, Son and Holy Spirit' means: the one God, i.e. the one Lord, the one personal God is what he is not only in one mode but ... in the mode of the Father, in the mode of the Son, in the mode of the Holy Spirit." And Barth interprets these modes not as "three divine attributes" or "three parts of the divine property" – and certainly not as a committee of three separate, willing persons or subjects – but as "the threeness of revelation, revealer, and being revealed, the threeness of God's holiness, mercy and love." Hence "this one God is to be understood not merely as impersonal lordship, that is, as power, but as the Lord, thus not merely as absolute Spirit but as person, that is, as *I* being in and for itself [*in und für sich seiendes Ich*]."[82] And this concept of the location of God's personhood persists throughout the *Dogmatics* and is stated explicitly in its last volume, "The Doctrine of Reconciliation": "If the essence of God existing in these three modes-of-being is one only [*ein einziges*], it is not that of three 'persons' in our meaning of the concept, but that of the one personal God."[83]

However much Kierkegaard would agree with and be heartened by Barth's identification of God's personhood with God's essential being-in-and-for-itself, he would be disturbed by Barth's refusal to see human personhood as the gift of God to the essential being of every human individual. Kierkegaard certainly agrees with Barth that a human-being can actualize this gift and become authentic person (self, spirit) only in relationship with God because this potentiality for personhood is "derived" from and hence dependent upon God. But Barth goes further.

80. CD 1–1:350–351; KD 1–1:369–370.
81. CD 1–1:488; KD 1–1:512.
82. CD 1–1:408, 412–413, 415, 412; KD 1–1:375, 379, 381, 378. Barth provides a cogent argument to support his thesis that his term and concept of *Seinsweise* is not a new concept but has been used "from the very beginning" (*von jeher*), indeed "is the literal translation of the concept τροπος ὑπαρξεως, already in use in the Early Church debates" (CD 1–1:359, which omits the final phrase from its translation, KD 1–1:379).
83. CD 4–2:44; KD 4–2:46.

Early in volume 2 of the *Dogmatics,* in section 28,"The Being of God as
the One Who Loves in Freedom," he sounds a theme, a major and ruling concept, which is repeated and radically developed throughout all
the remaining volumes. In expositing "God's being in act," he argues
that God's act is not "an event occurring through foreign impulses" because "God's being is self-moved being [*durch sich selbst bewegtes Sein*]."
And this fact distinguishes "the divine Person" from all other persons
because "no other being is utterly in its act." Therefore, "if the being of
a person is a being in act, and if a being in act can, in the strict and
proper sense, be ascribed to God alone, then it follows that under the
[category of] being a person, in the strict and proper sense, only the being of God can be understood." So "the human-being is not genuine
[*eigentlich*] person, but God is that."[84]

This lack of genuine personhood in human-being, however, is even intensified when Barth explains it in terms of the Trinity. In coming to
know God as Father, Son, and Holy Spirit (through revelation in Jesus
Christ), we come to know that "God is the one who seeks and creates
community [*Gemeinschaft*] between himself and us, without needing to do
so ... because he has in himself, so without us, that which he seeks and
creates between himself and us." Indeed, "as and before God seeks and
creates community with us, he wills and achieves it even in himself. ... So
that which he seeks and creates between himself and us is in fact nothing
other than that which he wills and achieves and therefore *is* in himself."[85]

The implications of this view become even more severe (definitive
and restrictive) when Barth then explains it in the context of God's absolute freedom, first within himself and then within and over all that
God creates. "God's freedom consists precisely in the intrinsic positivity
not only of his acts toward what is outside [himself], but also of his own
inner being." But this, his aseity, also means that "He is the one who is
free from all origination [*Begründung*], conditioning or determination
from without, from any other [than Himself]."[86] Nevertheless, Barth
says, God's freedom also means that God

can so indwell [*inseitig sein*] ... every other [being] so that, while he is its creator
and the giver of its being, ... he does not withdraw anything of his own divine
being, does not oppose it as an unconcerned stranger, but is present as the be-

84. CD 2-1:273–274; KD 2-1:304–305.
85. CD 2-1:273, 275; KD 2-1:306–307, 308–309.
86. CD 2-1:303, 307; KD 2-1:340, 346.

ing of its being. ... God can allow this other so utterly distinct from Himself (and which has originated by his will and subsists by his will) to live and move and have its being within Himself. ... [God can] in fact be nearer to [this other] than it is to itself, understand it better than it understands itself.[87]

Now, if we ask how this simultaneous transcendence and immanence is possible, how it is grounded in the very being of God, Barth returns to what we have called a major and ruling concept in all of his theology, namely, his very special interpretation of the doctrine of the Trinity. A few pages later in the same section 28 that we have been listening to, Barth declares that in God's self-revelation itself "the fact emerges that all the possibilities of divine presence and action have a very definite center, that is, they have their ground and their consummation, their meaning, their norm and their law in Jesus Christ." This is so because "the Son of God who became flesh in Jesus Christ is, as God's eternal mode-of-being, nothing more nor less than the principle of all world-immanence of God and therefore the principle of what we have called the secondary absoluteness of God." Then Barth makes his typical move from this secondary back into the "primary absoluteness" of God, into what he calls "the innertrinitarian life of the Father with the Son by the Holy Spirit."[88]

His central point is that God's communion with the created human-being "has its original truth" in "the relationship and communion" of the Father with the Son "before any world," indeed, "from eternity and in eternity." And from this eternal relationship, Barth derives a general principle: "The Son of God is the principal truth of an other in God himself. This other, as the Son of God, is God himself; but even God himself becomes as himself [*sich selbst*] an other in his Son. The world is not needed in order for there to be an other. Before any world he has otherness [*Andersheit*] in his Son, from eternity and in eternity in himself." Therefore, God's relationship and communion with the

---

87. CD 2–1:313–314; KD 2–1:353. I have taken some liberty in arranging the (partial) contents of these impossibly long and complex sentences of Barth's German text. As one who spent the year 1959–60 listening to Barth present in lecture form what was meant to be the beginning of the last volume of the *Dogmatics* (4–4, the "Ethics of Reconciliation"), I can profoundly sympathize with the original auditors who tried to capture the content of these sentences as they listened to Barth read them. I say "last volume" because Barth told me that he would get around to writing the intended last volume on Redemption (5) only in heaven. I guess he wanted to have a truly primary source on this topic.

88. CD 2–1:316–317; KD 2–1:356.

created world is not "an alien or contradictory but a natural ... manifestation of God's being externally [*nach aussen*]. The world is because and as the Son of God is." Therefore, in the incarnation of the Son of God, when the Creator "also became creature, it is clear that we have ... the essence and epitome of every conceivable [*in Betracht kommenden*] relationship and communion [between God and the world]."[89]

This interpretation of the "innertrinitarian life" of God gets formalized into a general concept about six or seven years later (ca. 1943) in Barth's first volume on God as creator (3–1), and this concept becomes a ruling principle that is applied throughout the rest of the *Dogmatics*. He calls it the "analogy of relationship" (*analogia relationis*) in contrast and opposition to the "analogy of being" (*analogia entis*).[90] Simply put, it states that the interpersonal relationship between one human being and another (which is the essence of being human) is analogous to the relationship and communion between God as creator and human being as creature, and that the latter relationship is analogous to the eternal innertrinitarian relationship between God the Father and God the Son by (or through) God the Holy Spirit. In this concept Barth does not mean analogy simply as a form of symbolic language or as a method of epistemological analysis used by human beings to interpret and to explain (and to control) their own experience of reality. Rather, Barth is making an assertion of *what* God has revealed (an assertion of content and substance) about the eternal being of God and about that God's relationship with all creation. And this revelation is not derived by humans on their own initiative through an analysis of the created world, but strictly and only by God's initiative in coming to us in the person of Jesus Christ, the incarnation of the eternal mode of God's being God called the Word or Son of God. Hence Barth claims that the truth and validity and meaning of this tripartite analogy is dictated and established by the grace of God in Jesus Christ (*analogia gratiae*) and comes to be known and understood in the faith relationship of the believer with Jesus Christ (*analogia fide*).

89. CD 2–1:317; KD 2–1:356–357.

90. I have treated this theme in Barth at some length in my *An Introduction to Barth's Dogmatics for Preachers*, pp. 59, 78, 145–150, 155–158. For earlier anticipations or versions of this concept and for its development within Barth's *Church Dogmatics*, see the following passages (with the German pages in parenthesis): 2–1:317, 667–673, (356–7, 752–759); 2–2:110 (117–118); 3–1:184–185, 194–197, 301–303 (206–208, 218–222, 226–229); 3–2:218–220, 323–324 (260–263, 370–371); 4–1:202–204 (221–223); 4–2:341–343 (381–383).

Kierkegaard would have grave difficulties with this entire conceptuality on at least two scores. First, the primary assertion (of Barth's theory of *analogia relationis*) is that, in their *primary* character, the relation between God and the human being and the relation of one human being to another are essentially the same as the relation between "Father" and "Son" within the eternal unity of the one and only God. So my I-thou relationship with God and with another human being is, in one (primary) way, nothing more (and in other ways much less) than the relationship between Father and Son within the Spirit-unity of God. (Hence an "analogy" that asserts both likeness and difference.) As we have just heard Barth say (at note 85 above), "that which [God] seeks to create between himself and us is *nothing other* than that which he wills and achieves and therefore *is* in himself" (first emphasis added). But we have also heard Barth insist (at notes 80, 82, and 84 above) that God is personal and has personhood not separately as Father or as Son or as Spirit as such but only as "the one single essence of God," and it is "this one God" who is to be understood "as person, that is, as *I* being in and for itself." Therefore, "under the [category of] being a person, in the strict and proper sense, only the being of God can be understood," and "the human-being is not genuine person, but God is that."

In other words, hidden within Barth's analogy of relationship is an analogy of being. That is, the element of *likeness* in the analogy is the positive characteristic of the human *being*'s total derivation from and dependence upon the *being* of God. The element of *unlikeness* in the analogy is the negative characteristic of the human being's inability to understand, to originate, and to enact anything on her/his own, and especially the negative element of the human being's assumption that one is free to do so and hence becomes lost in sin and nothingness.[91] It is this totally negative view of human freedom that would give Kierkegaard trouble.

For Kierkegaard every individual human being is given by God the built-in potentiality and task of becoming as authentic person, self, spirit. Therefore, Barth's analogy of relationships, which defines our relation to God and to other human beings strictly in terms of the relation of Father and Son within the triune nature of God, is tantamount to denying true

91. For an account of Barth's understanding and use of the concept of analogy, see my *An Introduction to Barth's Dogmatics*, pp. 142–151. There I also note that Barth became persuaded by Hans Urs von Balthasar that he misunderstood Aquinas' concept of *analogia entis* and that Aquinas actually meant something like Barth's *analogia relationis*; hence Barth ceases (from 1950 on) to contrast the two.

selfhood to the human individual and, for Kierkegaard, to contradicting the entire Biblical view of human nature and the heart of Christian faith. In my Christian faith-relationship with God-in-Christ, God addresses me as "thou" in the complete sense of person or self, as one who is "like" or "in the image" of God as person. In fear and trembling, in awe and wonder, I become conscious of my selfhood, my personhood, precisely in the event of God's pursuing and wooing me as lover to beloved (more exactly, in the event of forgiveness, acceptance, reconciliation). If God is person (as Barth says) in the unity of being, not separately in three different *modes* of being, then I am not a "thou" to God's personhood as the Son is a "thou" to the Father. The latter relationship is analogous not to my relationship with God as personal being or with another human being as a person but is analogous to my essential "I" being conscious of the active "me" within the inclusive unity of self.

Kierkegaard's second difficulty with Barth's theory is even more crucial for him. As we have heard (at note 79 above), Barth defines being-person (*Personsein*) as "being free subject, ... able to be in charge of its own existence and essence, ... able to choose new possibilities of existence and essence." For Kierkegaard, freedom is definitive of human selfhood, personhood. Certainly, human freedom is qualified and delimited, by being derived from and dependent upon an Other, by being in essential unity with finitude and temporality. Human selfhood is *not* like God's being-in-and-for-itself. Nevertheless, human freedom is true and real, the essential quality of being human, of being "in the image" of God.[92] This latter assertion is precisely what Barth's theory of *analogia relationis* prohibits and excludes.

A thorough analysis and critique of this theory of Barth is beyond the scope of the present interpretation of Kierkegaard as theologian, but a few remarks will help to clarify the uniqueness of Kierkegaard's own theological perspective. The essential elements of Barth's theory gradually emerge in *Church Dogmatics* in the development of his doctrine of the Trinity in volumes 1 and 2:1 and his doctrine of election in volume 2:2. But it is in the context of his doctrine of creation (volume 3, parts 1 and 2) that he pulls these elements together by means of the explicit theory of an analogy of relationship.

Barth borrows the phrase and some of its content from Dietrich Bonhoeffer's lectures on *Creation and Fall* (*Schöpfung und Fall*) delivered in

---

92. I have spelled out Kierkegaard's view of freedom in great detail in my volume on *Kierkegaard as Humanist.*

the winter semester of 1932–33 at the University of Berlin. Barth is seeking to clarify what Genesis means when it says that God made the human-being in God's "image" and "likeness." He finds it helpful when Bonhoeffer asks, "How can God see, recognize and discover himself in his work?" Bonhoeffer's answer is: "The fact that God creates his image on earth in the human-being means that the human-being is like the creator in that he is free."[93] But in what sense "free?" Barth accepts and repeats Bonhoeffer's interpretation (with his own additions). The human-being is not free "in itself" (*an sich*, "as such"), does not have freedom as "a quality, activity, disposition [*Anlage*], kind-of-being [*Wesenart*]," nor as "an intrinsic capacity [*eigene Fähigkeit*], possibility or structure of his being." Rather, "this created freedom finds expression in the fact 'that the [one] created-being is related to the other created-being, that the human-being is free for the human-being,'" just "as the Creator willed and always does will to be free for the creature." Then Barth makes his main point: "In this purely given and established relationship is revealed the freedom of the human-being and therefore the fact that the human-being is in the image of God [*die Gottebenbildlichkeit des Menschen*]. As God is for the human-being, so the human-being is for the human-being; that is to say, [only] in that God is for him, so that the *analogia relationis* as the meaning of the image-of-God [*Gottebenbildlichkeit*] cannot ever be confused with an *analogia entis*."[94]

Barth's own formulation of the principle of *analogia relationis* is much more inclusive and elaborated. Shortly before his explicit reference to Bonhoeffer (in a footnote), he gives this version. Here he also make the point that, for the human creature, being in the image and likeness of God does not consist in a "quality" or in "peculiar attributes or modes-of-behavior [*Verhaltungsweisen*]," not "in anything the human-being is or does." Rather, the image consists in the fact that God's own "form of life" is "repeated in the human-being created by Him," because "in God's own being and sphere there is an opposite [*Gegenüber*], [and therefore] a genuine but harmonious self-encounter and self-discovery, an open being-opposite and [yet] being-for each other." It is this structure within God that "is copied in God's relation to the human-being," and then this "co-existence and co-operation within God himself is repeated in the

93. Dietrich Bonhoeffer, *Creation and Fall*, p. 35 (*Schöpfung und Fall*, p. 41). This early theological creativity emphasizes the tragedy of his loss.

94. CD 3–1:194–195; KD 3–1:218–219. All of this material is contained in a long footnote. Compare with Bonhoeffer's own treatment of these themes in CAF, pp. 35–37; SUF, pp. 41–44. Bonhoeffer says quite bluntly, "Freedom is a relationship and nothing else."

relation of human-being to human-being." And "thus the *tertium comparationis*, the analogy between God and human-being, is simply the existence of I and thou in encounter" (or "in opposition," *Gegenüber*).[95]

Barth's major point in these statements is that my being in the image
and likeness of God does not consist in anything I *am* or *do*, but consists
in the *relationship* that God himself and God only establishes with me by
repeating in and with me that relationship that God already is in God's
own eternal inner being. And then this relationship is repeated and reflected at a third level (the *tertium comparationis*) in the relationship of
one human-being to an other, in the "co-humanity" (*Mitmenschlichkeit*)
which is definitive of what it means to be human. In other words, to be
human has nothing to do with a structure of selfhood or personhood
that is interior and integral to the individual human being but is composed simply of a relationship which God creates and sustains both between the human creature and God and between one human being and
an other. And these two relationships are derived from and reflective of a
third and eternal relationship that is interior to God's own "form of life."

In this passage Barth does not mention the Trinity or use the formula
of *analogia relationis*. But the same interpretation of the image of God in
human-being is repeated in the next volume of the *Dogmatics*, and there
he makes it clear that what he means by God's "own form of life" is that
of the Father, Son and Holy Spirit. He says, "God is ... in this triunity the
original [*Urbild*] and the source of every I and thou: the I which is eternally from and to the thou and precisely thus I in the most eminent
sense. And it is this relationship within the inner divine being that is repeated and copied in God's eternal covenant with the human-being as is
revealed and empowered in the humanity of Jesus." And "the humanity
of Jesus is not merely the repetition and copy of his divinity or of the will
of God ruling him, but the repetition and copy of God himself, no more
and no less." Hence "between the relationship of God and human-being
and the prior relationship of the Father to the Son and the Son to the
Father, i.e., the relationship of God to himself," one cannot speak of
"a correspondence and similarity of being, an *analogia entis*," but only
of "an *analogia relationis*, the correspondence and similarity of the two
relationships."[96]

95. CD 3–1:184–185; KD 3–1:206–207.
96. CD 3–2:218–220; KD 3–2:260–262. It is little wonder that Barth finally (about eight
years later) came to speak of "the humanity of God," that is, the identification of the eternal
Son of God with humanity in and through the eternal decree of the one God.

But as we have already seen (at note 91 above), the element of unlikeness in the analogy of relationship is negative, that is, the denial of any authentic selfhood and freedom in the human being as such. On the other hand, the element of likeness is indeed a kind of "correspondence and similarity of being"; that is to say, the relationship between God and the human being is a repetition and copy of the relation of Father and Son in the inner life of the eternal God. Hence original and authentic humanity is the humanity of the eternal Son which, through the Incarnation, is present and operative in Jesus Christ. And we finite, mortal, and sinful human beings share in Christ's true humanity only through our faith-union with Christ.

Barth at times clearly attributes authentic selfhood and freedom to the human being. In his treatment of ethics in the context of the doctrine of creation (vol. 3–4), freedom is the main topic. And in the final section (section 56) of that volume, he explicates the nature of "Freedom in Limitation." Kierkegaard and Barth agree on this basic character of human freedom.[97] Again and again both of them argue that freedom does not mean the right and ability to choose between good and evil, because that really means that the human being claims to be able to determine for itself what is good and what is evil. On the contrary, God alone is the source of that distinction because God alone is goodness as such, in God's own being. So human freedom is essentially the ability to recognize and acknowledge and then to affirm, accept, and enact that goodness – all of which a human being can do only upon the initiative and with the help of God.

But this delimited freedom is actual and operative because this "limitation is not negation but the [granting of] highest possible status [*Position*]," because it "means ... definition and accordingly determination. Only the negated [*das Nichtige*, empty of being and impossible] is undefined and therefore unlimited." In this way God differentiates the created human being from God and from and above all other creatures. Indeed, God differentiates each individual human being from all others, "regards only *this* [particular] human being ... and therewith treats her/him as soul, as subject, as self [*ihn selbst*], as 'I' who is to be addressed as 'thou.' "[98]

97. See the extensive treatment of Kierkegaard's concept in chapters 4 and 5 of my *Kierkegaard as Humanist*, especially the section entitled "The Resultant Nature of Freedom" in chapter 4.

98. CD 3–4:567; KD 3–4:651.

And in a section (section 41 of the earlier volume 3–1) on the topic, "The Covenant as the Internal Basis of Creation," Barth makes clear the central importance of this relationship between God and the human being: "by the power of this address and summons [to obedience] and the responsibility thus ascribed to him/her, the human being becomes and is free." Now, "the purpose of God in granting the human being freedom for the sake of obedience is to verify as such the obedience proposed in and with [the human being's] creation, i.e.. to confirm it, to allow it to become *event* in [the human being's] own decision. It is obvious that if this is [God's] will, God cannot [!] compel the human being to obey; [God] cannot as it were bring about [the human being's] obedience mechanically." Indeed, "God has not created the human being in this way, rather [God] has created [the human being] with the capacity [*Fähigkeit*] for confirmation and actualization [*Betätigung*] of one's obedience, [a capacity] for one's own [*eigener*] decision to obey."99

About ten years later Barth reaffirms this view of human freedom in his exposition of "The Holy Spirit and Christian Love" (CD 4–2, section 68). Barth is exploring the fact that "the covenant of grace becomes two-sided instead of one-sided." While he is careful to spell out that God and the human being are not equal partners in this relationship, he also insists that for the covenant to be consummated, the human being must contribute her/his part by accepting God's loving demand for obedience *freely.* "If it were not one's free action, if it would therefore occur naturally or inevitably or mechanically so that one must do what God wills under constraint and not as one's own willing and doing, – how then would it be obedience? A puppet does not obey." In other words, the human act of love toward God's "cannot be understood as a prolongation or emanation of the divine action, of God's love. The apparent grandeur of this theomonistic conception must not blind us to the fact that if it is true, then there can be no question of a free act of human love toward God, and therefore of an act of obedience enclosed within it and following it."100

Nevertheless, in spite of all these instances of glowing praise of human freedom and responsibility, the weight of Barth's entire interpretation of the Christian knowledge of God and of Christian faith minimizes the role of human freedom almost to the point of being inconsequential. In his depiction of the faith-relationship with God-in-Christ, Barth comes very close to, seems everywhere to assume, a doctrine of irresist-

99. CD 3–1:265, 264; KD 3–1:302, 301.
100. CD 4–2:790, 799, 800; KD 4–2:896, 906, 907–908.

ible grace. One clear instance occurs in the context of the very materials asserting human freedom and decision quoted in the previous paragraph. He asks, "What is the meaning of love for God, for Jesus? Just this: that God, Jesus, is so urgent and pressing toward a human being that [the human being] may and must [*darf und muss*] yield to this constraint of his [i.e., God's] love in the experience of its majesty/lordliness [*Herrlichkeit*]." A few pages later he adds, "We can and must emphasize by way of closer definition that the liberation of the human-being for the love of God encloses within it from the very first the liberation for obedience to God, so that it [the love] is ineluctably [*unweigerlich*, unresistingly, implicitly] followed by human obedience."[101]

Two pages later, Barth restates this view even more bluntly: "When the Christian loves ... God, he/she *cannot* choose or will or even imagine any other order of this relationship than that of obedience" (emphasis added). And why does the Christian love God? Barth says (replacing his "he" with "I"), "I do not love God because God commands me to do so, but on the basis [literally, out of the ground] of the electing, purifying, creative love with which God first loved me." And what are the implications of this relationship for human freedom? "In that I – not *have* – but *receive* this freedom to love God, I inevitably discover that even in this freedom there remains for me nothing other than to place myself under the will, the word, the command, the order of God as I hear it, and therefore to be obedient" (emphasis added). The reason for the inevitability of this discovery had been stated by Barth plainly and directly in his previous volume (4–1) when treating the topic, "Faith and Its Object." He asks how it is possible for "the sinful human-being" to believe for oneself that one's own "human situation" has been qualitatively transformed by God's presence and act in Jesus Christ? This "creative character" of one's faith certainly "cannot derive from the sinful human-being." It derives only from Jesus Christ. In the human-being's encounter with Christ, "He is the stronger in virtue of what He has done for all human-beings ... in His death [and] resurrection. ... He proves Himself to be stronger by the *irresistible* [*unwiderstehlich*] awakening power of His Holy Spirit. ... He creates the presupposition on the basis of which the sinful human-being can and does actually believe. ... When it is this One who closes the circle around her/him, a human-being may, can and must do that which one does in faith." (emphasis added)[102] It is clear,

101. CD 4–2:794, 798; KD 4–2:901, 905.
102. CD 4–2:800; KD 4–2:907; CD 4–1:752–3; KD 4–1:840–1.

then, that the word, concept, and reality of what Barth calls human *free-dom* refer *only* to this human response (of human love/faith toward God) that has been "received" from and "irresistibly" elicited by the prior, initiating, enabling, electing, creating love of God toward the human-being.

The key question for our purposes of comparison with Kierkegaard is this: does Barth assume and allow that the human-being is also free *not* to love God and hence not to be obedient to God's will and purpose? This is an important and very revealing question for the clarification of the uniqueness of Kierkegaard's thought, and therefore will be given a thorough analysis here. Since Barth obviously assumes that human beings as a race failed (and fail) to love and obey God, the answer would seem to be obvious. But not for Barth. For his answer let us turn to his only detailed treatment of this question.[103]

He is expositing his general thesis that the covenant is the "internal basis of creation," and he illustrates this thesis by the condition of the human-being in the Garden of Eden as the human-being confronts the two trees: the tree of life and the tree of the knowledge of good and evil. Like Kierkegaard, he argues that God alone is qualified to judge what is good because God *is* goodness itself, and in creation God has "negated and rejected" every other alternative as not-good and therefore as "impossible." The human-being, alone of all creatures, is created with the capacity to affirm God in the role of Judge of what is good and evil and thus to share in life and fellowship with God. This affirmation is what "freedom" is for. So if the human-being should claim the right and power to judge what is good and what is evil, this would be a claim to be equal with God. But this is not "a positive possibility to be realized by the human-being." It could only lead to death and destruction. Hence God prevents this possibility by issuing first the prohibition against such a claim and then also the threat of death if the human-being makes the claim.[104]

The problem seems to be resolved: the human-being simply *cannot* realize the impossible possibility. "The life of the human-being is destined for life in fellowship with God, that is, in acknowledgment of God's deity and therefore of God's judicial office in creation." But Barth does not

103. If there is any other explicit and extended treatment of this question (than the one I now use) in any of Barth's writings, I have not found it. The section is in CD 3–1:256–265; KD 3–1:293–302.

104. CD 3–1:257–260; KD 3–1:293–296. The quotation is from p. 258 (294).

avoid an urgent pressing question. He says, "Now we face the critical point: will [the human-being] come to that [acknowledgment] and will it have her/his acquiescence? ... Or will [the human-being] retreat in opposition to this offer of supreme fellowship between God and one's self, and thus lay down the impossible but indeed enticing condition that he himself must first know not only the good but also the evil?"[105] Obviously throughout the entire *Dogmatics* Barth assumes that every human-being does "retreat in opposition," fails to acknowledge and affirm God's exclusive "judicial office," does fall into sin. Yet not once does Barth explore the complexities and depths of the *human* side of this failure, but is intent on portraying God's cosmic drama of creation, human failure, covenant people, incarnation, cross and resurrection, reconciliation, redemption and consummation.

In the passage under consideration, Barth repeatedly makes two points. First, he affirms that God needs the human-being's free acknowledgment and acceptance of God's graceful offer of eternal life and fellowship. So God "leaves the door open" to the negative possibility; "the human-being is brought to a crossroads" where "a question is put to her/him." Hence the "divinely given life ... assumes the nature of a task." And "in this arrangement" made by God, obedience "is not made physically necessary," and disobedience "is not made physically impossible." So "room-to-play is given the human-being; freedom is ascribed to him/her."[106]

On the other hand (and secondly), Barth vehemently asserts that "this freedom is not a freedom-of-choice [*Wahlfreiheit*] between obedience and disobedience." God "has not allotted [the human-being] a place midway between obedience and disobedience, ... has not presented to the human-being, like Hercules at the crossroads, the choice between obedience and disobedience." And again, "The possibility of obedience presented to the human-being [is] not as the competition of one possibility as opposed to another, but as free decision for it [i.e., for

---

105. CD 3–1:260–261; KD 3–1:296–297.

106. CD 3–1:262–263; KD 3–1:298–300. Note Barth's use of "physically." He seems to assume that eating of the forbidden fruit was (and is) a *physical* act whereas this external figure is but a symbol or image of what is meant to be the profoundly inward, spiritual, and psychological struggle (as Barth himself puts it) to "acknowledge" and to "acquiesce" to God's juridical office and to resist the claim that the human-being can determine what is right and what is wrong for him/herself. As we will note later, this use of "physical" is precisely indicative of Barth's failure to take seriously the true and full nature of the human-being as spirit, as self, as person.

obedience]." And again, "No other decision than that of obedience will correspond with [the human-being's] place," that is, "with and before God." And again, "In the freedom given to her/him by God, the human-being could not possibly will to use it," that is, to choose "the possibility denied him/her." In other words, Barth transfers the principle that the human-being does not have freedom-of-choice between good and evil (because only God makes that distinction) to the principle that the human-being cannot even freely choose between being obedient to God and being disobedient.[107]

With the first principle Kierkegaard profoundly agrees; with the second he vehemently disagrees. He would argue that if one does not explore the complexity of the inward agony and travail of the human soul/mind in the event of "disobedience," of human failure to respond to the eternal when the human-being faces "the open door," faces the "task" of making "the free decision" of how to answer "the question put to him/her," then one will never uncover or face the profound complexities of the inward depths of what it means to be *human* spirit, human self, human person – which God in creation has given the human-being to be and which the eternal everywhere and always, and especially God-in-Christ, seeks to help the human-being to become.

Barth, in this passage, quite consciously and deliberately rejects the entire enterprise (which Kierkegaard undertakes throughout his authorship) of pursuing just such an exploration. In so doing, Barth makes an obvious allusion to Kierkegaard's well-known use of the image of "dizziness" in *The Concept of Angst*.[108] Barth is arguing that the human-being "does not need to grasp after this [negative] possibility," but if she/he does do so, "the human-being's decision will be a decision for evil, destruction and death." Then he adds, "Gazing down into the abyss on the left hand – which the decision of God has graciously obstructed [*verschlossen*] – the human-being would only become immediately dizzy and would immediately plunge down into it, from which God in his decision wills to hold her/him back. ... The door to this possibility was opened when God planted the second tree. But above this door there stands the inscription 'No entrance.' This possibility is not to be actualized." Of course, "some room-to-play is given to the human-being," but

107. The quotations in this paragraph are, in sequence, from CD 3–1:263, 264, 265, 266; KD 3–1:300, 301, 303.
108. *The Concept of Anxiety*, p. 55; (KW 8:61); SV 6:152–3; (4:331).

"no room-to-play is given her/him on the edge of the abyss. One is not allotted a place midway between obedience and disobedience."[109]

Kierkegaard's entire anthropology, and the entire theology which is reflected in it, centers around the assumption and the conviction that every human-being does play around on the edge of that abyss of innocence, does become dizzy in contemplation of the contradiction and conflict between the infinite and the finite, between the eternal and the temporal, between freedom-for and freedom-from – and it assumes that in that dizziness every human-being does plunge into the abyss of nothingness, impotence, despair, and the sickness-unto-death by *choosing* in favor of freedom-from (i.e., from the eternal, from God). For Kierkegaard, such is the actuality of authentic human freedom that is inherent in being created to be and to become spirit, self, person, in the image and likeness of and in fellowship with the eternal, with God. For Kierkegaard, all talk of sin and guilt is meaningless except on the presupposition of human freedom and responsibility in the event of human failure to use freedom to choose *for* that fellowship. And, as we shall see in the next chapter, this freedom is operative not only in the innocence of our original state but continues to operate in our mature failures of self-deception and taking offense before the mercy and love of God.

How, then, does Barth account for human failure and guilt, for the fact that every human-being lives in transgression? Beyond the question of why the human-being can not choose evil and still live, he recognizes a second and "more difficult" question. "Why was not this divinely given prohibition more effective? ... Why is there opened in a certain direction a door which the human-being should not smash down?"[110] Again we

---

109. CD 3–1:261–262, 263–264; KD 3–1:297–298, 300. That these allusions to Kierkegaard's concept of dizziness are not merely incidental is clear in the fact that Barth still has them in mind about ten years later in specific references to Kierkegaard. He warns against the horrible error of "the older Protestantism" in its emphasis first on "the individual experience of human grace" and only then on the community of the church. And then he warns that we should not "be crowded again into the same *cul de sac* on the detour through Kierkegaard." (CD 4–1:149–150; KD 4–1:165) More specifically, he argues that in order "to be clear that our life is a vacuum and darkness, we need the confrontation and comparison of our life with that Jesus Christ. ... Then we become aware of the abyss above which we unsuspectingly moved. But at the same time ... we now become aware of the fact that we are protected from and delivered from plunging into that abyss." (CD 4–3:84–85; KD 4–3: 93)

110. CD 3–1:262–263; KD 3–1:299.

hear Barth's insistence that if God wills (desires) that the human-being will enter into obedience freely, "in one's own decision," then "God cannot compel the human-being to obey, ... as it were ... mechanically."[111] But how then does the human-being fail to obey if one cannot choose freely to disobey? Barth's answer comes several pages later. As we have heard, "the violation [*Übertretung*] by the human-being cannot be derived from what God positively willed with [the open door] and with the freedom given to the human-being." Rather, "the tree of knowledge could become a danger to the human-being only when it confronted her/him in a freedom which she/he had used [*nehmen*] in the misuse of the freedom given to her/him."[112]

So when Barth says that we are not free to disobey, that "the human-being could not possibly make use" of that door that opens to the negative possibility, he simply means that what we get by disobedience is not what we intended (i.e., freedom to do whatever we desire), that the state of sin, destruction, and death that eventuates from disobedience hardly deserves the name of "freedom." But he finally does admit that we use the freedom, given to us by God for a positive purpose, in a *mis*use of that freedom by the negative act of disobeying, that is, by *choosing* not to affirm and to acknowledge and to acquiesce to God's sovereign right to define what is good and to God's invitation to a life of fellowship with God. This is a curious circumlocution, a convoluted play upon words in order to be able to say that humans are not free to disobey. It is a clear contradiction for Barth to say that the human-being's God-given "capacity [*Fähigkeit*] for confirmation and actualization of obedience" does not inherently carry with it the capacity for "the choice of ... disobedience."[113]

But the truly amazing and most significant characteristic of Barth's analysis is that he shows no interest, not anywhere in the *Dogmatics*, in exploring and depicting the human side of this event of disobedience. He affirms that "disobedience was not made physically impossible,"[114] but he never asks what are the inner, psychic conditions and makeup of the human self (person, spirit) that bring the self to the "crossroads" where the human-being faces a fateful choice between two paths, that

111. CD 3–1:264; KD 3–1:301.
112. CD 3–1:266; KD 3–1:303–304.
113. CD 3–1:264; KD 3–1:301.
114. CD 3–1:263 & 264; KD 3–1:300 & 301.

make the individual become conscious of an "open door" to an alternative that the self does not really understand and yet that enthralls the self in the ambiguity of fear/desire. Barth is not curious as to what it is in the given conditions and makeup of the human self that serve as the seedbed for human failure, for making the wrong choice. Nor does Barth explore the ramifications of this failure in all the stages of development that occur in both the inner and outer life of the individual self, as one becomes increasingly self-conscious and self-responsible in familial, social, economic and political relationships. Volume 3–4, "The Command of God the Creator" ("Ethics as a Task of the Doctrine of Creation") would seem to be an exception, but even here the conclusions are stated in formal terms of principles that are derived from the standard of authentic humanity found and revealed in the person of Jesus Christ. There is little depiction of or sympathy for the inner struggles of the human being (as Christian disciple) in seeking to incarnate in one's own life what one comes to know as authentic life in the Spirit of Christ.

In stark contrast to Barth's treatment of these issues, Kierkegaard turns his most intense concern and consciousness precisely to the character of the inner spiritual struggles of both the ordinary human being and, then, the Christian disciple – and in that order, because Kierkegaard never forgot that the most faithful and ardent Christian had first been and always remains an individual and very *human* being. Barth argues that the only "adequate concept for the whole arrangement [*Anordnung*] of the relationship between God and human-being" (that was established by God in creation) is the concept of *Bewährung*, that is, to affirm, authenticate, prove one's willingness to obey.[115] This kind of "fellowship, exercised in freedom with the God who had willed the good and rejected the evil, was the genuinely alluring and inviting thing in Paradise."[116] Kierkegaard sees the "paradise" of the "original," basic and essential condition of every human being to be a much more ambiguous and complex "arrangement" in which human freedom, given and shaped by God as the key factor in that arrangement, faces a task and a dilemma much more demanding, precarious, and perilous than Barth recognizes or deems important to explore. Kierkegaard

115. CD 3–1:264; KD 3–1:301.
116. CD 3–1:266; KD 3–1:304.

explores this "arrangement" in some depth and detail in *The Concept of Angst*.[117]

Kierkegaard agrees with Barth that "freedom's possibility is not being able [*at kunne*] to choose the good or the evil." That is too abstract and rational a concept of human freedom, and it assumes a position *above* the distinction that the human-being never possesses. Rather, this "possibility is [simply] *being able*."[118] And again Kierkegaard agrees with Barth that this free and responsible "being able" is a capacity given by God for one reason: (in Kierkegaard's words as spelled out in these sections of *The Concept of Angst*) for the human task of becoming a self in a loving relationship with God and neighbor. And the key question is how and in what way this possibility becomes actuality. Certainly the transition does not occur simply by logic or reason. But Kierkegaard would argue that Barth's concept of *Bewährung* is *not* "adequate" to the situation but is too one-sided, because it does not acknowledge and take seriously that the gift of this freedom to the human being inescapably involves every individual person in a crucial and portentous inner spiritual agony and struggle with the manifest possibility of failure.

Kierkegaard insists that "an intermediate-determinant is required" that takes account of the ambiguity (*Tvetydiged*) of this situation, and the term he proposes for it is *angst*. To know angst is not yet to be sinful or guilty. Indeed, it is not a "troublesome burden" because even "though it alarms one, it also captivates one by its pleasing apprehension."[119] Angst

117. The material that follows is from Kierkegaard's *The Concept of Anxiety*, sections 5 and 6 of chapter 1 and section 2 of chapter 2. A much more comprehensive analysis of Kierkegaard's concept of angst can be found in my *Kierkegaard as Humanist*, chapter 3, sections A, B, and C. I think it was a serious mistake that Reidar Thomte and Howard Hong did not use the word "angst" in the title and text of the 1980 translation of *Begrebet Angest*. According to Merriam Webster's tenth edition of the Collegiate Dictionary, angst entered the English language about 1942. It has been in several American-English dictionaries for at least the last thirty years, and it has been commonly used in American magazines and newspapers (even in cartoons) since the 1960s, often appearing in headlines even of the sports section. The connotations of angst are so diverse, rich, and ambiguous that neither "dread" nor "anxiety" are adequate, especially for understanding Kierkegaard's special meaning. So it is better to use angst itself.

118. *The Concept of Anxiety*, pp. 40, 44; (KW 8:44, 49); SV 6:138, 142; (4:315, 320).

119. Ibid., p. 38; (KW 8:42); SV 6:137; (4:314). The Danish verb for "alarm" (*ængste*) and noun for "apprehension" (*Beængstelse*) are the same word or root and have the same meaning; so even the Danish language does not connote the double-sided character of angst that Kierkegaard indicates by "antipathetic" and "sympathetic." I think that Swenson's "alarm" and "apprehension" better capture this ambiguity than Thomte's "causes anxiety" and "anxiousness." Kierkegaard wants to capture the dichotomy of human consciousness in being simultaneously allured and repulsed, excited and frightened.

is characteristic of the state of consciousness of every human-being as created by God in the state of innocence. In this state one has not yet become self (spirit); rather, one's self is a "dream," an alluring but undefined possibility. To become self one must relate to the Infinite, to the Eternal, to God, and as Barth and Kierkegaard agree, the human-being must do this willingly, freely, in one's own decision. But unlike Barth, Kierkegaard sees human consciousness of freedom, of "being-able," (to perform this task of becoming-self-in-relationship-with God) as situated intermediately between affirmation and negation, between actualization and failure. And therefore this awareness of being-able is experienced as angst, as feeling both sympathetic and antipathetic, both alarm and pleasing apprehension; "angst is a sympathetic antipathy and an antipathetic sympathy." So "the relationship of angst [and hence of freedom] to its object is altogether ambiguous [*tvetydigt*]."[120]

So angst "is an entangled freedom, where freedom is not free in itself but entangled, not in necessity but in itself."[121] That is to say, the human self is not free to determine for itself what is good and what is evil, and yet it is not determined from outside itself (necessity) but must face its agony of decision on its own and for itself. This decision is required by the self's inescapable, intrinsic "entanglement" in the dichotomy of its given nature as simultaneously finite and infinite, necessary and possible, temporal and eternal. The decision must be made as to which dimension of its being it will look to for the meaning of its existence and to which it will commit itself and one's future. So the self's freedom to become itself is ultimately "entangled" in the fact that this freedom has been given to it by an "other" (God), and the self must turn to the infinite, the possible, the eternal in order to get help to fulfill its freedom. Hence we will turn in our next chapter to a detailed analysis and depiction of the inner agony of the human self as it struggles – and fails – in making this decision, and in the chapter after that, we will arrive at Kierkegaard's understanding of how Christian faith/love resolves this agony and failure.

But one final question about Barth. Why does he not turn to, indeed, why does he deliberately avoid and ignore this question of the inner, personal dimensions of human failure, this agony of the human soul? We have heard him say (in note 109 above) that we must avoid the error of "the older Protestantism" and of Kierkegaard when they stressed the

120. Ibid., p. 38–39; (KW 8:41–43); SV 6:136–137; (4:313–314).
121. Ibid., p. 45; (KW 8:49); SV 6:143; (4:320).

individual experience of grace as taking place prior to the communal experience of the Christian church. But his more basic reason would seem to be that he does not really believe in the infinite and eternal significance of the human individual self as a distinct entity given *being* by God. He refuses to speak of human "spirit" because, as in the Hegelian school, "it involves at least an indirect identification of the human-being with God. ... The human-being as such cannot be characterized as spirit because in the Bible spirit denotes what God himself is and does for the human-being. ... The human-being has spirit [i.e., the Spirit of God]" in the sense of "something that comes to the human-being, something not essentially one's own, ... something that totally limits one's constitution and thus totally determines it. ... The human-being has [the Spirit] provided that he/she is one who is had by it."[122]

And how does one become possessed by the Holy Spirit? By being first of all a member of the Christian community. So, Barth says, "we have [first] to do with the occurrence of the reconciliation of the world in Jesus Christ and only in this larger context also then with the [reconciliation] of the individual human-being. ... The 'pillar and ground of truth' (1 Tim 3:15) ... is first of all the community of God and not the individual Christian as such. ... The work of the Holy Spirit ... is the historical actuality of the community."[123] Hence in this context Barth repeatedly defines sin (in its three forms: pride, sloth, and falsehood) as essentially the breaking of the original and continuing *covenant* of God with the human-being, with the human race, and thus reconciliation in Jesus Christ is the restoration and fulfillment of that covenant in the community of the church.[124] Amazingly, this point is simply the repetition of what he had already spelled out in the context of his earlier definition of sin as "the misuse of freedom" (at note 112 above).

Immediately after this seemingly most subjective, inward, personal account of the individual human transgression in the Garden of Eden, Barth argues that the real meaning and intention of God's creation scene with Adam and Eve only comes to light in the later understanding that Israel gains of "The Covenant as the Internal Basis of Creation," that is, "the covenant of God with Adam, the Patriarchs, Abraham and the people of Israel." The Garden of Eden is but an anticipatory image of the "holy land" promised and given to Israel. And "the decisive parallel ...

122. CD 3–2:354; KD 3–2:425–426.
123. CD 4–1:150–151; KD 4–1:165–166.
124. CD 4–1:138, 140–141; KD 4–1:152, 154.

consists in the relationship between the trees of the Garden ... *and* the revelation of God which ... formed the center of the 'holy' land and ... the life of the nation" (emphasis added). Both the Garden and the holy land/nation are the locale of life, but in both there is also present the danger of and the warning against the seeking of a knowledge and freedom in independence from Yaweh Elohim, with the threat of imminent destruction and death. From this perspective, human failure (of Adam/ Israel) is seen as real and actual but also as serving a purpose and goal that lie beyond and transcend the failure, indeed, as we shall see, that transcend the entire being and life of the human creature as such.[125]

Barth is amazingly frank and direct about this point. By divine decree and "deeply grounded in the development of all things," both the Garden and the Land are intended as only "provisional (interim)" places of residence. Neither one is the "final abiding place" in the divine plan. Indeed, "the removal of the human-being [Adam/Eve] and of Israel from their respective places is no doubt an act of God's judgment, but as such it is also an act of God's grace. What God genuinely has in mind for the human-being and for Israel will not happen in this particular place but precisely in and with their removal from this place."[126] In other words, God's judgment (and therefore human failure which it assumes) is a provisional step toward the ultimate event of God's grace.

Certainly, this failure does not derive in any way from God's wish or act. Barth reiterates once more that the failure occurs because God desires Israel's (the human-being's) "free obedience" so that God does not merely triumph but achieves "community" and "covenant" with Israel. But Israel, like Adam/Eve, misuse this freedom in seeking its own righteousness, and in so doing Israel "surely grasps failure" and causes "the destruction of the people." "From the very outset this people of Israel is at every point a chastised, suppressed, suffering and lost people, a dying and perishing people. It is with this people and under these conditions that Yahweh Elohim has formed a covenant. It is over it that first to last and step by step His grace undoubtedly rules. It is this people that he loves and commands to live."[127] Likewise, "God's covenant with Adam is at once fulfilled in such a way that the latter stumbles [*zu Falle kommt*] at the tree of knowledge, ... so that rather than being obedient to God's

125. On this topic one should read the entirety of the passage in 3–1:267–276 (KD 3–1:304–315), plus the long note of Biblical exegesis in 3–1:276–288 (KD 3–1:315–329). For the references in this paragraph, see 3–1:267, 269 (KD 3–1:304, 306–307).

126. CD 3–1:268–269; KD 3–1:305–306.

127. CD 3–1:271–272, 274; KD 3–1:310, 313.

gracious command he is disobedient ... and has to be removed from the tree of life also."[128]

Then Barth raises an ultimate question that allows him to propose his own conclusion. How can the actual existence of Adam and of Israel in sin, exile, destruction, and death serve the purpose of God in creation? "To what extent are Genesis 2 and all the corresponding prophecies of salvation more than a dream," more than "the expression of a bold hope that was never actually fulfilled, the document of a grandiose illusion?" Barth contends that the only answer to these questions does not lie within the Testament which contains these dreams. Rather, we must finally turn to "the objective Christological meaning" of this material. "The alternative answer is the Christian one." So it can only be said that "the creation saga is no illusion, and that the history of Israel recorded in the Old Testament is more than the history of a contradiction," because each "has actually and objectively found its goal, intended for it from the very outset, in the person and death and resurrection of the Jewish Messiah, Jesus of Nazareth."[129]

In other words, for Barth the ultimate purpose and goal of all creation – which is prefigured in God's covenant (or community) first with Adam and then with Israel, and which is the driving force and beckoning vision of the entire "holy-history" (*Heilsgeschichte*) from Abraham to the building of the second temple – is the achievement of the perfect God/human community (covenant) of love and obedience in the coming of God, in total divine Personhood, to dwell with humanity in the one human being, Jesus of Nazareth, and of course to share that community with those humans who are (ultimately and in the end) united with Jesus Christ in faith, namely, his "body."

In the sweep of this divine cosmic drama, the episode of original human failure (Adam/Israel) to accept God's gracious invitation to share in a communal life is (for Barth) ontologically and literally of no consequence. Nothing can come into *being* through this failure because the alternative to life with God is nothingness (*das Nichtige*), that-which-Being/God-has-negated, an impossibility. The attempt to be free *from* God is simply unfreedom, enslavement to nothingness, emptiness. The human refusal/failure to obey God can only be a failure; indeed, it is ultimately impossible. Hence the actual failure of Adam/Israel only serves as the occasion for God's light and life to burst forth into human actual-

128. CD 3–1:273; KD 3–1:312.
129. CD 3–1:273–276; KD 3–1:311–315.

ization in the incarnation, death and resurrection of God's own being in
the humanity of one human-being, Jesus Christ.

And so, in traditional Chalcedonian language, Barth argues that this
particular human is wholly (*ganz*) a human (*Mensch*) and at the same time
wholly God, in the sense that there is nothing lacking in his being-a-hu-
man and nothing lacking in his being-God, in the sense that he is not just
partly (*teilweise*) God and just partly a human. Indeed, Jesus Christ "is in
[true] identity [*Gleichheit*] of his being-human [*Menschsein*] with ours."
And Barth goes all the way: "to say human is to say creature and sin and
therefore limitation and suffering." But then Barth equivocates:

Jesus Christ is human quite differently [*anders*] than we others. ... In virtue of
the fact that God is one with him, he is the free human: wholly a creature but
wholly superior to his own creatureliness [*Geschöpflichkeit*], wholly bound by sin
but wholly blameless because he is not bound to commit it. ... In this he is ex-
alted above us because he is different from us. ... But he does precede us. ...
What has happened in him as the one true human is the turningaround of all of
us to God, the becoming-true [*Wahrwerden*] of all human-being [*Menschsein*].

Thus the Evangelists' "representation of the human-being [*Menschsein*] of
Jesus Christ ... left no doubt that it was a human-being as that of all other
humans, but yet therein even less [*weniger*], in that it was as such the human-being [*Menschsein*] of the true God, and therefore in spite of its likeness with that of all others, it was distinguished from all others in its
freedom in face of its limitation [*Bindung*] and its suffering." Thus the
"turning-around of the human to God took place in him," that is to say,
"the reconciliation of all humans, the fulfillment of the covenant."[130]

___

130. CD 4–1:130–132; KD 4–1:143–145. Barth's use of the phrase *Menschsein ... Gottes*
would seem to be a variation of the phrase *Menschheit Gottes* (humanity-of-God) used seven
pages earlier in this volume and, as indicated by Barth, derived from F.H.R. Frank (CD 4–
1:125; KD 4–1:137). And this latter term is clearly an anticipation of the phrase, *Menschlichkeit Gottes*, which was coined by Barth some three or four years later as the title of a lecture
delivered to the Swiss Reformed Ministers' Association in Aarau on September 25, 1965.
About the same time the phrase also appears, quite incidentally, in his lectures that later
comprised volume 4, part 3, of the *Dogmatics* (probably assuming the lecture at Aarau). In
the Aarau lecture he says, "When we look at Jesus Christ we know decisively that God's deity
does not exclude but includes [God's] *humanity*. ... Actually [God's] deity *encloses* humanity
in itself. ... It would be the false deity of a false God if in and with [God's] deity [God's] humanity did not also immediately encounter us. ... In [Jesus Christ] it is once for all decided
that God is not without the human [*den Menschen*]." [Karl Barth, *Die Menschlichkeit Gottes*
(*Theologische Studien, Herausgegeben von Karl Barth, Heft 48*), pp. 13–14; or in the English
translation of four years later, *The Humanity of God*, pp. 49–50].

In all this, Barth is clearly maintaining two theses. First, the limitations of our creatureliness and the potent actuality of our sinfulness are not to be taken seriously, because being-a-creature is no limitation for authentic human-being [*Menschsein*] as revealed in Jesus Christ, and sin itself simply does not touch his *Menschsein.* Of course, he "actually died as we must all die. But in dying he is superior to death, ... he is triumphant and alive."[131] Secondly, only the human-being of Jesus Christ is "true" (authentic) humanity because it is "the human-being [*Menschsein*] of the true God." So everything positive that Barth says about our humanity is true for us ordinary human beings *only* in so far as we participate, by the faith-relationship, in the human-being of very God as incarnate in Jesus Christ.

This second point is made explicitly by Barth even in direct connection with his strongest assertions of human individuality and subjectivity. We have heard above (at notes 97–100) that he clearly asserts that God created every human being to be free subject or self. But nowhere does he explore the inner character of the struggles of the individual in becoming that subject or self, because he assumes that all human beings fail in this task by misusing their freedom in their attempt to live their lives free *from* God instead of *with* God. So he comes finally to assert and to explore human subjectivity only in the context of Christian faith, that is, only as the inner life of Christian individual who is already connected with God in the faith relationship through Jesus Christ.

On the one hand he says, "Certainly the question of the subjective realization of reconciliation by the individual is absolutely indispensable. And it belongs properly to the concluding section of the doctrine of reconciliation." So he proposes that he will explore the individual Christian's "personal knowledge and experience of reconciliation" as being "awakened to faith" at the end of volume 4–1, as being "quickened in love" at the end of volume 4–2, and as being "enlightened in hope" at the end of volume 4–3.[132] And in his exposition of the nature of faith (at the end of 4–1) he says clearly,

There are no saints without the [Christian] community, but there is not community without the saints. If there is no Christian I and Thou and He outside the Christ-centered circle of the We and You and They of the race and the community, then the general no less than the particular is an abstraction, not to say an

131. CD 4–1:131; KD 4–1:143–144.
132. CD 4–1:150, 153; KD 4–1:165, 169.

illusion, since it does not become an event in the Christian I and Thou and He, in the personal faith of the members of the body of Christ.[133]

On the other hand, there immediately comes again his equivocation. "The alteration of the human situation" that occurs for the individual through Christian faith, love, and hope does not derive from the "human act" involved in this event. "As this human act it has no creative but only a cognitive character. As a human act it is simply the confirmation of a change that has already taken place, the change in the whole human situation that took place in the death of Jesus Christ and was revealed in his resurrection and attested by the Christian community." So how do human beings become "individual Christian subjects"? "It is not their faithfulness that makes them this (not even when it is understood as the act of their believing)." The "creative" character of faith "cannot derive from the sinful human-being." How then does the creative alteration of the individual take place? Simply from the fact that the individual "is encircled by [Christ]" through the witness of the Christian community. And (as already noted above) in that circle, Jesus Christ "proves to be the stronger by the irresistible awakening power of his Holy Spirit." It is this activity of Christ "in which He Himself is the mystery in the event of faith, in which He gives to this event a creative as well as a cognitive character."[134]

This point is made unequivocally clear at the very end of Barth's preliminary "overview" of the entire doctrine of reconciliation (§58). He says that faith, love, and hope – the essential form and content of the most inward and subjective being of the individual human-being as Christian – are all "relational concepts [*Beziehungsbegriffe*]."

The being of a Christian-human-being indicated by them is a being in relationship. ... Faith and love and hope in this relation to Jesus Christ are all primarily His own work, and His work first in the community of God, and only then His work in individual Christians. ... We speak correctly of faith and love and hope in the individual Christian only when it remains clear and constantly becomes clear that, although we are dealing with our existence, we are dealing with our existence in Jesus Christ as our true existence, that we are therefore dealing with him and not with us – and with us only in so far as wholly and exclusively with him.[135]

133. CD 4-1:751; KD 4-1:839.
134. CD 4-1:751–753; KD 4-1:839–842.
135. CD 4-1:153–154; KD 4-1:169–170.

In other words, the freeing of "humanity" from sin and the reconciliation of "humanity" to God (the fulfillment of the covenant-purpose of God in creation) occurs essentially and primarily in the humanity-of-God (*Menschlichkeit Gottes*) and only derivatively and secondarily and dependently in ordinary human beings. This point becomes overwhelmingly and numbingly clear in the remaining parts of volume 4 of the *Dogmatics*. All of Barth's talk (in §59) about human obedience is really about the obedience of Jesus Christ as "The Way of the Son of God into the Far Country." And (in §63) our act of faith is just a reflection of Jesus' act of obedience. All of Barth's talk (in §64) about the exaltation of humanity is really about the exaltation of Jesus Christ as "The Homecoming of the Son of Man." And (in §68) our act of love is just a reflection of the unity of the Son with the Father in the loving relation of the Holy Spirit. All of Barth's talk (in §69) about the glory of human life in the relationship of reconciliation is really about Jesus Christ as the true and only Son and Word of God shedding "The Light of Life" into all of creation. And (in §73) our "Life in Hope" is only a reflection of the victory of Jesus over sin and death and of the promise of his (God's) Spirit. So when one hears repeatedly that Jesus' humanity is the only "true" humanity, namely, the humanity which God has claimed from all eternity in God's trinitarian mode of being "Son," one gets the sense that my individual human self is totally engulfed in the "humanity of God," and my reconciliation and renewal is already an accomplished fact in Jesus' humanity, is indeed "inevitable and automatic," whether I know it or not. And Barth's speculative concepts of *analogia relationis* and *Menschlichkeit Gottes* intensify the notion of God's sovereign inclusiveness to the point of absoluteness.

This is no new theme or principle that develops in late volumes of the *Dogmatics*. Barth had laid out this perspective in direct and unexceptional language early on in his basic Doctrine of God, as presented in his Basel lectures in the late 1930s and early 1940s and then published as volume 2 of the *Dogmatics*. He remains faithful to it throughout. In part 1 of that volume, he ends his treatment of "The Perfections of the Divine Freedom" (§31) with the topic of "The Eternity and Glory of God." God's glory, he says,

can come to its end ... only as He becomes external in His Son, ... only as all things are to Him in His Son as they are also from Him. ... God's glory is the answer (awakened and evoked by God himself) of the worship offered Him through His creation to the extent that ... this is the echo of his own voice. But it is only in the light of ... Jesus Christ that we can be bold to say that there does exist this echo to be given by creation, and to be given only as the echo of God's voice. ... God magnifies himself through us.

So we must "look away from ourselves and all other created beings, looking to the creature which is God's own Son."[136]

So what does the creature do in and contribute to this relationship? "It serves God's self-glorification as an echoing wall can only serve to repeat and broadcast the voice which the echo 'answers'." How important is this function? "It is and remains God's self-glorification that is accomplished in his glorification through the creature. ... The divine glory *is* his self-glorification" (emphasis added).[137] Then Barth intensifies this divine narcissism with another image. He says,

The point to the whole of creation is that God should have a mirror [*Spiegel*] in which God himself is reflected, in which the image of God as the creator becomes visible, so that through it God is attested, confirmed and proclaimed. However, since [this reflection] is the center and epitome of creation, concretely in the existence of the human being, the point [to creation] is to show that the reflection (and so the image) of God that God chooses to repeat in an *other* is the same as that which he finds within himself from eternity and in eternity, namely: in his Son. [emphasis added][138]

So the normal creaturely human being fulfills its God-given nature and destiny in one's acquiescence to the task of serving as an echoing wall and a reflecting mirror in which God can hear the divine voice and

---

136. CD 2–1:667–668; KD 2–1:752–754.

137. CD 2–1:670, 672–673; KD 2–1:756, 758–759.

138. CD 2–1:673; KD 2–1:759. The second sentence in this quotation is divided into two sentences in the standard translation, as the translators often do quite helpfully with Barth's long and tortuous sentences. But in this case they miss an important point by doing so. Within half a page, Barth makes this point four times, namely, that the human-being is the image of God in creation *only* as and when that human-being is "a new creature" *in Jesus Christ*. And in this sentence (in German), Barth adds the point that Jesus Christ is the image of God *because* in Jesus "the Son of God became flesh," that is to say, the Son or "other" which God "finds within himself from eternity and in eternity." It is because of this relationship of Jesus Christ to the Son within the inner Trinitarian life of God that, many years later, Barth comes to speak of Jesus as the incarnation of the "humanity of God" (*Menschlichkeit Gottes*). Barth indicates this added point by the "however," which the translators omitted when they divided the sentence in two. My translation is admittedly a "free" one in an attempt to make Barth's point clearly.

see the divine image and hence fulfill the divine glory in *self-glorification.*
And a human being cannot freely acquiesce on one's own but only as
he/she becomes "encircled" in the life and being of the true human being, the "humanity of God" in Jesus Christ. And since God's self-glorification is "the whole point to creation," to the entire process of God's act
of externalizing in creation what is already eternally true in the internal
life of God, the failure of humankind to use its freedom to obey God,
and all the attendant human suffering in humankind's attempt to live
apart from God, only serve as an unpleasant but necessary and helpful
step in this process of God's self-glorification.

Barth, therefore, sees no point to exploring the inner agony and
struggle of human self in its original and qualitative failure, nor the inner structure and dynamics of the event of that failure. Nor does he see
any sense in analyzing the state and forms of despair that the human being experiences and lives in, both consciously and unconsciously, as a result of that essential failure. His treatment of sin as pride, sloth, and
falsehood (§s 60, 65, and 70) are from God's point of view, not that of
the human person who is living in them. And the reverse side of this position on human failure is that there is also no point in exploring the ag-
onies of the Christian individual's struggle to live in faith, love, and
hope. Barth cannot even admit let alone take seriously the fact that in
every moment of Christian living-in-faith one struggles with the possibility of "taking offense" at God's gracious loving offer of help. For Barth it
is not the ordinary human self *as such* who believes, loves, and obeys
God: it is only the "humanity of God" in Jesus Christ that has the freedom to overcome pride, sloth, and falsehood and to believe and love
and obey God. And the power of Holy Spirit in the encounter of God-in-
Christ with a sinful human being is "irresistible," and hence the human
being "may and must" yield to the reforming reconciling love of God in
Jesus Christ. There is no other alternative for human being.

With all of this Kierkegaard radically disagrees. In all of his writings
he focuses precisely on what Barth says is unimportant and inconsequential. This basic disagreement reflects essentially different concepts
of the human self and its relationship with God. As we have seen repeatedly above, Barth keeps saying that every human being is self, is person,
an "I" in relation to every other human "thou," and a "thou" in relation
to God as the true and supreme "I." But then Barth keeps taking it back
by insisting that "the human-being is not genuine person, but God is
that" (note 84 above). So he refuses to speak of human-being as "spirit"
because that seems to attribute being-as-such to the human-being

whereas only God is and has being-as-such. The human-being is, therefore, not a true *other* that has and lives any life of its own, which can
freely, though mistakenly, try to live without God. For Barth the principle of otherness or "the other" holds true and has meaning only as a differentiation *within* God, not between God and anything external to the
divine being. Its meaning obtains in the inner Trinitarian life of God.
"The Son of God is the principle truth of an other [*ein Ander*] within
God himself" (see note 89 above but also notes 86, 87, 88). And we
have just heard Barth say that the true image of God resides in "an
other" only in Jesus Christ, that is, "the same as that which [God] finds
within himself from eternity and in eternity, namely: in his Son" (see
note 138 above).

Kierkegaard speaks of the human-being as self and as spirit throughout his works from *Either-Or* onward, but in his definitive definition of
human-being (in the opening paragraphs of *The Sickness unto Death*) he
makes a direct equation of being "self" with being "spirit." And by
"spirit" he means specifically what Barth wants to deny to human nature,
namely, freedom to be and become one's own self consciously and in-
tentionally, *and* freedom to ignore, refuse, and reject a positive relationship with the power which has established human-being and on which
human-being depends for its being and for its capacity to become free,
conscious, responsible self/spirit.

In other words, to be human spirit or self means to be an "other" to
God not only in human creatureliness as delimitation within finitude,
necessity, and temporality, but also precisely to be "other" in what Barth
defines as God's *Personsein*: "being free subject, ... able to be in charge
of its own existence [*Dasein*] and essence [*Sosein*], ... also able to choose
new possibilities of existence and essence" (see note 79 above). In the
opening page of *Sickness*, Kierkegaard speaks only of God as being "an
other" (*et Andet*), which has "established" (*sat*) human-being and to
which the human self must relate in order to become self/spirit. But he
also directly implies that the human-being is also an "other" to God
since human-being is a synthesis of finitude *and* infinitude, of the temporal *and* the eternal, of necessity *and* freedom. Hence every human-being, like God, has structured into its being the God-given capacity for
infinitude, eternity, and possibility (freedom).

The fact that the human-being is created and regarded by God as
"other" in the sense of spirit/self had been established by Kierkegaard
before *Sickness*. In *Postscript* he returns again and again to the difference
between direct communication that is used and accomplished in the

spheres of aesthetic and intellectual matters, and indirect communication that is required in ethical matters which come into play when one is
relating to another human-being or to God not as object but as subject,
as spirit. There is, he maintains, a qualitative difference between what
and how one can come to "know" about things that are mere objects
and what and how one can "know" about things that are subjects or
selves (spirit). About impersonal objects we can have direct and immediate knowledge of what they are in themselves and can communicate this
knowledge directly to others. But about an other subject (self, spirit) we
can only know what it is in itself as a *possibility*. Why? Because in every
subject (self) there is an inward self-possession and self-determination
that must be honored, respected, and let alone; there is a certain mystery and unfathomableness that cannot be exhausted and totally comprehended, that remains ineffable at some depth even for the subject
itself as it seeks to share itself with another, that is, with an *other*. And if
one self does not honor the inward selfhood of another self, then that
other self is turned into an object, to be controlled, manipulated, and
used for one's own satisfaction.

Kierkegaard argues that it was *God* who, as the only and unconditioned being-in-and-for-itself, deliberately chose to reduplicate that *being*
in an *other*, in human-being so it would possess personhood like unto
God's, but unlike God, within the delimitations of finitude and temporality, and hence as derived and dependent being. Therefore, it is God
who first and qualitatively and unreservedly chooses to honor, affirm,
encourage, and enable the human self (spirit) as *other* to become itself
in the agonizing, strenuous, never ending but infinitely rewarding struggles of human existence. And this otherness resides essentially not in
human finitude/temporality but in human spirit (self) itself. Therefore
(as we have heard above at note 55), "not even God relates directly to
[such] a derived spirit" because "such a relationship ... means that one
part has ceased to be spirit." So Kierkegaard concludes that "to have a
self, to be a self, is [eternity's] great concession, an infinite concession,
given to the human-being, but it is also eternity's demand [or claim]
upon him."[139]

It is precisely because of this central controlling concept of the meaning of "the image of God" as consisting of the spiritual, personal otherness (selfhood) of every individual human-being, in relationship both to

---

139. *Sickness*, p. 154; (KW 19:21); SV 15:80; (11:135).

God and to other humans, that Kierkegaard's depiction of both human sublimity and human degradation, of both human creativity and human impotence and futility, is so much more immediate, profound, persuasive, and *real* than anything that is to be found in Barth's equally profuse writings. Kierkegaard was an avid reader of the literature and philosophy of every culture open to him. His knowledge of ancient Greek and Roman poetry, drama, histories, and philosophy was extensive. His analyses of the concepts of tragedy and comedy in Sophocles, Aeschylus, and Aristophanes are still arresting and stimulating. His knowledge and use of Plato and Aristotle are extensive, and of course he considers Sophocles to be a Greek messiah. We find quotations of and references to Marcus Aurelius, Apuleus, Diogenes Laertius, Cicero, Homer, Horace, Livy, Plutarch, Ovid, Boethius, Seneca, Longinus, Suetonius, Herodotus, Hesiod, Virgil, Xenophon, and many others. And he refers to these non-Christian thinkers not as mere examples of his own views but as sources of insight and wisdom about the human condition in its every aspect.

And from the Christian era Kierkegaard draws upon amazingly various sources in both literature and philosophy. Shakespeare is quoted throughout his writings, and frequent references are made to Lord Byron (both in German translation, of course). He was fascinated with the characters of Mozart's operas (which he heard and adored in Copenhagen), and makes repeated analyses of their relationships. He refers briefly to both Wagner and Gluck. He knew the works of Goethe, Heine, Lessing, and Schiller and makes reference to Cervantes, Fenelon, Moliere, and Swift. He draws important ideas from such diverse thinkers as Descartes, Böhme, Pascal, Leibniz, and Spinoza, and of course he was profoundly impacted by the systems of Kant and Hegel.

From all of these sources and many others, plus his own intentional daily conversations with people on the streets of Copenhagen, he was in intimate touch with and developed profound empathy and respect for the boundless diversity and totally unpredictable creativity of the human spirit. But the central insight that he comes to from all this testimony of the human spirit, *and* from his own corresponding exploration of his own personal subjectivity, is this: human freedom and creativity finds expression in diametrically opposite directions, both in startling sublimity and nobility and in frightening, horrifying depths of demonic degradation, but most of all in a third form: the deadening weakness of triviality, mediocrity, and "small-mindedness" (*Smaalighed*), the irresolute and lethargic conformity to the external demands of social propriety and tradition. Indeed, in the latter weakness he saw the real death of the human spirit, whereas he saw great promise in both its sublimity and its degradation.

SUMMARY OF KIERKEGAARD'S DOCTRINES OF GOD AND HUMAN NATURE

Finally, this point brings us both to the conclusion and back to the beginning of our summary of Kierkegaard's theology proper, that is, of his depiction of God as God (begun at note 15 above), namely: the otherness of the human-being is definable and meaningful only in the context of the otherness of God. Our explication of the two concepts (being-in-and-for-itself and reduplication) and the two analogies (infinite subjectivity and personal-individuality) which Kierkegaard uses to describe God began in an attempt to understand what he means by "the infinite difference of quality" between God and the human. We heard Kierkegaard say that God always acts only out of concern for what "pleases God's majesty," that God never acts to accomplish "purposes" or "causes" in the human sense of something external, because this would involve God in "having a relationship to an environment" and hence "within the realm of relativities" (see text from note 36 to note 38 above). And when he uses a very human analogy by saying that God is "infinite subjectivity," he stresses that in God "there is no imperfection to be taken away nor anything lacking that should be added, as is the case in human subjectivity." Likewise when he asserts that God is "infinite reduplication," he immediately adds, "which of course no human-being can be," and spells out in detail how reduplication in God and in the human-being differ: the human-being "can neither completely transcend [*overlegen*] himself in such a way that he perfectly relates objectively to himself, nor can he become subjective in such a way that he can bring to full consummation what he in his objective transcendence has understood about himself; he cannot see himself with unconditioned and perfect objectivity; even if he could, he still cannot unconditionally reproduce subjectively this view of himself."[140]

Nevertheless, when we got involved in our very lengthy exposition of the other analogy for God's own being, namely, God's personhood (*Personlighed*), we were inevitably required also to explore Kierkegaard's basic anthropology as implicit in his theology proper (contrary to our expectations as expressed in the paragraph following note 15 above). In

140. Ibid., 4571; XI^2 A 97.

other words, the very otherness of human selfhood, of human spirit, as distinct from God guarantees both the integrity of the human self and, at the same time, the transcendent uniqueness and otherness of God's being. Without the assumption of this absolute difference of quality between God and the individual human being (who also is subjectivity and capable of self-transcendence), the whole central and crucial Biblical-Christian piety of prayer and worship would be totally transformed if not obliterated, because the heart and substance of the event and relationship of prayer/worship consists of, first, confession of sin, and secondly, waiting upon God's own gracious, undeserved, even surprising act of forgiveness and acceptance.

That is the reason the bulk of this present exploration of Kierkegaard's Christian theology will comprise a treatment of "My Self: A Failure" (sin and despair), and of "My Self: In Need of the Eternal" (faith/love). And it will be in the treatment of faith/love, especially as the latter takes the form of forgiveness and reconciliation, that we will come to see that, for Kierkegaard, the concepts of being-in-and-for-itself and reduplication (as descriptive of God) are not rational, intellectual speculations, and that the analogies of subjectivity and personhood (as descriptive of God) are not simply human projections of human nature. Rather, we will see in detail how these concepts and analogies are phenomenologically derived from the impact of God's own presence in our faith encounter with Jesus as the Christ, the God/human-being. More specifically, they are derived from the very transformation of one's own self (personhood) that takes place in this encounter (see at note 51 above).

We are, therefore, now ready to begin our chapter on human failure, that is, on the Christian understanding of sin and despair. But first we must recall that in the same paragraph (following note 30 above) where we proposed the two concepts and the two analogies used by Kierkegaard to depict the nature of God-as-such, we also said that there are two terms that are regulative for Kierkegaard: the concept that God is "all-things-are-possible" and the analogy that God is "love." But these will be treated in chapter 4 on our need of the eternal, because faith is precisely the coming to believe that all-things are possible, and the faith relationship with God is precisely the product of our experience of God's love in forgiveness of our sin and in our deliverance from despair in reconciliation.

3

My Self: A Failure

THE MYSTERY OF HUMAN FAILURE

The mystery is not that humans
   dream
   dreams of greatness
   perform deeds of exceeding beauty
     of noble sacrifice
     of inordinate power
      and creativity
The mystery is that humans – these same humans
   explode into
     unspeakable horror
     incredible self-degradation
     vicious cruelty
      beyond imagination
The beauty and creativity
   disclose the wonder
     of immutable configuration at the heart
     of limitless promise
     in every human spirit
The horror and degradation
   crawl out of a yawning fathomless maw of
     darkness
      nothingness
       chaos
   a hidden maelstrom at the core of my being

So the question: why I am a failure –
   I cannot brush aside
      as inconsequential
I must look into this maw – with all honesty and acumen
     what is hidden must be revealed
     what is dark must be brought into the light
       it is the measure
       it is the mirror
         of my greatness

Kierkegaard helps us look into this darkness (expressed in the present author's own words) with greater honesty and acumen, with greater profundity and complexity, than most other philosophers and theologians in the history of Christianity. But those critics are seriously mistaken who claim that Kierkegaard's analysis and description of the human capacity for horrific degradation and overpowering despair constitute the dominant theme and irresistible conclusion of his entire authorship. They fail to note, or deliberately and willfully ignore, that it is precisely by the power of this negative vision that he sets off and emphasizes his central conviction of every human's infinite, eternal dignity and worth as the indestructible destiny set by creation for the human individual.[1] For Kierkegaard, Christian faith makes the demand for purity of heart absolute and uncompromising because that is the only alternative to becoming overcome by the power of emptiness and nothingness and hence enmeshed in the trivialities of finite pleasures and necessities, subservient to the criterion and demands of approval by the "crowd." Not that anyone achieves the absolute, but one must listen first and last to its voice as the truth and be always "on the way" toward the absolute as the telos, the home of the human spirit.

In the next chapter we will explore what it is like to be "on the way," that is, to experience God's love in deliverance from despair and hence to live by faith that all-things-are-possible. But the wonder of this deliverance and this faith can be witnessed only if we "walk through the valley of the shadow of death," that is, only if we first (in this chapter) listen to Kierkegaard's exploration of the nature of sin and despair.

1. I have in mind the views of such writers as Mark C. Taylor, Josiah Thompson, and Henning Fenger. See my commentary on them in my earlier volume, *Kierkegaard as Humanist*, chapter 3, note 73.

This approach might seem to be self-defeating for an age in which the older generations still want to hang onto "the power of positive thinking," and even most Christians do not want to hear the word "sin." And many in the younger and middle generations reject all absolutes in favor of some form of relativism (e.g., anything is acceptable if it doesn't hurt others) or of optimism that rejects all talk of guilt and despair. But among the youth throughout the world there is also a strong undercurrent of total nihilism and anarchy whose strength is hard to calculate. It is evident in some recent dramas and novels, but it also finds a frank and powerful expression in the form of some "industrial rock" music developed (according to one critic) from punk, heavy metal, and disco.[2] Some of the younger generation find its message too cynical and its music too wild and noisy, but they listen – and wonder. Most older people just turn a deaf ear and try to shrug it off as a madness that will go away or be suppressed if necessary. But if one will read the words (they cannot be heard through the music), one will find a crude but eloquent and brutal testimony precisely to one element in Kierkegaard's own vision of life, namely, the element of estrangement, doubt, guilt, and despair, leading possibly to horror, terror, and madness – that is, short of entrance into "the gentleness and love and compassion of Christianity."[3]

One of the more powerful rock musicians espousing this negative vision of humanity is Trent Reznor, the lead singer and composer for a group called Nine Inch Nails. In their latest album, "The Downward Spiral," the first piece is called "mr self destruct." This person says to his lover, "I control you," and claims to do so by using "religion's message" of "denial, guilt and fear," by appealing to "the prayers of the naive, ... the lies that you believe." In another piece, "heresy," Jesus is characterized as one who "sewed his eyes shut because he is afraid to see," as one who "dreamed a god up and called it christianity." The believer is chided, "if there is a hell i will see you there, burning with your god in humility," but really "your God is dead and no one cares." And yet in "closer," the poet, while crying out that "i want to fuck you like an animal," confesses to his lover that "my whole existence is flawed," and admits to her, "you get me closer to God." So he pleads with her, "tear down my reason" and "help me become somebody else." But the last piece in the album is called "hurt," in which the singer faces disillusion-

2. Michael Snyder, "Nails Pounds Out Industrial Angst," in the *San Francisco Chronicle,* October 3, 1994, p. E1.

3. *Practice in Christianity*, p. 72; (KW 20:68); SV 16:73; (12:65).

ment: "i focus on pain, the only thing that's real," and dreams of starting again "a million miles away" where "i would find a way."

Eight thousand college students packed an auditorium recently to hear Trent Reznor sing these kinds of words. The reviewer said, "No matter how hot and uncomfortable the environment or how noisy and unsettling the music and message of Nine Inch Nails, the young audience was rapt and supportive." The success of their latest album "says megabytes about the nature of modern life. Rock and roll has always been great for channeling youthful exuberance and letting off steam. Nine Inch Nails is a bleaker, darker beast that provides catharsis for the alienated, powerless and angry in the era of cybernet."[4] One might wonder if the audience was not moved primarily by the music and its passionate performance, since the words as sung are hardly understandable, and yet the mood and intent of these words is captured in that music and performance. So Kierkegaard's vision of lost and despairing humanity is ringing true at the close of the twentieth century, even if it is being heard only by a segment of the population.

Kierkegaard, however, would argue that what Reznor is expressing in his very personal way (despair) is universally true for every human being:

there is not a single living human being who does not ... secretly harbor an unrest, an inner strife, a disharmony, an angst about an unknown something or a something that one does not even dare to try to know, ... an angst about oneself, so that ... s/he walks around with ... a sickness of the spirit that signals its presence at rare intervals in and through an angst one cannot explain. In any case, no human being ever lived ... who has not despaired.[5]

Kierkegaard also describes how despair can take the form captured in Reznor's songs, that of self-centered anger, rage, hatred, and malice, which in turn deform love into a self-serving, manipulative, exploitative, and (in some) even a cruel and abusive relationship with the so-called "beloved." But Kierkegaard's total view is in utter contrast to Reznor's message of unrelieved pessimism, that begins and ends with wallowing in a mire of what Kierkegaard would call demonic, self-destructive despair,

---

4. Michael Snyder in the *San Francisco Chronicle*, October 3, 1994, pp. E1 and E4. Others see Reznor as an expression of shallow "Designer Nihilism" that is "covetous and materialistic" (NY Times Magazine, March 24, 1996, pp. 30, 32).

5. *The Sickness unto Death*, p. 155; (KW 19:22); SV 15:81; (11:136).

not able to "find a way" except in a fantasy of something "a million miles away." In total rejection of such a view, Kierkegaard insists on a positive interpretation of despair, on a creative possibility at the very depth of despair because, he insists, there is an infinite and absolute goodness that never leaves the human spirit alone but implants an inescapable angst at the core of human consciousness, an angst that beckons the spirit outward and onward. Already in *The Concept of Angst* his first chapter is entitled "Angst as the Presupposition of Hereditary Sin and as Explaining Hereditary Sin Retrogressively in Terms of Its Origin." But the last chapter is entitled "Angst as Saving through Faith," and in it he says, "Angst is freedom's possibility, and only such angst is through faith absolutely educative. ... Whoever is educated by possibility is exposed to danger, not that ... of going astray in various ways, ... but the danger of a fall, namely, suicide. If at the beginning of one's education one misunderstands angst, so that it does not lead one to faith, then one is lost."[6] And four years later in his definitive treatment of sin in *The Sickness unto Death*, he writes a prayer for the preface (but does not include it) in which he refers to this sickness as what "we all have but which [Jesus Christ] can heal only in those who are aware [*bevidste*] of being sick in this way."[7] And when considering the universality of this sickness, he notes that "this observation will strike many people as ... an overstatement, and also as a gloomy and depressing point of view." But he argues that it is none of these things "but instead is elevating, inasmuch as it views every human being under the destiny of the highest claim upon him/her, to be spirit." Indeed, "it is the worst misfortune never to have had that sickness: it is a true godsend to get it," because otherwise one goes on "living so deceived by life's joys or its sorrows that one never becomes decisively and eternally conscious as spirit, as self, or what amounts to the same thing, never becomes aware ... that there is a God and that [one] ... exists before this God – an infinite benefaction that is never gained except through despair."[8]

However, a humanist would probably speak up at this point and expostulate, "Wait just a holy minute! What's all this talk about sin and despair? Did you not encourage us in your treatment of *Kierkegaard as Humanist* to believe that every human being is capable of discovering one's self and of struggling to become oneself by achieving a positive re-

6. *The Concept of Angst*, pp. 139, 142; (κw 8:155, 158–159); sv 8:234, 237; (4:422, 424).

7. *Sickness*, κw 19:141; *Papirer*, viii[2] b 143; trans. in *Journals* 3423.

8. Ibid., pp. 155, 159–160; (κw 19:22, 26–27); sv 15:81, 85; (11:136, 140).

lationship of love with both the eternal and one's neighbor? Of course everyone must become aware of one's limitations and failures and must appeal to the inspiration of the infinite and eternal dimension of reality in order to do better. You spoke of 'total guilt-consciousness' but quoted Climacus to the effect that it does not have to end in despair.[9] Did you not argue, and give illustrations, to the effect that many human beings possess and practice 'gentleness and love and compassion' [see note 3 above] without having to be devotees of Religiousness B (Christianity)?"

All true. But in *Kierkegaard as Humanist* it was also specifically noted, first, that the presence of the infinite/eternal (god) is strictly immanent at the depth (or height) of human subjectivity and is therefore difficult to keep sharply defined; that is, it is difficult to keep the line of "infinite, qualitative difference" sharply drawn between the human and the divine. Secondly, it was acknowledged that the normal human impulse to do works of love is spasmodic and irregular at best because it lacks the repeated commitment to "love your enemies" that is demanded by the continuing objective presence of Jesus as the Christ. In other words, Climacus was specifically quoted as emphasizing that "the upbuilding element in the sphere of Religiousness A is that of immanence," whereas "in Religiousness B [Christianity], the upbuilding is something outside the individual; the individual does not find the upbuilding by finding the relationship with God within himself," and this upbuilding "therefore corresponds to the determinant of God in time as an individual human being [i.e., Jesus]." The result is that "Religiousness B ... makes conditions in such a way that the conditions are not the dialectical concentrations of inward-deepening [*Inderliggjørelsen*] but a definite something that defines eternal blessedness more specifically."[10]

It is precisely this more specific, Christian definition of eternal blessedness and the path to its attainment that Kierkegaard seeks to explore in his second authorship (beginning with *Upbuilding Discourses in Various Spirits*), the authorship that was initiated by his experience of the so-called "*Corsair* affair" in 1846.[11] As part of that definition he also gradually comes to a more profound understanding of despair and to a rather different concept of sin, achieving their consummate formulation two

9. *Concluding Unscientific Postscript*, pp. 492–493; (KW 12.1:554); SV 10:224; (7:484).
10. Ibid., pp. 497–498, 494; (KW 12.1:560–561); SV 10:229–230, 225; (7:489, 485).
11. See my account of this affair and its influence on his authorship in chapter 5 of *Kierkegaard as Humanist* (for page references see the topic, "The *Corsair* Affair," in the table of contents), and/or read the historical introduction by Howard and Edna Hong to their book entitled, "The *Corsair* Affair" (KW 13:vii–xxxviii).

years later (1848) in *The Sickness unto Death.*[12] For example, Climacus in *Philosophical Fragments* and Haufniensis in *The Concept of Angst* speak (in different languages) of the "fall" into sin as the universal state of all humans, and they both see this fall as occurring through the misuse of human freedom and therefore humans as being at fault or guilty. Climacus seeks to explain *why* God allowed (and allows) this failure to happen and how God sets about to correct it. Haufniensis provides a detailed analysis of *how* this failure happened (and continues to happen) through angst. But neither of them explore the state of despair that seizes and envelops the human being as a result of this failure.

In *Sickness* Anti-Climacus therefore assumes and incorporates, but also transforms, the concepts of his predecessors by injecting his analysis of despair as the universal intermediate state between innocence and salvation (healing), and reserves the word "sin" as applicable to despair only when despair becomes fully self-conscious defiance "directly before God," that is, when the human being becomes the "theological self" that has God as its "criterion." And (for those in the Christian tradition) "first-and-only [*først*] in Christ is it true that God is the human-being's goal and criterion." So we must see how every human-being (including everyone who becomes Christian) lands in *despair* through *failure* to become the self one is given to be, before we can understand how one becomes a *sinner* through *failure* to accept that help that is offered to the self that stands directly before God in Jesus as the Christ. "Sin is the intensification of despair."[13] So being a sinner is simply an intensification of being a failure.

In both *The Concept of Angst* and *Sickness* it is assumed that human beings in this intermediate state have lost their way but are also still loved and pursued by God because they still are able to be aware of the eternal in their lives, still seek to discover and, in measure, to achieve their destiny as unique individual selves, still capable of loving God and neighbor – even though they fail at it times without number. Despair, then, is the mediating concept by which Anti-Climacus makes the transition from

12. This development in his concepts of sin and despair is parallel with and intimately related to the shift in his concept of necessity from its formulation in *Fragments* to that found in *Sickness*. This latter development is traced in some detail in my earlier *Kierkegaard as Humanist*, and it is shown that this development was also a product of the new self-consciousness aroused in Kierkegaard by the *Corsair* affair.

13. *Sickness*, pp. 210, 245, 208; (KW 19:79, 114, 77); SV 15:133, 164, 131; (11:191, 224, 189).

Religiousness A to Religiousness B, but as despair is seen and defined from the vantage point of Religiousness B. For this reason despair could not be properly analyzed and understood within the scope of *Kierkegaard as Humanist,* even though much of the analysis in *Sickness* is clearly accessible at a purely humanist level.

Hence the title of this chapter indicates that it is concerned with my self as a failure rather than a sinner because "failure" is a more accurate term than "sin" to indicate *how* all humans end up in the state of despair. An analysis of the process of this "how" must account for the ambiguity of the state of despair, namely, that in it humans are innocent and yet guilty, are impotent and yet may become defiant, are lost and yet not beyond recovery, are capable and in danger of becoming sinners and yet rarely in open and final defiance and denial of Love-Itself. Granted, Kierkegaard does not generally use the word failure for this process. There is one passage in *Either/Or* where he describes the failure of the human being to "choose himself" properly as the "basic mistake" (*Grundfeilen*) of "choosing altogether abstractly," or "his mistake [*Feilen*] is that ... he has regarded himself within the category of necessity."[14] But in *Sickness* there is one startling passage that may serve as the key to Kierkegaard's total view of humanity's "fall" into despair and sin, and in it he uses the concept of failure.

The passage comes in the concluding sentences of the entire part one on despair. In this paragraph he gives a summary of his total analysis of the forms of conscious despair as (1) "not to will to be oneself" and (2) "to will to be oneself" demonically, that is, defiantly. But contrary to what he has said just five pages before, here he insists that the defiant self "does not want to tear itself loose from the power [God] that established it." Rather, out of spite and malice and "in hatred [and] ... rebellion against all existence," the defiant self "wants to force itself upon [that power]," because "it feels that it has obtained evidence against it, against all goodness," that "the person in despair ... is him/herself the evidence." Then Kierkegaard draws a startling analogy for God in this situation.

Speaking figuratively, it is as if a writing-error [*Skrivfejl*] has slipped in from an author, and it [the mistake] becomes conscious of itself as a mistake [*som*

14. *Either/Or*, pp. 235–236; (KW 4:231–232); SV 3:214–215; (2:207–208). He repeats this language on pp. 244–245; (KW 4:240–241); SV 3:222–223; (2:215–216).

saadan] – perhaps it actually was not a mistake [*Feil*] but in a much higher sense an essential constituent-element [*Medhenhørende*] of the whole production – it is as if now this writing-error would mount a rebellion against the author, out of hatred for him, forbidding him to correct it and in maniacal defiance saying to him: No, I refuse to be erased; I will stand as a witness against you, a witness that you are a second-rate author.[15]

In this homely but poignant analogy, Kierkegaard captures two profound ideas. First, that the human being as such, as created by God, is an ineluctable unity of noble possibility and promise on the one hand and of vulnerable fallibility and weakness on the other. Secondly, that this seeming tragic/comic combination is not an accidental mutation but is "something-that-belongs-to" (*Medhenhørende*) or a constituent element of the "author's" whole story about the meaning of the existence of the human race, that is, of human individuals, in the midst of the total created universe. It is the universal and perennial story of the innocent, precocious but unstable child and of the parent for whom the child is the most precious and beloved object of life, who surrounds the child with loving care day and night, and yet who knows that sooner or later the child must be allowed to slip away, to make its own mistakes and learn its own lessons, but with the parent always standing eagerly ready to help and to receive the mature child back into the loving fold but now as equal, responsible adult in an extended family.

But why *must* the child be allowed "to make its own mistakes?" Both Climacus in *Fragments* and Anti-Climacus in *Sickness* state baldly that there is *no other way* for God to secure the purpose and goal that God has set for humans than for God to allow humans to fail, as the reverse side of giving them the capacity to return God's love *freely*. Freedom, willingness, is at the heart of love, and God *is* love. At the conclusion of his parable of the king and the maiden Climacus says,

this is the unfathomableness of love, that in earnestness and truth and not in jest it willingly-desires [*ville*] to be equal of the beloved, and it is the omnipotence of love's resolve to be capable of [just] that. ... This is God, and [God's] eyes rest anxiously [*bekymret*] on the human race, for the individual's tender shoot can be crushed as readily as a blade of grass. ... [God] knows that the learner is untruth – what if s/he failed [*saae feil*], became weary and lost confidence!. ... Oh, to

15. *Sickness*, p. 207; (KW 19:73–74); SV 15:127–128; (11:184–185).

sustain heaven and earth – ... how easy ... compared with the possibility that the human race will take offense![16]

Anti-Climacus states the same position by exploring in detail the concept of offense, first briefly in *Sickness,* and then at great length in *Practice in Christianity* (which we will explore later). In *Sickness* he says that humans are often offended at the Christian claim that "every single individual human-being ... exists *before God,*" because this claim sets too high a goal and "makes too much of being human," because it demands that humans "live on the most intimate terms with God."[17] Hence "offense is the most decisive qualification of subjectivity," because Christianity demands that one *either* believe this claim *or* be offended. When one is encountered by this claim, one cannot moderate or soften or "mediate" it; every person must decide, choose one way or the other at the core and depth of one's being.[18]

In this sense, then, "the possibility of offense is the dialectical element in all that is [essentially] Christian," dialectical in the sense that the human self is designed with (and for) the noble possibility of life in and with the eternal but united with vulnerable fallibility and weakness, *and* the outcome hangs in the balance of the self's decision. This dialectic marks and reveals the fact that "God and human-being are two qualities between which there is an infinite difference of quality [*Qvalitets-Forskjel*]." But if the human individual self is to have and retain independent identity vis-à-vis God and hence be capable of entering (by definition, *freely*) into an eternal relationship of love with God and with other human beings, then there is no other way. In other words, "the possibility of offense is ... the guarantee by which God makes sure that the human-being cannot come too close," and hence be absorbed into the divine being.

So Anti-Climacus repeats the conclusion of Climacus:

In the infinite love of [God's] merciful grace, God makes one condition: [God] cannot do otherwise. Precisely this is Christ's grief, that "he cannot do

---

16. *Fragments,* pp. 39–40; (кw 7:32); sv 6:33–34; (4:200). The Danish of the 1st and 3rd editions both have *saae feil* but that would mean either "looked erroneously" which is nonsense, or "sowed a mistake" which is possible and which the Hongs simply translate "made a mistake," but I suggest that it is possible that the "l" was omitted from *slaa feil* which means simply "to fail."

17. *Sickness,* pp. 216, 214, 218, 216; (кw 19:85, 83, 87, 85); sv 15:138, 136, 140, 138; (11:196–7, 195, 199, 197).

18. Ibid., pp. 253, 229; (кw 19:122, 98); sv 15:172, 150; (11:232, 209).

otherwise"; ... the possibility of offense he cannot take away. Ah! singular work of love. Ah! unfathomable grief of love, that even God cannot – as in another sense neither will [God], nor can [God] will, but even if [God] wanted to – cannot make it impossible for this work of love to become just the opposite for a human-being, to become the utmost misery! ... Christ cannot, "love" cannot make this impossible. ... Oh! unfathomable contradiction in love! But still, in love he cannot find it in his heart to desist from completing this work of love ... even though it makes a human-being more miserable than otherwise one would ever have been![19]

A puzzling question still remains and is not answered by these wonderful words about love. Why, and how, may this basic human failure be regarded as "not a failure but in a much higher sense something-that-belongs-to the whole production?" Does this statement by Anti-Climacus mean that the human failure (to pass directly from innocence to self-realization) is only a possibility, that is, that it is also possible for humans to avoid the failure? Clearly not. As we have heard, he flatly asserts that every human person is in despair and needs to be healed. In this way he assumes what Climacus (in *Fragments*) says in principle and Haufniensis spells out in detail, that the human race as a whole and every human individually has "fallen" into the state of untruth or sin. Is, then, this universal human failure merely a learning episode that all individuals pass through on their way to fulfillment and therefore needs not be taken too seriously? Indeed not! Even when the human individual is personally encountered by the God of love in person, the final and ultimate failure of taking offense remains a tragic possibility. There is no guarantee that the mature child will understand and accept the Parent's loving help that it so desperately needs; rather, the child often sinks into petulance and suspicion, blaming the Parent for all its mistakes and suffering.

These questions are the primary focus of Kierkegaard's "total production" as author; he never forgets and seeks constantly to explore the anguish of the lost child, because (he claims) God's own focus is not on the race as a whole for the sake of God's own grand universal design and self-glorification (Karl Barth), but on the individual human self and its failure to use properly its freedom to become the loving companion of

---

19. Ibid., pp. 256–257; (KW 19:125–126); SV 15:174–175; (11:235–236). These words are mostly from the Hongs' translation but also partly from that of Alastair Hannay because the latter's more literal though awkward translation often captures better the urgency and intensity of Kierkegaard's original.

God and neighbor. Only in this setting does he turn to the task of depicting what it is like to experience the delivering and fulfilling power of repentance, forgiveness and reconciliation, supremely in *Works of Love* and *Practice in Christianity*, but also as those works are supplemented and interpreted in *Upbuilding Discourses in Various Spirits*, in *Christian Discourses*, and in all the discourses from *The Lily in the Field and the Bird of the Air* through *For Self-Examination* and *Judge for Yourself!* That task will be the subject matter of our next chapter.

But in this chapter we seek an answer to the question: how can I understand *my self* as one who is both guilty and yet not-guilty, both lost and yet not beyond recovery, capable and in danger of becoming sinner and yet not in final, hopeless, and incurable defiance of Love-Itself? And as we proceed, we should once more be reminded that Kierkegaard does not regard this task as gloomy or depressing. Rather, if you wait in utter stillness and hear "God's voice delivering judgment in stillness," and "if you fear this stillness, ... then keep on, then endure it; this stillness is not the stillness of death in which you perish, it is not the sickness unto death – it is the transition to life." Indeed, "the person who without affectation says that he is in despair is still a little closer, is dialectically closer to being healed than all those ... who do not regard themselves as being in despair." This is true of even the most intense form of despair, namely, *defiance*, "which is really despair through the aid of the eternal" and *therefore* "in a certain sense it is very close to the truth. ... The despair that is the thoroughfare to faith comes through the aid of the eternal; through the aid of the eternal the self has the courage to lose itself in order to win itself."[20]

To address these questions and to understand how Kierkegaard can regard the subject of despair as "elevating" and as the pathway to healing faith, we will attempt to clarify five of his major theses: (1) All human failure occurs in the context of an original innocence. (2) Innocence is inevitably disturbed by angst, and thereby the self is awakened to consciousness of its self. (3) The essential failure occurs when "freedom looks down into its own possibility," becomes "dizzy" and "lays hold of finiteness to support itself," and falls.[21] The human self arises from the "fall" conscious of itself as responsible, guilty. (4) The human state resulting from this essential failure is despair (disrelationship); it takes two

---

20. *Three Discourses on Imagined Occasions*, KW 10:11–12; SV 6:249; (5:179); *Sickness*, pp. 159, 201; (KW 19:26, 67); SV 15:85, 122; (11:140, 178).
21. *Concept of Angst*, p. 55; (KW 8:61); SV 6:152; (4:331).

universal forms regardless of human consciousness; it also takes two con-
scious forms in most people. (5) Despair becomes sin (in the strictly
Christian sense) when one takes offense at God's offer of help in Jesus
Christ.

Before we begin this lengthy analysis, it will be helpful to gain a perspective on a difficult and puzzling question, namely, at what stage (age)
in the child's development does the essential, qualitative failure ("fall")
of the human individual occur? Or, in other words, at what stage of individual development do the concepts of self-consciousness and guilt become applicable or operative? The answer will be decisive as to whether
the notions of freedom and responsibility play any role at all in that failure. In order to distinguish clearly Kierkegaard's own answer, let us first
take a look at one notable alternative.

EXCURSUS ON FREUD

Several recent psychologists (of a Freudian bent) insist that children develop a sense of self, of conscience and guilt as early as five or six years
of age by internalizing models of assertion and self-control. Some propose that there is awareness of a positive pole of initiative vis-à-vis guilt
even at three or four years old. The present author claims no compe-
tence as an interpreter of Freud based on a firsthand knowledge of his
writings or on expertise in the field, but will hazard a few comparisons
of Freud and Kierkegaard based on conversations with knowledgeable
Freudian psychologists and on reading two excellent secondary sources.
The major one is the highly regarded *Freud* by Richard Wollheim, who
provides a clear, nonintrusive, and highly sympathetic account of both
Freud's life and his thought. The second one is *The Problematic Self in
Kierkegaard and Freud* by J. Preston Cole, who seems to have a fairly comprehensive and direct familiarity with both writers.[22]

Drawing first on Wollheim's material, the following three points are
of crucial importance (unless indicated otherwise, all the quotations are
Wollheim's words, and all page references are included in the text).

22. To say that Wollheim is "sympathetic" to Freud puts it mildly. In his concluding es-
timate he says, "Freud was never a lover of humanity, but he did as much for it as any other
human being who has lived. And, if he could find little evidence for the goodness, he had
a sense, as no one else before him, of the richness and mystery, of the psyche" (p. 218). On
the first point, I am not sure that I would rank Freud along with Siddartha Gautama, Plato,
Aristotle and Jesus. On the latter point, I would argue that Kierkegaard had a much greater
sense of that richness and mystery.

(1) "Freud had, virtually from the beginning, made a distinction between two types of instinct – libido and ... the ego-instincts. ... Freud's distinction did not merely rest on observation, it was also required by his general psychological theory. ... Remove the duality, and the whole theory of the psycho-neurosis would surely crumble," because "any psychological theory must include some kind of dualism if it is to explain the facts of inner conflict" (pp. 179–80). With this point Kierkegaard is in fundamental agreement. While Climacus was writing *Philosophical Fragments*, Kierkegaard told his journal, "The view which sees life's doubleness [*Duplicitæt*] or duality [*Dualisme*] is higher and deeper than that which seeks unity."[23] But in spite of this basic agreement, each was interested in a different side of the duality. Freud spent most of his life's energies on exploring the complexities of the libido while Kierkegaard was almost wholly dedicated to delving into the mysteries of the ego (self).

However, in Freud's later thought, his interest in primary narcissism "gradually forced upon Freud two large issues, ... the classification of the instincts, and the nature of the ego" (p. 178). Earlier he had asserted three criteria for distinguishing an instinct: source, aim, and object. Whereas source had previously dominated in his thinking, now he sees that "the criterion of source was valueless in discussing the ego-instinct," whereas aim was clearly the appropriate one. One result was that he now assigned aggression and sexuality "to that part of the mind which is explicitly set over and against the ego: namely, the id" (pp. 182–83).

(2) In this way Freud came to a rather (for him) startling and rather reluctant conclusion, namely, that it must be possible to attribute to the ego, in "contrast or opposition to the sexual," certain functions and also "the energy necessary to carry out these functions." Gradually and slowly there emerged in his late works a definition of these special ego functions: perception, motility, and defense. That is to say, "it is in virtue of the ego that we perceive the world, that we can change the world, and that we adapt to the world." And it is precisely the perception of the world as external that reveals another type or nature of perception, one that does not disappear when our bodies move, a perception that is internal rather than external. "Awareness of this division [between external and internal] also contributes to our awareness of *self*" (emphasis added). Indeed, "in making the distinction between the outer world and itself, the ego must not be thought of as a mere neutral or passive observer. On the contrary, it is through making this distinction, through

---

23. *Journals*, 704; IV A 192.

developing an awareness of itself *over and against everything else*, that the
ego develops." In fact, "in the very earliest days of infancy, there is no
ego: it is only gradually, through perception, through *self-awareness*, that
the ego emerges from the id" (emphasis added). And this whole development of self-awareness and of the ego itself is "essentially bound up
with the development of the concept of the ego. Without such a concept
neither self-awareness nor, ultimately, existence itself could be attributed to the ego" (pp. 186–88).

On this point one would have thought that Kierkegaard and Freud
had had a conversation and agreed. Kierkegaard says, "[A] certain degree of reflection is present here, consequently a certain degree of pon-
dering over one's self. With this certain degree of reflection begins the
act of discrimination wherein the self becomes aware of itself as essentially distinct from the environment and the external-world [*Udvortesheden*] and [from] their influence upon it."[24] And Kierkegaard agrees that
integral to this process of differentiation is the emergence of a "concept" of self as such (*i sig*), because this type of reflection (perception) is
inwardly achieved by the imagination's "re-presentation of the self as the
self's possibility."[25]

Furthermore, Kierkegaard affirms Freud's emphasis on "the crucial
significance that attaches to the body in our growing consciousness of
the difference between the world and the ego." Obviously, the body is
"ancillary to perception," and hence "the concept of the ego will have
heavily corporeal overtones" and "contain bodily connotations" (Wollheim, pp. 188–89). At the heart of Kierkegaard's concept of the self is
his assertion that the self is an indissoluble synthesis of body and soul, of
the sensuous and the psychic, or in his favorite terms, of the finite and
the infinite. But the harmonious unity of the two is a task to be achieved.
So "the moment the spirit [self] posits itself, it posits the synthesis"
(never one without the other). "But in order to posit the synthesis, it
[the self] must pervade it [the synthesis] differentially [separately], and
the ultimate [expression] of the sensuous is precisely the sexual," while
the ultimate expression of the psychic is "selfishness," i.e., egocentrism.
Kierkegaard calls this separation of the sensuous and the psychic "sin."
But neither sensuousness nor egotism is wrong as such; it is the separation of them that is wrong. And it must be kept in mind that "sin [sepa-
ration] posits just as much a sensuous as a spiritual consequence." But

24. *Sickness*, p. 188; (KW 19:54); SV 15:110; (11:166).
25. Ibid., pp. 163–164; (KW 19:30–31); SV 15:88–9; (11:144).

there is a primacy in the sensuous, and so "it is in sexuality that the synthesis is first posited as a contradiction, but like every contradiction it is also a task." And "the task, of course, is to bring it [the sexual] under the determinant of spirit [i.e., self]."[26]

However, as already suggested, Kierkegaard never turned to a serious and extensive exploration of the role and impact that sexuality plays in the formation of self, and so in the last few years of his life he gave vent to a bitter and disillusioned attack on sexuality in general and on the Christian institution of marriage in particular. And Freud never achieved a detailed examination of the nature and capacities of the ego because, he claimed, he found no evidence that could provide an empirical avenue of analysis of the ego as such. Let us examine the latter point at some length.

(3) As we have noted above, Wollheim points out that when Freud came to the question of the nature of the ego (through exploring the hypothesis of primary narcissism) and proposed the existence of ego-in-stincts, he "had not merely been saying that there were instincts other than the sexual. Their postulation was also a way, if a confused one, of attributing to the ego certain functions, and also the energy necessary to carry out these functions." As we have seen, Freud had no trouble in defining the functions of the ego, but it was quite a different matter when he came to the task of "identifying the energy upon which they drew" (pp. 186–87). About twenty pages later (pp. 204–05) Wollheim explains why. This problem "did not arise for Freud in either the early or the middle phases of the theory," but when he assigned all instinct to the id and when the superego emerged, then the conundrum arose as to how both the ego and the superego could "be credited with the energies necessary to discharge" their assigned functions.

Freud had no trouble with the superego because, he said, "The superego merges into the id: indeed, as heir to the Oedipus complex it has intimate relations with the id." Therefore, Wollheim comments, "The energy of the superego is aggression. ... However, in the case of the ego no such ready answer was available." So Freud explores "tentatively the hypothesis of a neutralized or 'desexualized' libido." But his "scattered remarks" on the matter do not reveal a clear or consistent concept. One idea "seems to be of a libidinal impulse so heavily saturated in narcissism that it cannot attach itself to an outer object." In any case, "the

26. *The Concept of Angst*, pp. 44, 69, 72; (κw 8:49, 77, 80); sv 6:142, 166, 169; (4:319, 346, 349).

hypothesis [of a desexualized libido] is to be taken [only] on a highly theoretical level, and it has nothing to do with the observable or with behavior. More specifically, ... nothing follows from the hypothesis about the motivation of the individual and his capacity to transcend sexuality. For desexualized libido, however it is to be taken, is a feature solely of the ego. By contrast, the motivation of the individual is a complex product which arises out of the energies of the id as these are regulated or modified by the efforts of the ego."

One senses a genuine reluctance or even a dread on Freud's part to investigate the implications that an ego can transcend sexuality and how such an ego might have other sources of energy for its actions than the sexuality and oedipal aggression of the id. Does it not take powerful energy for the ego to "regulate or modify" the insistent motivational drive of libidinal passions? Why did not Freud take an interest in using his incomparable capacities of analysis in order to ferret out these other sources in the lives and the psyches of relatively healthy patients? If he had, he would have found that some human beings have relatively positive relations with their parents from infancy onward and that they absorb unconsciously positive energies of control and modification or redirection of their libidinal drives. Even more threatening to Freud would be the discovery that some human beings, who may indeed have very negative oedipal experiences, derive powerful psychic energy for control and redirection of such experiences from their awareness of and openness to an experience of the infinite, of the eternal, of God. Freud might have had to recognize that some forms of Near Eastern religions, including aspects of his own Jewish heritage, provide positive resources for understanding and directing the human spirit, so that he could not brush them aside with his facile and frivolous characterization as "presumptuous attempts to overcome the outer world of appearance by means of the inner world of wishful thinking" (p. 217).

In any case, it is precisely on this point that Kierkegaard parts company with Freudian analysis. For Kierkegaard it is precisely the capacity of the ego to transcend the self's integral sensuousness (including sexuality) that provides the energy to control and redirect the energies of the id because the ego achieves transcendence by turning inward and achieving infinite, personal, interested *passion* about and for one's relation with the eternal. That is to say, one achieves subjectivity in contrast to cold theoretical objectivity, and then "an objective uncertainty, held fast through appropriation with the most passionate inwardness, is the truth, and the highest truth there is for an existing person."[27] And out of this ego-passion for the eternal comes the ethical energy precisely to "regulate" and "modify" one's "observable" life, one's "behavior." For Kierkegaard this passion of the self, of the inward subject, for the infinite/eternal is a *fact* of human consciousness and experience as real and "instinctual" as the passionate drive of the sexual, and it can be verified phenomenologically in human experience as can the complex sexuality of our infantile relations with our parents. For Kierkegaard this infantile sexuality and its continuation into childhood precisely serves as the required *occasion* for the first stirrings of angst about one's own self and hence for one's opening up to fantasies of the infinite, as the occasion for the beginnings of awareness of the ego or self as (in Freud's own thinking) something different from the "outer world," as something "over and against everything else," with its own functions and its own energies.

Let us see how this difference between Kierkegaard and Freud works out in their interpretation of two common events in human experience. Freud argued that his hypothesis of the superego provides a better understanding of several of the paradoxes of our moral life than did traditional moral psychology. For example, "the peculiar harshness of the superego" is not to be explained by the traditional sense of "conscience" that is subject to an extreme and stringent moral standard from on high. Rather, "at the height of the Oedipus complex, the infant feels a deep hostility toward its parents," and it proceeds to project its own "unconscious aggression onto the parents" who then appear as very severe. This "turning round of aggression upon itself through the vehicle of the superego is one of the few methods by which man can gain some control of his destructive instincts," even though if carried to the extreme, it can result in melancholia (Wollheim, pp. 196–97).

On the contrary, Kierkegaard argues that the need for parental guidance and supervision need not take the form of guilt-inducing morbidity that he experienced from the impact of his own father's strict pietism. Rather, this need may serve as the occasion for the awakening self-consciousness of the child/adolescent to become aware of a superego, a source of judgment, that transcends the parent. In his upbuilding discourse, "On the Occasion of a Confession," he tells how the person who is suffering from misdirected wishes and desires can come to an experience of a faith/love that "does not disappoint," that does not

27. *Postscript*, p. 182; (KW 12.1:203); SV 9:169–170; (7:170).

separate or equivocate, but "in the decision of death [i.e., dying to one's self] there is born a love that ... is not until death, but on the other side of death *abides*; ... in the decision the suffering-one *abides* with the good." This love comes to one because in faith one "*grasps* the eternal and *holds it fast*," that faith "in which the suffering-one draws the eternal closer to oneself." And to arrive at this faith/love, everyone is provided with "two stern guides." On the one hand there is "governing necessity" that silently "leads [the suffering-one] on"; on the other, "duty, rigorous and earnest but not cruel, since it is never that, comes behind."[28]

Here Kierkegaard certainly does not specifically have in mind the sufferings of the child under the impact of infantile sexuality and its ambiguous relationship with its parents. But he does have in mind *all* of the kinds of sufferings that every human passes through under the impact of the angst of childhood innocence. And he is trying to describe the emerging subjectivity in which every child has fantasies of the infinite beyond the superego of parents, teachers, friends, and childhood heroes and idols. And as angst becomes the occasion for gradually becoming aware of self in contrast to everything else including one's parents, so this fantasy becomes the occasion for becoming aware of an introjection of a reality that is also distinct from the parent. As the psychiatrist W.W. Meissner has said,

There are no psychoanalytic "facts" that are not ultimately embedded in a context of meaning and relevance which bears an immediate relationship to the patient's subjectivity. There is a constant tension between the meaning of the events in themselves and the meaning attributed to them in the patient's mind. The ultimate explanation, then, does not lie so much in the determining causal effect of given factual sequences and their resultant effects in the patient's experience as in the meaningful construction given to such events and their integration in a pattern of relevance within the patient's experience. In a sense, the patient constructs a meaning out of his experience and it is this constructed meaning that serves as the basis for the sense of self to which he must ultimately commit himself.[29]

This ability to use the concrete, empirical parent relationship as the occasion of discovery of the infinite/eternal in one's being may be seen

28. *Upbuilding Discourses in Various Spirits* (Douglas V. Steere's translation as *Purity of Heart*), pp. 150–153; (KW 15:101–103); SV 11:95–96; (8:198–199).

29. In his essay, "Subjectivity in Psychoanalysis," in *Kierkegaard's Truth: The Disclosure of Self*, ed. Joseph H. Smith, p. 287.

at work in another common moral dilemma or paradox that Freud explores and seeks to explain. He suggests (in Wollheim's words) that

it is continuing evidence for the origins of the superego in the Oedipal drama that so many of the prohibitions to which the individual feels himself subject should have a partial or discriminatory character, and in this way fall short of the universality advertized by moral philosophy. And this is because the child's parent, or the parent as experienced by the child, not merely holds up as ideals some forms of behavior in which he engages, but often forbids other forms of behavior just because he engages in them himself and wishes to do so exclusively (Wollheim, pp. 199–200).

So the relation of the superego to the ego, Freud says, "also compromises the prohibition: 'You *may not be* like this (like your father) – that is, you may not do all that he does; some things are his prerogative'" (idem). For example (not suggested in Wollheim's text), a child may be told by its mother, "Never say 'shut up'," but then the mother tells the noisy child to "shut up!" The father may tell the child, "Stop swearing," or, "Don't let me catch you masturbating." Then the child is astounded when it catches the father swearing or masturbating. But Kierkegaard contends that these compromised prohibitions may serve as the occasion for the increasingly self-conscious child to become aware of another Superego beyond the parent. As in the myth of the Garden of Eden, the human psyche hears the Voice that forbids any attempt to determine for oneself what is "good" and what is "evil" (i.e., forbids "eating of the tree"), because there is a Totally Other who alone has that prerogative. And in the depth of this awareness the human psyche comes to self-consciousness of a dual angst: the lure of "being able" (freedom) and the threat of failure (sin) and retribution (death).[30]

Undoubtedly, Kierkegaard's life would have been very different if he had been able to analyze sexuality as honestly and completely as Freud did. He would have been better able to come to terms with his father's denial of a normal childhood to him, and the "earthquake" of his later discovery of his father's adulterous relationship with Søren's mother-to-be. Also, Kierkegaard would have better understood the inner crisis that led him to break his engagement with Regine, rather than camouflaging the event in various fanciful and delusory explanations that prevented a reconciliation and lodged him permanently in a sexually frustrated life.

30. *The Concept of Angst*, pp. 40–41; (KW 8:44–45); SV 6:138–139; (4:315–316).

And, on the other hand, Freud could have achieved a more hopeful view of the human self and of human life in general if he had been more faithful to his commitment to the duality of id and ego and had not been afraid to explore the inner life and passions that are peculiar to the ego, including the passion for the infinite and eternal.

The issue of whether psychoanalysis can be successfully conceived and functional within natural science (as Freud wished) or whether it must expand to include a humanist psychology was recognized by disciples of Freud by the close of his writing career (1925). W.W. Meissner traces the development of this issue, first through the works of Heinz Hartmann and D. Rappaport in support of Freud's ideal of a "natural science account of mental phenomena" that seeks "explanation" by means of "causal" sequences, as opposed to "understanding" which seeks to grasp "meaning structures," including the role of the "personal agent in the therapeutic technique." Then Meissner traces the rise of a critique of this view and the development of a humanistic psychology in the works of H.J. Home, H. Guntrip, Roy Schafer, and Donald Winnicott.[31] He concludes his essay with these words:

In the debate between the objective and subjective adherents within psychoanalysis, I have taken the position here that is intermediate and consequently open to ambiguity. ... [P]sychoanalysis cannot do without the inclusion of individual subjectivity within its scope. ... For the Hartmann school, the data of subjectivity and of meaningful content within psychoanalysis were regarded as nontheoretical. ... The contemporary argument, however, reaches further, since it demonstrates not only the operation of subjective factors within the analytic process but places a further demand that these elements be given theoretical recognition. ... The debate over subjectivity, as I have traced it above, labors under a theoretical framework or paradigm ... that did not reach beyond the merely functional, mechanical, and structural account provided by a systematized ego psychology. In such a theory, there was no place for the personal agent, the meaning-giving, meaning-taking, interpreting, and intentional source of individual responsibility and action. I would like to take the argument a step further by saying that a properly elaborated concept of the self may provide the overriding conceptual framework so that the elements of the objective structuralized account may take their appropriate place alongside the more subjective concerns we have been discussing.

31. "Subjectivity in Psychoanalysis," pp. 267, 271–282.

Then after specifying two other functions of such a concept of the self, he adds a third one:

The emergence of a self-concept provides a locus in the theory for articulating the experience of a personal self, either as grasped introspectively and reflexively or as experienced as the originating source of personal agency. As numerous criticisms have indicated, the conceptual apparatus having to do with the functions of id, ego, and superego cannot provide an adequate account of this sense of personal agency. However, the full understanding of the experience of selfhood involves various aspects of the integrated function of these respective psychic agencies, and something more. The something more has to do specifically with the subjectivity of the personal agent, the dimension of human experience so exquisitely addressed by Kierkegaard.[32]

It is precisely this "something more" in Kierkegaard's understanding and explanation of the human psyche that J. Preston Cole explores in comparison and contrast to Freud's views, and he agrees with Meissner that it is something that psychoanalysis must recognize and appeal to in order to achieve the full healing of the human psyche. He says that Freud rejects "the notion of an original state of innocence in which there is the absence of desire" because the "blissful state" of the prenatal period is brought to an end by the trauma of birth that produces an elemental anxiety as "an anticipation of impending danger." Cole finds in Freud certain similarities with Kierkegaard but, as we will see below, Kierkegaard's concepts of innocence, angst, self-consciousness, and guilt are qualitatively different from Freud's, and therefore for him human failure and "loss of self" is a different phenomenon and occurs at a different stage than the occurrence of innocence, angst, etc., as described by Freud. The root of these differences is indicated by Cole when he points out that Freud's "deterministic interpretation of selfhood" means that "the ego as well as the id comes into being by necessity," and therefore Freud's "ontological presuppositions will not permit him to appropriate fully the spiritual dimension of the self." On the other hand, he argues that "Kierkegaard's ontological commitment to Spirit, or freedom, prohibits an adequate appreciation of the deterministic factors in the dialectic of selfhood," as evidenced by his failure to appreciate Freud's concept of "identification" according to which "the content of the imaged self ... is acquired through the child's identification with his

32. Ibid., pp. 305–307.

parents. ... His image of his parents becomes the ideal image of the self by means of which he finds his identity" (pp. 65–67). So Cole's conclusion is that Kierkegaard and Freud do not so much contradict each other, but that they supplement each other in crucial and needed ways.

Our conclusion is somewhat different. Cole, in spite of his careful reading of Kierkegaard, works with an inadequate notion of Kierkegaard's concept of necessity as developed in *The Sickness unto Death*, and he does not appreciate Kierkegaard's insistence on the capacity of subjective reflection to discern the given, inherent potentiality of selfhood in every human being, that is, in one's own self. And if one takes seriously Kierkegaard's view of the role of human freedom in human failure, and of the role of human openness to the infinite/eternal as crucial to the recovery and healing process, then surely every assumption and every conclusion of Freud must be radically modified. The central role played by the concept of the Oedipal complex in every aspect of the Freudian analysis makes nonsense of the notion of individual freedom, because, as applied by Freud, every infant/child is fated, by the subconscious hostility and aggression arising from its complex sexual relations with its parent(s), to the "failure" of neuroses and a sense of guilt that will distort both the child's and the adult's ego.[33] As has been shown in detail in our earlier volume,

33. Freud's selection of a Greek myth, which was also the theme of two of Sophocles' tragedies, as the leitmotif of his theory is clearly indicative of his rejection of the notion of any significant kind of individual freedom. As Paul Harvey says of *Oedipus Tyrannus*, "It illustrates the Greek conception of human impotence in the presence of destiny, which may hurl a man, for no fault of his own, from the height of prosperity to appalling misery" [*The Oxford Companion to Classical Literature* (Oxford: Oxford University Press, 1984) p. 293]. Kierkegaard made this point vis-à-vis freedom in his fascinating essay, "The Tragic in Ancient Drama Reflected in the Tragic in Modern Drama" (*Either/Or, Part I*): "In ancient tragedy, the action itself has an epic element; it is just as much event as action. ... Even if the individual moved freely, he nevertheless rested in substantial determinants, in the state, the family, in fate. This substantial determinant is the essential fateful factor in Greek tragedy and is its essential characteristic. The hero's downfall, therefore, is not the result solely of his action but is also a suffering, whereas in modern tragedy the hero's downfall is not really suffering but is a deed." Kierkegaard argues that if a drama (and hence a psychological theory, perhaps?) portrays the individual at either extreme of absolute fate or total freedom, then there is no true element of tragedy. "It is, therefore, surely a misunderstanding of the tragic when our age endeavors to have everything fateful transubstantiate itself into individuality and subjectivity. ... This misguided enterprise may somehow have its basis in the working of the whole age toward the comic. The comic lies precisely in the isolation; when one wants to affirm the tragic within this isolation, one has evil in its badness, not the authentic tragic guilt in its ambiguous innocence [*Uskyldighed*, literally 'guiltlessness']" (pp. 141–142; (KW 3:143–144); SV 2:133–134; (1:121–122). It is precisely this concept of "ambiguous innocence" that Kierkegaard picks up and explicates as the context of human failure in *The Concept of Angst*.

Kierkegaard as Humanist, "the self is freedom" for Kierkegaard. In any case, our task here is simply to depict Kierkegaard's own understanding of how the self comes to consciousness and how the self never achieves its potentiality except through the trauma of crucial mistakes (failures) that threaten the whole process. Psychologists and psychiatrists will have to judge for themselves the helpfulness and usefulness of his understanding for contemporary psychology and psychoanalytic theory, but I personally find Kierkegaard's analysis and depiction to be much more resonant with common human experience than that of Freud's.

Thus comes to an end the excursus on Freudianism begun a dozen or so pages above in our study. We have not formulated a specific answer to the question with which we began, namely, at what age do responsibility and guilt emerge in the development of a child to mature adulthood, but clearly Kierkegaard's concepts of the conscious self and its freedom/guilt do not accord with the notion of an infant/child committed to a fate by subconscious, oedipal sexual drives. In order to spell out the details of Kierkegaard's answer we need to complete our analysis of his basic theses about human failure.

INNOCENCE AS THE CONTEXT OF FAILURE

The entire Christian experience and its interpretation (in a theology of creation, sin, and salvation) has as its absolute presupposition the conviction that at the base, at the heart, at the beginning of all human existence lies a Garden of Eden, a pure, unadulterated, yet complex state of being. With this Kierkegaard agrees. But as usual with every Christian doctrine and tradition, he transcribes the biblical story of this Garden into his own peculiar language and conceptuality, and thus he brings fresh and startling insights into old dogma. For him, every man is his own Adam, every woman is her own Eve. The Garden is a state neither of perfection nor of imperfection but of innocence. The temptation presented by the serpent is a conversation that one has with oneself, that goes on within the mind and heart of every human being. Adam's/Eve's failure is the same as my failure and vice versa.

Like some other biblical interpreters of the nineteenth century, Kierkegaard becomes convinced of the mythic-poetic character of many of the ancient Hebrew stories and traditions, but unlike some of them, he is also convinced that these stories and legends are rooted in the earliest memories that the human race has of its history and, likewise, in the earliest memories that every individual has of one's own history.

This double sensitivity is reflected in his interpretation of Adam/Eve and the Garden of Eden. He takes exception to much of the traditional interpretation because, he says, it views Adam/Eve as representative of the race as a whole and neglects their very real role as individuals. Then it exacerbates the situation by placing them in a realm of their own outside the human race as it has developed historically, because they (as racial figures) are represented as the only ones who sinned in a state of innocence, while all subsequent individual members of the race have become sinners by participating in a fateful inheritance through simply being born as human beings.[34]

34. In the first two sections of chapter 1 of *The Concept of Angst*, Kierkegaard presents a (to me) convincing engagement with traditional dogmatics by spelling out its confusions in the doctrine of hereditary or original sin. If he had read Calvin as assiduously as he had read Luther, he would have found a position that is, in some ways, nearer to his own. Calvin speaks of Adam as both "the first human-being" (*primo homini*, not *vir* for male) and as the race itself in the sense that "the Lord deposited with Adam whatever he chose to confer on human nature," and hence "it was ordained by God that the gifts conferred on the first man should by him be simultaneously possessed and lost both for himself and for his [descendants]" (*Institutes of the Christian Religion*, book 2, chapter 1, §7). Calvin also asserts (as does Kierkegaard) that Adam's sin of pride and disobedience had its origin in the fact that he was "contemptuous of the truth" and "turned to the lie," in that Adam was not satisfied to be "made in the likeness of God unless he could achieve equality [with God]" (2.1.4). Nevertheless, this basic error, from which "vitiation" and "corruption" flows into the whole of human nature, "did not flow from nature"; rather, "it is an adventitious quality which comes upon [*acciderit*, to happen or fall upon] human-being, rather than a substantial property that has been implanted from the beginning" (2.1.11) Indeed, Calvin is very clear that human failure is not "God's handiwork" but originates from "*our* original condition," that is, from "that pure [*integra*, morally innocent] and uncorrupted nature of Adam" (2.1.10; emphasis added).

However, as we shall see, Kierkegaard disagrees with Calvin on two important points. First, Calvin defends the traditional view that original human nature as created by God was not only uncorrupted but total and complete: "God provided the human soul with a mind, by which to distinguish good from evil, right from wrong. ... To this he joined the will, under whose control is choice. Human-being in its first condition excelled in these pre-eminent endowments, so that [the human's] reason, understanding, prudence, and judgment not only sufficed for the direction of his/her earthly life, but by them humans mounted up even to God and eternal bliss. Therefore Adam could have stood if he wished, seeing that he fell solely by his own will. ... The highest rectitude was in his mind and will, and all the organic parts were rightly composed to obedience, until in destroying himself he corrupted his own blessings" (1.15.8). On the contrary, Kierkegaard argues that in original innocence of the human-being, selfhood (spirit) is only a given potentiality with the task of coming into existence, and the human-being is still ignorant of the what and the how of becoming. Secondly, Calvin argues that human-beings subsequent to Adam/Eve lack that original innocence and righteousness because Adam/Eve's sin and corruption have been devolved on the very nature of all their inheritors by God's ordination. And "although God's image was not totally annihilated and destroyed" by this sin and corruption (1.15.4), yet (as Lombard says) we do

The way Kierkegaard makes this point is a telling example of his phenomenological method, as well as of his unique contribution of a profoundly personal anthropology as the focus of and key to an authentically Christian theology. In discussing Adam's fall into sin, he says that the Bible often has "a harmful effect" when one assumes that one can come to an "explanation and knowledge" of some matter by simply making an arrangement of a set of Biblical passages on the topic – as if, before making the arrangement, "the whole matter were something foreign for the one" making the arrangement. Such a method places one "in the awkward position of having to understand the explanation before one has understood what it should explain." On this false assumption there have been "many a learned theologian" who claims to have "known how to explain the teachings of the Bible ... on hereditary sin without having occupied him/herself at any time in tracing the influence [*Virkning*] of hereditary sin in her/his own ... consciousness. And yet this is the first thing that every human-being is assigned to do, and every human-being, if one carefully examines oneself, possesses within oneself a more complete expression for everything human than the *summa summarum* of all the knowledge one gains in the above manner."[35]

In other words, Kierkegaard contends that all human beings have at least some dim idea that something has gone wrong with their own human existence, that all humans fail repeatedly in doing what they know

---

not now have free decision (*arbitrium*) in the sense that "we are equally capable of doing or thinking good and evil, but merely that we are freed from compulsion." So we have a kind of free decision "not because one has free choice [*liberum electionem*] equally of good and evil, but because one behaves evilly willingly [*voluntate*], not by compulsion." (2.2.6–7) Kierkegaard, on the other hand, asserts that the first human-being and every subsequent human-being start from the same state of innocence, and that Adam's failure and mine are qualitatively the same. And Calvin warns against "inordinate curiosity" about why God did not prevent Adam's fall by "sustaining him by the virtue of perseverance"; the "why," Calvin says, "is hidden in [God's] own counsel [*consilio*]," that is, in "God's secret predestination" (1.15.8; 2.1.10). Kierkegaard does not hesitate to locate the "higher sense" in which human failure is "an essential constituent-element of the whole production," namely, to find it in the demands of God's purpose ("hidden counsel") of achieving a relationship of love between God and the human-being and among all human beings. [For the Latin of Calvin's *Institutes* I used the Barth-Niesel edition (Monachii {Munich}: Chr. Kaiser, 1928). For the English I consulted (but did not always use) the text as edited by John T. McNeil and translated by Ford Lewis Battles (Philadelphia: Westminster Press, 1960.)]

35. *The Concept of Angst*, p. 36–7; (KW 8:40); SV 6:134–135; (4:312). The last quotation is from a longer draft that Kierkegaard made for this passage, and it may be found in *Papirer*, V B 53:6; a translation is provided in the *Supplement* to KW 8 on pp. 184–185.

is ethically right, that below the order and civility of human society is a seething and threatening cauldron of chaos, that human history is constantly replete with inexplicable horrors of human devising. Hence when the Bible speaks to us in a way that attempts to explain our existential situation, the matter is not foreign or strange to us, even though the explanation will seem to be so, at least to begin with. And the truth of what the Bible has to say on this matter gains its power as revelation and enlightenment by giving us an "explanation," a vision, that convicts the heart and thus convinces the mind – *if* we let it in.[36]

In this way the story of Adam/Eve becomes my story. "Every subsequent individual is essentially as original as the first," because like Adam "every individual is both oneself and the race" and hence "not essentially different."[37] The key term is "essentially," because Haufniensis strongly affirms that later individuals of the race are very different from Adam/Eve *quantitatively.* That is to say, although "every subsequent individual begins in the very same way" as Adam/Eve, our beginning is "within the quantitative difference that is the consequence of the relationship of generation and the historical relationship." Hence, "just as the sinfulness of the race moves in quantitative determinations, so also does angst," and thus "angst will be more reflective in a subsequent individual than in Adam."[38]

Nevertheless, his main point is that these quantitative differences do not change or modify, let alone negate, the *qualitative identity* of the way that every single human being becomes involved in the actuality of failure (sin). This theme runs throughout *The Concept of Angst.* Unless one wants to resort to the concept of fate or of predestination or to one of strict determinism, then "innocence is always lost only by the qualitative leap of the individual," that is, "innocence is lost only by guilt;" hence "every human being loses innocence essentially in the same way that

36. Kierkegaard's point here on the topic of hereditary sin is a good example of the general point we made in chapter 1, namely, that for him the "truth" of Christian revelation is not a set of doctrines, and faith is not rational assent to and acceptance of the doctrines. Rather, "you will know the truth, and the truth will set you free" in the sense that Christ will reveal to you who you are as the image and the child of God, Christ will help you to see what is wrong with your life and will offer to help you to become that self that God has given you to be. *Then* you can say that Christ is "the way, the truth and the life."

37. *The Concept of Angst,* pp. 57, 88; (KW 8:63, 98); SV 6:155, 185; (4:334, 368).

38. Ibid., pp. 81, 47; (KW 8:90, 52); SV 6:178, 145; (4:360, 323). Note that Kierkegaard spends the whole of chapter 2 of *The Concept of Angst* exploring this difference. In other words, he takes very seriously the matter of individual differences that are due to the specific and unique historical, social, and physical conditions of each individual.

Adam lost it," because "the guilt that breaks forth in angst by the qualitative leap [in us] retains the same accountability as that of Adam, and the angst [retains] the same ambiguity." So we must "hold fast to the distinction ... between the quantitative accumulation and the qualitative leap," because "every individual becomes guilty only through oneself."[39] Therefore, "if I can explain guilt in a subsequent person [me], I can explain it in Adam as well," because Adam "is himself and the race. Therefore that which explains Adam also explains the race and vice versa." If this were not so, "Adam would actually stand outside the race, and the race would not have begun with him but would have had a beginning outside itself."[40] Haufniensis therefore concludes: "By a qualitative leap sin entered into the world, and it continually enters into the world in that way. ... In the qualitative leap they [Adam and every subsequent individual] are completely alike."[41]

What then does it mean to say that every human individual comes into being in an original state of innocence? And how is it that human failure within innocence possesses both "accountability" (*Tilregnelighed*) and "ambiguity" (*Tvetydighed*)?[42] In this language Kierkegaard is clearly talking about the state of awareness that gradually emerges in a child,[43] when it is no longer an infant suckling at its mother's breast and yet has

39. Ibid., pp. 34, 33, 54, 48; (KW 8:37, 36, 60, 53–54); SV 6:132, 131, 152, 146; (4:309, 308, 331, 324).

40. That is to say, the state of sinfulness, which Adam did not know but brought into the world, becomes the presupposition ("outside") of the race, for which the race has no responsibility. Kierkegaard rightly holds that this is nonsense that explains nothing. The only recourse then open would be to "explain" the situation as inexplicable fate or as God's secret predestination – which of course is to despair of any explanation.

41. *The Concept of Angst*, pp. 35, 27, 99–100; (KW 8:38, 29–30, 111–112); SV 6:133, 125, 196–197; (4:310, 302, 379–380).

42. *Tilregnelighed* is an interesting variation of Kierkegaard's usual *Ansvarlighed*. The latter means that you are responsible in the sense that you are held accountable for your actions, while the former has the added sense that you are of a sound mind, in full possession of your faculties, and *therefore* to blame and accountable. This is actually more than Haufniensis asserts about innocence, but it does emphasize Kierkegaard's insistence that original and essential human nature is not and never is evil as such. These two words quoted in the previous paragraph are from the quotation designated in note 27 as: p. 54; (60); 152; (331).

43. See *Johannes Climacus*, KW 7:167; *Papirer*, IV B 1:145–146.; also *The Concept of Angst*, pp. 38, 61, 64–65, 67–68, 112; (KW 8:42, 68, 72–73, 75–76, 126); SV 6:136–137, 159, 162–163, 165–166, 209; (4:314, 337–338, 341–342, 344–345, 393); *Sickness*, p. 183n; (KW 19:49n); SV 15:106n; (11:162n.); also *Journals*, 91; II A 18. Some of these passages will be quoted below.

not become fully adult, when it first enters the outer precincts of that bewildering, frightening, exciting trauma of becoming *self* conscious, that is, when "I" (as a totality) first begin to distinguish "me myself" from everything external to my own body (of which I now become overwhelmingly and embarrassingly conscious), when I first begin to contemplate my self and ask all kind of inchoate questions about that self.

In this intermediate state, then, what is the awareness of a child before it becomes an adult? Can we really know? Someone has said that by the time we are able to ask this question in all self-consciousness, we have "forgotten" the answer. That is to say, a veil has dropped down, and we can see (remember) that other world only dimly, partially, uncertainly, in images distorted by our present consciousness. Yet we do have these dim memories, and we observe and empathize with our own (and others') children. And whatever the joys we experience in the company of children, we do know that they are incapable of fulfilling the role of companions and friends, which we desperately need and desire at the level of adult self-consciousness. And out of both this positive and this negative relationship with children (and our own childhood), we can try out hypotheses and stories and images in an attempt to depict and to understand that Garden of Eden into which we were born – *and* that Serpent that spoke to us in the midst of our blissful innocence.

Indeed, we must make this attempt because psychologists generally agree that all that we are as adults, in both our most promising potentialities and our direst capacities for self-destruction, is shaped and given direction (but not determined) by what went on in that hidden, secret garden. And Kierkegaard was one of the first and one of most sensitive and insightful explorers of this terrain. His story, his picture, and his hypotheses are among the more intriguing and persuasive of our modern age, and they are intimately reflective of and have fundamental implications for his particular Christian theology.[44]

For Kierkegaard, original human innocence is not homogeneous, simple, unqualified, or uncomplicated. He says it is both immediacy and transcendence, neither perfection nor imperfection, both peaceful repose or bliss and yet disturbed and anxious longing, a knowing and yet an ignorance, a state or quality that may endure and yet is filled with the agony of incompleteness. It is this peculiar dialectic or polarity that

44. The cluster of ideas that we will use here have been explicated in part in my earlier volume, *Kierkegaard as Humanist*. I will use some of the material developed there as found on pp. 29–31, 47–67, 455–457. For a fuller account of "angst" see especially pp. 47–64.

makes possible the emergence of a consciousness of self as a task to be accomplished in freedom and responsibility. So "in innocence, a human-being is not merely animal, for if one were at any moment of one's life merely animal, one would never become a human-being;" yet, "the moment one becomes human, one becomes so by being animal as well."[45] And within the perspective of Christian experience, one comes to the overwhelming conviction that this unique character of the human species (within our ken of the universe[46]) is not *merely* the product of an evolutionary accident but manifests itself with the quality of being a special gift. Moreover, this quality asserts the startling, seemingly absurd claim to embody the very likeness and image of the Giver, the claim that the fundamental capacity for reduplication (self-consciousness and self-differentiation) that defines Being-In-And-For-Itself is shared with and is inherent in being-human.

As Anti-Climacus summarizes it, "primitively every human-being is naturally fitted [*anlagt*] to be a self, appointed [*bestemt*, fixed] to become oneself;" moreover, this capacity "to have a self, to be a self, is the greatest concession, the infinite concession, given to the human-being, but it is also eternity's claim upon her/him."[47] In other words, every human being who awakens to consciousness of this ultimate concession or gift is not free to forget or ignore it, nor to use it and manipulate it as one wills. Rather, that person experiences that eternity (the giver) pursues every human being in order to claim, to require, to demand that one use this ineffable gift, ultimately, for one thing and one thing only: to love and be loved, to relate to and with God and neighbor in love. And woe to the one who fails or refuses! because that path leads not to

---

45. *The Concept of Angst*, pp. 39, 44; (KW 8:43, 49); SV 6:137, 142; (4:315, 319).

46. The noted paleontologist, Stephen Jay Gould, argues that even the scientific search for the origins of our particular species has the value and task of providing us "with crucial clues in the oldest quest imposed by our altered style of mentality – to know ourselves." He describes that mentality as "a symbolic capacity based on a kind of mental modeling performed either temporally or geometrically." Presently paleoanthropology claims to have discerned some of the gains that this capacity produced in *homo sapiens* and describes them as the capacities "to envision a geometric order in living space, ... to calculate complex degrees of relationship, and the establishment of a notion of futurity," the last one being "the ability to think about futures and to plan for events to come," including "a view of oneself as a moving dot in time, with a past on one side and a future in front" (In an article about the present status of research on neandertals, in *The New York Review of Books*, October 20, 1994, pp. 28, 27).

47. *Sickness*, p. 154; (KW 19:21); SV 15:80; (11:135).

freedom but to slavery, not to hope but to despair, not to life but to the sickness unto death.

Now let us see how Kierkegaard (Haufniensis) spells this out.

The original human state (Garden of Eden) has often been character- ized as ideal perfection (e.g., Calvin in note 22 above), which has been lost through sin and must be regained (in salvation). So, in Milton's po- etic rendition, "Paradise Lost" and "Paradise Regained." Likewise, child- hood has often been idolized, and it is sometimes averred that our only hope is to find our way back to the sweet innocence of that "secret gar- den."[48] On the other hand, some theologians and philosophers have re- minded us that the Serpent was an original inhabitant of that Garden, and therefore, they argue, evil has its esoteric origins in the unfathom- able depths of God's own being, or in the eternal struggle of God with uncreated conditions of chaos, a kind of Anti-God, an Ahura Mazda ver- sus an Ahriman. And human existence reflects not only the image of the Creator but also the presence of that chaos and corruption from the moment of creation and from every subsequent moment of conception of a human being. Kierkegaard shares neither of these pictures.

In *The Concept of Angst* (as already noted above at note 26), it is indeed acknowledged and repeatedly asserted that every infant is born into a world of sinfulness that operates both in individuals (e.g., one's parents) and in the structures and events of society.[49] And Haufniensis affirms that the quantitative increase of this evil environment intensifies the angst that impinges on all children and on some more than others. One must, he says, take note of "the relation of the particular innocent indi- vidual to his/her historical environment," because "the most dissimilar things may produce the same effect. ... The sight of the sinful may save one individual and bring another to fall. ... Speech and silence can pro- duce an effect opposite to what was intended." The ultimate example for Kierkegaard (out of his own life, no doubt) occurs when "an individ-

---

48. This view continues to capture the imagination of humans who believe that they have observed childlike innocence and purity among certain island or jungle tribes more or less isolated from human history. In spite of recent rejection by some anthropologists of Margaret Mead's idyllic picture of natives, *Coming of Age in Somoa* (1928), casual visitors still often claim to observe and continue to admire this apparent quality of primitive life. But as we will see, Kierkegaard contends that original innocence in the child is always qualified with angst, and that "in all cultures where the childlike is preserved as the dreaming of the spirit, this angst is found" (*The Concept of Angst*, pp. 38–39; [KW 8:42]; SV 6:137; [4:314]).

49. See *The Concept of Angst*, chapter 2, especially the concept of the "more" in succeed- ing generations.

ual from his earliest awakening is placed and influenced in such a way that sensuousness for her/him has become identical with sinfulness, and this ultimate more will appear in the most painful form of collision if in the whole surrounding world he finds nothing that can give him support." So in a very early journal entry (1837) he warns that "one ought to be very careful with children, never believe the worst and by untimely suspicion or by a chance remark ... occasion an anxious consciousness in which innocent but fragile souls can easily be tempted to believe themselves guilty, to despair" and hence "give the kingdom of evil ... an occasion for reducing them to a kind of spiritual paralysis."[50]

Nevertheless, in spite of this quantitative difference, Haufniensis insists that every human being shares originally and essentially in the same qualitative innocence. This innocence is "a quality, ... a *state* that may very well endure." It is a state of "peace and repose" insofar as "the human-being is not [yet] formed [or qualified, *bestemmet*] as spirit [i.e., self] but is psychically formed in immediate unity with one's natural condition." Indeed, "spirit is present" as a potentiality, otherwise humans would be merely animals. But it is present "as immediate, as dreaming."[51]

This state of the human spirit (self) as "dreaming" is crucial to Kierkegaard's understanding of the difference between childhood and adulthood. It assumes that the child is still "psychically formed" so that the ego or self is not conscious as such, that is, as something more than its bodily-psychic unity, as something distinct from its total environment.

---

50. Ibid., pp. 66–67; (KW 8:74); SV 6:164; (4:343); *Journals*, 91 (or KW 8:169); II A 18. One wonders what Kierkegaard would make of the "spiritual paralysis" that is evident in the children born into modern urban slums, where poverty, hunger, drug-use, crime, physical violence, terror, fear, and often the total lack of "family" rob both children and adults of any sense (even a "dream") of self. Letty Russell, one of the early workers in the East Harlem Protestant Parish, once told some of us that their first task was to scrape off, patiently and gently, layer after layer of terror-induced psychic numbness that possessed the people who lived there, before they could finally touch and evoke a sense of self, before they could even begin to convince them that God is love and that each one of them was a precious child of God, of great dignity and eternal worth. With many, they never succeeded. But without at least some success in this endeavor, the workers were helpless in any attempt to lead the people into endeavors for breaking out of their enslavement to their environment. Only then could political leaders like Andy Young arouse a movement among blacks to fight for racial equality and justice. Some of us once asked Young how he and others in the movement could keep up the spirit and hopefulness of poor oppressed blacks. "Very simple," he said. "We just keep telling them, over and over again, 'You are a child of God! You are a child of God!' "

51. *The Concept of Angst*, pp. 34, 37–38, 39; (KW 8:37, 41, 43); SV 6:132, 135–36, 137; (4:309, 313, 315).

Yet the child is not totally without selfhood because it is present like a "dream." So the child can appear to be conscious of being threatened and of feeling guilty, but, Kierkegaard would argue, these are strictly reflexive attitudes, induced by one's environment. These attitudes are neither authentic *self*-consciousness, nor are they guilt in the sense of selfdetermining responsibility.

Here is the root of the basic and definitive ambiguity of selfhood. On the one hand, at the very origin of life as infant/child, innocence is a given and unadulterated immediacy of body, psyche, and the world around, in "peace and repose." On the other hand, human immediacy in innocence "is by no means the pure being of the immediate," because in sheer immediacy the "difference between myself and my other" (the duality of id and ego, or of my present immediacy and my future, potential self-consciousness) would not be operative at all. It would, in Kierkegaard's analogy, be "sleeping" or "suspended." Rather, he avers, "in this state of peace and repose, ... there is simultaneously something else. ... Dreamily the spirit [self] projects its own actuality." Clearly, in such a projection the self is not "sleeping," but neither is it "awake" as when one is fully conscious of the "difference;" it is "dreaming." But this dream of selfhood is not "an immanent movement within immediacy" such as happens in the annulment of immediacy by mediacy. Rather, there is a gulf or gap between the dreaming possibility of self and the actualization of self, and hence "innocence is canceled by transcendence." That is why "the concept of immediacy belongs in logic; the concept of innocence belongs in ethics."[52] And this fact means that the childhood

---

52. The quoted phrases in this paragraph are from ibid., pp. 32–34, 37–38; (KW 8:35, 37, 41); SV 6:130–132, 135–136; (4:307–308, 313). In a formulation of his concept of immediacy a year or so before *The Concept of Angst* (in his account of the philosophical musings of "Johannes Climacus"), Kierkegaard explicitly says, "There is consciousness in the child but this has doubt outside itself." In other words, "the child's consciousness ... is not qualified [*bestemmet*]" but is "immediate" in the sense of "indeterminateness," because "there is no relation, for as soon as there is a relation, immediacy is canceled." The relation he has in mind is that of "contradiction" between immediacy as "reality" [*Realitet*] and mediacy as the "ideality" [*Idealitet*] of language or expression in word. Hence consciousness occurs neither in reality nor in ideality, and "yet consciousness does not exist without both, and this contradiction is the coming-into-existence [*Tilbliven*] of consciousness and its nature." So the "I" that becomes conscious comprises a *third* that comes into existence through the interplay or contradiction between the dual elements of mere awareness in immediacy/reality and of the ideality of language/reflection. (*Johannes Climacus, or De omnibus dubitandum est*, KW 7:167–69; *Papirer*, IV B 1, pp. 145–48; see also the draft for this passage in *Papirer*, IV B 14:6, translation in *Journals*, 2320, or in KW 7:255).

dream of self is not altogether a peaceful one but is a disturbing one. So it is this disturbance that brings us to our second thesis (see p. 143 above).

Why is the presence of the potentiality and possibility of selfhood disturbing? Because "dreaming, it is an adumbrated [*antydet*] nothing." Indeed, "the spirit projects its own actuality, but this actuality is nothing," that is, it is undefined and, for the child, undefinable because "innocence always has this nothing outside itself," that is to say, authentic and operative consciousness of "the difference between myself and my other" is beyond the capabilities and experience of the child. From this perspective, then, while agreeing with Freud that this potentiality for selfhood has "sources" (certainly parents but ultimately God), Kierkegaard would want primarily to emphasize Freud's later insight that for the ego instincts, aim should "replace source as the dominant criterion," because "the ego itself is an agency identified by reference to aim" (Wollheim, pp. 182–83). But if this "aim" is beyond the child's capability to grasp, if the innocent child has its undefined self "outside itself," then "what effect does nothing have? It begets angst. This is the profound secret of innocence, that it is at the same time angst."[53]

As we have noted in *Kierkegaard as Humanist* (p. 48), Kierkegaard's analysis of the role that angst plays in the movement out of innocence into true *self*-consciousness is one of his more significant accomplishments, and the twentieth century is indebted to him for its awareness of being "the age of anxiety." But our concern here is not the total process of coming to self-consciousness (see chapter 3 in *Kierkegaard as Humanist*). Rather, we are seeking to understand how innocence with its "ambiguity" is still the context of human failure with "accountability," and in what follows, we shall see that the process, in which one moves from an original sense of peaceful immediacy to a full consciousness of responsible, adult selfhood (including failure), moves (in Kierkegaard's account of it) through four distinguishable stages and consumes from ten to fifteen years (at least) of a person's life. The clue as to how this development gets its start lies in what Kierkegaard means by saying that the self that one is aware of in innocence (childhood) is a "nothing" that "begets angst."

53. *The Concept of Angst*, pp. 37–38; (KW 8:41); SV 6:135–136; (4:313).

Kierkegaard insists that in this first stage, "the angst that is posited in innocence is ... no guilt, ... no troublesome burden, no suffering that cannot be brought into harmony with the blessedness of innocence." He says that the angst we observe in children is usually "a seeking for the adventurous, the monstrous, and the enigmatic." And "this angst belongs so essentially to the child that he cannot do without it." Why? Because sooner or later the child experiences this same angst when s/he dreams about one's own participation in some vague and undefined adventure. And then angst manifests its inherent dialectical character. "Though its alarms [*ængster*] him, it captivates him by its pleasing anxiousness [*Beængstelse*]." The English words "anxiety" and "dread" do not usually capture this double meaning but only the negative sense of alarm and fear, although we can speak of being "anxious to get going" on some project. Kierkegaard's usage of angst stresses its "dialectical determinants" that have "psychological ambiguity." He puts it most succinctly by saying: "Angst is *a sympathetic antipathy* and *an antipathetic sympathy.*"[54]

The child "cannot do without" this dialectic and its angst *if* it is to have that minimum of reflection by which it can take the first steps out of that undifferentiated immediacy of innocence into which it was born, and thereby can initiate the process of actualization of its potential self that is as yet undefined, a nothing. Actually, no child can escape this angst because there is a dialectic built into the given structure of every human being. "The human-being is a synthesis of the soulish [i.e., the psychical] and the bodily [i.e., the sensuous]. But a synthesis is unthinkable if the two are not united in a third. The third is the spirit [i.e., the self]." But as we have heard, in this first stage of innocence the self is "immediate, dreaming." And in this dream of selfhood, "the spirit's actuality constantly shows itself as a shape that tempts its possibility but disappears as soon as it [the dreaming self] seeks to grasp for it [the actual self], and it is a nothing that can only bring angst." In other words, in this peculiar presence of selfhood the dialectic becomes even more intense because the self's actuality presents itself both as "a friendly power, which precisely wants to constitute the relationship," and as "a hostile power, for it constantly disturbs the [immediate] relationship between soul and body [ego and id]." What a dilemma! "Do away with itself, the spirit cannot; lay hold of itself, it cannot, as long as it has itself outside itself." What agony! when angst is most intensely sympathetic/antipathetic: "flee away

54. Ibid., p. 38; (KW 8:42); SV 6:136–137; (4:313–314).

from angst, one cannot, because one loves it; really love it, one cannot, because one flees from it." Now "innocence is at its apex [*Spidse*]," its point of crisis. It knows itself as a dreaming presence, yet "as the enormous nothing of ignorance," with "no knowledge of good and evil."[55] Innocence is no abiding place. As Johannes Climacus says: to ask, "Cannot consciousness remain in immediacy?" is a foolish question "because if it could, there would be no consciousness at all."[56] What, then, makes any movement possible?

A new (second) stage of development now appears, but still within innocence. Kierkegaard describes it this way. The "nothing" of the dreaming self, which "passed by innocence" (i.e., was "outside itself," beyond its "grasp"), "now enters into [the human-being]." And instead of being a "tempting possibility" external to one's consciousness, the potentiality of selfhood takes a strange new shape: "innocence can speak, inasmuch as in language it possesses the manifestation [*Udtrykke*] for everything spiritual." Indeed, "innocence still exists, but only a word is required and then ignorance is concentrated. ... Instead of nothing, it [the angst of innocence] now has an enigmatic word." And the first word that innocence hears is one of permission ("you may freely eat of every tree") but with the final hook of prohibition ("but of the tree of the knowledge of good and evil you shall not eat" [Gen 2:16]). Kierkegaard assumes that "the human-being [Adam] is talking to himself," listening to an infinite depth within, not to some external command.[57]

This internal conversation is analogous to but qualitatively different from hearing the external parental order, "You may go out to play," but "you may not go out of the yard," or as Kierkegaard heard it from his own father, "You may travel anywhere you choose, but I will take you there through my imagination by describing the trip in detail, as we walk up and down the floor of our drawing room."[58] Rather, the internalization of the external transcendence of the parent finally awakens innocence to a voice within that infinitely transcends parental authority, that relates with power and force to the dream of selfhood. Kierkegaard says that the definitive mark of this event is that the inward word of prohibition awakens not "the desire" to *use* freedom to do whatever one

55. Ibid., pp. 39, 38, 39–40; (KW 8:43, 42, 43–44); SV 6:137, 136, 137–138; (4:315, 313–314, 315).

56. *Johannes Climacus*, KW 7:167; *Papirer*, IV B 1, p. 146.

57. *The Concept of Angst*, pp. 40–41; (KW 8:44–45); SV 6:138–139; (4:315–316).

58. These are not Kierkegaard's words, but for his account see *Johannes Climacus*, p. 105; (KW 7:120); *Papirer*, IV B 1, p. 106.

chooses for oneself as the good, but awakens simply a sense of the non-specific "possibility of freedom," that is, awakens "the anxious possibility of *being able*." Yet innocence has "no conception of what one is able to do," because one still has no knowledge of and no power to distinguish for oneself between what is good and what is evil. "Only the possibility of being able is present as a higher form of ignorance, as a higher expression of angst, because in a higher sense it [the possibility of being able] both is and is not, because in a higher sense one both loves it and flees from it."

The word of prohibition, however, is followed by a second word, "a word of judgment: 'You shall certainly die.' " But just as the human-being in innocence has "no conception of *what* one is able to do," so also Adam/Eve, the essential human-being, "does not know what it means to die." Yet as one in innocence is powerfully excited and allured by the freedom's possibility, so now one is also terrified and repelled by the possibility of failure. "The infinite possibility of being able that was awakened by the prohibition now draws closer, because this possibility points to [another] possibility as its sequence," namely: *failure*. In this situation "there is nothing but the ambiguity of angst," enticement/alarm, fearful-fascination, because "in angst [innocence] is related to the forbidden and to the punishment." So "in this way, innocence is brought to its extremity [*Yderste*]."[59] And Kierkegaard reveals just how extreme this ultimate form or stage of innocence is by one final analysis of the absolute intensity of human angst.

At this point, he says, "[innocence] is not guilt, yet there is an angst as though it were lost." Or as he puts it later in the context of his discussion of the temporal/eternal in the human-being, "The difference between Adam and the subsequent individual is that for the latter the future is more reflective than for Adam. ... The highest difference in relation to Adam is that [for the subsequent individual] the future seems to be anticipated by the past, or [is] the angst [felt by the subsequent individual] that 'possibility' is [already] lost before it has been."[60] How is that possible? Kierkegaard recognizes that "in each subsequent individual, angst is more reflective," and hence "the nothing that is the object of angst becomes, as it were, more and more a something." Nevertheless, it does

---

59. *The Concept of Angst*, pp. 40–41; (KW 8:44–45); SV 6:138–139; (4:315–316).

60. Ibid., pp. 41, 82; (KW 8:45, 91); SV 6:139, 179; (4:316, 361). The last part of this sentence is impossible to translate literally from Kierkegaard's Danish. It means that the subsequent individual is sometimes seized by the feeling that, for him/her, all possibility has been lost prior to the actual fact of losing it, and this feeling fills the person with angst.

not "actually become a something," because essential innocence is the same for both Adam and the subsequent individual, and this means that the whole complexity of angst in innocence simply sets the stage for freedom, that is, for the critical moment when "the single individual [*den Enkelte*] posits sin by the qualitative leap."

In this situation, at the moment when the last extremity of angst in innocence has been reached but has not yet found its only resolution in a conscious, responsible (though utterly ambiguous) act of freedom, in this moment of crisis "the nothing of angst is a complex of presentiments, which, reflecting in themselves, come nearer and nearer to the individual, even though again, when viewed essentially in angst they signify nothing; yet, mark well, not a nothing with which the individual has nothing to do, but a nothing which communicates vigorously with the ignorance of innocence."[61] In fact, Kierkegaard concludes, this reflection and communication of this complex of presentiments is so vigorous that "the state that precedes sin, psychologically speaking predisposes more or less to sin."[62] For Kierkegaard these "presentiments" clearly include (1) the frustrating inability of the child to depict and to grasp its illusive dream of self, (2) the mysterious "hearing" of the transcendent words of prohibition and judgment, (3) the alluring and fascinating sense of *being able* to do something, (4) the threatening, frightening, repelling sense of possible, almost inevitable failure and loss, and (5) as we shall see, the first intimations of sexual differentiation. As we have heard, at this critical moment "innocence still exists" but its ignorance now becomes infinitely "concentrated," because "instead of nothing, it now has an enigmatic word" (note 57 above). A crisis indeed! when the inner consciousness of the child has become such a chaotic maelstrom of conflicting forces.

But, says Kierkegaard, "further than this psychology cannot go."[63] Why not? Because, as he repeats again and again throughout *The Concept of Angst*, the most intense, quantitative buildup of presuppositions and predispositions never explains the qualitative event of the self-conscious leap-of-freedom involved in the attempt of the potential self to "posit [actualize] the synthesis" and thus bring the self from a dreaming potentiality into a conscious actuality. "It would never occur to the [psychological]

61. For the quotations since the last note see ibid., p. 55; (kw 8:61–62); sv 6:166; (4:345).

62. Ibid., p. 68; (kw 8:76); sv 6:166; (4:345).

63. Ibid., p. 41; (kw 8:45); sv 6:139; (4:316).

explanation [of the ambiguity of angst in innocence] that it should explain the qualitative leap." The passage from possibility to actuality is assumed as inherently normal in a logical system, but "in actuality [of the human psyche] it is not so convenient," because "the intermediate term is angst, but it no more explains the qualitative leap than it can justify it ethically."[64]

Now, finally, we have the specific materials at hand to provide an answer to the question which was raised when we first outlined the main theses in our earlier analysis of Kierkegaard's concept of human "failure" (p. 144 above) and again at the end of the section on Freud (p. 155 above), that is, the question: at what stage (age) in the child's development do the concepts of self-consciousness and guilt, the concepts of freedom and responsibility, come into play in the emergence of "the sickness unto death," that is, in the failure of the human being to achieve selfhood?

For Kierkegaard, the five-fold "concentration" of the nothing of innocence described above is what sets the stage for the decisive event in which the child/youth will become *conscious* of being constructed as a unity of both the sensuous (finitude) and the psychic (infinitude), namely, when the child/youth is able to "pervade [the synthesis] differentially", will then be aroused by the passionate determination to *posit* or actualize that synthesis, and hence, in this way, will seek to *become* her/his potential self. Just as clearly, this complex event assumes that, when the individual begins to talk to him/herself, there arise the first traces of a distinction within oneself between the word spoken and the hearing of the word, that is, a rudimentary, initial form of conscious reflection which produces a sense of a "third," of an "I" (see note 52 above). For Kierkegaard this form of "consciousness," this vivid differentiation of sensuous and psychic, the emergence of this defined "I" through the power of language, does not occur except at the very outer, most extreme edge of innocence, when one stands at the verge of puberty and the first appearances of a new sexuality. And at the end of the next section (on the "fall") we will discover precise evidence for this thesis.

It must also be noted that this complex event marks the end of innocence. But the end comes not by "an immanent movement within im-

64. Ibid., pp. 39, 44–45; (kw 8:43, 49); sv 6:137, 142; (4:314, 320). For other examples see pp. 27, 29, 31, 55, 82; (kw 8:30, 32, 33, 61, 92); sv 6:126, 127, 129, 153, 179; (4:302, 304, 305, 331, 362).

mediacy" such as a subconscious impact of an oedipal complex on the
dim awareness of an infant or child. Rather (as we have heard above at
note 52), "innocence is canceled by transcendence," and the transcendence that is required for this end to occur is not, for Kierkegaard, that
of Freud's superego in any of its forms, but the transcendence of a Word
that has infinite and universal authority and that awakens the dreaming
self through the angst of hearing the words of prohibition and judgment as addressed to the "I" who hears, the angst that comes with the
startling intimation of my "being able" (freedom) and with the frightening possibility (*almost* inevitability) of my failure.

Again, it would seem that Kierkegaard is talking about the years of puberty. He states the difficulties involved in analyzing and depicting this
event in this way: "Just as the relation of angst to its object, to something
that is nothing, ... is altogether ambiguous, so also the transition that is
to be made from innocence to guilt will be so dialectical that ... the explanation ... must be psychological." Nevertheless, "the qualitative leap
stands outside all ambiguity," and the psychological explanation by
means of angst is only the last approximation to it and hence would
never try to "explain the qualitative leap." In this setting, "now occurs
the fall; ... the fall is the qualitative leap."[65] And this brings us to
Kierkegaard's third major thesis about human failure and despair
(p. 143 above), and hence to the next (third) stage of development of
self (see p. 165 above) from "dreaming" to authentic consciousness,
from potentiality/possibility to actuality. The thesis is this: the basic, essential human failure occurs as a responsible misuse (failure) of freedom
at that juncture when the potential self merges into *self*-consciousness
and makes its first moves to achieve self-actualization.

However, before we begin this analysis, it must be remarked that we
are here interpreting the thought of Kierkegaard as Christian theologian, as one who has been baptized in infancy and nurtured in childhood as a member of the community of Christian faith, and for whom
this nurture has had a profound effect on the form and content of the
psychological event in which such an individual becomes self-conscious.
When in the angst of innocence the "adumbrated nothing" of the self
begins to "speak" the words of prohibition and judgment (note 57
above), this "enigmatic word" for the Christianly-nurtured child comes,
in its address to the embryonic "I," with a definite content and intona-

65. Ibid., pp. 39, 43; (KW 8:43, 48); SV 6:137, 141; (4:314, 318).

tion which profoundly shape that "complex of presentiments" that "communicate vigorously with the ignorance of angst." This content and tone derive from the profundity and power of mythic pictures of legendary events caught in magical language and expressed in moving, passionate drama and song. And this particular form of the Word speaks not only in the primitive forms of prohibition and judgment but also in tales of heroic deeds and of high, noble callings. And *ultimately* this Word is carried in a message of a mystical love that "passes understanding," beyond the capacity of human imagination, a message, a Word of love that becomes incarnate in a *life.*

In this way, through the medium of this complex and variegated "word," the mystery that has been forbidden (the knowledge of the distinction between good and evil) is revealed, but not as a harsh legalistic code of moral absolutes. Rather, this knowledge comes to human consciousness and conviction through "the way," a way of living, as a growing, developing, ever-enriching *relationship* expressed and actualized in "works of love." And this way, this word, comes to be known not at some mystic depths or heights of human imagination or of inner self-contemplation. It comes in the humblest human form of a seemingly simple human being, a member of a poor family of an obscure tribe of a minor people that emerged from a remote desert region of the world. And this human being had a name, Jesus, and had a life: an infant born, a child growing, an adult with a calling, a failure in the eyes of the world, a criminal executed, a corpse dead and buried.

How this particular form of the Word comes to dwell within the consciousness of the adult human being will be the subject of the next chapter. But how that Word understands the human *need* that is universal and is a "sickness unto death" must first be clarified. And here it must be noted that Kierkegaard was such an infant and child whose coming to self-consciousness was profoundly formed by his Christian nurture. And although, as a young adult in university, he went through a period of aggressive rejection and critique of the particular Christian piety that he was subjected to by his father, and although he had to fight his way out of the suicidal depression in which his distorted childhood left him, and although he leveled a scathing attack on "childish Christianity" in the concluding chapter of *Postscript,* yet he devoted the major energies of his adult life to a clarification of what he considered to be authentic Christian faith. First, he did so from the perspective of one who is not yet a Christian in his own experience (Climacus), and hence from the open-

ing pages onward, even his personal journals are replete with explica-
tions of what he understands authentic Christianity to be.[66] Then later
he develops an entirely different explication of the same materials from
the perspective of one who is a hyper-Christian (Anti-Climacus). Eventually he identifies himself as one on the way, somewhere in between
Climacus and Anti-Climacus, as is true of everyone who takes one's
Christian faith seriously.

The point is this: the analysis of universal human failure ("fall" into
"sin") that follows draws from both the pre-Christian and the super-
Christian "Kierkegaard," as well as from discourses by the ordinary-
Christian Kierkegaard. And one of the issues which will be addressed at
a number of points will be whether and how far Kierkegaard's explication of this fall is accessible and meaningful for those who do not participate in the uniquely Christian form of the general human experience
of the infinite/eternal. We must wait and see.

THE FALL: FREEDOM AND GUILT

When Haufniensis says, "Now follows the fall," by "now" he means "the
moment" when the dreaming self comes awake and wants to become itself in the act of "positing the synthesis."[67] The given, potential, dreaming self is as such a construction (*Anlæg*) or compound (*Sammensætning*)
of the infinite and the finite, of freedom (possibility) and necessity, of
the eternal and the temporal, but "the synthesis is not actual." So by
"positing" the synthesis Kierkegaard means that the individual becomes
aware of or awake to the dialectic inherent in this primal duality, that is,
aware of the contradiction and contrast between the two inescapable elements or dimensions of each of the three dyads inherent in one's being, and in becoming conscious *in this way,* the individual confronts the
crisis of having consciously to *choose* to exist and to live in the harmonious interplay of the three dyads. In the language of the first paragraph
of *Sickness,* the given, established synthesis or relation (between these elements) must "relate to itself." This is the event of "becoming my self."

66. For example, see the entry in *Journals,* 273; I A 53 (dated November 26, 1834, at the
age of 21), which begins: "Christ's whole life in all its aspects must supply the norm for the
life of the following Christian and thus for the life of the whole Church." Then he stresses
the point (which repeats throughout his entire authorship) that it is Christ's *activity* that is
"the principle thing."

67. *The Concept of Angst,* pp. 43–44; (KW 8:48–49); SV 6:141–142; (4:319).

And to "choose" it consists of "the qualitative leap" of freedom. Hence, one is *responsible* for what one chooses.[68]

However, as we have been hearing throughout this chapter thus far, Kierkegaard (Haufniensis) stresses the dynamic instability of this given "construction" of self as a "compound" of three different explosive dyads.[69] It is precisely this instability that creates what he calls "the gap" of indeterminateness between possibility and actuality where "choosing" (freedom) finds its responsibility and comes into play. But, as we have also noted, the precondition of this moment, namely, the dialectically sympathetic/antipathetic angst of innocence, is so volatile and precarious that it comprises a kind of "weakness" that "predisposes more or less to sin [i.e., failure]." Or as he puts it in other words, "whoever is educated by possibility is exposed to danger, not that of ... going astray in various ways, ... but the danger of a fall, namely suicide. If at the beginning of one's education one misunderstands angst, so that it does not lead a person to faith, then that person is lost."[70]

Four years later Anti-Climacus makes the same analysis of human failure but in different language and conceptuality. He repeats Haufniensis' concept of the self as the unity of finitude and infinitude (the sensuous and the psychic) and the unity of the temporal and the eter-

---

68. An exploration of the infinite complexities of this event comprise the substance of the five hundred pages of my earlier volume, *Kierkegaard as Humanist.* There I spell out in great detail how each of the three dyads indicate very different aspects and functions of the human self as it becomes self-conscious and as it becomes itself in freedom. Obviously, each of the three dyads also plays a different role in human failure, which will become clear as we proceed on our present topic. In that volume, I also explain why I prefer to translate *forholder sig til sig selv* as "relates to itself" in place of the Hongs' translation, "relates itself to itself" (pp. 8–9).

69. But also see *Postscript* where, in speaking of the duality of abstract (objective) thinking and subjective thinking, Climacus says, "[T]o remain in existence in such a way that one understands one thing at one moment, something else the next, is not to understand oneself. But to understand extreme opposites together, and existing, to understand oneself in them is very difficult." And, earlier, he applies this principle to the duality of human finitude/infinitude: "The question is ... how can one simultaneously speak from the standpoint of the infinite and the finite and think the two together in the one moment? ... [W]here is the place that is the unity of the infinite and the finite, where one, who is simultaneously infinite and finite, can speak simultaneously of one's infinitude and one's finitude, and whether it is indeed possible to find this dialectically difficult place, which is nevertheless requisite?" *Postscript*, pp. 316, 156; (KW 12.1:354, 175); SV 10:55, 9:146; (7:307, 145).

70. *The Concept of Anxiety*, pp. 55, 68, 142; (KW 8:61, 76, 158–9); SV 6:153, 166, 237; (4:331, 345, 424).

nal, but he elaborates at some length a more sophisticated interpretation of the self as a dialectic of possibility (freedom) and necessity.[71] In this setting he develops the concept of the self not only as a synthesis but especially as a *relationship* of the elements of the three dyads. Then he is able to devise his definitive formula for the self as this very complex, triadic relation "which relates to itself." This act of "relating to itself," he says, "is freedom. The self is freedom." And this concept of relationship provides a new way of speaking about and of understanding failure or sin. Here he speaks not of angst predisposing to sin, nor of a possibility that exposes one to the danger of a fall. Rather, he says that "in the synthesis lies the possibility of disrelation [*Misforhold*]." That is to say, there is the built-in threat of a dissolution of the given unity of the sensuous (finitude) and the psychic (infinitude), of necessity and possibility, of the temporal and the eternal. Instead of "fall" and "sin," he speaks of the failure of a relationship, and the result is called despair. "Despair," he says, "is the disrelationship in a relation (within a synthesis), which relates to itself." And how widespread is this disease and its "sickness unto death"? He answers, "[N]o human being ever lived ... who has not despaired."[72]

Then he asks, "Where, then, does the despair come from?" His answer is that it comes only from "the relation in which the synthesis relates to itself," that is, from the self, because this capacity of the human self (freedom) is a gift of God "who constituted the human being [as] a relation" and "released it from his hand, as it were." That is, God gives every human being this freedom to become one's self, and therefore "upon it rests the responsibility for all despair at every moment of its existence." At this point Kierkegaard offers no analysis of the details of this human failure, except to say that it has many analogies to "dizziness."[73] In this way he is pointing the reader back to *The Concept of Angst* where he had formulated a key concept of essential, original human failure

71. See chapter 5 of *Kierkegaard as Humanist*.
72. *Sickness*, pp. 146, 148, 155; (KW 19:13, 15, 22); SV 15:73, 75, 81; (11:127, 130, 136). For my reasons for translating Kierkegaard's key definition of the self as a relation "which relates to itself" instead of the Hong translation, "that relates itself to itself," see my *Kierkegaard as Humanist*, pp. 8–9. Also, I translate *Misforhold* as "disrelation" (in preference to the Hongs' "misrelation") because in English the prefix mis- connotes "badly, wrongly, unfavorably," while dis- connotes "to do the opposite of, deprive of, exclude, expel." So dis- is more active and negative, while mis- is passive. *Misforhold* for Kierkegaard is not a misfortune or a mistake but is a broken relation traceable to human failure. This concept will be more fully developed in the next section (of this chapter) on despair.
73. Ibid., p. 149; (KW 19:16); SV 15:75; (11:130).

that is assumed throughout the rest of Kierkegaard's writings and journals. And that concept gives quite another perspective on what Kierkegaard means when he suggests that in an ultimate sense human failure is
an "essential constituent element of [God's] whole production" of human existence (see text at note 16 above).[74] He asserts (in *Sickness*) that
for the human-being "*to be able* to despair is an infinite advantage" because "it indicates infinite ... sublimity, that [the human-being] is
spirit," even though "*to be in* despair is not only the worst trouble and
misery – no, it is ruination [*Fortabelse*, that is: forfeiture, damnation, an-
nihilation]" (emphasis added).[75] Without the capacity to fail, the human-being would not have the capacity freely to become spirit or self,
that is, the capacity to *relate* freely and lovingly to God, to neighbor, and
to one's own self. But, Kierkegaard contends, because of the particular,
peculiar circumstances in which this option, this possibility, first presents itself to each human-being, no human being succeeds in achieving
mature self-actualization in faith/love except through the experience of
its opposite, and hence failure is "a constituent element of the whole
production."

Let us return, then, to *The Concept of Angst* and to "the moment" described in the opening paragraph of its section on "the fall." The moment occurs at the first awareness of the definite possibility of becoming
one's self, of achieving in actuality the synthesis of the dichotomies that
are inherent in the self. But first the self "must pervade [the synthesis]
differentially" so that, through the reflection made possible by the contrasts between the elements, the dialectical fearful-fascination of the
angst of innocence may become conscious of those dichotomies, and
hence is confronted with the horrendous task of holding them together
in harmony, a task that requires a decisive, qualitative choice (leap).[76]
At this point, Haufniensis says, one may say that the angst of innocence
is transformed by taking on the character of "dizziness." How does this
happen?

74. Later in *Sickness* he provides a new and very complex analysis of self-deception as the
source of a human being's continuing involvement in failure as sin against God, but he
does not apply this concept to the human being's initial step out of innocence into conscious and responsible failure because self-deception assumes an original knowledge of the
difference between good and evil.

75. *Sickness*, p. 148; (KW 19:15); SV 15:74; (11:129).

76. *The Concept of Angst*, p. 44; (KW 8:49); SV 6:142; (4:319). For the nature of reflection and its relation to consciousness see also *Johannes Climacus*, KW 7:169; *Papirer*, IV B
1:147–8.

As a purely psychical phenomenon, dizziness occurs when one's "eye happens to look [*skue*] down into the yawning abyss." But the source of this dizziness "is just as much one's eye as the abyss, because what if one had not stared [*stirret*] down?" Now we can draw the analogy for angst. In this moment "when the spirit [self] wants to posit the synthesis," and the self becomes aware that one must choose (freely) to do so in spite of angst's sense of possible failure, precisely then the failure occurs, namely: instead of keeping its "eye" focused on the task at hand, "freedom looks down into its own possibility." In other words, the self becomes enamored with its capacity of "being able," of being free to choose, *as such*, as a thing in itself rather than as a means to an end. But the human being comes to consciousness of its freedom only in the dynamic instability of the tension between finitude and infinitude, between possibility and necessity, between the temporal and the eternal. In this unstable and ambiguous situation, angst experiences "the dizziness of freedom," and "freedom succumbs [falls] in this dizziness." And then angst is no longer innocent. "In that moment everything is changed, and freedom, when it again rises, sees that it is guilty. Between these two moments lies the leap."[77]

We are faced with two questions. Just what is wrong with "freedom looking down into its own possibility"? Why and to what extent does the human being become "guilty" as a result?

For the answer to the first question, it must be noted that Kierkegaard uses the phrase "freedom's possibility" in two senses because "possibility" has two senses. On the one hand, "freedom's possibility is not being able to choose the good or the evil" but is the simple capacity of "*being able*" to choose, that is to say, possibility in the sense of an inherent potentiality. On the other hand, this potentiality does have a proper object: to choose to posit or become one's self, and hence to choose to risk an attempt to harmonize the conflicting elements of the synthesis, and hence to run the risk of failure. In this sense, "the possible corresponds exactly to the future. For freedom, the possible is the future." And in this relationship, the self's freedom has to do with the eternal, "because the future is the [first] incognito in which the eternal ... preserves its association with time."[78]

"Freedom looking down into its own possibility" clearly means "possibility" in the first sense, that is, becoming absorbed in one's given poten-

77. *The Concept of Angst*, p. 55; (KW 8:61); SV 6:152–153; (4:331).
78. Ibid., pp. 44, 82, 80; (KW 8:49, 91, 89); SV 6:142, 179, 177; (4:320, 361, 359).

tiality of freedom as such and for itself, without reference to the future and its task, and hence without reference to the eternal or to ethical decisions. In other words, in the very first stage or moment of reflection and self-consciousness, the self fails to hold together the dialectic of its given nature; as we will see in what follows, the self engages in "disrelation" by withdrawing its attention from the duality of its being (possibility *and* necessity, infinitude *and* finitude, the eternal *and* the temporal), and by staring at one side of the equation, at the one nearer and more congenial and less disturbing, namely, at one's immediate sense of *being able.* And this single moment and this simple, seemingly innocent act become the source and cause of that "dizziness" in which the self loses itself.[79]

Why is this seemingly innocent failure of attention so crucial, so destructive? Already in *Either/Or* (in the essay, "The Balance between the Aesthetic and the Ethical") Kierkegaard defines the problem. Ideally, the self posits itself in the act of *choosing* to be that "rich concretion, a multiplicity of qualities" which "the self contains;" and when "I myself choose absolutely, ... this absolute choice of myself is my freedom." Then a significant thing happens: "[O]nly when I have absolutely chosen myself have I posited an absolute difference: namely, the difference between good and evil. ... The good is because I will it, and otherwise it is not at all. This is the expression of freedom, and the same is also the case with evil. ... The good is the being-in-and-for-itself, posited by the being-in-and-for-itself, and this is freedom." But a few pages later, he warns that in this choice I can make a fatal error, that is, I may then assume, "Now I possess myself; ... I am the person I am." In this case "my basic-failure [*Grundfeilen*] would really be that I had not, strictly speaking, chosen myself, ... had not chosen in such a way that ... I remained in myself [i.e., in my duality]." Truly, "I have grasped myself in my eternal validity," and

---

79. The notion of dizziness runs throughout Kierkegaard's entire corpus. It appears already in *The Concept of Irony* where he notes Socrates' attraction to "the game of life" with its "dizziness" produced by the opposites of life/death, lightness/darkness, infinitely real/infinitely nothing, pain/pleasure, which opposites comprise "a syllogistic *aut/aut*" (the first appearance of "either/or" in Kierkegaard's writings) [p. 117; (KW 2:81; see also note 221 on p. 502); SV 1:131; (13:173)]. In *Either/Or:1* he says that boredom is "the demonic side of pantheism" and produces an infinite dizziness "like that which comes from looking down into a bottomless abyss" of "the nothing that interlaces existence" [p. 287; (KW 3:291); SV 2:268–269; (1:263)]. The most extensive treatment comes in *The Book on Adler*, written in 1846–47. Besides its key usage in *The Concept of Angst*, it appears incidentally but significantly in *Discourses on Imagined Occasions; Upbuilding Discourses in Various Spirits; Works of Love; The Sickness unto Death*; and *Judge for Yourself!*

"this overwhelms me with its fullness. Temporality vanishes for me," and I have a sense of bliss and security. Then comes the moment of fatal temptation: "if I now begin to stare [*stirre*] at it [i.e., my eternal validity] one-sidedly, the temporal asserts its claims. ... Everything comes to a standstill. ... I sink into contemplation, stare fixedly at myself, but this staring cannot fill up time. ... I have not chosen myself; like Narcissus, I have become infatuated with myself. Such a condition ... ends in suicide."[80]

The complexity of the destructive results of this original qualitative failure, as reflected in each of the three dyads that compose the identity of self, is not spelled out by Kierkegaard until his analysis of the forms of despair in *Sickness* (which we will come to in the next section, "The Human Condition: Despair"). But how this one-sided "staring" at "freedom's possibility" or one's "eternal validity" produces the "dizziness" in which one loses that freedom and validity was spelled out by Kierkegaard a year or so before *Sickness* in *The Book on Adler*. There he says that "in a physiological sense ... dizziness results when the eye has no fixed point on which to rest," and hence "the infinite, the unlimited, ... indeterminacy is the ground of dizziness ... because indeterminacy is contrary to the human-being's nature." By analogy, then,

spiritual dizziness ... may be occasioned by the fact that a human-being has so wandered wildly in the infinite that nothing finite can acquire substantial existence [*Bestaaen*] for him/her, that s/he can get no standard of measurement. This kind of dizziness consists rather in an excess of imagination, and inasmuch as one conceives of dizziness metaphorically in relation to the eye, one might call it *single-sighted dizziness*. ... Salvation from all dizziness, spiritually understood, is essentially to seek the ethical, which, by qualitative dialectic, disciplines and limits and thus sets the tasks for the individual.

And in so doing, "the ethical ... by qualitative dialectic knows well how to make the instant important as *decision*." All this is possible because "ethics lives and has its being [*er*] in the distinction between good and evil."[81]

80. *Either/Or:2*, pp. 227, 228; (KW 4:222, 224); SV 3:206; 208; (2:199, 200–01). I have continued the use of the first person "I" from the first quotation into the second quotation, thereby avoiding the awkward "he/she."

81. *The Book on Adler*, pp. 127–129, 132–133; *Papirer*, VII² B 235, pp. 161–162, 165–166, using variant B 261:24 on p. 298. The idea of going wild in an unrestricted exploration of the infinite through the imagination is picked up and elaborated as a central factor in Anti-Climacus' analysis of despair in *Sickness*.

However, in several different writings Kierkegaard makes clear that the failure involved in this single-sighted dizziness consists of much more than simply a contradiction of human nature as such or a violation of a purely human ethical standard of measurement. It essentially consists of a denial of the eternal as transcendent to and yet inherently conditional of human nature. It is a rebellion against God. In other words, the human failure that occurs when "freedom looks down into its own possibility" is to be understood ultimately not in the terms of the ethical sphere but of the ethical-religious sphere. Human failure consists not simply of a disrelationship in the relation of the self to itself or in the relation of self to another human being. Rather, the failure is "a disrelation in a relation which relates to itself and [which] has been established by an Other, so that the disrelation in that relation existing-for-itself [*for sig værende*] is also reflected infinitely in the relation to that Power which established it." And this negative statement is simply the reverse entailed by the earlier statement that the self is "a derived relation" that "in relating to itself relates to an other," and hence the self is unable "to be in equilibrium and rest by itself, but only ... by relating to that which has established the entire relation."[82]

This point is already made in *The Concept of Angst* but not in theological language. Haufniensis spells out what Anti-Climacus assumes, namely, that the human self is composed of two different yet interdependent syntheses: "the human-being is a synthesis of psyche and body, but s/he is also a *synthesis of the temporal and the eternal.*" But "the latter synthesis ... is formed differently from the former," because it was said that the synthesis of the psychical and the sensuous dimensions is actually accomplished only in a third, "and the spirit [self] is the third." But in the synthesis of the temporal and the eternal, "where is the third? And if there is no third [factor], there really is no synthesis." His answer is "faith," but this is only indirectly said in the last chapter as a kind of postscript to the book. However, this answer is specifically and clearly formulated in *Fragments* as the companion volume that was published at the same time by Kierkegaard.[83] And Haufniensis also makes the point that the two syntheses are inseparable in that the latter synthesis "is not another synthesis but is the expression for the first synthesis ... of

---

82. *Sickness*, p. 146–147,; (KW 19:13–14); SV 15:73–74; (11:128).

83. See *Fragments*, pp. 59f., 67, 73, 101; (KW 7:47f, 54, 59, 81f.); SV 6:47, 52, 56, 74; (4:214f., 220, 224f., 244f.). This material is analyzed in *Kierkegaard as Humanist*, pp. 305–09.

psyche and body that is sustained by spirit." In other words, the achievement of the unity within the human self requires that the self be in unity with the transcendent eternal.[84]

Soon after these two works, in a discourse "At the Graveside," Kierkegaard derides the common attempt to avoid the true crisis of death by speaking of it as a place of "rest" and quiet "sleep," a "hiding place" from the world of woes. This attitude is nothing but "depression's escape from life, and in this way to be unwilling to fear death is rebellion." Death's touted equality "is in nothing, in annihilation." Such a mood "is a cowardly craving of depression to want to become dizzy in the emptiness, and to seek the final diversion in this dizziness; it is envy in rebellion against God to want to damage one's soul." And a year or so later, in a discourse entitled "The Gospel of Sufferings," Kierkegaard is noting that "in daily life a person more or less lives in the stipulations of human criteria – whereas the fundamental relation measures the person with God. But that does not mean that the fundamental relation is absent." So "when confusion is about to intrude, when impatience wants to stare [*stirre*] itself dizzy at a particular thing and thereby finally turn everything around – then the fundamental relation asserts itself. When impatience wants to rebel, as it were, against God, wants to quarrel with God as one quarrels with one's equal by insisting on being in the right, then something else happens; then the fundamental relation rebels against the impatient one and teaches her/him that in relation to God a human being is essentially guilty, thus *always* guilty."[85]

These passages, clearly, are not describing the original, qualitative failure and its dizziness, but they do indicate that in Kierkegaard's mind the dizziness and confusion that accompanies the attempt of human freedom to be totally self-determining and self-contained signifies a rebellion against and a denial of every human being's essential, given, inescapable relationship with and dependence on the eternal, on God. In this "moment" the dreaming self comes awake (1) by being able to reflect about the dichotomies of its inherent synthesis, (2) by becoming aware that it is able and eager to achieve that synthesis by its own decision and choice, (3) at the same time being frightened by the implicit possibility of failure and hence becoming aware of the radical distinction between good and

84. The material in this paragraph from *The Concept of Angst* is from pp. 76, 79; (KW 8:85, 88); SV 6:173, 176; (4:355, 358).

85. *Upbuilding Discourses in Various Spirits*, pp. 89–90 of trans. by Aldworth & Ferrie; (KW 15:285–286); SV 11:264; (8:367).

evil, (4) yet being overwhelmed by its infatuation with its own freedom's possibility as "being-*for*-itself," (5) then becoming confused and dizzy as the self's inherent finitude/temporality reminds the self that it is not "being-*in*-and-for-itself"[86], (6) finally, making the fatal error (failure) in this moment of crisis by not immediately turning its attention ("eye") back to the eternal but rather "lays hold of finiteness to support itself" and thus "falls."[87]

As we have heard, "Freedom succumbs in this dizziness. ... In that very moment everything is changed, and freedom, when it again rises, sees that it is guilty. Between these two moments lies the leap. ... The one who becomes guilty in angst becomes as ambiguously guilty as it is possible to become." This is the case because "he who becomes guilty through angst is indeed innocent, for it was not he himself but angst, a foreign power, that laid hold of him. ... And yet he is guilty, because he sank in angst, which he yet loved even as he feared it. There is nothing in the world more ambiguous."[88] In other words, qualitative human failure occurs in a psychic-physical condition which was not of our choosing and which cannot be escaped, a condition of volatile, complex instability that holds great promise but also great danger. For us it is a condition of fearful fascination, both sympathetic and antipathetic. But at a certain stage in our psychic-physical development, the very complexity and instability of our condition, of our given nature, open up to our consciousness an awareness of certain options and of our capacity to choose.

Even at this point, however, Kierkegaard says that "the egoistic infinity of possibility ... does not tempt like a choice but ensnaringly disquiets [*ængster*] with its sweet anxiousness [*Beængstelse*]." So he says (twice) that I (or "freedom") sink, succumb, fall (*synke, segne*), or faint (*daane*). On the other hand, he insists that I "leap," that is, I make a "decision." Yet, whatever the ambiguity, I end up with a profound sense of guilt, of being in the wrong, because I misused by freedom in turning my attention solely to my own "infinity of possibility." And, as we have heard, this amounts to "quarreling with God ... by insisting on being in the right" but ending up with being taught that "a human being is essentially guilty" (note 85 above). Kierkegaard could have used the conversation between Eve and the serpent to make this point, because even though

86. See section on "God as Being-in-and-for-itself" in chapter 2 above.
87. *The Concept of Angst*, p. 55; (KW 8:61); sv 6:152; (4:331).
88. Ibid., pp. 55, 39; (KW 8:61, 43); sv 6:152, 137; (4:331, 314).

he says that he is not able to "connect any definite thought with the serpent," he does go on to say that it is not God who tempts but "each person is tempted by oneself" (quoting Jas 1:13–14). If one assumes the latter point, then the temptation took place as a conversation of Eve with herself as follows (Gen 3:1–7).[89]

Eve must have gotten bored with the easy life, and so she began to review the rules of the game. She asks herself, "Did God say, 'You shall not eat of any tree of the garden'?" Just the asking of this question is itself a sign of mistrust. And of course she remembers that God did say that there was one tree they must not eat of "*lest you die.*" Then comes the fateful and fatal temptation: she muses, "Will I really die? Or will I be like God, knowing good and evil?" So, according to the account, she convinced herself that coming to this knowledge was "good" and "desirable" and "a delight." And within this naive and relatively innocent self-deception lies hidden the more profound and cataclysmic deceit that the human being has life in itself, that this entails the power and right to define good and evil for itself, with the implication that the human being has unrestricted autonomy and freedom. In Kierkegaard's words, the human being is unconsciously, by implication, claiming to be not only a conditional "being-*for*-itself" (which it is) but an unconditional "being-*in*-and-for-itself" (which it is not). And in so doing the human being is declaring its independence of the source of its existence, is effecting a qualitative and disastrous "disrelation" with its creator.

89. Ibid., p. 43; (KW 8:48); SV 6:141; (4:318–319). Kierkegaard seems to have considered this use of the serpent but rejected it, as is indicated in his deletion of a draft-sentence, which was preserved by Kierkegaard and is found in *Papirer* V B 53:11, with a translation provided in KW 8:185. Admittedly, interpreting the serpent as part of the "language" of innocence is more difficult because of the Genesis account's description of it as one of the "wild creatures" of the Garden and because of God's separate curse on the serpent (Gen 3:1, 14–15). But to attribute separate existence to the serpent as a "creature" of God in the original Garden is totally contradictory of Kierkegaard's view of God, as well as of the general biblical view of God, as sheer goodness and love. On the other hand, it is imperative, for Kierkegaard's view of God's relationship to the human creature, to acknowledge the possibility of a negative, erroneous conversation as going on within and being entertained by Eve/Adam, because as we have seen, Kierkegaard believed that God's pure and unqualified goodness contains within its eternal selfhood an essential, ontological distinction between what God is and what God is not, between what is good and evil (see chapter 2, note 40, above and the text immediately before and after it). And the reflection of this distinction within the human being created in God's image is surely the grounds of Kierkegaard's belief that the inherent human capacity for failure is a "constituent element in the whole production" of God's creation.

It must be stressed again, however, that Kierkegaard views this qualitative failure, in the initial attempt at achieving the actualization of the potential self (the unification of the dichotomous synthesis), as occurring at the outermost edge of the angst of innocence, when the self first comes to possess that capacity of reflection that produces self-consciousness. So, as we just heard, the infinity of freedom's possibility at this point "does not tempt like a [clear-cut, conscious, informed] choice." Indeed, "the [first, qualitative] fall into sin always takes place in weakness," because "angst is a feminine weakness in which freedom faints [*daaner*]."[90] But *how*, then, does the self (freedom), when it arises again from the fall, recognize that it is guilty? Is it just some intuitive feeling, as vague and ambiguous as the "decision" (leap) to stare down into freedom's possibility? Kierkegaard's answer to this question marks the beginning of the fourth and final stage of that complex process of transition from the infant's/child's sense of peaceful immediacy to full consciousness of adult selfhood. First, that immediacy was disturbed by the sense of self as an undefined nothing which begets angst (p. 165 above). Then innocence began to speak to itself, hearing the words of permission, prohibition, and judgment (p. 167 above). Then freedom succumbed in dizziness when it looked down into its own possibility, and arose guilty (pp. 170, 175 above). And now finally, Kierkegaard says, the self is no longer dreaming but is rudely startled awake, not by just a vague feeling of guilt but by undeniable indications that something has radically gone wrong. What are they? He answers that there are three concrete, interconnected signs that the individual has *attempted* the qualitative leap in order to posit the synthesis, and yet has *failed* to become in actuality the self that one has been in potentiality and possibility from the beginning. They are: sensuousness as sexuality manifests itself as sinful; temporality becomes sinful; egoism as self-concern becomes sinful.

The key to this answer lies in the point we have heard before, namely, that in order for the dreaming self to come awake and posit the synthesis of the sensuous and the psychic, the self "must first pervade [the synthesis] differentiatingly, and the ultimate [point] of the sensuous is precisely the *sexual*. ... The synthesis is posited as a contradiction *first of all* in sexuality" (emphases added). So, in *The Concept of Angst*, at the beginning of this extended fourth stage in coming to consciousness, Kierkegaard explores the fundamental and primary role that sexuality plays in this event. He mentions, without development, that temporality also acquires

90. Ibid., p. 55; (кw 8:61); sv 6:153; (4:331).

a sense of sinfulness, but he does not go on to discuss what the ultimate expression of the psychic is as sinfulness, namely, the hubris of the claim of self-autonomy and absolute freedom. He believes that the sense of our failure and guilt comes immediately in the form of regarding sexuality as sinful, but the awareness of the sinfulness of self-centered and self-asserting egoism only comes gradually with a more mature development of self-consciousness. In *The Concept of Angst* Kierkegaard (as Haufniensis) is primarily concerned with "the state that precedes sin and ... predisposes more or less to sin," and with the very first concrete manifestation of sin.[91]

It is left to Kierkegaard as Anti-Climacus to explore the mature forms of sinfulness under the category of despair. He, indeed, makes the point that the ultimate form of despair is precisely, by a "misuse [*Misbrug*] of the eternal within the self, to will in despair to be oneself," that is to say, on its own and by itself because it assumes that the eternal belongs to one's own being. "[S]evering the self from any relation to a power that has established it, ... the self in despair wants to be master of itself or to create itself, to make one's self into the self *it* wants to be" (emphasis added).[92] But before we go on to look at his characterization of the failed life as a life of "despair," we are finally in a position to clarify at what age in human development Kierkegaard assumes that this crucial event of original human failure occurs. And the key to this issue lies in what happens to our sexuality.

Kierkegaard and Freud agree on certain basics about sexuality. About fifty years before Freud begins to focus on infantile sexuality and its impact on one's total life, Kierkegaard writes, "The whole question of the significance of the sexual, as well as its significance in the particular spheres, has undeniably been answered poorly until now." He condemns the "witticisms" of the stage for "turning the sexual into a joke," and he condemns the "admonishments" of the pulpit because its "rigorism made life melancholy and made sexuality into sinfulness," while the usual alternative of silence ruined "many a young life ... because no mention was made of the sexual at all." He insists that "psychology is what we need, and, above all, thorough knowledge of human life as well as sympathy for its interests." Then he warns: "until this [task] is

---

91. Ibid., pp. 44, 68; (KW 8:49, 76); SV 6:142, 166; (4:219, 345). A brief treatment of egoism in *The Concept of Angst* may be found on pp. 69–71; (KW 8:77–79); SV 6:167–168; (4:346–348).

92. *Sickness*, pp. 201–202; (KW 19:67–68); SV 15:122; (11:178–179).

resolved there can be no question of completing a Christian view of life."93

While Kierkegaard never mentions infantile sexuality, he explicitly "assumes the presence of the sexual difference before the fall," that is, in the state of childhood innocence, because he sees the body and all its forms of sensuousness as integral to the human individual "synthesis," and "the ultimate [form] of the sensuous is precisely the sexual." So the child has a kind of "knowledge of the generic difference," as evidenced in its sense of modesty or shame, but not "in relation to its other," not as "a relation to a generic difference, which is to say, the sexual urge [*Drift*]" or "sensuous lust [*Lyst*]." So, just as the presence of the self's potentiality in innocence evokes angst because it is an undefined "nothing," so too the "prodigious ambiguity" of the child's sexuality evokes angst as a sense of shame about an undefined "nothing."94

In this context Kierkegaard repeatedly asserts that sensuousness or sexuality in itself is not sinfulness, but it becomes so only at the moment in which the human being attempts the synthesis and fails. This essential failure of the human being as *self* has repercussions throughout the structure of the self, first in each factor of the synthesis (psyche and body) and then in every relationship in which it stands: to itself, to the Power that established it, to other humans. So "only at the moment that sin is posited is the generic [sexual] difference posited as a drive [*Drift*]." And although "sensuousness is [not] sinfulness," in the same moment "sin makes it into that [*dertil*]." Precisely because the human being is "a synthesis of psyche and body sustained by spirit," so "one [event] can ... have two consequences," namely, "sin came into the world and ... sexuality was posited; the one is truly [*skal være*] inseparable from the other." And this inseparable connection will follow every person throughout life. So Kierkegaard follows up his statement that it is first of all in sexuality that "the synthesis is posited as a contradiction"

93. *The Concept of Angst*, p. 60; (KW 8:67); SV 6:158; (4:337); but mostly from a draft version of this page as found in *Papirer* V B 53:29, pp. 118–119; translation in KW 8:190–191. In this draft Kierkegaard vows "forthwith to draw up a number of sketches that will exhibit the prodigious conflicts that may arise in this area." To my knowledge Kierkegaard never fulfilled this intention. There are several other brief passages about sexuality in *The Concept of Angst*, but they hardly comprise the sketches promised.

94. Ibid., pp. 44, 61; (KW 8:48, 68); SV 6:142, 159; (4:319, 338). In the pages following the second reference, Kierkegaard makes an interesting analysis of shame and compares it with the Greek sense of the erotic as innocent and urges us to be more Greek in our attitude toward the sexuality of childhood.

by saying, "like every contradiction it [i.e., sexuality] is a task," and the "history" of every individual's task "begins at that same moment."[95]

For Kierkegaard, then, the "moment" in which the self comes "awake" – that is, becomes self-conscious in its freedom and fails to achieve actualization of the synthesis (as described in the five-dimensional event at note 87 above) – coincides precisely with the age at which a human being becomes sexually aware of the generic differentiation in which it stands, at which one is powerfully motivated by one's sexual urge and lust in relation to an "other." For Kierkegaard it is only in this moment that "self-consciousness" and "freedom" take on their definitive meaning and come into being and operation in their truly authentic form. And it is only in this moment that feelings of "guilt" are appropriate as connected with one's acknowledgement of being in the wrong or having done something wrong for which essential responsibility is traceable to one's own self alone. As in the biblical story, the first manifestation of this qualitative human failure is: "they knew that they were naked," and tried to cover their bodies with leaves. Then with a guilty conscience, "they hid themselves from the presence of the Lord God." (Genesis 3:7–8) Before this age of sexual awareness, a child's sense of self is largely defined by external relations, and the line between the child's fantasies and the external world, between inner and outer, between psyche and body, is blurred. It is only as such distinctions and contrasts become consciously possible that *self*-consciousness becomes possible, in the sense of "self" that Kierkegaard believes the term deserves and demands.

Freud certainly agrees with this timetable on the issue of sexual development. He accepts that there is almost no direct evidence for infantile sexuality, because "for most, though not all, of us, the earliest years, up to the sixth or eighth are buried in amnesia" (Wollheim, pp. 111–12). At that age "infantile sexuality ... undergoes ... a massive repression and the period of latency sets in." This period continues until the onset of puberty when "with the revival of sexuality the adolescent is presented with the problem of object-choice at the very point at which it was broken off nine or ten years previously." But now with a qualitative difference: one is "in command of 'the sexual products' which gives a physical urgency to [the] situation," and even more notable, one must find a "love object" other than one's father and mother, and one might add,

95. Ibid., pp. 71, 66, 43–44; (KW 8:80, 73, 48); SV 6:169, 164, 141–142; (4:349, 343, 319).

other than one's own self who now finds narcissistic auto-eroticism still intriguing but ultimately unfulfilling. (pp. 119–21)

However, it is not clear from Wollheim's account (pp. 186–90) whether Freud agrees with Kierkegaard's assumption that authentic self-consciousness, with a sense of responsibility and guilt (failure and sin), emerges simultaneously with the new sexual consciousness that arises in puberty and beyond. Kierkegaard would certainly agree with Freud that "the origins of the ego lie in perception" because "it is through perception that awareness develops of the difference between the outer world and the ego." He would agree that two types of perception can be distinguished by their fundamental "nature," namely, "external" and "internal" perceptions (roughly, Kierkegaard's more sophisticated differentiation between objective reflection and subjective reflection). And he would strongly agree that "awareness of this division contributes to our awareness of self," because "in making the distinction between the outer world and itself, the ego must not be thought of as mere neutral or passive observer. On the contrary, it is through making this distinction, through developing an awareness of itself over and against everything else, that the ego develops."

But then Freud develops some other ideas that confuse the picture for Kierkegaard. Agreeably, Freud asserts that "without a *concept* [of the ego] neither self-awareness nor, ultimately, existence itself could be attributed to the ego" (emphasis added). But then he goes on to insist that, in addition to "a period at which there was no ego," there is also "a period at which there was no concept of the ego. Indeed, the distinction between auto-eroticism and narcissism requires there to be a moment before which the concept does not exist, and after which it does exist, in the *infant's* mind" (emphasis added). What Freud means by a "concept" existing "in" an infant's mind is not clear in the materials provided by Wollheim. If it amounts to no more than what Kierkegaard means when he attributes an unconscious and undefined but disturbing presence of the self's potentiality in the given structure of a human being from its beginning, then there is no apparent conflict between Kierkegaard and Freud on the presence of such a concept.

For Kierkegaard, however, the conscious entertainment of a "concept" requires and assumes that measure of reflection about the dichotomy of inner and outer, of subjective and objective, that comes only with consciousness of being a *self* as a maturing adolescent, indeed, a self that must be consciously, deliberately and willingly *chosen* by the individual. As we have seen in the earlier section on Freud in this chapter, becoming one's self involves, for Kierkegaard, the crucial element of a free decision that resembles a "leap." And there is no trace of this element in Freud's analysis. Rather, Freud is more interested in exploring the thesis that significantly informs most of his thinking, namely, "[t]he Ego is first and foremost a bodily Ego." This thesis results in the theory of the "sexualization of thought," because "the corporeal concepts that the ego employs in its growing self-awareness will reflect the dominant organization of the libido. Initially they relate to the mouth, then to the anus, then to the genitals." In this way "sexuality and thinking can become equated with the same bodily activity – and hence one with the other." From this perspective, self-awareness obviously begins its gradual development in infancy.[96]

Our conclusion here is: if other psychologies wish to speak of self-awareness and responsible actions and guilt as occurring in infants and children, then they simply mean something else than what Kierkegaard means by these terms at the adult level. As we have seen earlier, Kierkegaard of course recognizes that children are conscious in a general sense, and that even in their state of innocence their consciousness is pervasively and profoundly disturbed by an ambiguous angst in which one is both enticed and repelled by the dim adumbration of the possibility of becoming a self which is as yet an undefined nothing. He insists that the sexual revolution that occurs in puberty and adolescence signals a radical and total transformation in self-awareness, and that only then do his own peculiar concepts of self-consciousness, responsibility, and guilt come into play.

Finally, let us remember that, for Anti-Climacus, despair may be, should be, "the thoroughfare to faith," and that in this sense human failure and the fall into sin (despair) comprise "an essential element in the

96. Two additional notes on Freud. (1) As noted in the earlier section, Freud simply avoided exploring the capacities and energies peculiar to the ego as such. Wollheim refers to "our awareness of *self*" and to "the ego's *self*-awareness" (p. 188; epmhasis added), but nowhere does he clarify how self-awareness differs from and transcends ego-awareness. It is probably true that, as Freud himself said, "The Ego is first and foremost a bodily ego," (p. 189) but it is equally true that the ego is ultimately "aimed" to be a *self*-ego. (2) In the material referred to above about the shift in object-choice at the time of puberty, one of the limitations of Freud's entire conceptuality on sexuality and the ego becomes obvious, namely, that it applies almost wholly to the male. This is obviously true of the Oedipus complex, but here also the shift in object-choice is said to occur because "now *he* is in command of 'the sexual products,'" and because "the *male* adolescent ... must detach his libidinal wishes from his mother, ... must reconcile himself to his father, and ... must try to find a love object similar to, but not identical with, his mother" (p. 121, emphasis added).

whole production" of God's dealings with human beings.[97] Haufniensis makes this point indirectly by two interesting statements. While discussing the fact that sin makes sensuousness sinful, he says, "to speak foolishly for a moment and by way of accommodation, let us suppose that Adam had not sinned: then the sexual would never have come into being as a drive." And while making the point that sin also makes temporality sinful, he says, "to speak foolishly and by way of accommodation, had Adam not sinned, he would in the same moment have passed over into eternity."[98] But nowhere does he make the corresponding statement that, if Adam had not sinned, he would automatically have achieved the harmonious synthesis of the sensuous and the psychic, and hence would have become his potential self without any trouble.

Kierkegaard cannot make this latter statement, because we have heard him stipulate that "in order to posit the synthesis [the self] must *first* pervade [the synthesis] differentiatingly," that is, disjunctively or separately (*adskillende*). This exploration of each of the self's given polarities by and in itself is necessary for the kind of reflection that is crucial for becoming self, namely, reflection that, first, produces self-consciousness and then, secondly, sets the task of becoming one's self freely and hence not automatically. But this exploration also opens up the possibility of a divisive disjunction within, instead of the desired unification of, the elements of the synthesis, of the self. And as we have heard several times above, Kierkegaard believes that this necessary differentiation takes place in a context of inherent instability and weakness, at a point in the self's development when the self's awakening occurs in a state of riotous confusion and commotion of sensuous drives and passions and of exalting spiritual visions of infinite and eternal possibilities.

Furthermore, consideration of "possibility," which must be chosen and enacted, opens one's consciousness to the "future" and to the future in relation to one's "past." And "future" reveals itself as the incognito of the "eternal," so that the human-being becomes aware of the dialectic of time and eternity. In other words, temporality, time, proves to be as much a constituent element or factor in the given, created human-nature as are finite/infinite and possibility/necessity. Without temporality, becoming one's self would not be a task involving the definitive element of freedom; there would be an immediate and automatic trans-

97. *Sickness*, pp. 201, 207; (KW 19:67, 74); SV 15:122, 128; (11:178, 185).
98. *The Concept of Angst*, pp. 71, 83; (KW 8:79, 93); SV 6:168–169, 180; (4:348, 363).

ference from innocence into non-sexual eternity. Stated in still another way, God created the human-being in such a way that becoming self requires time, involves a task, because to achieve the intended relation of love with God and neighbor, the human-being has to become fully conscious and has to enter into the love relationship freely, and this condition exposes human beings to the possibility of failure in a context so unstable that failure is unavoidable and has to be dealt with as part of the maturing process. Indeed, the need and the task of *dealing with* this inevitable failure is of ultimate and central importance in the process of becoming self – if the self is not to be lost "eternally."

In other words, this exposure of the human-being, by God, to these risks and dangers is required and motivated by God's own desire and intention: to confer being on an other in such a way that that being possesses personhood or selfhood for itself (in the image of God) and hence is able to return God's love freely and (in one sense) equally. As Climacus says in *Postscript* and as Kierkegaard repeats in *Works of Love*, "not even God relates directly to a derived spirit (and this is the wondrousness of creation: not to produce something that is nothing in relation to the Creator, but to produce something that is something ...); even less can one human being relate in this way to another *in truth*. ... With regard to the essential truth, a direct relation between spirit and spirit is unthinkable. If such a relation is assumed, it actually means that one party has ceased to be spirit."[99]

To put it succinctly: no sin, then no sex; no sin, then no time; no sin, then no task; therefore, no "self" as conceived in the Christian vision of this human possibility, no self in the image of God. And the depth and complexity of sin's threat and peril are only hinted at in Haufniensis' analysis of human failure. Kierkegaard's full and final plumbing of these depth's comes four years later in Anti-Climacus' concept of despair.

THE HUMAN CONDITION: DESPAIR

1 Despair as a New Category

In his depiction of universal human failure as ending in universal despair, Kierkegaard as theologian comes to a radical alteration of the views of Kierkegaard as humanist. From the humanist perspective, a person

99. *Postscript*, pp. 220–221; (KW 12.1:246–247); SV 9:206; (7:207–208); cf. *Works of Love*, p. 253; SV 12:261; (9:253).

does indeed need a relation with the eternal, but only to be enabled to resolve one's sense of total guilt-consciousness, which simply means one's sense of inadequacy to fulfill the ethical demands of the absolute on our own. As theologian, Kierkegaard comes to perceive that the qualitative and universal human failure (as described by Haufniensis) has as its most profound consequence a deformation of human nature which is best described as "despair." This new understanding of the human condition came to him in the experience of a radical transformation both of his own self-understanding and of his relatively optimistic view of human nature, both of which came as a result of his sufferings during the *Corsair* affair,[100] and more particularly, as the product of his reflections on the meaning of suffering in the light of new meditations on Scripture and the Christian faith.

The outcome of these reflections was an unexpected second authorship (beginning with *Upbuilding Discourses in Various Spirits*). In retrospect, in an article published in *Fatherland* in May of the last year of his life, Kierkegaard declares that "I have finished and left behind me" the first authorship that climaxed in Climacus' *Concluding Unscientific Postscript*, in order, he says, "to get further forward in the direction of bringing to light [*opdage*] the Christianity of the New Testament." To say that he "left behind" his previous writings is an exaggeration to indicate how radically new he considered the insights of the second (Christian) group of writings.[101] As has been repeatedly shown in *Kierkegaard as Humanist*, numerous ideas, formulations and phrasings from the first authorship have been brought forward and specifically used or assumed throughout the entirety of the second authorship. In another article in *Fatherland* just a month before the one above, Kierkegaard himself lumps *Concluding Postscript* together with *The Sickness unto Death* and *Practice in Christianity* as sources which his critics should consult if they want to understand his concept of "The Moment." And the year after writing

100. See my brief account of the *"Corsair* affair" in *Kierkegaard as Humanist*, p. 191, but especially see Howard and Edna Hong's historical introduction in their volume on *The Corsair Affair*, KW 13; they also supply very pertinent comments in the historical introduction to *Upbuilding Discourses in Various Spirits*, KW 15, and in the historical introduction to *Postscript*, KW 12.2, pp. xi–xiii.

101. See especially *Journals*, 6238, 6356, 6361, 6501; *Papirer*, IX A 227, X[1] A 138, 147, X[2] A 66, where Kierkegaard specifically expresses his own wonderment at the new insights he came to, especially in *Sickness* and *Practice*. In many other journal entries, he also expresses his wonderment at his own dramatic deepening in Christian faith so that for the first time in his life he could say with some confidence that he was a pilgrim on the path of Christian faith, though not at all anywhere near the ideal described in these two books.

Sickness and *Practice*, he is defining, in a journal entry, what he means by designating "the Christian-religious [as] a unique sphere" and adds parenthetically, "as I have so often pointed out in *Concluding Postscript.*"[102]

Nevertheless, as we shall see in the next chapter, in the post-*Corsair* writings Kierkegaard did get "a new string on my instrument" and claimed a disclosure (in *Sickness*) of "crucial categories" which, he felt, enabled him "to illuminate Christianity on a scale greater than I had ever dreamed possible" (see note 101 above). One of those crucial categories certainly was that of "despair."

Some have claimed that Kierkegaard's new analysis of sin as despair was not just a "radical transformation" but a total rejection and denial of his pre-*Corsair* depiction of human nature. They claim that Kierkegaard as a person was a sexually frustrated manic-depressive who was totally alienated from the human community, and that, reflecting his own life, his vision of Christianity ended in one of terror, horror, and madness. In contradiction to this view, it was promised in *Kierkegaard as Humanist* that in this present volume "it will be shown that Kierkegaard's central understanding of Christian faith does not end in a vision of terror and madness and despair but in a positive, liberating, and creative experience of loving forgiveness and renewal."[103] The burden of proof will be faced in the next chapter, but much depends on correctly depicting and understanding Kierkegaard's concept of despair.

Before we begin that depiction, however, one question must be asked: how much of his analysis and depiction of despair in *Sickness* is accessible to what he calls "the natural human-being"? In his introduction he seems to give a blunt, unqualified answer. He says that "the natural human-being ... is ignorant of what is truly horrifying," whereas "Christianity has discovered a miserable condition that humanity as such does not know exists. ... Only the Christian knows what is meant by the sickness unto death. As a Christian, one gains a courage that the natural human-being does not know, and he gains this courage by learning to fear something even more horrifying" (that is, to fear the sickness of the spirit that is a perpetual dying, rather than the physical sickness that is ended and escaped in death). Later he adds, "[T]o be aware of [*opmærksom*, observant of] this sickness is the Christian's superiority over the natural

102. For a translation see Walter Lowrie's *Kierkegaard's Attack upon Christendom*, pp. 52, 40–41; sv 19:69, 53; (14:76, 42–43).

103. *Kierkegaard as Humanist*, p. 81n73; for a discussion of the negative views see pp. 79–81, especially n73, and pp. 309–310.

human-being; to be cured of this sickness is the Christian's blessedness." And how is one cured (or healed: *helbrede*)? In a prayer that Kierkegaard wrote as a part of the preface of *Sickness* but did not include, he first addresses "Father in heaven" and prays: "[G]rant that each one of us may rightly become aware [*opmærksomme*] of which sickness is the sickness unto death, and of how we are all sick in this way." Then he addresses "you, our Lord Jesus Christ, you who came to the world to heal those who suffer from this sickness: ... help us in this sickness to turn to you to be healed." Finally he addresses "you, God the Holy Spirit, you who come to us for help in our sickness, if we genuinely [*oprigtigt*] want to be healed: be with us so that we ... remain with [the physician, i.e., Jesus]. ... For ... only when we are with him are we saved from the sickness!"[104]

In this rare Trinitarian prayer, Kierkegaard is clearly saying that human beings become "rightly aware" of true sin as despair only "before God," and that we become healed and saved "only when we are with [the physician]," that is, with Jesus Christ present in the power of Holy Spirit. So it is not surprising that later (in his section on "Despair is Sin") he bluntly asserts that "if sin is ignorance [as Socrates says], then sin does not really exist." And "Christianly, this is quite in order. ... It is specifically the concept of sin ... that most decisively differentiates Christianity from paganism," because "neither paganism nor the natural human-being knows what sin is; ... there has to be a revelation from God to show what sin is." In other words, "the pagan and natural human-being have the merely human self as their criterion," and so "the sin of paganism was essentially despairing ignorance of God, [ignorance] of existing before God. ... Therefore, ... in the strictest sense the pagan did not sin." It would be "a dangerous objection to Christianity if paganism had a definition of sin that Christianity would have to acknowledge as correct." Why? Because "a pagan, the natural human-being, is very willing to admit that sin exists, but this 'before God' that actually makes sin into sin, this is too much for the [human-being]."[105]

Taken at face value, these assertions imply that only Jews and Christians know what sin/despair truly is because only they are "before God," and that only Christians are healed because only in Jesus Christ has God provided a healer, and therefore only Christians, who by definition are

104. Ibid., pp. 145, 148; (KW 19:8, 15); SV 15:70, 74; (11:123, 129); *Papirer*, VIII² B 143; translation in KW 19:141 or *Journals*, 3423.

105. *Sickness*, pp. 220, 211–212, 218; (KW 19:89–90, 81, 87); SV 15:142, 134, 140; (11:200–201, 193, 199).

"with Christ," are "saved." And while Kierkegaard was writing *Sickness* and *Practice* (in 1848), and especially as he mounted his "attack upon Christendom" in the 1850s, he seems increasingly to suggest that very few of those who take the name of "Christian" really come to know God in Jesus Christ, confess their sin "before God," experience reconciliation in faith, and walk in the way that Jesus has opened up and for which he set the example.

The radicalness of this stance, however, is modified by the fact that Kierkegaard was very aware that in *Sickness* and *Practice* (taken together) Anti-Climacus was presenting Christian faith in its absolute, pristine form, which admittedly is not to be found fulfilled in anyone (certainly not in Kierkegaard himself, as he frequently insisted). Yet he also insisted that his presentation was not an "exaggeration" but simply the Christianity of the New Testament, which, contrary to what was being preached in his day, is precisely "God's word … for us." Hence "it is important that the ideal picture of a Christian be held up in every generation, that it be illuminated particularly in relation to the errors of the times."[106] And in a series of journal entries during the month prior to the publication of *Sickness* (July 30, 1849), he reflects about the character of Anti-Climacus and his writings. He notes that Climacus (author of *Fragments* and *Postscript*) "said he was not a Christian. Anticlimacus is the opposite extreme: a Christian on an extraordinary level – but I myself manage to be only a very simple Christian, … higher than Johannes Climacus, lower than Anti-Climacus" – hence "I use a pseudonym for it." But Anti-Climacus plays an indispensable role because "Christendom does indeed greatly need to hear the voice of such a judge," and "anyone who cannot present ideality so high so that he is judged by it himself must have a poor understanding of it."[107]

Furthermore, Kierkegaard gives some indications (in *Sickness*) of quite another perspective, which continues to assert the uniqueness of the Christian experience of God and yet does not see it as condemning the rest of the human race to damnation or annihilation, or even to total ignorance of one's selfhood and one's despair. He readily admits that this Christian exclusivity poses a very "strange dilemma [*Vanskelighed*]."

106. *Journals*, 6677; x³ A 434 (n.d., 1850); *Armed Neutrality*, p. 37; *Papirer*, x⁵ B 107, p. 292. This brief essay or declaration was written just after Kierkegaard finished *Sickness* and *Practice* in December 1848, but it was never published.

107. *Journals*, 6431, 6433, 6442; *Papirer*, x¹ A 510, 517, 536. On this point one should read the entire series of entries in *Papirer* from A 510–A 567, from which H. and E. Hong provide a selection of the more important ones in *Journals* 6431–6451.

According to that view, "Christianity regards everything as under sin; we have tried to depict the Christian point of view as rigorously as possible – and then this peculiar outcome emerges, this odd conclusion that sin is not found at all in paganism but only in Judaism and Christendom, and there again very seldom." Assuming this lack of a sense of sin and despair in an extreme form, one could even say that such humans live "in a kind of innocence." On the other hand, some pagans have enough "depth" and "ethical qualities" to have a limited sense of sin and despair, even to the point of "despairing ... over [their] sin." And this sense may be "dialectically understood as pointing toward faith," as being "the first element of faith." So Anti-Climacus agrees with Haufniensis that "paganism in the stricter sense ... does indeed lack spirit but that it is qualified in the direction of spirit."[108] But do any of these points modify the claim that only Christians are conscious of that despair that comes from being conscious of the fact that they are suffering from a sickness of spirit (selfhood), that they have a "sickness unto death"?

Kierkegaard's analysis of the levels of consciousness, both of self and of despair, suggests some ambiguities in his answer to this question. He begins by acknowledging that "actual life is too complex" to find anyone who, in regard to being in despair, is "completely unaware of being so" or is "completely aware of being so." Many have "a dim idea" of being in despair but even here "the nuances are myriad." And many of these may try to "keep [themselves] in the dark" about their despair through various diversions, but they are "not clearly conscious about what [they] are doing," how despairingly they are conducting themselves. Next he asserts that "a rise in the consciousness of the nature of despair" and "that one's state is despair" is directly proportionate to "a rise in consciousness of the self." Later he repeats this view but adds another qualification: "the greater the conception [*Forestilling*] of God, the more self there is; the more self, the greater the conception of God."[109]

So the question is: when and how does any human being get a great enough conception of God in order to acquire that intensity of self-consciousness that leads one to the awareness of being in despair? Is the "natural human-being," within the confines of religiousness A, capable of such consciousness? Or does Anti-Climacus, with his declaration of

108. *Sickness*, pp. 231–232, 175, 247n, 180; (KW 19:101, 42, 116n, 47); SV 15:152, 98, 166n, 103; (11:211, 155, 226n, 158).

109. Ibid., pp. 181, 182, 211; (KW 19:48, 49, 80); SV 15:104, 105, 134; (11:160, 161, 192).

the uniqueness of the Christian understanding of sin and despair, totally and rigorously reject Johannes Climacus' attribution (to the natural human-being) of both an authentic consciousness of the eternal and an authentic consciousness of being a *self*, which then make possible both "a relationship with God ... in the inwardness of subjectivity" and "the totality of guilt-consciousness" as "the most upbuilding element in Religiousness A?"[110]

For our answer, the controlling point is made at the beginning of part 2 of *Sickness* on the topic, "Despair Is Sin." There Anti-Climacus flatly declares that the entire preceding section, "Despair Defined by Consciousness" (of the self, that is) falls strictly within the limits of "the consciousness of the self ... within the determinant of the human self, or the self whose criterion is the human" (in contrast with the "theological self" whose criterion is the revealed God). This means that whatever is said there about the eternal (God) and about consciousness of despair is attributable to the "natural human-being," including the relationship with God as experienced within religiousness A. By implication, we would argue, the same thing should be said about the entire preceding section, "Despair Considered without Regard to Its Being Conscious or Not," because "the constituents of the synthesis" (infinitude/finitude and possibility/necessity) that are used there to analyze despair are the universal elements of the self that have been embedded in human nature by "the power that established it."[111]

Let us begin, however, by seeing how natural human consciousness of God and of despair is described simply within the section, "Despair Defined by Consciousness." Even in his consideration of despair in weakness (i.e., in not willing to be oneself) Kierkegaard insists that there is "a

110. The quotation is from *Postscript*, p. 497; (KW 12.1:560); SV 10:229; (7:488–9). In *Kierkegaard as Humanist* I have attempted to demonstrate that Climacus in *Postscript* clearly adopts and persuasively defends both of these attributions, and I support this contention with materials from various of Kierkegaard's discourses, as well as some even from *Sickness*. See especially pp. 130–135, 281–309.

111. In *Kierkegaard as Humanist* I have used this distinction as the key to the entire thesis of that book, namely, that Kierkegaard, in the totality of his writings, has posited and developed a very sophisticated humanism, which, however, integrally and essentially *includes* religiousness A. Louis Dupré supports this thesis when he says, "Kierkegaard regards the instant not as an element peculiar to Christianity, but as a central element in every type of religion. The religious life on a sheerly natural basis, the so-called religiousness A, culminates in the consciousness of guilt before God. In this affirmation of oneself before God, natural religion arrives at an instant in which eternity touches existence in time, but without penetrating it." (*Kierkegaard as Theologian*, p. 94)

consciousness of having a self in which there is something eternal." And he sees three levels of such consciousness. The first occurs "when immediacy is assumed to have some reflection; ... a somewhat greater consciousness of self comes about, and thereby of the nature of despair and of one's condition as despair. ... With this certain degree of reflection begins the act of discrimination wherein the self becomes aware of itself as essentially distinct from the environment and external-world [*Udvortesheden*] and [from] their influences upon it," and thereby "[it] has a dim conception that there may even be something eternal in the self." But at this level of weakness in despair, "one does not dare to let it come to a decision" in order that "the life of the spirit can break through," so that "consciousness of the eternal in the self breaks through."[112]

But even in the state of weakness and lack of resolve, a second form of despair is possible when "consciousness ... rises to a new consciousness – that *of* one's weakness" (emphasis added). This intensification of consciousness brings with it an awareness of "despair *over* one's weakness," and in turn, "one now becomes more clearly conscious of one's despair, that one despairs *of* the eternal, that one despairs over oneself" (emphases added). But to no avail. In weakness one fails to "turn away from despair to faith," and thus "entrenches oneself in despair," taking one's attraction to earthly finitude as "the despairing sign that one has lost the eternal and oneself." Such a person does not lose the sense of self, but hides it, "shares it with no one," keeps it behind "a carefully closed door, and behind it sits the self, so to speak, watching itself, preoccupied with or filling up time with not willing to be itself and yet being self enough to love itself."[113]

Finally, the "natural human-being" is capable of a third and even more intense combination of awareness of self and of despair. This level is reached when, in rebellion against the eternal, the self "is unwilling to begin with losing itself ... in order to win itself." Rather, in defiance and in despair, "one wills to be one's self," that is to say, by one's own powers and on one's own. "In this form of despair, there is a rise in the consciousness of self, and therefore a greater consciousness of what despair is and that one's state is despair." And one knows that this despair is an "act" that "comes directly from the self. Therefore, defiance, compared with despair over one's weakness, is indeed a new qualification."

112. *Sickness*, pp. 188, 193; (KW 19:54–55, 59–60); SV 15:110–111, 115; (11:166–167, 171–172).

113. Ibid., pp. 195–196; (KW 19:61, 63); SV 15:116–117, 118; (11:173, 174–175).

And in order to fuel this defiance of the eternal in willing to be and to become one's self on one's own, "there must be consciousness of an infinite self," of "the most abstract possibility of the self," of "the infinite form of the negative self." Why? Because it is this infinite form that one uses to "sever the self from any relation to a power that has established it, or to sever it from the concept that such a power exists." In this way, the self believes it is free "to be master of itself or to create itself, to make one's self into the self one wants to be, to determine what one will have or not have in one's concrete self." It is precisely this illusion, Kierkegaard maintains, that lands the human being in the hopelessness of despair, because "one does not want to put on one's self, does not want to see one's given self as one's task," and because "no derived self can give itself more than it is in itself by paying attention to itself; ... in its self-reduplication it becomes neither more nor less than itself." So in striving to become an other self, "it really becomes no self."[114]

In these attributions of consciousness to the self which has only the "human self" as its criterion, it would seem that Kierkegaard belies his contention that only those humans who are "directly before God" by being "before Christ" know what despair is or what it means to be in despair as a "sickness unto death." If the purely "human self" can achieve a consciousness of itself as distinct from everything external and a consciousness of the presence of the eternal in itself, if the human self can continue "to love itself" behind a "closed door" even while conscious that it is in "despair of the eternal," if the human self is capable of a defiance in which one is conscious of one's "infinite self" and therewith deliberately "severs the self from any relation to the power that established it," then surely this purely human self must be said to be capable of some intimation, some level of awareness that its essential failure to achieve a positive relationship with the eternal carries with it a despairing foreboding of its own doom, of a dreaded and dreadful illness of the human spirit that amounts to a qualitative alienation from life, an alienation from the eternal, alienation from all loving human companionship, and – most profoundly – alienation from one's own true being: one's self.

Kierkegaard tries to resolve this apparent contradiction in *Sickness* by minimizing what he has attributed to the "natural human-being." "The majority," he says, "have not gone particularly deep in despairing. There are very few persons who live even approximately within the qualification

---

114. Ibid., pp. 201–202; (KW 19:67–69); SV 15:122–123; (11:178–80).

of spirit; indeed, there are not many who even try this life, and most of
those who do soon back out of it. ... [T]o be concerned about one's soul
and to will to be spirit seems to be a waste of time in the world. ... [M]ost
people virtually never advance beyond what they were in their childhood
and youth: immediacy with the admixture of a little dash of reflection."
And the "higher form" of despair ("of the eternal or over oneself") "is
quite rare in the world."[115] If Anti-Climacus really means these statements, then he is indeed "leaving behind" Johannes Climacus and everything that the latter said about the "God-relationship" and the Socratic
analogue to "faith" that are possible within the immanence of religiousness A.

If even Climacus (in *Postscript*) is interpreted by some as shrugging off
these possibilities of religiousness A as nothing more than a humorous/
ironic theory about the *ideal* capacity of natural human-beings, such an
interpretation does not succeed. As has been argued in *Kierkegaard as
Humanist*, Climacus himself takes human achievement of religiousness
A seriously when he insists that "religiousness A must first be present in
the individual before there can be any consideration of becoming aware
of the dialectical B."[116] There it is also demonstrated that the possibilities of the human spirit to attain to significant depths and heights of a
kind of faith and self-realization in the God-relationship within the immanence of religiousness A, including forms of self-sacrificing love, are
expounded by Kierkegaard himself in numerous upbuilding discourses
that are clearly meant to describe religiousness A. Even in the first production within the "second" and specifically Christian authorship, *Upbuilding Discourses in Various Spirits*, Kierkegaard reserves the subtitle
"Christian Discourses" for part 3, "The Gospel of Sufferings." And he
pointedly notes that "An Occasional Discourse" in part 1 (on purity of
heart) "is decidedly upbuilding" but "in the religiousness of immanence."[117] A noted Jewish neurologist recently commented on this particular discourse: that Kierkegaard provides in the first half a brilliant
analysis of human neurosis and in the second half a profound and prac-
tical prescription for its healing – an insight that clearly did not require
one to be "before God in Christ."

115. Ibid., pp. 190–191, 199; (KW 19:57–58, 65); SV 15:112–113, 120; (11:169–170,
177).

116. *Postscript*, p. 494; (KW 12.1:556); SV 10:226; (7:486).

117. *Journals*, 5975; VIII[1] A 15; or KW 15:389.

Kierkegaard was, in a certain way, disturbed by this entire issue. In his introduction to the consideration of conscious despair, he mentions a certain problem which he promises to address later but never did: "To what extent perfect clarity about oneself as being in despair can be combined with being in despair, that is, whether this clarity of knowledge and of self-knowledge might not simply wrench a human-being out of despair, make one so terrified for oneself that one would stop being in despair, we will not determine here; we will not even make an attempt in that direction, since this whole investigation will be taken up later."[118] This same question is still nagging at him when he comes to the topic of "despair of the eternal or over oneself." In a footnote he muses, "[P]urely philosophically it could be a subtle question whether it is possible that one can be in despair along with complete consciousness of that whereof one is in despair."[119]

Was Kierkegaard afraid of pursuing this question? Did his knowledge of Euripides, Plato, and Aristotle, of Descartes, Spinoza and Leibniz, of Shakespeare, Goethe, and Mozart disconcert him about his claims of the exclusivity of revelation that comes with being "before God in Christ?" What if he had known in depth of Buddhism and its diverse formulations in China and Japan? What if he had known in depth of the mystical forms of Judaism and Sufism? What if he had lived to see the spread and adoption of the Judeo-Christian vision of the radical individual (as of infinite worth and dignity) throughout populations of the world which are largely untouched by Christian faith? Did the fact that the *Corsair* affair drove him off the streets of Copenhagen and thus ended his constant conversations with the whole range of humanity that he met on those streets have something to do with his increasing pessimism about the capacities of the "natural human-being"? Did his deepening determination to attack the false Christianity of Christendom blind him to the simple but profound Christian faith of many of the unknown and unsung members of the church and readers of the Bible? In the second, specifically Christian authorship, one does not find stories to match the one in *Postscript* about the despairing old grandfather counseling his despairing young grandchild before the new grave of the one's son and the other's father.[120]

118. *Sickness*, pp. 180–181; (KW 19:47); SV 15:104; (11:160). See KW 19:177 for a note about an apparently contemplated section that was deleted in Kierkegaard's outline of this part of *Sickness*.

119. Ibid., pp. 194n; (KW 19:61n); SV 15:116n; (11:173n).

120. *Postscript*, pp. 210–216; (KW 12.1:234–242); SV 9:196–202; (7:197–203).

Whatever the answers to these questions, now, with this problem (of
the Christian exclusivity vis-à-vis the human universality of Kierkegaard's
interpretation and depiction of human despair) before us, let us look at
his analysis of despair in some detail. And even where it seems that there
are elements that are uniquely Christian (or Judeo-Christian), we will
want to ask whether or not even these are accessible to humans in general once they have been enunciated. We will ask that question even
though (let it be clear) this entire treatment of Kierkegaard as theologian agrees with Kierkegaard in his conviction that the Judeo-Christian
experience of God has yielded and continues to yield a unique understanding of God, creation, human nature and destiny, human failure
and its healing. This understanding stands in constant encounter, more
so in our world than in Kierkegaard's, with the uniqueness of the experience of other religions and philosophies. It is not the burden of this
present study to compare these diverse experiences or to judge among
them. But those Christians are not faithful to their own faith if they believe that they can shrug off or combat or abolish all other faiths merely
by labeling them "pagan," "demonic," "untrue."[121]

2 Basic View of Despair

For his primary analysis and depiction of despair in *Sickness* (section C
of part 1), Kierkegaard provides two introductory paragraphs in which
he states some basic, unifying insights in the light of which alone can be
understood the extremity, both the dire threat and the potential promise, of human desperation in the state of despair.[122]

First and last, it must be stressed that authentic, qualitative despair is a
function of the human-being as self. It is to be understood only in terms

121. In the background of this entire discussion of what Kierkegaard says about the limitations of the experience of the natural human-being, there are two issues that must be
faced. First, in all his references to "pagans" we must ask just how much did he know about
the history of religions and about the then current practice of other religions and philosophies, especially in India and Asia? (See, for example, his brief notes on this subject from
Schelling's Berlin Lectures, *Papirer*, XIII, pp. 320–329, translation in *The Concept of Irony*,
KW 2:403–412) Secondly, in Kierkegaard's references to the limitations of the experience
of all "natural" human beings, we must ask if his insights were not at least partially limited
by those of his own western European culture, and distorted by the intensity of his very
pious-Christian upbringing under the domination of his father?

122. For basic material in the next three paragraphs, see *Sickness*, p. 162; (KW 19:29);
SV 15:87; (11:142). The additional material in each paragraph will be accounted for in following notes.

of the structure and the operation of the self. Structurally "the self, as synthesis, ... is composed of infinitude and finitude." These two elements are neither blended indistinguishably nor separable independently, but each subsists in a *relation* to each other, so that "the one constantly is its opposite." But this relation has another peculiarity, namely, the capacity to "relate to itself." In this peculiar event and act (of a relation [of two] relating-to-itself), the self is no longer simply a built-in potentiality (what Haufniensis describes as the self "sleeping," what Anti-Climacus describes as the self κατα δυναμιν). Rather, the self becomes "the third" in which the synthesis of the two becomes consciously operational. In this act/event of becoming, "the self is freedom."[123]

In thus becoming "awake" and functional in this act of freedom, the self moreover becomes conscious of being caught and involved in a second opposition or relation, because "freedom is the dialectical in the determinants possibility and necessity." And for human freedom, for human choosing, possibility is future. And in facing the future, the self becomes involved in the third set of those determinants that comprise the human identity, namely, the temporal/eternal (see first paragraph of *Sickness*). For Kierkegaard, the future is the "first expression" or "incognito" of the eternal, and the immanence of the eternal in the self is the first expression and incognito of the God-relationship for the human self. On the other hand, the "necessity" that correlates with and sets limits to the self's possibility is comprised not just of the external, sensuous, and contingent conditions of the self's particular finitude; rather, this unique, particular necessity manifests itself more especially as that "inner necessity" that inheres in the self's task to become itself, and in the self's need for help from the Eternal in the accomplishment of this task.[124]

It is precisely this threefold complexity of the self that is operative in human freedom and therefore in what we have called the self's failure. And it is this same complexity that Kierkegaard uses as explanatory of

123. Note 122; also ibid., p. 163; (19:30); SV 15:88; (11:142–143); *The Concept of Angst*, p. 38; (8:41); SV 6:136; (4:313).

124. Note 122; also, for the concept of the future/eternal, *The Concept of Angst*, pp. 80–81; (KW 8:89–91); SV 6:177–178; (4:359–361); for "inner necessity" see *Journals*, 1269; X⁴ A 177. Actually, the last three paragraphs contain aphoristic references to many main themes that are explicated extensively in *Kierkegaard as Humanist*, particularly the definition of the self on the first page of *Sickness*, the nature of freedom and its limitations, human temporality and its relation to the eternal, and specifically the concept of the "inner necessity" of the self (for the last item, see pp. 200–221).

that human condition or state that comprises authentic, qualitative despair, which qualifies and modifies every single dimension of the selfhood of every single human being. Even though many of those "in whom [despair] resides, who rightly understood must be called despairing," are not conscious of it, nevertheless "all despair, grasped in its [essential] concept, is conscious." This is so because "generally speaking, consciousness – that is, self-consciousness – is decisive with regard to the self. The more consciousness, the more self."[125]

It is also on the basis of the first two emphases of this complexity (on the given structure of the self and on the decisive role of self-consciousness) that Kierkegaard divides his treatment of despair into two parts: "despair considered … only with regard to the constituents [*Momenter*] of the synthesis," and "despair as defined by consciousness." And it is the third emphasis (on the presence and need of the Eternal) that leads to his separate and third treatment of despair as sin.[126] The way in which Kierkegaard develops each of these parts makes each part fascinating in itself. But by becoming absorbed in his series of fine distinctions and their dialectical interplay within each part, the reader can easily lose sight of what the totality is all about, what is its unifying theme and subject.[127] As Kierkegaard warns us in the preface to *Sickness*, "[O]nce and for all may I point out that in the whole book, as the title indeed declares, despair is interpreted as a sickness, not as a cure."[128] So in the interpretation that follows, we will keep to the main theme and try to see how the details of its treatment in each part are interrelated. Indeed, we will try to bring all the details to bear on the primary focus of "the whole book": the diagnosis, by this consummate physician of the human spirit, of the spirit's primary and all-consuming illness of despair (even though

125. See note 121.

126. We will show in the next and last section of this chapter that the entirety of part 2 of *Sickness* ("Despair Is Sin") is a further specification of the last paragraph of part 1. As Kierkegaard says in the opening paragraph of part 2, "[S]in is intensified weakness or intensified defiance: sin is the intensification of despair."

127. Kierkegaard was enamored with categories, classifications, sharp definitions, the isolation of the "ideal," and what he called "algebraic" formulations (*Bogstavregning*, e.g. see *Journals*, 6137; VIII[1] 652). He immediately bought and avidly read Trendelenburg's *Geschichte der Kategorienlehre* when it was published in 1846. But he also emphasized that categories and the ideal do not exist as such, and that knowing a definition does not mean that one "knows" the actuality for which it stands, and that knowing something in actuality is always qualitatively different from knowing it in imagination.

128. The cure, of course, is treated in *Practice of Christianity*. Anti-Climacus's *Sickness* and *Practice* should be regarded as a single, two-volume work.

the "editor" [Kierkegaard] claims, "I am not the physician, I am one of the sick"[129]).

3 Disrelation as the Key to Despair

For the section that seeks to delineate the forms of despair simply "by reflecting upon the constituents [*Momenter*] of which the self as synthesis is composed," one needs only to look at the table of contents to see what this approach yields. As just noted, it assumes a diversity within the unity of a synthesis (at note 123 above). But the unity is both an ontological given and also a functional requirement. The given unity is inescapable and indestructible, but its functional success is only a possibility, that is, it may or may not come into operation. The main point to this entire section (in *Sickness*) is this: for the human individual to fail to achieve functional, operational unity as a self is to be in despair: "insofar as the self does not become itself, it is not itself; but not to be itself is precisely despair."[130] And Anti-Climacus' key term to indicate the nature of this failure is "disrelation" (see text above at notes 72–75). Several of the leading characteristics of this phenomenon must be noted if we are to understand our human despair.

The term "disrelation" (*Misforhold*) is often used by Kierkegaard in his earlier writings in its simple sense of a disparity, disproportion, or imbalance between two elements within an entity (e.g., thinking and existing), or between two different entities (e.g., male and female, the comic and the tragic). But in *Postscript* there is a shift in his usage that partly anticipates the application in *Sickness*. Climacus argues that when a human being becomes ethically aware, then "one comprehends the contradiction [*Modsigelse*] between the mode in which one exists in one's inner being and one's not expressing it in outer appearance." This is inevitable because "what makes the ethicist an ethicist is the movement by which he inwardly joins his outward life together with the infinite requirement of the ethical, and this is not directly apparent." The fact that this inward movement is not observable to others leads the ethicist to perceive this contradiction also as a "disrelation" inherent in the fact that "what engages him absolutely does not engage others absolutely."[131]

129. In an "Editor's Postscript" that was never added to *Sickness*; see *Journals* 6277 or KW 19:162; IX A 421.
130. *Sickness*, p. 163; (KW 19:30); SV 15:88; (11:142).
131. *Postscript* pp. 450–451; (KW 12.1:504–05); SV 10:181–182; (7:438–439).

And this perception leads to still another intensification of the ethicist's sense of disjunction because one's desire and drive to engage absolutely in one's own relation to an eternal blessedness inevitably produces a sense of impotence, of inability to enact the absolute within the conditions of actual, concrete existence. This sense of impotence in turn leads to an awareness that the solution to the ethical demand (inherent in one's vision of an eternal blessedness) is the suspension of the ethical *as* ethical, to an awareness that what seemed possible is impossible, that one needs help from beyond the ethical, from another sphere: the religious. At this juncture the self gains a new and unexpected consciousness: that of essential, total guilt-consciousness, and (potentially) that of being in *sin*.[132]

This line of analysis yields for Climacus a new quality in the disrelation. An essential (i.e., not comparative or relative) guilt-consciousness does not necessarily lead to despair, because in religiousness A the eternal remains immanent and "embraces the existing person everywhere." Indeed, one's "relation [to an eternal blessedness] always carries the disrelation," that is, between what the absolute telos demands and what one can do on one's own. But even though "the existing person cannot get a firm hold of [this] relation because the disrelation continually places itself in between as the expression of the relation," nevertheless, "they still do not repel each other (the eternal blessedness and the existing person)." Rather, "it is only by being held together that the disrelation repeats itself as the decisive consciousness of essential guilt," and thus the existing person must (i.e., may) turn from one's own self to look for help from the eternal.

At this point Climacus prepares for his later distinction between religiousness A and B by pointing out that, in B, the disrelation becomes intensified as "a breach in which the paradoxical accentuation of existence consists." When "the eternal define[s] itself as a temporality, as in time, as historical, ... the existing person and the eternal in time have eternity between them," that is to say, a radical breach becomes manifest and expresses itself in that the guilt-consciousness of immanence becomes "the consciousness of sin" before God, and this consciousness (unlike the guilt consciousness of immanence) "make[s] the subject into someone else."[133]

132. Ibid., pp. 237–239; (KW 12.1:266–267); SV 9:222–224; (7:225–227).

133. For the last two paragraphs, ibid., pp. 473–474; (KW 12.1:532); SV 10:204–205; (7:464–465).

This latter, Christian perception of the nature of the disrelation is what lies at the base of and makes possible Anti-Climacus' definition and description of the essential human condition as *despair.* Climacus' analysis and use of the concept of disrelation in the above context certainly points to something more than mere disparity, disproportion, or discrepancy (the Swenson/Lowrie translation in *Postscript*). He calls the disrelation a "contradiction" between the inner and outer dimensions of human existence. Even within religiousness A he clearly describes a conflict between human allegiance to an absolute telos and to relative ends, between ethical aspiration and ethical impotence, so that the total disrelation expresses and repeats itself as total guilt-consciousness. But Christian religiousness B goes all the way to label the relation quite frankly for what it is: a break or breach between the human self and "the power that established it"; furthermore, religiousness B uncompromisingly asserts that the human being is the source of and hence responsible for this fundamental breach and has no resource for its fundamental healing. Within the limits of religiousness A, the human being is left to struggle desperately to hold together the two sides of the contradiction, finding the only assuagement for one's despair in the commitment of one's heart to the continuing, accepting, affirming immanence of the eternal.[134]

Anti-Climacus affirms as actual what is proposed as only a "hypothesis" by Climacus in his "thought-project" in *Fragments,* namely, that if the human being is to experience qualitative healing that "make[s] the subject into someone else," then that human being must find (or be found by) one's Healer in that paradoxical presence of the eternal that has entered into time in the humblest, most self-effacing, most compassionate human being that ever lived in the dust of this earth: Jesus the Christ.

It is from this perspective that Anti-Climacus comes to perceive and describe fundamental, qualitative, universal human despair as a "disrelation," and by this term he certainly does not mean simply an "imbalance or disproportion" among the constituent elements that comprise the human being.[135] Rather, the term signifies the essential breach or brokenness, the alienation, the estrangement that is at the heart of the existence (life) of every individual human being. In *Sickness* "disrelation"

134. For an extensive exposition of Kierkegaard's exploration of the possibilities of religiousness A, see the index of *Kierkegaard as Humanist,* but especially pp. 129–134, 281–323.

135. This is the translation used by Alastair Hannay in his excellent translation of *Sickness* (1989). See his defense of this translation in note 7, p. 168 (of this translation).

signifies a basic breakdown in the functioning and operation of the given potentiality of selfhood, and the breakdown is reflected in every dimension of the human being. One particular form of this breakdown is considered as primary.

Kierkegaard stresses the fact that "the disrelation of despair is not a simple disrelation but is a disrelation in that relation which relates to itself and [which] is established by an Other, so that the disrelation in that relation being-for-itself [*for sig værende*] is also reflected infinitely in the relation to the Power that established it."[136] In other words, the brokenness of human despair is simultaneously a breakdown within the structure and operation of the self *and* in the relation of the self to God. A correlative point (as noted above at notes 72, 73) is that this dual breakdown is traceable purely and only to the failure of "the relation in which the synthesis relates to itself," because "the synthesis [was] originally from the hand of God in the right relationship." In other words, disrelation and its despair are not inherent, are not a given of human nature. "The synthesis [as such] is not the disrelation." Certainly, "the possibility of the disrelation lies in the synthesis," but "if the synthesis were [itself] the disrelation, then despair would not exist at all, then despair would be something that lies in human nature as such. ... [I]t would be something that happens to a human-being."[137] Rather, disrelation (despair) is a discord, an opposition or antagonism to the point of a broken relation (between the constituent elements of the self and between the self and God) that is traceable to a subtle desire (will) to avoid the "demand" (*Fordring*) and the difficult task of becoming one's own unique self by living in the dialectic of finitude and infinitude, of necessity and possibility, and ultimately the dialectic of one's temporality and one's need of the eternal. As we shall see, everything that follows in *Sickness* consists simply of a complex, interrelated series of illustrations of this one main point.

4 *Omission of Relation to Neighbor*

At this point, however, we must note that, in his analysis of the brokenness of the human self in despair, Kierkegaard makes a serious omission of one of the main categories that he had developed in his previous analysis of the way or path to fulfillment of human selfhood: the love of

136. *Sickness*, p. 147; (KW 19:14); SV 15:74; (11:128).
137. Ibid., pp. 148–149; (KW 19:15–16); SV 15:75; (11:130).

neighbor.[138] Our consideration of this significant topic will form an extended excursus from our exposition of despair but is required for a proper understanding of despair (as exposited in *Sickness*).

In *Works of Love*, Kierkegaard elaborates an ontology of love in which he asserts that to be "before God" involves a human being in a triadic relationship, because love is always "a relationship among: humanbeing-God-humanbeing." In other words, in every relationship of one human being to another, "God is the middle-determinant [*Mellembestemmelse*]" or the "third-party [*Trediemand*]." Hence "the love-relationship requires [*hører til*] threeness: the lover, the beloved, love; but love is God. Therefore, to love another human-being is to help [that human-being] to love God, and to be loved is to be helped." Granted, "no human-being is love. ... Yet love is everywhere present where there is a lover," because love is not just "a relationship between two" but "also a relationship among three. First there is the lover, next the one or the ones who are the object; but love itself is present as the third."[139]

In other words, the requirement (in *Sickness*) of being "before God" in order for the self to become itself should have compelled Kierkegaard also to make explicit the requirement of loving one's neighbor in order for the self to be "before God." In *Works* he specifically says that authentic love (i.e., love at the level of spirit/self) must have both God and neighbor as a middle-determinant, and only then can the self "love

138. For a fulsome analysis of this category in Kierkegaard's thought, see *Kierkegaard as Humanist*, chapter 7. For what follows, see especially the section on Love's Triad, pp. 350–359; the following section, "Love Presupposes Love" also bears on this issue, especially pp. 370–376. The omission of this category (love of neighbor) from *Sickness* has also been noted by Sylvia Walsh in her article, "On 'Feminine' and 'Masculine' Forms of Despair" in *IKC: The Sickness unto Death*. She, too, finds this omission "rather puzzling" in the light of its development in *Works of Love*. And she also speculates, as I do, on the reasons, and concludes that even if one assumes that "the insights of the earlier work are somehow implied in the later one, ... [s]till, one wishes that Kierkegaard had addressed the matter of relatedness to others more directly in defining the structures of the self." (pp. 125–126) In what follows here, I suspect other reasons for the omission and find its ramifications even more serious than Walsh does. In her more recent work, *Living Poetically*, Walsh concludes her book with a five-page comment on "The Neighbor as the True Other," and my interpretation of this concept in the chapter of *Kierkegaard as Humanist* (referred to above) is in remarkable agreement with hers. She makes a very helpful application of this concept to the general subject of "gender differences as modes of selfhood and despair," and reference will be made to her view in chapter 5 of this present work.

139. *Works of Love*, pp. 112–113, 124, 280; (KW 16:107, 121, 301); SV 12:107, 120, 289; (9:104, 117, 287).

itself truly."[140] Surely, this view is implicit in one of Kierkegaard's basic contentions in *Sickness*: that God has built into the very fabric of the human creature the potentiality of being spirit/self so that no human can ever get rid of this "concession" and "demand" from the Eternal, because if spirit-love (*Kjerlighed*) to both God and Neighbor is the fulfillment of selfhood, then an essential relation to neighbor is a given relationship just as is the relation to self: in the very "fabric" of existence. If Kierkegaard had made this insight explicit in *Sickness*, he would have defined the self as a relation that relates to itself and, in so doing, also relates simultaneously to *both* the Power that established it *and* to its neighbor. Correlatively he would have defined disrelationship not only as a duality of broken relations with self and with God but also as including a third broken relation: with fellow human-being[s]. This inclusion would have vastly enriched his concept of despair/sin in *Sickness*, as well as his concept of the form and content of the Christian way of life in *Practice in Christianity* – in which there is also no mention of love of neighbor.

The fact is, Kierkegaard had not forgotten this triad. About the time he was finishing the composition of *Practice in Christianity* (December 1848), he projected a new series of seven discourses on the general theme, "Let Not the Heart in Sorrow Sin." The "sin" is for a person to believe that "for one's pain, one's sorrow, there is no cure, ... neither from God nor from humans, neither in time nor in eternity." He declares that this sin "is the highest form of despair" and that "no sin [is] as common as this one." He proposes to use the topics of faith, hope and love to illustrate how sorrow can so easily turn into sin. In the last three, he intends to show that if you sin in sorrow, then "you abandon love *to God*, ... you abandon love *to human-beings*, ... you abandon love *to your self* [*Dig selv*]."[141] So the question presses as to why he did not include the relation of self to other humans in his definition of self and in his definition of disrelation/despair?

One factor may have been that, during the period from the completion of *Works of Love* in August of 1847 to the completion of *Practice* in December of 1848, Kierkegaard had an increasing sense of urgency to make his critique ("attack") of the church and Christendom more explicit and more uncompromising. In December 1848, he wrote in his

140. Ibid., p. 113; (KW 16:107); SV 12:107; (9:104).
141. *Journals*, 6277–280; translation also in KW 19:163–165; *Papirer*, IX A 421, 498–500.

journal a note headed, "To be a Christian involves a double-danger" – a concept he had developed in *Works*.[142] In the journal entry he describes the two dangers as, first, "the intense internal suffering involved in becoming a Christian," and secondly, "the danger of the Christian's having to live in the world of secularity and here express that he is a Christian." But in *Works* he spells out what will inevitably happen to the Christian who risks the second danger, namely, since "the world's opposition stands in an *essential* relationship to the inwardness of Christianity," the Christian must "put up with being abominated almost as a criminal, insulted, and ridiculed." This theme is expanded in *Christian Discourses* (which immediately followed *Works*). For example, "Joyful Notes in the Strife of Suffering" ends with the thesis that "Misfortune is good fortune," and "Thoughts which Wound from Behind" contains the thesis that "It is blessed nevertheless – to suffer derision in a good cause."[143] So (in the journal entry) he defines his task as this: "Christianity must be presented as the difficult thing it is." And he sees his entire "later productivity" after *Postscript* as dedicated to this end and as culminating in what he then (1848) had ready for publication, namely, *Sickness*, the discourses that would eventually be put together as *Practice in Christianity*, and the article "Armed Neutrality."[144]

The point is this: in letting Anti-Climacus present the "difficulty" of being a Christian with uncompromising rigor and portray the state of human sin and despair in absolute, unmitigated terms, Kierkegaard perhaps did not want any of the gentleness and compassion of his views

142. *Journals*, 493; IX A 414; *Works of Love*, pp. 185–188; (KW 16:191–195); SV 12:185–189; (9:182–186). It should also be noted that Kierkegaard's qualitatively intensified sense of the failure of the Christianity of his day, and therefore his critique of it, are inextricably bound up with the *Corsair* affair. At the end of 1849, four years after the *Corsair*'s first attack on him, the whole prolonged affair still rankles deep in his consciousness, and his sense of its importance for him personally increases, as indicated in a journal entry entitled, "An Accounting of My Action Against the Corsair." There he lists six "consequences for me." Number 3 is: "If I had not taken this action, I would have escaped completely the *double*-danger connected with the essentially Christian, I would have gone on thinking of the difficulties involved with Christianity as being purely interior to the self." (*Journals*, 6548; X² A 251) Hence he views his suffering of public rejection and ridicule as an example of the second "danger" that is an inherent, inevitable, and inescapable dimension of Christian witness.

143. See *Christian Discourses*, trans. by Walter Lowrie; SV³ 13, SV¹ 10.

144. See *Journals*, 6271, 493; IX A 390, 414. But at this time (1847–1848), Kierkegaard was not yet ready for a frontal assault and hence delayed publication of *Sickness* until July 30, 1849, *Practice* until September 27, 1950, and *Armed Neutrality* was published only posthumously in 1965.

of human love (as expressed in *Works of Love*) to soften or dilute the message of Anti-Climacus to the purveyors and promoters of what Kierkegaard considered to be an apostate Christianity.[145] So the human-to-human relation is omitted.

Another more serious and fundamental possibility must also be considered. Kierkegaard may have been reluctant to recognize that the human-to-human relationship is a given dimension of essential humanity, because it could lead to two conclusions that he considers to be gross and dangerous errors: (1) the assumption that human beings as such and on their own have the capacity to discover and to define what is true and what is good for human existence, and (2) the assumption that this truth/goodness presupposes and requires an integrally "social" character to being human and becoming self. We have seen at length that Kierkegaard rigorously denies the first assumption by insisting that even the highest and best human ethical capacity must finally appeal for help from the eternal in order to achieve the ethical telos. We will consider Kierkegaard's position on the second assumption directly in chapter 5 of this volume, but we have already heard him decry dependence on crowd or mass humanity as a source for meaning and guidance, whether the "crowd" is simply at the social, tribal, familial level or at the political, national level, or indeed even (or especially) at the communal level of organizations such as "church" and "congregation." His category is, first and last, the individual (*Individ*), the particular, unique, individual self (*Enkelte*).[146] Whether Kierkegaard's view actually denies any positive role to this social character of being human is an open question and will be considered later.

There is still a third possible, and probably subliminal, motivation for Anti-Climacus' neglect of the self's human-to-human relation. And this source is potentially even more inimical to the cogency and persuasiveness of Kierkegaard's entire interpretation of human nature than the accusation that he is fundamentally "anti-social."

On the surface, this factor appears innocent and unexceptionable (from a Christian point of view). Kierkegaard resists, in fact abhors, any

---

145. It should be noted that Kierkegaard considered *Works* also to be polemical. And certainly among its more generous views of humanity, there is a continuous emphasis on the essential element of offense in the Christian gospel, and hence he flatly states that "the highest responsibility" of Christians is "to preach *against* Christianity in *Christian* sermons." (*Works of Love*, p. 191; [KW 16:198]; SV 12:191; [9:188]).

146. See Gregor Malantschuk's very perceptive and complex analysis of this distinction in his *Fra Individ til den Enkelte* (København: C.A. Reitzels Boghandel, 1978).

attempt to define and to explain the human at a purely sensuous/psychic level. While clearly insisting that this level is a given, essential, integral and "good" dimension of being human, he sees it as a constant temptation to reduce basic humanity to it, and to regard all talk about even the ethical let alone the spiritual as suspect, as romantic delusion. He rightly regards this view as the total denial of the Christian experience and understanding of reality. He contends that living life purely at the level of what he calls "finitude" and "immediacy" leads to utter failure and despair as a human being, indeed, consists in the destruction and damnation of the authentically human. But the problem arises when this emphasis is made by Kierkegaard, from 1848 onward, in increasingly ascetic[147] terms, which is evidenced in his writings and journals (especially in the last three or four years of his life) as an intensifying bitterness against the sensual, sexual, and social dimensions of human existence, ending in a mood of world-weariness. And this mood has at least two uncharacteristic and even ominous expressions, which run counter to and even contradict some of the fundamental concepts and categories of Kierkegaard's general understanding of human selfhood and its relations to God and to creation as a whole.

The first such expression is the obvious one, much noted and often misused to ridicule the entire Kierkegaardian corpus, namely, late journal entries that deride and demonize sex, marriage, the breeding of children, and women in general. This emphasis can be shown to be in flat contradiction to concepts worked out both in the pseudonymous writings up through *Postscript* and in the discourses up through *Works of Love*, as well as in certain key ideas of *Sickness* itself.[148] And it is quite possible that its source does not lie at all in the conceptual shift about the human-to-human relationship noted in *Sickness*, but in certain biograph-

147. This term pops up often in late journal entries – the earliest ones are from late 1849 (see the index of the Hongs' *Journals and Papers*, or see *Askese, asket, asketisk, Asketiske* in N.J. Cappelørn's index to *Papirer*). By asceticism Kierkegaard generally means the externalization of spiritual inwardness (see 6646; x^3 A 190), and he often takes medieval asceticism to task for seeking outward recognition and honor for itself. But he himself labels the direction of his late life as ascetic when (after *Postscript*) he gave up the notion of a country pastorate and accepted Governance's guidance to resume his authorship, when he saw that this decision would mean a life of poverty, when he concluded that he must resist reconciliation with Regine because it "would signify to me that I am deciding ... to make [my task] a finite endeavor." And he is clear that this whole trend started as a result of "the lines I wrote about *The Corsair*" (see 6843; x^5 A 146, dated October 13, 1853).

148. I believe that I have clearly demonstrated this point at great length in *Kierkegaard as Humanist*.

ical factors that intensify during those last five years of his life (e.g., the unresolved animosity of the Copenhagen public, his inability to walk the streets and converse with people, his decreasing circle of friends, the end of any hope of reconciliation with Regine, failing health, financial bankruptcy, and his failure to "awaken" the church.)[149]

The other not so obvious but more important expression of his late ascetic mood concerns a central issue in the whole history of Christian thought and piety, namely, the nature and role of uniquely Christian suffering. In the treatment of this theme, there is an important shift of emphasis between the *Works of Love* and the two volumes by Anti-Climacus. In *Works*, as we have seen, there is a strong recognition of Kierkegaard's new emphasis on the "second danger" of suffering the world's opposition, but the main focus remains on the suffering of the "first danger," that is, the suffering involved in the internal struggles of the self's becoming Christian. And the main point to the entirety of *Works* is that this latter suffering is not experienced simply in the self's struggle to believe in and to become reconciled with God, in a strictly bilateral relationship between self and God. Rather, the essential suffering to which a Christian disciple is called, which is demanded of every Christian, is the suffering involved in that very inward, unseen, unseeable act ("work") of the heart/spirit: "give up your self-loving desires and cravings, give up your self-seeking plans and purposes so that you truly work unselfishly for the good."[150] And that "good" is precisely the loving of one's "neighbor," that is, of every human person who is in need, who is in need of knowing that he or she is the child of God, of infinite worth and eternal dignity, and in need of the love of God. And unlike ascetic suffering, one must manifest this kind of love without the least hope or expectation of recognition or the return of such love from the human being(s) toward whom it is being expressed. It is only in this trilateral relationship that one is reconciled to God in forgiveness, that the self finds (is given) itself in the "like-for-like" from God.[151]

149. For example, see Kierkegaard's journal entry of September 1849 where he says: "Economic concerns came suddenly and all too close. I cannot bear two such disparate burdens, the hostility of the world and concern for the future, at the same time" (*Journals*, 6501, or KW 20:288; X² A 66). As the other elements mentioned gradually increased this "burden," it is no wonder that Kierkegaard's spirit became world-weary.

150. *Works of Love*, p. 188; (KW 16:194); SV 12:188; (9:185).

151. This point will be explored and explicated at length in the next chapter on faith/love.

The emphasis is directly reversed in the writings of Anti-Climacus. As Kierkegaard's sense of being ostracized as a result of the *Corsair* affair intensifies, and as he becomes increasingly convinced that he should make his attack on apostate Christendom more openly and directly, he begins to describe essential Christian suffering almost exclusively in terms of the "second danger," namely, that of being tried and tested by being "abominated ... and ridiculed" by the "world." In *Sickness* and *Practice* there is no mention of the triad of self-God-neighbor and no treatment of the relationship of love with neighbor. The Christian relationship with God is described in terms of faith as believing rather than in terms of mutual and reciprocal (even though infinitely different) love. And the God of faith is God who is "all-things-are-possible" rather than "Love-Itself."

So it is not surprising that in Kierkegaard's last two brief works (written in the year 1851) we hear some extreme expressions of this emphasis. In *For Self-Examination*, he speaks of the love that the Holy Spirit brings: "Not until you have died to the selfishness in you and thereby to the world so that you do not love the world or anything in the world, do not selfishly love even one single human-being – not until you in love of God have learned to hate yourself, not until then can there be talk of the love that is Christian love." Similar words can be found in *Works of Love* but they are surrounded and interpreted by a radically different emphasis. And he brings *Judge for Yourself!* to a close by specifying the preeminent Christian suffering, beyond the suffering of "an anguished conscience, fear and trembling," beyond the suffering of "the deep and perilous collision of the essential Christian" when it becomes "an offense to the Jews and a foolishness to the Greeks" – namely, "suffering for the doctrine." Such a mind-set is certainly a far cry from his constant insistence, throughout his earlier writings, that faith consists not of consent to doctrine but of enacting the truth in living relationship with God and fellow human beings.

It can, quite properly, be argued that the perspective of *Works of Love* is implied and assumed throughout *Sickness* and *Practice*. In *Works* Kierkegaard adopts as a basic principle the following thesis: "[I]f one has the courage to be oneself before God, then one has distinctiveness [*Eiendommelighed*]", that is to say, I "become something in myself," I attain authentic individuality that belongs to me alone. And when one says, "*before God* to be oneself, the emphasis is on 'before God'." But Kierkegaard immediately completes the triadic relationship of love by adding, "To have [such] distinctiveness is to believe in the distinctiveness of everyone else." And it is precisely "true love, self-sacrificing love, that loves every human being according to her/his distinctiveness," and such love is "willing to make every sacrifice" to help every other human being to discover and to become his/her authentic, unique self "before God" – "love seeks not its own."[152]

The same emphasis on the centrality of being "before God" is made in both *Sickness* and *Practice*. The entire analysis of the types and levels of despair in *Sickness* comes to its climax in the thesis that "sin is: *before God,* … in despair not to will to be oneself, or in despair to will to be oneself." And the opposite of sin is faith, that is, the relationship of forgiveness and reconciliation with God. And faith is: "in relating to itself and in willing to be itself, the self rests transparently in the power that established it."[153] So if one simply assumes that Anti-Climacus means that being oneself "before God" entails, by definition, loving both God and neighbor, then everything that *Works* says about love of neighbor is implied in *Sickness*. This implication is drawn even more clearly in *Practice*. There Anti-Climacus asserts that for a being (in this case, God-in-Christ) "truly to draw to itself" "that which … is in itself a self," that Being must first help the other one to become itself, and only then is able to draw to itself that other as "a free being, … that is, through a choice."[154] This statement is just a more complicated interpretation of what it means to have "the courage to be oneself before God."

Then Anti-Climacus makes the point that Christ as the God-humanbeing is able to draw others to himself in this complicated way only by virtue of his being a "composite" (*Sammensat*) of lowliness and loftiness, not "a single-thing" (*et Enkelte*) but "a duplexity" (*en Dobblethed*). It is only by the indirectness of being "abased" that "spirit can draw spirit to itself."[155] As we shall see at length in the next chapter, this point is key to the whole nature of faith/love, but here we want to see its connection with Anti-Climacus' other concept of Christ as the "prototype" for the disciple's "imitation." He stresses that in order for God to help humans to fulfill themselves as spirit (self), God's "loftiness must not be of the direct kind," but must be "more deeply pressed down into abasement and lowliness than any other human being … in order to be able to capture

152. *Works of Love*, pp. 253, 255; (KW 16:271, 274); SV 12:260–261, 262–263; (9:258–258, 261).

153. *Sickness*, pp. 208, 262; (KW 19: 77, 131); SV 15:131, 178; (11:189, 241).

154. *Practice in Christianity*, pp. 159–160; (KW 20:159–160); SV 16:155–156; (12:149–150).

155. Idem.

and include all." Hence, Jesus as the Christ "lived poor, abandoned, despised, abased." And he called his disciples to be "followers" and "imitators" only in the sense of "imitators of a life," that is, of his own life of suffering: "the correlative of abasement and lowliness is: imitators."[156]

This theme is announced in the opening pages of *Practice* where Anti-Climacus draws a qualitative contrast between mere "human sympathy" that "willingly does something for those who labor and are burdened: we feed the hungry, clothe the naked, make philanthropic donations, build philanthropic institutions." But we, "living in abundance," do not even consider that we should "reside together in a house and live together in a common life and in daily association with the poor and wretched." But he who said "come here to me, all you who labor and are burdened, and I will give you rest" also understood that "if someone wants to invite the sufferer to come to him, one must either alter one's condition and make it identical with the sufferer's, or make the sufferer's identical with one's own."[157]

It would seem self-evident that if the disciple is called to be an imitator precisely of this "lowliness" in Christ, then Anti-Climacus is implying and assuming that true Christian suffering lies in the self-negation inevitably involved in this identification with the condition of the poor and wretched of this earth – whether their "wretchedness" is the despair of physical poverty or of spiritual poverty. And yet this is not the suffering that Anti-Climacus concentrates on, even in a book that is concerned with the "practice" of Christian faith. Rather, he is mainly absorbed with the fact that, when Christ and his followers do practice this "divine compassion," this "unlimited *recklessness* in concerning oneself only with the suffering," then they suffer under the ridicule and derision of the general populace who consider them laughable and mad.[158] And this theme receives even greater emphasis when it becomes clear that the misery and wretchedness that Christ comes to assuage is not physical at all but spiritual. Christ does not come with "either money or medication or any such things," but rather he only "promises them the forgiveness of sins." It is in this sense that "Christianity came into the world as the absolute, not, humanly speaking, for comfort; on the contrary, it continually speaks about how the Christian must suffer, ... must endure sufferings that one could avoid simply by refraining from becoming a

156. Ibid., pp. 231–232; (KW 20:237–238); SV 16:221–222; (12:217–218).
157. Ibid., pp. 12–13; (KW 20:13); SV 16:21–22; (12:8).
158. Ibid., p. 62; (KW 20:58); SV 16:65; (12:55).

Christian."[159] In Christendom "authentic Christian suffering has been abolished, suffering 'on account of the Word,' 'for righteousness sake'."[160] If one is a contemporary (a follower) of Christ, then one must "suffer with him, ... nailed to the cross beside him," in that, one shares giving offense to the world and accepting its rejection and hatred.[161]

From this entire foregoing analysis of Christian suffering, it would seem that Kierkegaard's growing determination to mount his final attack on the apostasy of Christendom led him to emphasize the element of suffering from the world's rejection and ridicule over the element of suffering involved in self-negation in the service of bringing God's loving forgiveness to the lost and lone. "Carrying Christ's cross" becomes too closely identified with this negative suffering, and hence suffering is in danger of becoming an end and a good in itself.[162] This conclusion certainly was not Kierkegaard's intention. In the journal entry, "The New Pseudonym (Anti-Climacus)," just referred to (in note 160), he insists that the "qualitatively rigorous" thesis, that "Christ came into the world because he was the absolute ... 'you shall'" and "not out of human compassion," is only a half truth, because "it holds true Christianly that Christ came into the world out of love *in order* to save the world," and hence Christianity is proclaimed as *grace* and not merely as *law*.

In what follows, therefore, we must understand and interpret Anti-Climacus' analysis of despair in terms of this dual kind of suffering; that is to say, we must understand despair as involving the whole self, including not only one's private relation with one's self, and one's inner, indirect, hidden relationship with God, but also including the self's finitude in its relations with the world and especially with fellow human beings. The disrelation of despair occurs and is manifest not only in our guilt and sinfulness before God and in our failure to choose to be and become our God-given self (which are actually one and inseparable). Rather, these two dimensions of disrelation/despair actually become manifest, and their tragedy revealed, only in the brokenness of our relation with neighbor, our relation with friend, our relation with spouse and family, and therefore in the brokenness of our sexual life, our economic life, our social/political life, and ultimately in the brokenness of

159. Ibid., p. 64, 67; (KW 20:60–61, 63); SV 16:67, 70; (12:57, 60).
160. Ibid., p. 110; (KW 20:108); SV 16:109; (12:103).
161. Ibid., p. 171; (KW 20:171); SV 16:166; (12:160); also see the summary of this theme in all three parts or books of *Practice* in *Journals*, 6528, or KW 20:294–295; X² A 184.
162. In the next chapter we will see that Kierkegaard's general concept of Christian suffering is quite different, as exposited in other works, e.g., in "The Gospel of Sufferings," the third part of *Upbuilding Discourses in Various Spirits*.

our intellectual and aesthetic life, and of our life of phantasy and dream. There remains no little hiding place, no idyllic Eden, in any area or phase or dimension of human being that remains untouched, pure, and undefiled. Only with such a vision of *despair* will we come also to an awareness and a comprehension of (and longing for) the authentic plenitude of *healing* that comes in believing, hoping, loving.

All this must be read into Anti-Climacus' exposition of human despair in terms of the constituent elements of the individual human self and their interaction at the level of self-consciousness – *if* Anti-Climacus is to be read as remaining faithful to the total Kierkegaardian interpretation of Christian faith/love. And with this point we come to the end of our excursus and are ready to return to the exposition of despair in *The Sickness unto Death.*

Assuming, then, that the human condition of despair is primarily distinguished as a breakdown and brokenness (disrelation) within the inherent and human-defining structure and operation of the self, a brokenness that is manifest in each of the self's trilateral relations (to self, to God, and to other humans), what then does Anti-Climacus have to reveal to us about this fundamental and universal condition of despair (beyond the points made in the first ten pages of this section)? To answer this question we will first interrelate the materials of the two sections (on despair without regard to consciousness, and despair as defined by consciousness), and then consider separately despair as sin.

Kierkegaard says that "all despair is, in its concept, conscious," and hence "despair must be considered under the determinant of consciousness," even though not all those who are in despair are conscious of it.[163] So we will follow the outline of Kierkegaard's section, "Despair as Defined by Consciousness," and feed into it the appropriate materials from the first section on despair defined in terms of the constituent elements of the self. Accordingly, Kierkegaard considers: the despair of ignorance, the despair of weakness, the despair of defiance.

5 The Despair of Ignorance

The ignorance referred to is that of having "no conception of being spirit" or self, even though "every human being is naturally fitted to be spirit." Some humans "prefer to live in the basement, that is, in sensate

163. *Sickness*, p. 162; (KW 19:29); SV 15:87; (11:142).

categories, ... the pleasant and the unpleasant." Such a person easily "merges into some abstract universality (state, nation, etc.)" and "regards one's capacities merely as powers to produce." This form of despair is "the most common in the world."[164] "Most human beings live with all too little consciousness of themselves to have any idea of what consistency is; that is, they do not live *qua* spirit. Their lives ... are made up of some action of sorts, some incidents, of this and that. ... They play along in life, so to speak, but never experience putting everything together." So for them "the whole becomes a chaos in which the capacities in mutiny battle one another and plunge the self into suffering."[165]

Kierkegaard usually characterizes this kind of existence as one lived in "immediacy." When human beings cease to be "defined by spirit," then they are regarded "only as a psychical-physical synthesis," and "health is an immediate qualification."[166] But in such immediacy "there is no infinite consciousness of the self, of what despair is, or of the condition as one of despair. Despair is only a suffering, a succumbing to the pressure of external factors." Hence "the *person-of-immediacy* is only psychically determined, ... is an accompanying something within the dimensions of temporality and secularity. ... The self is bound up in immediacy with the other in desiring, craving, enjoying, etc. ... Its dialectic is: the pleasant and the unpleasant; its concepts are: good luck, bad luck, fate." Indeed, "immediacy has no self, it does not know itself; thus it cannot recognize itself. ... One quite literally identifies oneself only by the clothes one wears, one identifies having a self by externalities."[167] This, says Kierkegaard, is "despair at its minimum;" in fact, one is tempted to say that it is "a kind of innocence" in which one "does not even know that it is despair."[168]

Then why is it despair? Why should such persons be branded as living in a state of resignation, hopelessness, and depression? Are they not often happy? Do they not arrange their lives, cleverly and assiduously, so as to make happiness their daily occupation and ultimate goal? Yes, says Kierkegaard, many such people achieve, at least for a while, a life that, "humanly speaking, is beautiful and lovable – a youthfulness that is per-

164. Ibid., pp. 176, 179, 178; (KW 19:43, 46, 45); SV 15:100, 102, 101; (11:156, 158, 157).
165. Ibid., p. 238; (KW 19:107); SV 15:158; (11:217).
166. Ibid., p. 158; (KW 19:25); SV 15:84; (11:139).
167. Ibid., pp. 184, 186–187; (KW 19:50–51, 53); SV 15:106–107, 109; (11:162–163, 165).
168. Ibid., p. 175; (KW 19:42); SV 15:98; (11:154–155).

fect peace and harmony." But this "happiness [*Lykke*] is not a qualification of spirit," because "deep, deep within the most secret hiding place
of happiness there dwells also angst, which is despair," that is, there
dwells in every human heart "an allusion to some indefinite something,"
a dim awareness of another self that demands attention and that disturbs the simple, child-like innocence of the happiness of immediacy.[169]
Then humans may get some perspective or at least an occasional insight
that they are living a life of "childish naiveté or shallow triviality" in
which there is no consistency, no substantive core of unity or identity:
"now they do something good, and then something stupid; ... now they
are in despair for an afternoon, perhaps for three weeks, but then they
are jolly fellows again."[170] Such a life is suffering from the sickness of despair, because "despite its illusory security and tranquility, all immediacy
is angst," which is despair. This "sickness of despair is totally dialectical,"
and therefore "it is the worst misfortune never to have had this sickness:
it is a true godsend to get it, even if it is the most dangerous of illnesses."[171]

The key to Kierkegaard's analysis and critique of immediacy as despair is the term "dialectical." By this he means that those who try to live
in immediacy succeed in doing so only by denying, by shutting down
and repressing their sensitivity to, a whole other dimension of their very
being, namely: their openness to and longing for an infinite that breaks
the limits of their finitude, their coming awake to possibilities that
beckon them to bring into being something new in the midst of the necessities of their given existence, the shattering of their plodding temporality by the invasion of a vision of something eternal. Kierkegaard
admits that the idea of there being individuals who are gripped in "a despair that is completely ignorant of being so" is an abstraction for the
sake of his definitions, and that "very often the person in despair probably has a dim idea of one's own state, although ... the nuances are myriad."[172] In other words, the dialectic of finite-infinite, necessary-possible,
temporal-eternal remains at work below the surface no matter how hard
they try to deny and repress it.

Nevertheless, he believes that most individuals in our western culture
"try to keep [themselves] in the dark about [their] state ... through work

169. Ibid., p. 158; (KW 19:25); SV 15:84; (11:139).
170. Ibid., p. 238; (KW 19:107); SV 15:158; (11:217).
171. Ibid., pp. 158–159; (KW 19:25–26); SV 15: 84–85; (11:139–140).
172. Ibid., p. 181; (KW 19:48); SV 15:104; (11:160).

and busyness as diversionary means." An individual "may even realize that he is working this way in order to sink his soul in darkness, ... with a certain keen discernment and shrewd calculation, with psychological insight; but he is not, in a deeper sense, clearly conscious of what he is doing, how despairingly he is conducting himself."[173] One succeeds in suppressing this discernment by concluding that one's best interests lie in yielding to the demands of one's external, social environment in order to adapt and survive in a very competitive and difficult world. In this way one can

go on living fairly well, seem to be a [real person], be occupied with temporal matters, marry, have children, be honored and esteemed – and it may not be detected that in a deeper sense one lacks a self. Such things do not create much of a stir in the world, for a self is the last thing the world cares about and the most dangerous thing of all for a person to show signs of having. The greatest hazard of all, losing the self, can occur very quietly in the world, as if it were nothing at all. No other loss can occur so quietly; any other loss – an arm, a leg, five dollars, a wife, etc. – is sure to be noticed.[174]

Kierkegaard's point is that, no matter how successful, how rich and powerful, how much in control such a person might appear to be and might even think s/he is, that person is actually in despair. Why? because

that person ... went on living so deceived by life's joys or its sorrows that he never became decisively and eternally conscious as spirit, as self, or what amounts to the same thing, never became aware and in the deepest sense never gained the impression that there is a God and that 'he,' he himself, his self, exists before this God. ... What wretchedness that so many go on living this way, cheated of this most blessed of thoughts! What wretchedness that we are engrossed in, or encourage the human throng to be engrossed in, everything else, using them to supply the energy for the drama of life but never reminding them of this blessedness.

From this perspective, then, in spite of the fact that it is "the most dangerous of illnesses," it is indeed a "true godsend" to become aware of

173. Idem.
174. Ibid., p. 165; cf. 189–190, 197; (KW 19:32–33; cf. 55–56, 63–64); SV 15 10; cf. 111–112, 118–119; (11:146; cf. 168, 175).

our state of despair in order at least to have the possibility of becoming awakened to the authentic human task of becoming a self in the presence of the eternal, "before God." And so Kierkegaard ends his section, "The Universality of ... Despair," with that ominous peroration in which he says, "[W]hen the hourglass [of temporality] has run out, ... when the noise of secular life has grown silent, ... eternity asks you, as every individual in these millions and millions, about only one thing: whether you have lived in despair or not."[175]

In other words, truly human fulfillment, what Christianity calls "blessedness" or "salvation," requires a person to welcome that sense of desperation which emerges inevitably when one becomes gladly aware of the multiple dialectic of which every human being is constructed and in which every human must struggle in order to achieve that high destiny given our species: to become free and loving individuals in human community, and in communion with all creation and its Creator. Surely, then, Kierkegaard is right in insisting that to be unaware of and to be unable to recognize this multiple dialectic operating in one's total existence comprises the most serious illness a human being can have, an illness from which one must recover, a sickness for which one must find healing if one is not to be lost in "the sickness unto death," the death of meaning, of infinite worth and eternal dignity as a unique, individual self. The nature of the struggles involved in the despair that precedes this healing Kierkegaard spells out in his description of the despair of weakness and the despair of defiance.

6 *The Despair of Weakness*

Kierkegaard immediately admits that his distinction between the despair of weakness and that of defiance (Despairingly to Will to Be Oneself) is not absolute because, on the one hand, "no despair is entirely free of defiance," and "on the other hand, even despair's most extreme defiance is never really free of some weakness."[176] This is true because both forms of despair come down to the same thing: not to will to become the self that *kata dynamin* (potentially) one has been given to be. Out of weakness one wills simply to remain the self one already is in

175. Ibid., pp. 159–160; (kw 19:26–27); sv 15:85–86; (11:140–141). Here "blessedness" is the Danish word *Salighed*, in deliberate contrast to "happiness" (*Lykke*) on the previous page. Also, please read in its entirety the peroration mentioned.

176. Ibid., pp. 182–3; (kw 19:49); sv 15:105; (11:161).

immediacy (a false self), whereas in defiance one wills to use one's own conception of what one wants to be (the infinite, abstract, negative self) to redefine and to reshape the self that *kata dynamin* one has been given to be (thus also ending with a false self). But the differences that Kierkegaard spells out are also intriguing and revealing.

Within the despair of weakness, the first level is despair over the earthly which arises when one experiences "a suffering" caused strictly by "the pressure of external-factors [*Udvortesheden*]."[177] This experience comes to those who have just a minimal degree of self-reflection, by which one begins to differentiate one's self from its "environment and external-world [*Udvortesheden*]" but never achieves a concept of "the infinite self" which could serve as "the advancing impetus in the whole process by which a self infinitely assumes responsibility for its actual self with all its difficulties and advantages." Rather, while trying to become "responsible for the self," the self "comes up against some difficulty or other in the structure of the self." But this "makes it recoil" because "the difficulty one has run up against requires a total break with immediacy." So "one makes concessions" because "one does not have the self-reflection or the ethical reflection for that" (i.e., for the total break). The result is that "one despairs, and one's despair is: not to will to be oneself."[178]

For example, you believe that males and females should have equal opportunity in the work place. But your boss, who is the same gender as you, wants to promote you in advance of a coworker of the opposite gender who is clearly better qualified for the job. To tell your boss that the other person should get the job would require you to break totally with all the "normal" standards of social behavior: desire for more power and money, respect for those in authority, loyalty to your own gender, et cetera. But what about your belief? Well, just this one time you will make a concession to simply being human. What's wrong with that! It's what everyone else would do. What is wrong is that the central core of beliefs that defines who you are is engaged in a battle with other sub-systems that comprise your total existential being, and you do not will, do not desire and *choose*, you do not have the courage: to be your real self. So you do not break with the immediacy of your more physical, external human impulses and your desire for social approval.

Does one get a guilty conscience about this failure and suffer inwardly? Not most people, because "little by little, one manages to forget

---

177. Ibid., p. 184; (KW 19:51); SV 15:107; (11:164).
178. Ibid., p. 188; (KW 19:54–55); SV 15:110–111; (11:166–167).

it," and "over the years, an individual may abandon the little bit of passion, feeling, imagination, the little bit of inwardness one had and embrace as a matter of course an understanding of life in terms of trivialities." The so-called self that one appropriates consists merely of one's "capacities, talents, etc.," but all "in an outward direction, ... as they say, toward the real life, the active life." So "the whole question of the self becomes a kind of false door with nothing behind it in the background of one's soul."[179]

However, when one comes to despair in this way, by despairing over some "earthly" or finite difficulty as too great a barrier to becoming oneself, "despair in a higher form" remains a possibility for some. If one retains a measure of imagination and inwardness and does not "sink into the most trivial kind of despair," then one's despair over something earthly is transformed. One's "infinite passion changes this particular thing ... into the world *in toto*." But "the category [*Bestemmelse*, determinant] of totality is a thought category. Consequently, the self magnifies the actual loss and then despairs over the earthly *in toto*." And making this distinction between the particular and the whole means that "there is also an essential advance in consciousness of the self," because despair over the whole of one's existence "is in reality also despair *of* the eternal and *over* oneself." The advance is manifest in the fact that previously one's despair was "despair *in* weakness" but now is "despair *over* one's weakness." Hence there arises this "new consciousness – that *of* one's weakness" (emphases added). In this way "one's whole point of view is turned around: one now becomes more clearly conscious of one's despair, that one despairs of the eternal, that one despairs over oneself, over being so weak that one attributes such great significance to the earthly, which now becomes the despairing sign that one has lost the eternal and oneself."[180]

There follows a very sensitive analysis of the most intense form of the despair of weakness: that of an "enclosing reserve" (*Indesluttethed*). But before we consider it, there is one serious problem with this analysis: how did the determinant or category of "the eternal" get into the picture? In the opening paragraph of *Sickness*, Kierkegaard's definition of the self as a threefold relation (or synthesis) includes "the temporal and the eternal," but his analysis of despair strictly in terms of "the constituents of the

---

179. Ibid., pp. 189, 192; (KW 19:56, 59); SV 15: 111–112, 114; (11:168, 171).
180. Ibid., pp. 194–195; (KW 19:60–61); SV 15:115–117; (11:172–173); also read Kierkegaard's note about the difference between despairing *over* and despairing *of*.

synthesis" includes only "the infinite and the finite" and "possibility [free-dom] and necessity." The point is that the eternal is not a constituent el-ement of human nature *as such* (by itself). On the other hand, human nature, in the image of God, possesses an inherent potentiality for relat-ing to the eternal, and in order to achieve selfhood consciously and freely, the individual human being is in absolute need of relating to the eternal. And as has been noted, possibility is a category of futurity, and the future is the first incognito of the eternal in human experience.[181]

In other words, here Anti-Climacus is assuming everything his like-minded predecessor, Vigilius Haufniensis, had written in *The Concept of Angst* about the temporal/eternal relation as "an expression for that first synthesis according to which a human-being is a synthesis of psyche and body" (i.e, of infinite/finite).[182] The allusion is clear here in the comparison of "despair over the future as the present *in futuro* [in the future] that one is not willing to take upon oneself," and "despair over the past *in præterito* [in the past] that refuses to recede further into the past," that is, refuses to be forgotten. In either case, "there is never a metamorphosis in which consciousness of the eternal in the self breaks through so that the battle can begin that either intensifies the despair in a still higher form [i.e., defiance] or leads to faith."[183]

Contrary to Anti-Climacus, Haufniensis flatly declares that "inward-ness is ... the constituent [or determinant, *Bestemmelse*] of the eternal in a human-being," and however much one denies the eternal, "one will not be able to kill the eternal entirely."[184] But Anti-Climacus does say that, even here at the lowest level of conscious despair, "one has a dim idea that there may even be something eternal in the self."[185] And he explores the form of this presence in his definitions of despair as "the lack of infinitude" and, especially, as "the lack of possibility."[186]

181. This point is explicitly made in *Kierkegaard as Humanist* on p. 24 and explored ex-tensively throughout chapter 4.

182. *The Concept of Angst*; the entire section (KW 8:85–93) on time and the eternal is rel-evant, but read especially pages 85 and 88.

183. *Sickness*, p. 193; (KW 19:59–60); SV 15:115; (11:171–172).

184. *The Concept of Angst*, p. 134–5; (KW 8:151–2); SV 6:231; (4:417).

185. *Sickness*, p. 188; (KW 19:55); SV 15:111; (11:167).

186. And we will see that just as the source of the despair of weakness is to be traced to a lack of infinitude and possibility, so the source of the despair of defiance is to be traced to the lack of finitude and necessity. This is the hidden connection between Kierkegaard's consideration of despair "considered only with regard to the constituents of the synthesis" and despair "as defined by consciousness."

To have a sense of the infinite and to be open to the infinite manifests itself in one prime and basic attitude, one dominating spirit: to dare, to risk, to venture *everything*. And to have this attitude and spirit means, Kierkegaard says, that one possesses one's self "before God." To lack this attitude and spirit condemns a person to a reduction of one's humanity to the intellectual and aesthetic dimensions and to a neglect of the ethical and spiritual dimensions. The result is that one actually loses self-hood by being "completely finitized, by becoming a number instead of a self, … just one more repetition of this everlasting sameness [*Einerlei*]." Such "despairing narrowness" signifies that one has "robbed oneself of one's primitivity, to have emasculated oneself in a spiritual sense." One "does not dare to be oneself, finds it too hazardous to be oneself and far easier and safer to be like others, to become a copy, a number, a mass human-being." Especially it is prudent to keep silent and not speak out because "having spoken can involve one in difficulties." Such people are rewarded by being "publicly acclaimed, honored, and esteemed;" they "amass money, carry on secular enterprises, calculate shrewdly, etc., perhaps make a name in history." But: "they have no self."[187]

But what does it mean to possess one's self "before God," and how does this give one the daring to risk and venture all? It means to believe that "for God all things are possible." Indeed, one can say that "God is this: all things are possible." To believe in possibility, to have the sense that in spite of one's failure and downfall, there is help from on high to make things possible, this will "teach [us] to fear and to hope." Indeed, "possibility is the only saving thing," because "then the person in despair breathes again, revives again." This openness to possibility is what Anti-Climacus means when he speaks of an awareness of "having something eternal in the self." To lack possibility dooms a person to fatalism and determinism because "the fatalist has no God, or, what amounts to the same thing, one's God is necessity." This attitude produces what Anti-Climacus calls "the philistine-bourgeois mentality [*Spidsborgerlighed*]" which revels in "triviality" and "is completely wrapped up in probability." Such a mentality amounts to "spiritlessness" in which one "has lost one's self and God." Ultimately, "the one for whom everything became necessity overstrains himself in life and is crushed in despair."[188]

187. *Sickness*, pp. 168, 166–168; (KW 19:35, 33–35); SV 15:92, 90–92; (11:148, 146–148).

188. Ibid., in order of quotations, pp. 171, 173, 172, 173, 174, 175; (KW 19:38, 40, 39, 40, 41, 42); SV 15:95, 97, 96, 97, 98; (11:151, 153, 152, 153, 154).

So we have seen how Anti-Climacus includes the dialectic of tempo-ral/eternal (as operative in human despair) within his analysis of "the lack of the infinite" and "the lack of possibility." But even in all this de-spair of weakness, there is one special case that he deals with more sym-pathetically, and although he says it "less frequently appears in the world," it can serve as a key to a much broader and more inclusive phe-nomenon of despair that Kierkegaard was well aware of, namely, depres-sion. As mentioned above (following note 180), this despair of weakness takes the form of what is called "enclosing reserve."[189]

In *Sickness* it is pointed out that there are those who are too weak to resist the demands of the world to live in conformity with its standards of proper social and economic conduct, and yet who retain a significant awareness of the importance of self as having eternal significance. This form of the despair of weakness is "qualitatively a full level deeper than the one described earlier" (despair over the earthly). In the latter de-spair, one "turns away completely from the inward way," and "the whole question of the self becomes a kind of false door with nothing behind it in the background of one's soul."[190]

In despair over oneself or of the eternal, however, "that false door ... is here a real door, but a carefully closed door, and behind it sits the self, ... watching itself, preoccupied with ... not willing to be itself and yet being self enough to love itself." And because this "enclosing reserve ... is the very opposite of immediacy and ... has a great contempt for it, ... this matter of the self s/he shares with no one." This person appears to be like everyone else, and "outwardly ... looks every bit 'a real human-being'." The only sign of this person's "deeper nature" is the desire for "solitude, ... a sign that there still is spirit in a person," so that "one's hours have something to do with the eternal and are concerned with the relation of one's self to itself."[191] For such a one, "the more spiritual the despair becomes and the more inwardness becomes a peculiar world of

189. This is the Hongs' translation of *Indesluttethed*. As with many words that are in com-mon, everyday usage (in Danish), Kierkegaard here also attaches very special meaning to this one. Alastair Hannay has a very good note on this particular word in his translation of *Sickness* (pp. 172–173). I use Webster's preferred spelling of "enclosing" rather than the Hongs' "inclosing," because it connotes better the notion of the deliberate act of "confin-ing" or "shutting in" that Kierkegaard has in mind. The Hongs' use of the word "reserve" (which Hannay says is the everyday meaning) is also important because it suggests the sense of "hiddenness" and "reticence to admit or talk about" that Kierkegaard attaches to the Danish word.

190. *Sickness*, pp. 196, 189; (KW 19:63, 55–56); SV 15:118, 111; (11:174, 168).

191. Ibid., pp. 196–198; (KW 19:63–65); SV 15:118–119; (11:174–176).

its own in enclosing reserve, the more inconsequential are the externalities under which the despair conceals itself." And yet in the end, out of weakness, such a one's spirituality is "inwardness with a jammed lock," incapable of breaking the door down to find expression in the external world. So "one goes out, as it were," back to being a loving spouse and parent, a friend to one's friends, a responsible citizen, a dedicated worker in the world of business, even while "paying more attention to neutralizing the externalities, making them as insignificant and inconsequential as possible."[192]

The present author would argue that this kind of spirituality is much more common than Kierkegaard ever realized, that Judaism, Christianity, Islam, and the many forms of Hinduism and Buddhism as practiced throughout the world today are much more effective in helping their adherents to retain this level of spirituality than is generally recognized. In fact, this sense of the infinite dignity and eternal worth of one's own self is kept alive at diverse levels of intensity by a variety of cultural expressions only indirectly related to these religious traditions: in literature, drama, music, painting, sculpturing, and other art forms; in psychological interpretations of the human self at both technical and popular levels; even, in obscure and distorted forms, in some political ideologies. All of these forms may have little or no conscious or explicit reference to those traditions and yet have a profound impact on the self-image of millions who have no formal participation in any religious tradition. Indeed, as we have heard, Kierkegaard (Haufniensis) argues that below (more basic than) these formal religious expressions, there remains in every human being that angst that is aroused "in all cultures where the childlike is preserved as the dreaming of the spirit [self]," even though the self of such a dream "is an adumbrated nothing."[193]

Immediately following these words, Haufniensis comments that in later or more sophisticated cultures, "when freedom ... in the profoundest sense will come to itself," then "angst has the same meaning as depression [*Tungsind*]." And in a footnote, he suggests that for clarification of this point, one "should consult *Either/Or,* especially if one is aware that the first part expresses depression [*Tungsindighed*] in its anguished sympathy and egotism, which is explained in the second part." In order to understand Anti-Climacus' concept of the despair of enclosing reserve as

192. Ibid., pp. 206, 198, 206; (KW 19:73, 72, 64, 73); SV 15:127, 126, 119, 127; (11:183–184, 176, 184).
193. *The Concept of Angst,* p. 38–9; (KW 8:41–42); SV 6:136–137; (4:313–314).

a form of depression, let us now turn to that explanation of the despair involved in depression in the second part of *Either/Or,* and then to a clear definition of their relation in *Stages on Life's Way.*

Kierkegaard (Judge William) is describing the general life-view that "we are to enjoy life" in the unfolding of whatever talents we happen to possess, and this means, "live for your desire." But this view is "only a finite reflection, and the person remains in one's immediacy," and sooner or later most persons (even Nero) experience trials and tribulations. Many of these become depressed. In fact, Kierkegaard notes, "[T]his sickness is very prevalent in our day," and "all of young Germany and France are groaning" under it.[194]

"What, then, is depression?" It is, he says, a sickness of the spirit, not just of the body or psyche – just as he traced the origin of despair to a failure of human spirit. Depression is a symptom of the suffering of spirit's longing to come into being when it is buried, imprisoned, immobilized, paralyzed by "immediacy." In this condition "the spirit requires a higher form," but it finds itself "bound up with all the earthly life, and now spirit wants to gather [*samle*] itself together out of all this dispersion [*Adspedthed*], and to transfigure itself in itself [i.e., to come to self-understanding, or to be understood in and for itself]; personhood wants to become conscious in its eternal validity.[195] If this does not happen, if the movement is halted, if it is repressed, then depression sets in." So Kierkegaard unequivocally asserts that we must not assume, "as do many physicians, that depression inheres in the physical," and he notes that "physicians nevertheless are unable to eliminate it. Only the spirit can eliminate it, for it inheres in the spirit."[196]

This contention goes to the heart of the current debate about the cause and cure of our late twentieth century epidemic of depression. It is indeed too simplistic to explain every type or case of depression in

194. *Either/Or* 2, pp. 187–188, 193; (KW 4:183–184; 189); SV 3:172–173, 177; (2:165–166, 170). Kierkegaard immediately equivocates on this judgment by saying that "*generally* it happens only with the most endowed natures" (emphasis added). He does so because he believes that it has become fashionable to complain of being depressed, so that people with nothing but indigestion claim to be depressed. But in our own "age of anxiety" psychologists take very seriously the widespread phenomenon of depression among all social levels of the population, as witnessed to by the prevalence of the use of drugs to counteract it, especially the most popular one, Prozac.

195. This concept is picked up and repeated in the same language by Kierkegaard in his discourse on purity of heart in *Upbuilding Discourses in Various Spirits.* See text and note at note 207 below.

196. *Either/Or* 2, pp. 193–194; (KW 4:188–190); SV 3:177–178; (2:170–172).

terms of failure of spirit (self), but this explanation is true for what Kierkegaard considers to be authentic depression worthy of the term. Just as he argues that when people say they are in despair over their marriage, their children, their economic state, et cetera, they are not in the existential despair of the spirit that is "the sickness unto death," so also being depressed because of one's indigestion, or even because of war, environmental pollution, et cetera is not that qualitative depression that comes with failure to become one's self in its eternal validity. The qualitative difference of this latter depression is clear, Kierkegaard argues, in the fact of its "infinitude." "There is something unexplainable in depression. ... If a depressed person is asked what the reason is, what it is that weighs on him, he will answer: I do not know; I cannot explain it." And this is totally correct because "as soon as one becomes aware of [*veed*] what it is, it is eliminated." On the contrary, "a person with a sorrow or a worry knows [*veed*] why one sorrows or worries," but "sorrow ... is not eliminated by one's knowing why one sorrows."[197] Admittedly, Kierkegaard's "as soon as" is a seriously foreshortened account of the therapy of self-understanding that leads to deliverance from radical depression, a therapy that must include becoming aware of one's eternal validity, believing in it, "bowing in true humility before the eternal power," and then finding some form of concrete embodiment or enactment of that selfhood in the world of which one is a part because "the person who possesses oneself in one's eternal validity certainly does find one's meaning in *this life*" (emphasis added).[198] Nevertheless, Kierkegaard's main point holds.

What then is the relation of this undeniable, highly conscious experience of depression to that more elusive, repressed state of the despair of weakness in its form of enclosing reserve? For Kierkegaard, they obviously have the same root cause: living one's life in immediacy and thus failing to live out and enact one's consciousness of "one's eternal validity." So he says that depression consists in "the sin of not willing deeply and inwardly,"[199] just as he defines the despair of weakness as "not willing to be oneself." So there is no essential difference between the two, in that both have an awareness of being in a state of radical despair.

197. Ibid., p. 193; (KW 4:189); SV 3:177; (2:171).
198. Ibid., pp. 193–194; (KW 4:189–190); SV 3:177–178; (2:171–172).
199. Idem.

In *Either/Or* he contrasts depression with the immediacy of an aesthetic lifeview, because in the latter view one is certainly in despair but does not know it. The occurrence of depression awakens one to the fact that one has been and is now in despair. "But when one knows this, ... then a higher form of existence is an imperative requirement." In *Sickness* he contrasts the despair of weakness with the despair of ignorance. In not willing to be oneself because of weakness, especially in the form of enclosing reserve, "one now becomes more clearly conscious of one's despair, that one despairs of the eternal, that one despairs over oneself, ... that one has lost the eternal and oneself."[200] But in between these two pseudonymous works Kierkegaard had already worked out the concept of enclosing reserve, under the guise of two of his more obscure pseudonyms who are closer to his own identity.

In *The Concept of Angst*, Haufniensis identifies enclosing reserve as the "demonic," in the sense that one is in "angst in-relation-to [*for*]" the good, and rather than willingly embracing the good in freedom, one is possessed by unfreedom that "wants to close itself off [*afslutte*]" from the good and thus "closes itself up within itself." So it "does not want communication. ... Enclosing reserve is precisely muteness." In contrast, "the good ... signifies disclosure. ... Disclosure is the good, because disclosure is the first expression of salvation."[201] In *Stages on Life's Way*, Frater Taciturnus initiates the subject of enclosing reserve in his opening "notice." Then as author of the diary, he frequently refers to Quidam's enclosing reserve, and at the very end he states flatly that Quidam's life-view was "that I would hide my depression in my enclosing reserve." This statement is then carefully explicated in his "Letter to the Reader."[202]

His explication is summarized in this way: "enclosing reserve is essentially a form of depression, and [one's] depression in turn is the concentrated possibility that must be experienced through a crisis in order that [one] can become clear to oneself in the religious." But this happy eventuality does not occur for Quidam. He is not clear exactly what this reserve contains or means, except that its concentrated possibility is a vague "anticipation of religious subjectivity," and hence for him "remains the intimation of a higher life." So his reserve remains a delimiting "boundary" that he does not dare cross; rather, by definition, "it

200. Ibid., pp. 196–197; (KW 4:192); SV 3:180; (2:173–174); *Sickness*, p. 195; (KW 19:61); SV 15:117; (11:173).
201. *The Concept of Angst*, pp. 106, 110–111, 113; (KW 8:119. 123–124, 127); SV 6:203, 206–207, 210; (4:387, 390–392, 394).
202. *Stages*, pp. 183, 359; (KW 11:189, 394); SV 8:13, 195; (6:179, 367).

encloses [*indeslutter*] itself" and "holds him fast";[203] hence it is a "limitation of understanding that posits the misunderstanding," and he fails to "become clear to himself in the religious." Little wonder then that "he is depressed in his enclosing reserve," and does not know why. But Frater Taciturnus knows why: "all enclosing reserve is involved in a dialectical reduplication."[204]

In the foregoing paragraph two very technical phrases have been used by Kierkegaard to explicate the relation between enclosing reserve and depression: "condensed possibility" and "dialectical reduplication." Both of them indicate what he means by saying that "religious subjectivity has one more dialectical element than all actuality has," and that by means of this element "one can struggle ahead to religious transparency; this is what he [Quidam] has to do. But this he does not know." Let us see how each of these phrases define that missing dialectical element. The best enlightenment comes from three sets of discourses that Kierkegaard produced two years after writing *Stages*.

We must begin by assuming Haufniensis' series of equations: (1) "the possible corresponds exactly to the future;" (2) "the future is ... the first expression of the eternal and its incognito"; (3) "the eternal is the present" as that "moment" in which there is "the fullness of time," in that "this eternal [as the true present] is also the future and the past." Therefore: "possibility is the weightiest of all categories."[205] So *concentrated* possibility in the person of enclosing reserve means that one has reached that intensity of consciousness of "having a conception of the self, that there is something eternal in it."[206]

This is the consciousness that Kierkegaard describes so well in his *Occasional Discourse* (on "purity of heart is to will one thing"). At its very end he is recalling for "my listener" ("That Single Individual" [*Hiin Enkelte*] to whom the discourse is dedicated) that the discourse began with

203. So *Grændse* is a "boundary" in the sense of a "limit" rather than a "frontier" (Hongs' translation) which beckons.

204. Ibid., pp. 387–388; (KW 11:427–428); SV 8:224–225; (6:388–389). In the last quotation, I translate the Danish verb *ligger i* as "involved in" rather than Lowrie's (and Hongs') "is due to" because enclosing reserve, as explicated by Taciturnus, is not *caused* by the dialectical reduplication but actually ignores and contradicts it. In any case, what Kierkegaard really is saying is that "enclosing reserve is-to-be-understood-in-terms-of a dialectical reduplication," as will become clear in what follows. It should also be noted that SV³ (mistakingly) begins the sentence with *at* rather than *al*, as is found in both SV¹ and SV².

205. *The Concept of Angst*, pp. 81–82, 77, 81, 140; (KW 8:91, 86, 90, 156); SV 6:179, 174, 178, 235; (4:361, 356, 360, 422).

206. *Sickness*, p. 195; (KW 19:62); KW 15:117; (11:173–174).

the point that the temporal is always with us but "the eternal must also have time." And "since no human life is conducted in perfection but each one in weakness" (the weakness of sin and guilt), the eternal can be approached only in the moment of repentance and confession. But that act "requires a collected [or concentrated: *samlet*] mind that has collected itself from all distraction [*Adspredelse*], from every relation, in order to concentrate [*samle sig*] on its relation to itself as the single-individual [*Enkelte*] who is responsible before God; a mind that collected itself from all distraction and thus also from all comparison," (either to those above or to those below). And "by doing this [he] become[s] eternally responsible for every relation he is in ordinarily," because "the one confessing wins the eternal in that he is confirmed in the consciousness that he is a single-individual and in the task of willing one thing in truth."[207]

But: when one has achieved a "concentrated mind" and faces the "concentrated possibility" of embracing the eternal, does one automatically humble one's heart and turn to God in confession? In the discourse, Kierkegaard immediately notes that at this critical juncture the individual faces "the strait gate and the narrow way" (Mt 7:14). That is to say, one faces a very difficult decision, because what makes the way narrow is that one must choose it by oneself, on one's own, with no comparison with or help from anyone else. And going off in the opposite direction is clearly in view "the broad way" where one will have many companions: "the way of the crowd is always broad."[208]

Both Taciturnus and Anti-Climacus insist that the person of enclosing reserve fails, out of weakness (i.e., lack of inward depth and determination), to follow the strait and narrow path. Taciturnus says that in enclosing reserve, one "is unwilling to relate to oneself in one's religious idea," one retreats "in silence," and so one becomes depressed in one's reserve that "closes itself in," hidden within "in the quiet form of mental derangement, perhaps even in the form of guilt, ... the essential forms of consolidated enclosing reserve."[209] As we have seen (note 192 above), Anti-Climacus states, even more clearly, that sooner or later most persons of enclosing reserve leave their solitude behind and join the crowd on the broad path of "happy," successful living in the

---

207. *Upbuilding Discourses in Various Spirits*, pp. 215–217; (KW 15:152–153); SV 11:138; (8:240).

208. Idem.

209. *Stages*, pp. 387–389; (KW 11:427–429); SV 8:224–226; (6:398–400).

multitude of finite social relations. They carefully lock their concern for self behind a closed door and break out of the inner life. They "hurl themselves into life, perhaps into the diversion of great enterprises," or they "will seek oblivion in sensuality, perhaps in dissolute living." They "want to go back to immediacy, but always with the consciousness of the self [they] do not want to be." So either dimly or vividly they know they are living a life of despair. "The self does not want to acknowledge itself after having been so weak. In despair it cannot forget this weakness; it hates itself in a way, will not in faith humble itself under its weakness in order thereby to recover itself." So underneath it all, "one becomes more clearly conscious of one's despair, that one despairs of the eternal, that one despairs over oneself" and hence "has lost the eternal and oneself."[210]

The nature of this double loss is indicated again by Taciturnus when he says that enclosing reserve essentially involves "a dialectical reduplication." Since this is Kierkegaard's first use of this peculiar phrase and the first significant use of the term reduplication, we will interpret it in the light of his later development of the concept as has been discussed above in chapter 2 (at note 35 and pp. 72–76). In contrast with immediacy, Taciturnus says one's consciousness is disturbed by a dim awareness of the possibility of "religious transparency," or as Anti-Climacus would say, that there is "something eternal" in one's being. And since one is overwhelmed by the demands of one's finite, everyday, immediate relationships, this "reduplication" of the infinite/eternal in one's existence sets up an unsettling dialectic. This presence is the "one more dialectical element" that must be operative in one's actuality if one is to achieve "religious subjectivity."[211] But in the case of the despair of weakness, one does not have the daring to venture into this unknown realm of becoming a self before God. So the only solution is to close the door on this awareness, to hide it deep within, lock that door securely, and throw away the key. So the possibility of becoming self in relation with the eternal is lost.

Little wonder, then, that the despair of enclosing reserve often manifests itself at some level of depression. Kierkegaard warns that "if enclosing reserve is maintained completely, ... then the greatest danger is suicide." At this stage, most people today seek help, if only by using

210. *Sickness*, pp. 199, 196, 195; (KW 19:65–66, 62, 61); SV 15:120, 117; (11:177, 174, 173).
211. *Stages*, pp. 387–388; (11:427–428); SV 8:224–225; (6:398–399).

drugs.[212] And Kierkegaard says that if such a person "opens up to one single person," then the chance of moderating the condition is possible, and suicide can be avoided.[213] But for him such methods are only stop gaps and do not even touch the primary cause: "the loss of the eternal and one's self." And the human condition of despair can know even one more intensification: despair over one's weakness can turn into the despair of defiance

7 *The Despair of Defiance*

The three levels of despair (ignorance, weakness, defiance) were once presented to a group of pastors as representing three types of problems they face every week in presenting the gospel of hope and love, of forgiveness and renewal: the problem of *awakening* people to the possibility of self-fulfillment, the problem of *encouraging* them to work hard at it, the problem of *helping* them to see that they need the *help* of *God* to achieve it. They were asked which of the three tasks is the hardest. They replied unanimously that they could handle the first two fairly well, but the third one is very, very difficult, often impossible. Kierkegaard explains their difficulty this way.

He insists that the distinction between despair of weakness and of defiance is relative, that they are always mixed, with more or less of one and the other. But the basic principle is that the greater the degree of self-consciousness, the greater the despair.[214] And when one takes "one single dialectical step further" and reaches a certain intensity of self-consciousness, then there occurs "a shift" and weakness turns into defiance. Such a person recognizes "the eternal within the self," becomes aware of the infinite possibilities of the self, and accepts the challenge (demand) to become that self. Then the fatal error occurs when such a person refuses to recognize that the eternal transcends self, that one "needs the help of the eternal," that the self needs "the courage to lose itself," – to submit itself to the eternal – "in order to gain itself."[215]

---

212. Reports confirm that millions of cases of depression, at all levels, in the United States are routinely treated by prescribing Prozac or other similar drugs, and that the patients include large numbers from every level of the economic and social scale. Pharmaceutical companies are making the drugs available without cost for homeless and indigent people, and they are being used on a continuing and daily basis by top leaders of corporations and of other organizations in our society.

213. *Sickness*, p. 200; (KW 19:66); SV 15:121; (11:177–178).

214. Ibid., pp. 182–183, 175; (KW 19:49, 42); SV 15:105, 98–99; (11:160–161, 154).

215. Ibid., p. 201; (KW 19:67); SV 15:122; (11:178).

Instead of submitting to the eternal, the self "misuses the eternal." How? It assumes that "the infinite self" is within its own power to control and to direct. It "severs the self from any relation to a power that has established it," even "from the idea that such a power exists." It seizes the "infinite self, ... the most abstract possibility of the self," and uses it to become "master of itself or to create itself, to make one's self into the self that *s/he* wants to be, to determine what *s/he* will have or not have in one's concrete self." In other words, such a person "does not want to put on one's [own] self, does not want to see one's given self as one's task."[216]

In these words Kierkegaard describes perfectly the self-confident person, determined to assert oneself and to dominate whatever social grouping, professional field, or business operation one participates in, and thus to achieve power and recognition, even if one lacks the innate abilities, even if such activity contradicts one's own inner self-understanding. In his own world of the first half of the nineteenth century, Kierkegaard saw such "defiance" as characteristic of masculinity, seeing "devotedness, givingness" as typical of the feminine. But in the late twentieth century, women are in the process of freeing themselves from this stereotype and often manifest the same characteristics as the ambitious male in social, business, or professional situations. And at the same time an increasing number of men are gladly abandoning the model of dominance that has been projected upon them by most traditional societies. Even Kierkegaard admits that "I am far from denying that women may have forms of masculine despair and that men may have forms of feminine despair," although, he insists, these are "the exception." The ambiguities and inconsistencies in his uses of this masculine-feminine distinction have been carefully analyzed and noted by Sylvia Walsh, and hence in what follows here the distinction will be largely ignored.[217]

---

216. Ibid., pp. 201–202; (KW 19:67–68); SV 15:22–23; (11:178–179).

217. Ibid., pp. 182–183; (KW 19:49–50); SV 15:105–107; (11:161–163). See Sylvia Walsh's treatments of this theme first in her essay, "On 'Feminine' and 'Masculine' Forms of Despair" in *IKC: The Sickness unto Death*, pp. 121–134, and secondly in her recent book, *Living Poetically*, pp. 251–262. These superb materials can (and must) serve as the beginning point for an urgently needed and undoubtedly fascinating study of Kierkegaard's diverse treatments of the masculine/feminine distinction throughout the works and journals, in order to see what changes and development occur. For example, in *The Concept of Angst* he says, "[I]n spirit there is no difference between man and woman" p. 63; (KW 8:70); SV 6:161; (4:340). But in *Sickness* he says, "masculinity essentially belongs under the determinant spirit, while femininity is a lower synthesis," and hence he can adopt the absurd Pauline thesis that "in most cases the woman actually relates to God only through the man" just after having admitted that "in the relationship to God ... the distinction of man-woman vanishes" pp. 200,

In either case, he argues that any such attempt at self-transformation or self-redefinition is an impossibility, is doomed to failure. "No derived self can give itself more than it is in itself, ... it remains itself from first to last." Here Kierkegaard is assuming everything that we have spelled out in chapter 2 above under the topic, "The Gift and Givenness." But he is also recalling those powerful words in *Either/Or* about the task of choosing to be the very concrete specific self we have been given, as well as his exposition (earlier in *Sickness*) of the complex concept of the self as given κατα δυναμιν (potentially).[218] Granted this givenness of the self as a potentiality that one must become in order truly to be one's self, then it follows (Kierkegaard argues) that this attempt to redefine one's self produces nothing but a "negative self" or "hypothetical self;" it consists of "imaginary constructions," of "merely building castles in the air, ... merely shadowboxing." They may "look splendid," but "in the final analysis, what [the self] understands by itself is a charade. ... The whole thing can dissolve into nothing." Indeed, "it really becomes no self."[219] In other words, as we have noted, this defiant assertion of self in "willing to be itself" actually amounts to "not willing to be itself," namely, to be the self that it has been given to *become*. So when the self assumes that "the self is its own master," then it is in defiance of "the power that established it." And this can only end in despair, because the only alternative to being is non-being.

Then Kierkegaard spends about four pages at the conclusion of part 1 of *Sickness* exploring the most intense form of this despair, what he calls "demonic" despair, which serves as a clue to the fundamental character of all despair. Sooner or later the ontological emptiness and impotence of choosing to be the master of one's own self-definition, rather than choosing to explore the infinite possibilities of the self one has been given to be, manifests itself. In most dramatic form Kierkegaard saw it in Nero's burning Rome or Caligula's wishing that the Roman populace had one neck to be cut off with a single stroke (see *Either/Or*). We have seen it in Napoleon's trudging home from defeat before Moscow after

---

184n; (κw 19:67, 50n); sv 15:121, 107n; (11:178, 163n). Walsh's materials will be referred to more explicitly in chapter 5 under the section on "Relevance of the Triad of Self-God-Neighbor: Transforms Forms of Preferential Love."

218. For an exposition of both concepts, see *Kierkegaard as Humanist*; for choosing the self, see the section, "Freedom in Relation to the Past" in chapter 4, pp. 118–125; for the self κατα δυναμιν, see the section, "Necessity Internal to Becoming Self" in chapter 5, pp. 203–210.

219. *Sickness*, pp. 203; (κw 19:69–70); sv 15:123–124; (11:180–181).

the vain sacrifice of his troops, or in Hitler's final withdrawal into his bunker while Berlin went down in flames. In these extreme examples Kierkegaard sees the despair of enclosing reserve taking the demonic form of "rage against everything," of "hatred of [and] rebellion against all existence." But even simple and powerless persons can feel this existential rage against what they perceive as a cruelty at the heart of life. Kierkegaard says that such a self wants to use its own suffering as "evidence against ... the goodness" of "the power that established it," defiantly and in malice hurling its denunciation against that power.[220] "Life is not fair!" Or in the colloquial language of our day, "Life is shit!"

Kierkegaard insists that at the base of such rage is an unacknowledged refusal of help, a fervent desire not to be helped, masking a fear of the eternal, a fear that if a person listens to the offer of help, then one "would not be able to ... prove to oneself that one is right," or then perhaps one would have to face the denial of one's "infinite superiority over other human-beings." Here lies the heart of all despair: not wanting to admit that one "needs help." As we will see in the next chapter, at the heart of the Christian understanding of love lies the gracious offer of help (from God to self, from self to neighbor, from neighbor to self), and all renewal and recovery hangs on, waits upon, the humble acceptance of help.

It is precisely in this context that Kierkegaard suggests the perplexing perspective that we introduced at the beginning of this chapter (pp. 139–142), namely, the idea that the tragedy of human failure and despair is "actually not a mistake but in a much higher sense an essential constituent-element of [God's] whole production." In other words, there is no other way for humans to learn that they need help, that they are designed to live *only* in loving relationship with God and neighbor, that to try to live on their own, to live by and unto themselves alone, leads *only* into a state of emptiness and despair, into the nothingness and the self-destructiveness of anger, malice, and hatred. So human failure and despair may indeed be "something-that-belongs" essentially to God's whole creative process for humankind, *but*: the resolution of the failure (the renewal and recovery from despair, the fulfillment of this process) hangs on the narrow thread of the offer of loving help being *made*, being *listened to*, and ultimately being *accepted* in gladness and gratitude. In other words, Kierkegaard's justification of his thesis, that the inescapable failure and despair of every human being is part of "God's whole

220. Ibid., pp. 203–206; (KW 19:70–73); SV 15:124–127; (11:181–184).

production," is to be found and clarified (if at all) only in the exposition of his understanding of the nature of that faith/love relationship with God that opens up within the impact of God's presence in Jesus as the Christ.

Before we attempt this exposition, however, we must briefly note one final intensification of despair as characteristic of "My Self: A Failure."

IN OFFENSE DESPAIR BECOMES SIN

To repeat: "Sin is: *before God … in despair not to will to be oneself, or in despair to will to be oneself.* Thus sin is intensified weakness or intensified defiance: sin is the intensification of despair. The emphasis is on *before God.*" To put it even more strongly: to be "directly before [*lige over for*] God" is "the decisively Christian qualification."[221] This means to be *consciously* face-to-face with God, and such a relationship is not possible within religiousness A where the eternal is strictly immanent. It is precisely the paradoxically objective-subjective presence of God in a historical event/person that distinguishes the Judeo-Christian consciousness of the eternal. In this relationship, Kierkegaard argues, there is the qualitative shift from having "the human self" to having "the theological self" as one's "goal and criterion." And, as we have seen above (at notes 10–13 above), this involves also a shift in the meaning of the term sin. In *Either/Or* and in the works of Haufniensis and Johannes Climacus, the term sin is used to designate a universal state or condition of every human being. But in the exploration of religiousness B (Christianity), especially by Anti-Climacus, sin is restricted to a particular "position" taken by the individual who has come into a self-conscious relationship with God, particularly through encounter with Jesus as the Christ, and particularly the individual who, in and through that relationship, has experienced the offer and demand of a faith/love relationship with God.[222]

But why does the offer and the possibility of such a positive and promising relationship (faith/love) serve as the decisive context of the occurrence of *sin* and hence of ultimate despair? Because as we shall see at length in the next chapter, this offer or invitation *must* – in accordance with the essential nature of the One who offers and with the require-

---

221. Ibid., pp. 208, 214; (KW 19:77, 83); SV 15:131, 136; (11:189, 194).
222. Ibid., pp. 210–211; (KW 19:79–80, 113–114); SV 15:133, 163–164; (11:191–192, 223–224).

ments of its fulfillment – provide time and space (psychic distance) for the offer to be accepted in *freedom*. And the negative possibility, inherent in the possibility of acceptance, is refusal, or in the language of Anti-Climacus, is "the possibility of offense." Two years later he spells out this idea even more explicitly (in relation to "absurd" and "paradox").²²³ He says, "the absurd is the expression for despair: that humanly it is not pos-sible – but despair is the negative sign of faith. So it is with offense and faith – offense is the negative criterion which confirms the quality between God and human-beings." So "the believing-person [*Troende*] is not offended – [the believer] expresses just the opposite of offense [i.e., faith], yet [the believer] always has the possibility of offense as a nega-tive determinant." In other words, "in as much as the believer believes, the absurd is not the absurd – faith transforms it, but in every weak mo-ment it is again more or less absurd to [the believer]. The passion of faith is the only thing that masters the absurd."

This explication of offense, however, is much more complex than it appears to be on the surface in this abbreviated form. In it Kierkegaard is assuming and implying a whole range of ideas that he has developed previously: the infinite distinction of quality between God and the hu-man-being, the inseparability of love and freedom, the peculiar nature of God's sovereignty, the notion of God's reduplication, the ubiquitous presence of the negative as an indicator of the positive, and ultimately the question of theodicy: is such a risky undertaking (of human fulfill-ment as requiring human freedom) worth the cost of the suffering in-volved? In other words, human failure and human despair at their ultimate intensity in *sin* (that is, in weakness or defiance, taking offense when God out of love offers help and healing in face-to-face encounter) are really to be understood only in the context of that encounter.

That is to say, sin is not a concept, to be grasped by and in its defini-tion as such. "Christianity," says Kierkegaard, "*must* be believed and not comprehended [*begribes*]" through speculation or abstract thought.²²⁴ Sin is ultimately "understood" only in its experience, in its conscious-ness, only as the human spirit is brought to the point of confession in the face of the offer of forgiveness and reconciliation. So Socrates is wrong: sin is not ignorance, is not the lack of understanding. Sin is a po-sition, it is a stance, it is a determination or willing that takes shape at

---

223. In some notes he wrote as a possible reply to an attack by Theophilus Nicolaus (pseudonym of Magnus Eiriksson): *Journals*, 9, 10; x⁶ B 78, 79.

224. *Sickness*, p. 229; (KW 19:98); SV 15:150; (11:209).

the depth of human self-consciousness in the inward depths and the
heart of the self.[225] It is "a refusal to hear anything about repentance
and grace,"[226] a hardening of the heart against the truth and a withdrawal from the freeing, renewing, empowering relationship of love. So
sin finally takes the form of "despairing over one's sin" and "despairing
of the forgiveness of sins." And as such "the category of sin is [strictly]
the category of individuality; ... sin is a determinant of the particular individual [*den Enkelte*]." Hence, "if this 'particular individual' is to feel in
kinship with God (and this is what Christianity teaches), then [that indi-
vidual] also senses the full weight of it in fear and trembling and must
discover ... the possibility of offense."[227]

So sin in this eminent sense is the opposite of faith, and as such is very
close to faith, even though separated by a yawning gulf. In fact, "despair
over sin is dialectically understood as pointing toward faith. ... Indeed,
offense as annulled possibility is an element of faith, but offense directed away from faith is sin."[228] So Kierkegaard draws to a close his
treatment of despair and the entirety of *The Sickness unto Death* by emphasizing that the possibility of sin as offense is "the dialectical factor in
faith" and "is related primarily to the paradox (Christ) and thus arises
with every determination of the essentially Christian." And in his concluding words he notes: "the contrast [sin/faith] has been advanced
throughout this entire book, which at the outset introduced the formula
for the state in which there is no despair at all: in relating to itself and in
willing to be itself, the self rests [is grounded] transparently in the
Power that established it. This formula ... is the definition of faith."[229]
In other words, I really come to know my self as sinner, and what it
means to sin, only in the moment of my forgiveness, in relationship with
the Forgiver. So we are led inevitably to our next chapter on the heart of
the Christian experience of God and of the recovery of the self: faith/
love.

But let us close this contemplation of "My Self: A Failure" by recalling
some words from the opening pages of part 2 of *Sickness* (on "Despair Is
Sin"): "God is not some externality ... like a policeman." The point is that
the self has a real sense of being in relationship with God "and yet does

225. See *Sickness*, part 2, section A, chapters 2 and 3.
226. Ibid., p. 241; (KW 19:110); SV 15:160; (11:220).
227. Ibid., pp. 250–251; (KW 19:119–120); SV 15:168–170; (11:228–230).
228. Ibid., p. 247n; (KW 19:116n); SV 15:166n; (11:226n).
229. Ibid., pp. 259–260, 262; (KW 19:129, 131); SV 15:177–178, 180; (11:238–239, 241).

not will as [God] wills, and thus is disobedient. ... [W]hat really makes human guilt into sin is that the guilty one has the consciousness of existing before God. ... Only when [*først naar*] a self, as this specific individual, is conscious of existing before God, only then is it the infinite self; and [it is] *this* self [that] sins before God" (emphasis added).[230] For Kierkegaard (Climacus in *Postscript*), "totality of guilt-consciousness" consists in coming to the consciousness that one cannot fulfill the absolute ethical demands of the eternal (the teleological suspension of the ethical), and hence one must turn to the eternal for help.[231] But coming to a qualitative sense of *sin* occurs only in the consciousness that my *self* as such, as personal, subjective, responsible being, has hardened its heart against the demands of love and must now turn to the Power that gave it life for forgiveness and renewal, for recovery from its essential failure.

Anti-Climacus asserts that "only in Christ is it true that God is the human-being's criterion and goal," because "the greater the conception of God, the more self," and "a self directly before Christ is a self intensified by the inordinate concession from God, intensified by the inordinate accent that falls upon it by the fact that [*derved at*] God, for this self's guilt, could also be born, become human-being, suffer, and die."[232] In other words, only a Christian knows what it truly means to be in sin, because only a Christian has that intensity of self-consciousness before God that is required for the defiance of taking offense. But even Kierkegaard, immersed in the Scriptures as he was, must recognize one exception. On the one hand, his perspective on sin, as requiring a profoundly self-conscious presence before God, is beautifully expressed by the Christian mystic named John who wrote:

> God is light
>> and in God is no darkness at all.
> If we say we have fellowship with God
>> while we walk in darkness
>> we lie and do not enact the truth.

230. Ibid., p. 211; (KW 19:80); SV 15:134; (11:182).
231. See *Kierkegaard as Humanist*, pp. 291–294.
232. *Sickness*, pp. 244–245; (KW 19:113–114); SV 15:164; (11:223–224). The Hong translation inexplicably omits the word "guilt" from the phrase *for dette Selvs Skyld*. Also, the reflexive *lade sig* means "it can be." Kierkegaard's point is not that God "allowed himself" to be born, etc., but the startling fact that it is consistent with the very being of God that God could be born, etc., and actually was so.

> But if we walk in the light as God is in the light
>> we have fellowship with one another
> And the blood of Jesus (God's son) cleanses us from all sin.
> If we say we have no sin
>> we deceive ourselves
>> and the truth is not in us.
> If we confess our sins
>> God is faithful and just and will forgive our sins
>> And will cleanse us from all unrighteousness. (1 Jn 1:5–9)

On the other hand, Kierkegaard's claim of Christian exclusivity on this perspective must acknowledge the fact that the same intensity of consciousness of being before God, and the same intensity of self-involvement with the judgment and forgiveness of God, were expressed even more beautifully and poignantly by a psalmist one thousand years before Jesus:[233]

> Have mercy on me, O God, according to thy steadfast love;
>> according to thy abundant mercy, blot out my transgressions. ...
> For I know my transgressions, and my sin is ever before me.
> Against thee, thee only, have I sinned,
>> and done that which is evil in thy sight. ...
> Behold, thou desirest truth in the inward being;
>> therefore teach me wisdom in my secret heart. ...
> Hide thy face from my sins,
>> and blot out all my iniquities.
> Create in me a clean heart, O God,
>> and put a new and right spirit within me.
> Cast me not away from thy presence,
>> and take not thy holy Spirit from me.
> Restore to me the joy of thy salvation,
>> and uphold me with a willing spirit. ...
> The sacrifice acceptable to God is a broken spirit;
>> a broken and contrite heart, O God, thou wilt not despise (Ps 51).

In spite of the scholars' view that in this psalm the "I" is corporate Israel pleading for the purification of both the house of God and of the

---

233. I side with the judgment that the author belonged to the original David cult rather than to the promoters of the second temple.

nation, it has always been read by both the Jewish and Christian communities as a cry from the heart of the personal "I."[234] And it captures perfectly Kierkegaard's sense of the individual human's failure as sin before God and of his contention that the only resolution lies in accepting the help of God's Spirit at the depth's and in the heart of individual human spirit. But we must stress once more that, for Kierkegaard, sin before God does not consist in the breaking of rules of behavior or simply in being rebellious. Rather, in its essence sin is the failure to become self, either in despairing weakness or in despairing defiance. The reason "[God's] eyes rest with concern on the human race" is that God knows that "the individual's tender shoot can be crushed as easily as a blade of grass." And the reason God/Christ "cannot remove the possibility of offense" is the "unfathomable conflict in love," namely, that God/Christ longs for the human heart to return God's love but knows that to compel it would be to destroy it: love can be returned only *freely* – or it is not love.[235] So the key to the recovery of self lies in the mystery of the divine-human interchange through encounter with the sovereign love of God as known in the relationship of faith. Again, we are brought to our next chapter.

234. For example, Abraham Heschel comments on the psalm in his book, *A Passion for Truth* (p. 97). In one of his comparisons of the thought of Reb Menahem Mendl of Kotzk and that of Kierkegaard, he comments that, like Kierkegaard, "The 'I' becomes the central problem in the Kotzker's thinking; it is the primary counterpart of God in the world. The sin of presumptuous selfhood is the challenge and defiance that God faces in the world. The clamor for purity of heart, which has been heard throughout the history of Jewish reflection, often sounds like a signal of distress. 'Create in me a clean heart, O God, and put a new and right spirit within me,' says the Psalmist (51). This cry reverberates throughout the Bible and Jewish liturgy. But modern Judaism has not concerned itself sufficiently with the uncleanness of the heart."

235. *Fragments*, p. 40; (KW 7:32); SV 6:34; (4:200); *Sickness*, p. 257; (KW 19:126); SV 15:175; (11:235–236); cf. also *Practice*, pp. 159–160; (20:159–160); SV 16:155; (12:149–150).

4

My Self: In Need of The Eternal

THE DIALECTIC OF THE HUMAN-DIVINE
IN THE ENCOUNTER WITH GOD

For Kierkegaard, Jesus as the Christ is the source and the content, "the criterion and goal," of spiritual truth for the human being. Jesus is such because "only in Christ is it true that *God* is the human-being's criterion and goal" (emphasis added).[1] We have argued that Kierkegaard surely must grant that such consciousness was and is also possible for those of the Jewish faith. After all, Jesus himself came to such consciousness of God by steeping himself in the Bible and the traditions of the Judaism of his day. Yet Kierkegaard insists that "Abraham is called the father of faith in the New Testament" because "Abraham's faith is the formal determinant of faith," but "it is very clear that the content of his faith cannot be the [essentially] Christian, [namely] that Jesus Christ has existed [*har været til*]," that is, God has entered time.[2]

Climacus saw this difference as a matter of degree. He granted that Religiousness A is like (Christian) Religiousness B in that it is dialectical, but it possesses only "the dialectic of inward deepening" and hence "is not paradoxically dialectical." Religiousness B on the other hand "makes conditions" that are "a definite something that determines the eternal blessedness more specifically."[3] In contrast to Climacus, Anti-Climacus stresses

1. *Sickness*, p. 245; (KW 19:114); SV 15:164; (11:224).

2. *Journals*, 12; X^6 B 81.

3. *Postscript*, p. 494; (KW 12.1:556); SV 10:225; (7:485). Of course, neither Jesus nor Paul considered Judaism to fall under the category of universal religiousness A. And Kierkegaard certainly read the Jewish Scriptures as having the same authority as the New Testament, but to my knowledge he did not treat the question of the difference between the "revelation" of the Old and the New Testaments.

the qualitative newness of the presence of God in Jesus as the Christ. And the key to and evidence for all claims of Christian uniqueness lie precisely in the "content" of that faith-relationship with God that is opened up through the encounter of a human being with Jesus as the Christ. And in spite of current attempts to demonstrate that all major religions are fundamentally the same in essential content, and that all are equally reliable guides to the same goal of life in and with the eternal, the present author believes that Kierkegaard succeeds in depicting a Judeo-Christian experience of God and of life with God that is qualitatively unique among the religions of the world. And whatever of value Christianity may learn from dialogue with other religions, it should and must maintain its witness to its own uniqueness for the cause of salvation of all human beings from the despair of "the sickness unto death."[4]

Kierkegaard's second (Christian) authorship is dedicated to this depiction, and it seeks to plumb the depths and heights of the individual human self's experience and appropriation of that faith and life made possible by Jesus as the Christ. The present author also believes that Kierkegaard's analysis and depiction of the inward, personal, subjective

4. This assertion requires two explanations. First, the Judeo-Christian religion has been profoundly influenced in its formation by the impact of other religions and philosophies which it has encountered along the way. To name only a few: the Gilgamesh epic, the Zoroastrian concept of evil, the Greek concept of a universal logos, the notions of being and non-being. But these many sources have not been simply incorporated as such but have served to stimulate the peculiar perspective of the Judeo-Christian tradition to enlarge and to refine itself. Secondly, to say that this tradition is "unique" does not mean "totally different." All human beings have been born into the same universe and face essentially the same conundrums and mysteries of human existence. And as I have shown at great length in *Kierkegaard as Humanist*, Kierkegaard assumes that the eternal has been and is present and knowable at profound depths for all human beings. So what he regards as the essentially Christian must have and does have profound resonance with much in the very different perspectives of other religions. Yet when that particular Jew, Jesus of Nazareth, put together as one law the great *shema* of Deut 6:4–5 on the love of God in combination with that pedestrian advice of Lev 19:18, 34 on the love of neighbor and stranger, and then said, "On these two commandments depend all the law and the prophets" (Mt 22:40), Jesus had created the revolutionary insight that you cannot separate the love of God from the love of neighbor, nor from the love of self. And the author of John's gospel heard Jesus saying, "I give you a new commandment, that you love one another" (Jn 13:34). On this basis Jesus was able to say, "Think not that I have come to abolish the law and the prophets; I have come to fulfill them," and then to go on to make that revolutionary intensification of the law by saying, "You have heard it said of old ... , but I say to you ..." (Mt 5:17, 21–48). In this kind of "newness" there is both continuity and radical transformation. As suggested in note 121 of chapter 3 above, one wonders what Kierkegaard would have made of the extensive comparisons of similar but also different elements in the world's religions as done in the writings of Joseph Campbell.

dimensions of this appropriation are more subtle, more sensitive, and more complex than that of any other theologian he is aware of. In any case, all followers of "the way" that Jesus opened up, at whatever level of commitment, are bound to be challenged and startled as they test their own understanding of that way with that of Kierkegaard. And it is the hope of this present exposition that even those who are seekers of *a* way will find this presentation accessible, suggestive, stimulating, that it will lead seekers (as well as followers) to the place where they become filled with "fear and trembling," which (Kierkegaard says) signifies not that they have been persuaded but that they (for and by themselves) have become aware simultaneously of the judgment of the eternal *and* of their need of the eternal – and in this moment they will have to decide, for themselves and by themselves. This applies, Kierkegaard says, equally to seekers and followers because followers are always on the way, never at the end, never in possession of God nor fully possessed by God. Followers also continue to be seekers, who each day must freely turn again to the place where they meet the eternal. For Christians that "place" is the encounter with Jesus as the Christ.

Before we spell out Kierkegaard's analysis and depiction of the "content" of Christian faith, we must emphasize one of his major assumptions about the nature of the encounter. Throughout the history of Christianity, it has been a constant temptation for Christians to assume that the incarnate Christ has been replaced by the risen and glorified Christ, that the members of his body, the church, are redeemed and saved (even though remaining sinners), that the believer stands in direct and unambiguous relationship with the Son of God and no longer with the ambiguous rabbi of Nazareth named Jesus, and finally that regular participation in the worship and sacraments of the church establishes and constantly deepens this direct relationship. So they sing, "Blessed assurance! Jesus is mine! Oh, what a foretaste of glory divine!" Here is the attitude of what Roman Catholic theologians call "triumphalism." It was this attitude in the church of his day that so scandalized Kierkegaard, because the result was that Christians were encouraged by the clergy to regard God as their buddy and friend, or at the very least, their doting and ever indulgent Father who might scold his children but never demand or expect any rigorous or whole-hearted obedience.

In utter contrast, Kierkegaard lays as the bedrock foundation, as the absolute, unavoidable, and permanent presupposition of everything Christian this hard fact: God is present to us and with us (in the Christ event) only in and through the utter, paradoxical ambiguity of the lowly common humanity of Jesus as the Christ, the chosen and anointed one. And not just once, for only a few years long ago and far away in a remote province of the Roman Empire, but continuously throughout all time and in every land where his story is retold – and in every hour of every day during the entire life of the most devout follower. As we have heard Kierkegaard say in *The Book on Adler* (chapter 1, note 48), "[T]he paradox itself did not last throughout many years; it existed when Christ lived, and since that time it exists only each time someone [either] is offended or in truth believes."

He makes the point even more clearly in *Practice in Christianity*. He says that Christ "wants to draw the human being to himself, but ... he wants to draw the human being as a free being to himself, that is through a choice." But Christ "is in lowliness and in loftiness one and the same. ... Christ is not divided. ... Christ is a composite [*Sammensat*] and yet one and the same, is the abased and the lofty one, and thus specifically prevents choosing one of the two parts. ... If he could truly draw to himself without a choice, he would have to be a single one [*et Enkelte*], either the lofty one or the abased one, but he is both." Let us remember the apostles "who knew nothing and wanted to know nothing except Christ and him crucified."[5] And as we have heard (at chapter 3, note 223 above), this dual, composite nature of the Christ we encounter means that, while faith masters and transforms the absurd so that it is no longer absurd, yet "in every weak moment it is again more or less absurd to [the believer]," that is to say, the believer "always has the possibility of offense as a negative determinant." Even in the passion of faith we are not given direct objective certainty. After all, faith *is* faith.

Perhaps the most important implication of this paradoxical character of the Christian's daily encounter with Jesus as the Christ is this: that one does not meet (or is not met by) God first as wrathful judge who condemns sin, and only then as loving forgiver and reconciler. Rather, both seekers and followers come to know the true character and the depth of human failure only in and with the complex and ambiguous offer of loving forgiveness and acceptance, and with that offer, the possibility of the "recovery of my self." In what shape and with what substance does this offer come?

Our summary of Kierkegaard's answer will have two parts. In part 1 we will follow his exploration of the elements of what the old Protestant theological systems of the seventeenth century called the *ordo salutis* in

5. *Practice*, pp. 160, 178; (кw 20:160, 178); sv 16:155–156, 172; (12:150, 166).

terms of three topics: (1) the nature of confession, (2) the dynamics of forgiveness/reconciliation, (3) the imitation of Christ. A full exposition of Kierkegaard's treatment of this topic would require (and deserves) a book by itself. So what follows is only a brief description of the essential elements that would appear in such an exposition. In part 2 we will consider two problematic aspects of these three same elements: (1) the complementarity of love and faith, (2) the nature of human freedom in the faith/love relationship.

PART ONE: KIERKEGAARD'S *ORDO SALUTIS*

1 The Nature of Confession

"No one can achieve cognition [*tage Kjende*] of God without becoming a sinner."[6] Here Kierkegaard is saying two things: the moment I come into the presence of God, I immediately become aware of my self as a failure, as sinner in despair; in fact, I do not really know myself as sinner except in the presence of God. He is convinced that this highly self-conscious, double-sided cognition or awareness is the beginning point, the first step of a human being on "the way" that leads to healing, to recovery, to wholeness, to salvation, to blessedness. And this fact is especially and absolutely true for the person who is encountered by Jesus as the Christ, that is, when Jesus' words and Jesus' life serve as the occasion for one's awareness of being "directly before God." The phrase "consciousness of sin" (or "sin-consciousness") reappears throughout Kierkegaard's major writings, from *Either/Or* to *Practice in Christianity*, and many important things are said about it in the first authorship up through *Postscript*.[7] These things reflect the fact that Kierkegaard was nurtured from his earliest years in his father's piety of the Herrnhuter "Congregation of

6. *Three Discourses on Imagined Occasions*, p. 25; (KW 10:28); SV 6:263; (5:28). This quotation is from the first discourse, "On the Occasion of a Confession." This title is repeated by Kierkegaard for the first discourse in *Upbuilding Discourses in Various Spirits*, the well-known one on "purity of heart." The intensity and profoundness of the sense of being "directly before God" in the latter discourse is a good example of how Kierkegaard began to explore and to express his new Christian self-consciousness in the second authorship just six months after the first attack on him by *The Corsair* (January 2, 1846). Hence, in all that follows, the term "sin" must be understood in terms of the materials in chapter 3 concerning disrelation and offense.

7. In between these two, the phrase appears in *The Concept of Angst, Philosophical Fragments, Three Discourses on Imagined Occasions, Concluding Unscientific Postscript*, and *Upbuilding Discourses in Various Spirits*. We will refer to some of these below.

Brothers,"[8] and that, from that perspective, he absorbed much of his university theological teachings into his own way of thinking, but it took much longer for these influences to become absorbed and active as his own personal convictions. We can observe this latter step rapidly taking place as the second authorship takes shape during the *Corsair* affair.

Already in *Upbuilding Discourses in Various Spirits* Kierkegaard brings into play a new tone and new concepts. His reflections are more personal, more passionate and intense, explored with a greater sense of inward urgency and spiritual need. The dialectical relation and interdependence between the human sense of sin before God and divine grace becomes a ruling principle. These reflections are clearly impacted and shaped, in both form and content, by the turning of his spiritual awareness ever more specifically toward the New Testament witness to Jesus as the Christ. What form, then, does this sin-consciousness before Christ first take – not in an abstract sense as caught in a general definition, but in the specifics of the individual's inner sensitivities and heartfelt self-awareness? And what (in the language of Climacus) is "the definite something" in Jesus' objective teachings and life that evokes this sin-consciousness by "qualifying more specifically the eternal blessedness"? Or how (in the language of Anti-Climacus) does the fact that "in Christ" the self for the first time has *God* as "[its] criterion and goal" have the effect that "a self directly before Christ" becomes "intensified" and thereby "the more intense is sin"?[9]

On the character of the first step into confession/repentance, Christian faith agrees with Religiousness A.[10] They agree that one must enter in solitude and silence, that one faces a complete halt, a stop, a pause, because one is at the edge of a breach or chasm, marking an end, like dying. It is a moment filled with fear and trembling.

When a human being faces the eternal in any religious experience, one is possessed by a profound sense of isolation, of being alone. When a "knight of faith" (in *Fear and Trembling*) faces the judgment of reason and of the world that his ideal love is impossible, then one seeks a love that is "transfigured into a love of the eternal being" that "would assume a religious character." In that moment, "one becomes very quiet,

8. See Bruce Kirmmse, *Kierkegaard in Golden Age Denmark*, pp. 30–35.

9. *Postscript*, p. 494; (KW 12.1:556); SV 10:225; (7:485); *Sickness*, pp. 244–245; (KW 19:113–114); SV 15:164; (11:223–224).

10. For this step in Religiousness A, see the section on The Breach in Religiousness A in chapter 6 of *Kierkegaard as Humanist*, especially on isolation and silence. Some of the material used there is repeated below.

one dismisses [those judgments], one becomes solitary [*ene*]." One is "alone" in the sense that one is deserted by one's usually dependable sources of truth (reason, immediate sensation); one is left to make a decision all by oneself. One is required to venture, to risk all, because one is faced with "an intervening yawning chasm as the scene for the passion of infinitude, a gulf which reason [*Forstand*] cannot go over either forward or backward." This halting before the chasm fills one with fear and trembling, because it is "comparable to a fish's being taken out of water and having to breathe in the air." And one "shudders at this [new and strange] element," because one senses that "an enormous power resides in 'the halt'," and its power is limitless. And facing "the limitless, the infinite, the eternal-as-standing-still within the halt is like dying."[11]

But "the stopping is not indolent repose. The stop is also movement; it is the inward movement of the heart; it is self-deepening in inwardness."[12] But how does this movement in face of the eternal take place? Kierkegaard tells his journal, "Every human being who knows how to keep silent becomes a divine child, because in silence there is a concentration upon one's divine origin; one who speaks remains [simply] a human being. How many know how to keep silent, how many understand what it means simply to be silent?" In the same year, Johannes de Silentio says in *Fear and Trembling*, "[S]ilence is divinity's mutual understanding with the single individual [*den Enkelte*]." But why is silence so important? For an answer, Kierkegaard recommends that we turn to the lilies and the birds and from them "learn to be silent. ... You shall in the deepest sense make yourself nothing, become nothing. ... In this silence is the beginning," that is, the "fear-of-God" and hence "the beginning of wisdom." "In this silence the many thoughts of wish and desire fall dumb out of godly fear. ... Only in much fear and trembling can a human being talk with God," even though it "makes the voice fall dumb in silence."[13]

Why, then, does one learn wisdom in silence? Because when one stops listening to the voices of traditional wisdom (reason and immediate sensation), when one no longer seeks "to hear oneself speak," the one becomes "the opposite of a speaker, one becomes a hearer," one *listens* for

11. *Fear and Trembling*, pp. 53–54; (KW 6:42–43); SV 5:40–41; (3:93–94); *Postscript*, p. 379; (KW 12.1:423–424); SV 10:113; (7:367).; *Journals*, 4798; X³ A 47.

12. *Upbuilding Discourses in Various Spirits*, "An Occasional Discourse" on the occasion of confession (purity of heart), p. 217; (KW 15:153); SV 11:139; (8:241).

13. *Journals*, 3978; IV A 28; *Fear and Trembling*, p. 97; (KW 6:88); *The Lilies of the Field and the Birds of the Air*, in *Christian Discourses*, pp. 332–333; SV 14:135–136; (11:14–15).

another voice; one "wait[s] until one ... hears God." In fear and trembling you are "alone in the whole world, you ... are alone in the vicinage of the solemn silence, so alone that every doubt, and every objection, and every excuse, and every evasion, and every question, in short, every voice, is reduced to silence in your inward [self], every voice, that is, every voice but God's, which around you and within you talks to you by means of the silence." And this silence is "the first condition for being able to obey," because "when all around you is solemn silence, and when there is silence within you, then do you ... sense with the force of infinitude the truth of the saying 'you shall love the Lord your God, and [God] only shall you serve,' and you sense that it is *you*, you who shall love God, you, you alone in the whole world."[14]

All this talk of solitude and silence, however, applies for Kierkegaard to Religiousness A's inward deepening as much as to the consciousness of the person "directly before Christ." How, then does the presence of God-in-time (in Jesus) give this encounter more specificity? In his very last brief books, Kierkegaard treats the subject of Christian piety in two series *For Self-Examination*. And in the first series he begins with the admonition of the Apostle James, "Be doers of the Word, and not only hearers of it" (Jas 1:22). But then he avers that, of course, "in order to become a doer of the Word one must first of all be a hearer of it." And where does the Christian turn to hear the eternal Word of God? Not immanently, in an inward deepening of one's own subjective self-consciousness to the point where the omnipresent eternal manifests itself. No, the Christian turns to the objective medium where the Word may be read: Holy Scriptures.[15]

But Kierkegaard makes it immediately clear that it is not the mere, fallible, human *written* words that one listens to, but to the eternal Word of God speaking directly to the individual hearer in and through the written words. And he slices through all the higher-critical problems of

14. Ibid., p. 336; SV 14:148; (11:27–28). In the Biblical quotation in the concluding sentence ("you shall love the Lord your God, etc."), Kierkegaard typically gives a free rendering of Deut 6:13; in fact, he has transferred the word "love" from the more famous verse 5 and substituted it for the word "fear." So he is saying that "love" from the human being toward God actually is the sense of awe and wonder, the fear and trembling that one knows when being "directly before" the Giver of one's being and life, the One in whose image we are created and yet the One who is infinitely and qualitatively different from us. Hence "fear" of God is the beginning of wisdom (note 12 above). The primitive Hebrew root for "fear" is ירא, and it can mean to reverence, to have a sense of dread, terror, wonder.

15. *For Self-Examination*, p. 23–4; (KW 21:25); SV 17:68–69; (12:315).

reading the Bible ("Which books are authentic? How much belongs to 'God's Word'? Are they really the apostles, and are the apostles really authentic?" And how about the strange languages? Which translation do you trust?) Having pursued all the advantages (and confusions) of the scholarly approach is no guarantee that one will hear God's Word. Rather, having done all that, or having had someone else do it for you, you yourself must then turn and *listen* for God to speak. How?[16]

Kierkegaard has several pieces of advice. First, leave behind "the ten dictionaries and twenty-five commentaries." Rather, "take Holy Scripture and lock your door" until you are "alone with God's Word! ... The person who is not alone with God's Word is not reading God's word." And be forewarned: "being alone with God's Word is a dangerous matter. ... It is an imperious book – if one gives it a finger, it takes the whole hand; if one gives it the whole hand, it takes the whole person and may suddenly and radically change my whole life on a prodigious scale." If you are not ready for this, "put it in some out-of-the-way place, ... refuse to be alone with it." Now being alone, what then? Again, Kierkegaard insists on the need for silence. In fact, "the first thing, the unconditional condition that must be done is: create silence, bring about silence; ... if in order to be heard in the hullabaloo [God's Word] must be shouted, ... then it is not God's Word; create silence."[17]

Granted, then, that you are alone and have gained silence, how do you read Scripture in order for it to hear God's Word? The prime requirement is to regard it as a mirror. But "you must not look at the mirror ... but must see yourself in the mirror. ... [R]emember to say to yourself incessantly: It is I to whom it is speaking; it is I about whom it is speaking." And the result will come in this form: "provided you keep on reading God's Word this way, ... you will read a fear and trembling into your soul so that, with God's help, you will succeed in becoming a human-being, an authentic-person [*Personlighed*], rescued from this dreadful nonentity into which we humans, created in the image of God, have been bewitched, an impersonal, an objective something. ... If God's Word is for you merely a doctrine, something impersonal and objective, then it is no mirror. ... [I]t takes an authentic-person, an *I*, to look at oneself in a mirror."[18] For illustration of this point, Kierkegaard uses the Biblical stories of King David and Bathsheba and of the priest, the Levite, and the Samaritan on the

16. Idem.
17. Ibid., pp. 32–34, 56–57; (KW 21:31–32, 47); SV 17:74–75, 88; (12:320–321, 334).
18. Ibid., pp. 39, 50–51; (KW 21:35, 43–44); SV 17:78, 85; (12:324, 331).

road from Jerusalem to Jericho; to both, he says, one must respond, "It is *I* who stole Bathsheba! It is *I* who passed by on the other side of the road!"

Kierkegaard could have illustrated how God's Word leads us into a profound experience of personal conviction and repentance of sin "directly before God" by using more fully some of Jesus' own words that he had briefly referred to just a few pages before his King David illustration. In the (so-called) Sermon on the Mount, Jesus is declaring that he has come not to abolish the law and the prophets but to fulfill them. Indeed, he insists that instead of relaxing the law, we must exceed the righteousness of the scribes and Pharisees (who claim to keep the law to the letter). Then he proceeds to give these startling precepts:[19]

(1) – you have heard it was said to those of old:
    "You shall not kill."
  – but I say to you:
    "Every one who is angry with his brother … is liable to the hell of fire."
(2) – you have heard that it was said:
    "You shall not commit adultery."
  – but I say to you:
    "Whoever looks at [another] with lust has already committed adultery in [one's] heart."
(3) – it was also said:
    "Whoever divorces his wife [or husband], that one shall give her [him] a certificate of divorce."
  – but I say to you:
    "Whoever divorces his wife and marries another, commits adultery against her; and if she divorces her husband and marries another, she commits adultery."
(4) – you have heard that it was said:
    "An eye for an eye and a tooth for a tooth."
  – but I say to you:
    "Do not resist one who is evil. But if anyone strikes you on the right cheek, turn to him the other also."
(5) – you have heard that it was said:
    "You shall love your neighbor and hate your enemy."
  – but I say to you:
    "Love your enemies and pray for those who persecute you."

19. See Mt 5: 21f., 27f., 31f., 38f., 43f.; except that for Jesus' reply on divorce, I use Mk 10:11–12.

What is the total force of this piling of one shattering antiphony upon another and another and another? I must cry out: "What does Jesus think he is saying? Never be *angry*? Never feel *lust*? Never *divorce*? Never demand *vengeance*? Love my *enemy*? He's crazy! It's impossible!" Jesus would then reply: "*Now* you've got the point!" Once he told his disciples that "it is easier for a camel to go through the eye of a needle than for a rich man to enter the kingdom of God." The disciples "were greatly astonished saying, 'Who then can be saved?' But Jesus said to them, 'With human beings this is impossible, but with God all things are possible.'" (Mt 19:24–26) Here is a perfect statement by Jesus of what Kierkegaard calls "the absolute" which Christian faith will not compromise and a perfect example of the role that the proclamation of this absolute has to play according to Anti-Climacus.

In fact, this verse of Scripture, with its notion of the impossible/ possibility, with its statement that "with God all things are possible," became a central theological concept, indeed, the definition of God for Kierkegaard in *The Sickness unto Death*. And in his journals he reveals that these words became his own personal watchword and consolation as his own Christian faith deepened and the troubles in his life intensified.[20] And it is one of Kierkegaard's central convictions that the deepest and truest cry of confession and repentance of human failure, despair, and sin is possible *only* in the very moment that one also encounters and becomes aware of God's infinite, passionate, agonizing love expressed in the offer of forgiveness and reconciliation – "agonizing" because it must be offered with all the exquisite, hesitant delicacy of indirectness because of God's "unfathomable grief of love" that must leave room for human freedom to accept that love, knowing that in that moment the human heart may take offense, and refuse.[21] This dual and simultaneous consciousness – of one's own failure and of God's forgiving love – is at the heart of Kierkegaard's analysis and definition of the uniqueness of the experience and understanding of the encounter of the human being with God made possible in and through Jesus as the Christ.

20. *Sickness*, pp. 172–173; (KW 19:39–40); SV 15:96–97; (11:152–153); and see for example *Journals*, 6135, VIII¹ A 650; 6229, IX A 216 (written in May and July of 1848 as he finished writing *Sickness*).

21. See the descriptions of this moment first in *Fragments*, pp. 39–40; (KW 7:32–33); SV 6:33–34; (4:200), and then in *Sickness*, p. 257; (KW 19:126); SV 15:175; (11:235–236). Louis Dupré spells out this interdependence of consciousness of sin and God's loving grace in Kierkegaard's thought (see Chapter 3, sections 1 and 2).

Indeed, as will become clear throughout the rest of this chapter, for Kierkegaard the substance or content (the "meaning") of the "faith-relationship" (of living "before God," of "resting transparently in God," of "reconciliation" with God) is this: the human self willingly becomes itself in the event of confession and forgiveness, and in the obedience-to-God (or the imitation-of-Christ) that is integral to that process of reconciliation. And at the heart of this event or process comes the revelation that God is: "all-things-are-possible." Of course, this phrase does not mean that I can do or be or become anything I fancy (fantasize). As Kierkegaard has stressed (in *Sickness*), the self's fantasies that ignore one's finitude and the self's possibilities that do not relate to one's necessity lead not to self-actualization but to the destruction and loss of self.

Jesus's other two uses of this phrase are indicative of Kierkegaard's meaning. To the father who pleads with Jesus to heal his son who is possessed with a "dumb spirit," Jesus replies, "all things are possible to the one who believes" (Mk 9:23). In other words, "all things" are defined by one's self-consciousness in the faith-relationship with God. And in that relationship a further refinement is made. As Jesus struggles with his own agonizing consideration of other possibilities than suffering death on the cross, he prays, "Abba, Father, all things are possible to you; remove this cup from me; yet not what I will, but what you will" (Mk 14:36; cf. Mt 26:39; Lk 22:42). In other words, what is good and right (God's "will") for a particular, unique individual in a particular situation must be defined by the absolute of God's goodness and righteousness – about which the believer has no choice, even though s/he must choose it, if it is to become actual in the individual's life and being.

So "all things" are possibilities of *my* self in the sense that, even though *who I am* (including, ultimately, the presence of the Eternal within my temporality) defines and hence limits my future possibilities, yet who I am does not predetermine which future possibility I will actualize. At any one moment in the process of my life, an authentic possibility of my self remains unrealized. And God holds open my future so that "all the things" I choose (in accordance with my self and with God's goodness/righteousness) remain possible. And I live in and by *hope*. This is the point that was anticipated at the end of chapter 2 above when it was said (in the last paragraph) that "faith is precisely the coming to believe that all things are possible," and that "the faith relationship with God is precisely the product of our experience of God's love in forgiveness of our sin and in our deliverance from despair in reconciliation." So this point brings us to our next topic.

2 *The Dynamics of Forgiveness/Reconciliation*

The first element in this dynamics, therefore, is the paradoxical interplay of the "lowliness" and "loftiness," of the ordinary individual humanity and the presence of God, that operates initially and continuously in
every human being's encounter with Jesus as the Christ – the point that
was briefly stated in the introduction of this chapter (at note 5 above).
The "situation" for every such human being is the same as that of that father who brought his son (possessed of a "dumb spirit") to Jesus and
said, "If you can do anything, have pity on us and help us." As we have
just heard, Jesus replied, "All things are possible to one who believes."
And the father cried out, "I believe! Help my unbelief!" (Mk 9:14–29)
Or as Anti-Climacus puts it, "the *situation*" of the encounter with Jesus is
this: "that an individual human being who is standing beside you is the
God-humanbeing."[22]

So Jesus was this very ordinary human person, unknown and unher-
alded, self-taught, with no standing or authority, a people's guru (rabbi),
an itinerant with no possessions and no place to lay his head – and *yet*:
this same one filled his contemporaries with wonder and puzzlement,
possessed a magnetism that no one could explain, drawing thousands
after him along the lake, up into the hills, out into the wilderness. Why?
How? Anti-Climacus puts it this way: "What truly can be said to draw to
itself must be something in itself or something which is in itself. So
it is when truth draws to itself; because truth is in itself, is in and for
itself – and Christ is the truth."[23] And it is precisely this paradoxical, contradictory ambivalence, this mixture of belief and unbelief, this sense of
both wonder and puzzlement, that fills the consciousness of the most devout and confirmed Christian every time s/he opens the Bible in solitude and silence and – *listens.*

This point may seem to be a simple, irreducible surd (radical, element), the ultimate unanalyzable mystery of the so-called "incarnation."
But for Kierkegaard the human encounter with "the paradox" or "the
absurd" is not an intellectual conundrum to be solved. He is interested
not in a conceptual and/or physical explanation of how this presence of
God-in-time is accomplished, but in what phenomenological shape the
human encounter with God-in-time takes in human self-consciousness.
So he leads up to the statement about Christ as "the truth" (near the

22. *Practice*, p. 84; (KW 20:81–82); SV 16:85–86; (12:79).
23. Ibid., p. 160; (KW 20:159); SV 16:155; (12:149).

beginning of no. 3 of *Practice*) with a twenty-page analysis of the relation-ship between taking offense and indirect communication (at the end of no. 2). He makes the following three points.

First, when the followers of Jesus became aware of this duality in their impressions about him, they felt that they were witnessing an event whose significance escaped them. Jesus was a "sign" of some strange and disconcerting happening. A sign, says Kierkegaard, is not what you see and look at – not the piece of paper or wood, nor the letters or the draw-ing on it. A sign has a meaning, it points to something not itself. So a sign is a contradiction. Jesus' words and acts were ordinary human things, as he was an ordinary man, the son of Mary and Joseph. But they projected the profoundly disturbing sense of containing and expressing an ultimate and absolute truth, *the* truth as a glittering, shattering, un-bearably brilliant light that uncovered all the hidden dark secrets of their past, and that yet embraced and disclosed the epiphany of their ev-ery human dream of and yearning for blessedness. So the contradiction possessed by the figure of Jesus as the Christ, the anointed of God, is "the infinite qualitative contradiction" of the presence, in the life of a mere human mortal, of God, of *the* God above all the mere gods of hu-man devising and invention.[24]

Secondly, then, why does the truth come in this kind of existential con-tradiction? If the almighty God, the creator and ruler of the universe, wants human beings to know and to worship God in order to share in eternal blessedness, then why does not God appear in all the divine glory and power? The secret lies, Kierkegaard says, in the fact that the truth that has to do with a human being as spirit, as self, as person must come in the form of "reduplication."[25] The meaning of this peculiar require-ment becomes evident when one considers "the relation between the communication and the communicator." It is assumed that the commu-nicator is in possession of (that is, "exists in") the truth to be communi-cated; in other words, "the communicator is the reduplication of the communication," because "to exist in what one understands is to redupli-cate." It is also assumed that, as an existing human being, "the communi-cator himself is dialectically defined and his own being is based on reflection." Therefore, when the communicator seeks to reduplicate (to

24. Ibid., pp. 124–125, 131; (KW 20:124–125, 131); SV 16:122–123, 128; (12:117, 123).

25. For precedind and following treatments of this concept, see listings under "redupli-cation" in the index.

share) this truth in and through communication with an other, "the
communication contains a contradiction," namely, "it confronts you with
a choice: whether you will believe or not." In other words, the communication "becomes indirect communication," that is (in the language of
Climacus), the recipient must "appropriate" the shared truth for himself, through his own reflection, and decide for himself whether to accept it and to "exist in it."[26] So it is this contradiction and its requirement
of indirect communication that is assumed when Kierkegaard (later)
says that when Christ (as "the truth" that is "in and for itself") seeks to
draw to himself an other who is also a self, then this "drawing" (commu-
nicating) must take into consideration that "a self is a reduplication, is
freedom; therefore in this relation truly to draw to itself means to posit a
choice."[27]

Finally (thirdly), Anti-Climacus makes the point that this kind of and
need for indirect communication is the key to Christ's sufferings and to
the sufferings that must be expected by all who follow him. He calls it
"the suffering of inwardness," in contrast to the outward observable sufferings of being mocked and crucified. Christ must resist the temptation
to please his followers by demonstrating in an outward recognizable way
that he is "the truth." Out of agonizing love, he must make himself to
appear to be nothing, he must avoid showing any "purely human compassion and solicitude," even to the point of self-negation where "no
personal human-being" can be known. And he does all this with the loving hope of "dialectically luring forth faith" in his followers, but carefully "keeping them at a distance" in order to leave room for them (to
require them) to reach out and appropriate the truth for themselves,
and thus, believing, come to faith.[28]

But "the most grievous suffering" comes to Christ (and his followers)
with the simultaneous awareness that in the moment of this distance, in
the void of this lack of outward human compassion, there lies not only
the possibility (and hope) of faith but just as intensely the possibility
(and fear) of offense. Indeed, for every human being, "the possibility of

26. *Practice*, pp. 133–134; (KW 20:134); SV 16:130–131; (12:125). It is clear that Anti-
Climacus is consciously recalling and using all the materials on indirect communication developed by Climacus in *Postscript*, as indicated on the previous page where he refers to the
notion of "double-reflection" in "some pseudonymous writers." The latter phrase originally
read, "This is what I am accustomed to calling. ..." See the Hongs' notes on this matter.

27. Ibid., pp. 159–160; (KW 20:159); KW 16:155; (12:149).

28. Ibid., pp. 136–137, 133; (KW 20:136–138, 133); SV 16:132–133, 130; (12:127–
128, 124).

offense ... is present at every moment, confirming at every moment the chasmic abyss between the single individual and the God-humanbeing, over which faith and faith alone reaches." Leaving room for the possibility of offense *in order* to leave room for the possibility of faith is precisely what requires the use of indirect communication and dictates the denial of direct communication. In other words, "to deny direct communication is to require *faith.*" And all this happens because "[God] is love," and "out of love [God] becomes human" – and hence "unrecognizable." "But if [God] does not become the object of faith, that one is not true God," and "then that one does not save people either. Therefore, by the step [God] takes out of love, [God] at the same time plunges that person, humankind, into the most horrible decision. ... And [God] does it out of love, ... to save people."[29]

With these three points, then, Anti-Climacus analyzes the shape or the mode of the human being's encounter with God-in-time. But they leave unanswered the central and substantive question: what kind of "love" is it that accomplishes its purpose by deliberately positioning the object of love (every human being) in such a perilous situation? What does it mean to be "saved"? Or in the language of the *ordo salutis*, what happens to me in the event of forgiveness and reconciliation and how is it related to my repentance and confession?

In *Sickness* Anti-Climacus defines sin unambiguously: "Sin is: before God ... despairingly not to will to be oneself, or despairingly to will to be oneself." And he repeats again and again that the opposite of and the deliverance from sin/despair is faith, which he defines in this way: "in relating to itself and in willing to be itself, the self rests [is grounded] transparently in the power that established it," that is, "in God."[30] In other words, sin and salvation have to do with one thing: the self, its failure, and its recovery – always in relationship with God (and therefore with neighbor). This focus on the-self-before-God is repeated by Anti-Climacus in *Practice* in a key passage (that we have referred to a number of times) in part no. 3. Let us remember that part no. 1 is about The

29. Ibid., pp. 136–139; (KW 20:137–140); SV 16:132–134; (12:127–130).

30. *Sickness,* pp. 208, 213, 262; (KW 19:77, 82, 131); SV 15:131, 136, 180; (11:189, 194, 241). Louis Dupré, in his chapter on The Dialectic of Sin, clearly states Kierkegaard's thesis that human existence is a task, namely, of becoming "a relation to oneself and simultaneously to God" (p. 41), and that this task means that "I am, myself, the choice, ... I am essentially *freedom*" (43–44). But then Dupré delimits man's failure: "to sin means to take a stand against God." And throughout the rest of the book, he does not relate this "stand" to man's failure-to-become-self (in all its finitude as well as in its infinitude).

Invitation, that is, Jesus' first encounter with his contemporaries when he says, "Come here, all you who labor and are burdened, and I will give you rest," that is, when a human being is confronted with the assertion that the "burden" of human misery is not the usual trials and tribulations of human existence but is *"sin [as] a human being's corruption."* Part no. 2 is about Jesus' warning, "Blessed is he who is not offended at me," that is, the moment of crisis when the hearer of the invitation must *decide*, to believe or not to believe, to accept the implied demand for repentance, for admission of one's need for divine help, or to be offended. So part no. 3 is about the resolution of this crisis in the event of Jesus' "drawing" a human person unto himself "from on high," that is, the event of forgiveness and reconciliation. So let us see how, in this event, Anti-Climacus again focuses on the-self-before-God.

He describes the event of "drawing" as a dialectic and interplay between what the one who draws *is*, and what the one who is drawn *is*. On the one hand, Jesus as the Christ has the power and the right to draw because as we have just heard (note 21 above) "Christ is the truth," in the sense that "truth ... is in and for itself [*er i og for sig*]." This definition of truth and its designation as definitive of Jesus as the Christ is a powerful way of indicating what it means to call Jesus the God-humanbeing. It means that God is present in God's own distinctive being, totally distinct from human being (existence), and yet compatible with it. As we have spelled out above[31], Kierkegaard uses this Hegelian phrase (being-in-and-for-itself) to indicate his own understanding of God's being as "the unconditioned" (*det Ubetingede*), as having no "objective-element" in it "because ... that would limit [God] and set [God] down into the realm-of-relativities [*Relativiteterne*]." In this sense, then, Jesus as the Christ (that is, Jesus as the humble, ordinary human being who serves as the medium of the presence of the being of God) fulfills what is required of "the one who draws," namely: "What truly can be said to draw to itself must be something higher, more noble, which draws the lower to itself."

On the other hand, what is required of "the one who is drawn"? Anti-Climacus answers: "If [what is to be drawn] is in itself a self, then to draw to itself cannot truly mean merely to draw it *from* being itself ... in such a way that it has now lost its own continuing-existence [or objective-subsistence: *Bestaaen*]." Rather, "when that which is to be drawn is in itself a self, then truly to draw to itself means *first* to help it truly to become

---

31. See text in chapter 2 from note 30 through note 36. Hegel's German is *Anundfür-sichseiende*; Kierkegaard's Danish is *Iogforsigværende*.

itself in order *then* to draw it to itself. ... Therefore, truly to draw to itself means something twofold" (emphasis added). And what does it mean for a self to "become itself"? As we have just heard above (at notes 23 and 25), "a self is a reduplication," and this means (among other things) that "a self can truly draw another self to itself only through a choice." Applying this principle to Jesus and to our encounter with Jesus as the Christ, Anti-Climacus says, "Christ also first and foremost wants to help every human being to become a self, requires this of him/her first and foremost, requires that s/he, by *repenting*, become a self, in order to draw him/her to himself. ... [B]ut in order truly to draw him/her to himself he wants to draw the human being only as a free being to himself, that is, through a choice" (emphasis added).[32]

In this passage two very significant things are said about the Christian event of forgiveness and reconciliation, about how encounter with Jesus as the Christ delivers the human person from sin and despair. First, at the heart of this event, of this encounter, lies the act of repentance. Secondly, God's forgiveness and acceptance affirms, respects, calls into play, demands that the human being will repent and believe voluntarily, freely. In these (apparently) simple declarations Anti-Climacus – that is, Kierkegaard himself in his ultimate and definitive deliverances (in *Sickness* and *Practice*) of the "idea" that has been his guide and goal from *Either/Or* onward – is recollecting and assuming and bringing forward everything that he has explored and developed on these topics throughout both the pseudonymous works and the discourses. We must look at some of this material in order to flesh out that "idea."

Obviously, we will be looking again at the subject of the previous section, "The Nature of Confession." But we noted in that section's last paragraph that in Christian faith the truly profound sense of sin and repentance occurs only in the context of, in encounter with, the love of God as God offers forgiveness and reconciliation. In other words, in Kierkegaard's *ordo salutis* the "order" is not sequential, and we will see that this characteristic holds true also of "The Imitation of Christ" (our next main topic). If the order is not sequential, then what is it? Is it an order of simultaneity?[33] Do repentance, reconciliation, and the new life in Christ all happen in one blinding flash of a miracle by the Holy

32. For quotations since the last note, see *Practice*, pp. 159–160; (KW 20:159–160); SV 16:155–156; (12:149–150). Louis Dupré makes this point by stressing the "subjectivity" of the event of faith/salvation. See his chapter 4, sections 1 and 2.

33. With some refinements, this is essentially Karl Barth's view. See his *Church Dogmatics*, 4–2:502–503, 507–511; *Kirchliche Dogmatik*, 4–2:658–659, 574–578.

Spirit? Not if we take seriously the struggles and sufferings of that one human life – that started in a manger in Bethlehem and ended on a cross on Golgotha – as the life of Immanuel, God-with-us. Not if we take seriously the story (told in Acts of the Apostles) of the struggles of faith that the first disciples of Jesus suffered from the experience of the resurrection to the day when Paul was bound in chains in the city of Rome. Not if we take seriously the reports of Paul's own inner struggles of faith that Paul poured out in his letters to the disciples in the emerging congregations throughout the Roman empire (e.g., Ro 7:7–25).

What then is the order of the experience of repentance, forgiveness, and new life as reported by the first Christians? As we shall see, Kierkegaard describes it as a "way" and a "life" in which each of the three elements is repeated again and again, in such a way that each of the three feed upon and enrich the other two. The order is circular, or is a spiral that goes through the same elements repeatedly, but each time at a greater depth (or height) – but is never finished, consummated, or perfected. This view agrees with Luther's *simul justus et peccator*, that is, we remain simultaneously saint and sinner to the end of our days. It agrees with Calvin's insistence (as a corrective to the Lutheran "by faith *alone*") on treating first, at great length, the topic of "regeneration" (the new life of obedience to Christ) before turning to the topic of "justification by faith." This view was already captured, before the Reformation, in the motto of medieval monkish orders: *ora-et-labora*, written in a circle so that it appeared continuous as *oraetlab* or *laboraet*. In other words, prayer (*ora*) is expressed in work (*labora*), and work is motivated internally by prayer.

So let us recollect Kierkegaard's treatment of the relation between repentance (consciousness of sin before God) and forgiveness/reconciliation in a few examples from his writings (both pseudonymous and acknowledged) that preceded those of Anti-Climacus. Already in *Either/Or*, he sounded his prime theme, his leading "idea," the central concern of his entire corpus: choosing to become one's self. The complexity of this unifying concept, of this defining task of every human being, has been explored at great length in *Kierkegaard as Humanist*. Here we wish only to see how Kierkegaard initiates this theme in its relation to sin and faith at the very beginning of his authorship, and continues to explore it throughout that authorship.

In *Either/Or* we read, "[W]hile I myself as immediate personhood am created out of nothing, I as free spirit am born out of the principle of contradiction or am born by the fact that I choose myself." The contradiction is this: what I choose "comes into existence through the choice," but "if what I choose did not exist but came into existence absolutely through the choice, then I did not choose – then I created. But I do not create myself – I choose myself." The meaning of this contradiction consists of the fact that "this 'my self' " that I choose "is my self in my eternal validity." That is to say, in becoming my self through a choice, I come to see that I must relate to the eternal which created me and gave me existence. But

now one discovers that the self one chooses has a boundless multiplicity within itself inasmuch as it has a history, ... and this history contains many painful things. ... That is why it takes courage to choose oneself. ... This makes one uneasy, and yet it must be so, for when the passion of freedom is awakened in a person, ... one chooses oneself and struggles for this possession as for one's salvation, and it is one's salvation. One can give up nothing of all this, not the most painful, not the hardest, and yet the expression for this struggle, for this acquiring, is – repentance. One repents back into oneself, back into the family, back into the race, until one finds oneself in God. ... [O]nly in this can one choose oneself absolutely.

Then it must be noted that for me to repent back into myself "before God" is another expression for the fact that "I love God." Indeed, "this love has only one expression in language – it is 'repentance.' If I do not love [God] in this way, then I do not love [God] absolutely, out of my innermost being. ... As soon as I love freely and love God, then I repent. And if there were no other basis for repentance as the expression of my love for God, it is this – that[God] has loved me first." It would seem that "one's self, so to speak, is outside him/her, and it has to be acquired, and repentance is one's love for it, because one chooses it absolutely from the hand of the eternal God."[34]

In all this language that Kierkegaard puts into the mouth of Judge William, there is a startling anticipation of everything he has to say about the relation between the repentance of sin and the forgiveness from God throughout the authorship, including the works of Anti-Climacus. Elsewhere in *Either/Or* Judge William specifically says that repentance "seeks

34. For the last two paragraphs see, *Either/Or*, 2:219–221; (KW 4:215–217); SV 3:200–201; (2:193–194).

forgiveness," indeed, repentance is "an expression for reconciliation."[35] In other words, the Christian event of repentance and confession is inseparable from being "before God," as God is present in the offer of loving forgiveness and reconciliation in Jesus as the Christ.

Two years later in *The Concept of Angst*, Haufniensis notes very briefly this ambiguous relationship of interdependence between repentance of sin and the forgiveness of sin. He asserts flatly that "sin ... is posited by the individual as actuality in repentance," but that "repentance does not become the individual's freedom," because "repentance [by itself] cannot cancel sin, it can only sorrow over it." At this juncture two things can happen. Repentance can become a "crazed repentance" that ends in dejection and despair, because one stands in "the highest ethical ambiguity," that is, "ethics requires ideality" which one cannot perform. Or it can become a "true repentance" with a profound and serious "consciousness of sin," which turns in its angst to faith in the eternal. Thereby one is given "courage to renounce angst without angst. ... Only faith is able to do this, because only in faith is the synthesis eternal and at every moment possible."[36]

The significant thing in these comments for our purpose here is to note that Haufniensis sees the problem of sin and repentance as related to that of freedom. That was spelled out in the previous chapter of *Angst* this way. He says that "the concepts of sin and guilt posit precisely the single individual as the single individual." How does this work? When the individual turns inward, "s/he discovers freedom, ... and freedom is for him/her one's bliss, not freedom to do this or that in the world, ... but freedom to know by oneself that s/he is freedom." But "to the degree one discovers freedom, to the same degree the angst of sin is upon that person in the state of possibility. S/he fears only guilt, for guilt alone can deprive one of freedom." So "the opposite of freedom is guilt [not necessity], and it is the greatness of freedom that it always has to do only with itself, that in its possibility it projects guilt and accordingly posits it by itself." Hence "the relation of freedom to guilt is angst." And "freedom, as soon as guilt is posited, returns as repentance." For Haufniensis, then, repentance and its resolution in faith (reconciliation) has essentially to do with the problem of the self becoming itself in the dialectic of the temporal in relation to the eternal.[37]

35. Ibid., pp. 2:242, 180; (KW 4:238, 175); SV 3:220, 165; (2:213, 159).
36. *The Concept of Angst*, pp. 102–105; (KW 8:114–117); SV 6:199–201; (4:382–385).
37. Ibid., pp. 88, 96–97; (KW 8:98, 108–109); SV 6:185, 193–194; (4:367, 376–377).

About the same time, Kierkegaard makes this point in more personal language in *Three Discourses on Imagined Occasions* ("On the Occasion of a Confession") when he muses about the phenomenon of wonder (*Forundring*). He is saying that among all the many goods, God is the highest.

[W]here the wish draws its deepest breath, where this unknown seems to manifest itself, there is wonder, and wonder is immediacy's sense of God and is the beginning of all deeper understanding. ... [A]nd the expression of one's wonder is worship. Wonder is the ambivalent state of mind containing both fear and blessedness. Therefore worship is simultaneously a mixture of fear and blessedness, ... blessedness in [midst of] fear and trembling, trust in mortal danger, bold confidence in the consciousness of sin. Even the most purified and reasonable worship of God has the fragility of wonder; ... the most powerful person is the most powerless; the most devout person sighs out of deepest distress.[38]

In the same discourse we hear that with sin comes "sorrow" and "trembling" and a sense of being "nothing," because "the sorrower is the seeker who is beginning to become aware of God." And the requirement for discovering God "is that the person become a sinner." And this sense of sin is not "as humanity in general or as a human being, but of oneself as an individual [*enkelte*] human being." Indeed, "the person who comes to be alone with the consciousness of sin will certainly feel ... that s/he is the greatest of sinners, because directly before the Holy One one will be conscious of oneself as the single individual [*den Enkelte*] and of the essential magnitude of sin within oneself." So this mixture of blessedness with fear and trembling comes from "being directly before the Holy One and being silent."[39]

This description is mostly in the terms of Religiousness A, but when Kierkegaard uses the expression "directly before" (*lige overfor*) God, he also has in mind Religiousness B (Christianity), that is, directly before God in Jesus as the Christ. And in *Postscript* Climacus makes a very deliberate transition between, through a comparison of, A and B on this issue of the relation between repentance and forgiveness, between sin and faith. On A, he says that the fact that repentance is a contradiction does not make it a comic matter for the religious, because "the religious knows of no remedy for repentance that disregards repentance. On the contrary, the religious continually uses the negative as the essential

38. *Three Discourses on Imagined Occasions*, p. 12; (KW 10:18); SV 6:255; (5:185).
39. Ibid., pp. 26, 28; (KW 10:29, 31); SV 6:2646; (5:193–195).

form. Thus, the consciousness of sin definitely belongs to the consciousness of the forgiveness of sin. The negative is not once and for all and
then the positive, but the positive is continually in the negative." That is
to say, the "order" between the two is not temporal or sequential so that
first one and then the other. Nor is the order simultaneous in that the
polarity between the two is obliterated. Rather, each is inherent in (or
implies) the other; in a life-process, each continues to define and to enrich the other more profoundly in a cyclical movement.[40] And, as we
shall see, it is precisely this dialectical or cyclical movement that involves, requires, and guarantees the factor of human freedom.

Climacus, however, does not treat the subject of forgiveness or how it
can occur within the immanence of Religiousness A. In fact, in the context of A, he more typically speaks of "the totality of guilt-consciousness."
But when he comes to Religiousness B, he spells out how the encounter
with God-in-time provides a "more closely defined" view of the human
condition. "In the totality of guilt-consciousness, existence asserts itself as
strongly as possible within immanence," but in sin-consciousness there is
a "break" or "breach." That is, with "the appearance of God in time," the
individual is prevented "from relating himself backward to the eternal."
Rather, in the encounter with the eternal as a power "outside the individual," the human becomes aware of sin-consciousness for the first time,
and something new happens.

On the one hand, "in guilt-consciousness the subject's self-identity
is preserved in oneself" and hence accomplishes only "a change of
the subject *within* the subject him/herself." On the other hand, sin-
consciousness signifies "a change of the subject him/her*self*," because a
power "outside the individual ... makes clear to him/her that s/he by
coming into existence has become an other [person] than s/he was,
that s/he has become a sinner" (emphases added). Climacus means to
say that every human being is capable of the totality of guilt-consciousness when one admits that one cannot fulfill the ethical absolute on
one's own strength, but that only the presence of God in the Judeo-
Christian religious experience reveals to us the direness of the human
condition as a rebellion against the very Source and Sustainer of our
being, that is, imparts sin-consciousness. And as we have just heard
Climacus say, this "consciousness of sin definitely belongs to the consciousness of the forgiveness of sin." That is to say, in the Judeo-

40. *Postscript*, p. 467; (KW 12.1:524); SV 10:198; (7:457).

Christian tradition, it is the presence of God as redeemer and savior that makes clear the absolute depths of human loss and despair in sin.[41]

However: it is as we now turn to the second and deliberately Christian authorship of Kierkegaard that we find a whole new depth and intensity of insight into the relationship between sin-consciousness and forgiveness/reconciliation. And only in this new understanding does it become clear how forgiveness from God and reconciliation with God – that is, how the love of God – enables the human being, the human person or self, to accomplish its God-given task of becoming itself by "resting transparently in the power that established it." We will concentrate on a few of Kierkegaard's discourses that are clearly labeled "Christian."

We look first, however, at the first discourse in *Upbuilding Discourses in Various Spirits*, namely, the one concerned with the thesis that "purity of heart is to will one thing," which can be read within the confines of Religiousness A. Kierkegaard is reminding his listener that he is talking about the occasion of confession, and he insists that in this situation certain "self-activity" is required in order "not to draw attention away from the decisive issue." We must avoid all "double-mindedness" that makes us subject to "errors, delusions, deceptions, and self-deceptions." On this occasion we concentrate on confession of sin, "and while the consciousness of sin sharpens the need for the one thing necessary, while the earnestness of this holy place strengthens the will in holy resolution, and while the presence of the Omniscient One makes self-deception impossible, *consider your own life*" (emphasis added). Then, "the earnestness is to will to pay attention [*høre efter*] in order to do accordingly."[42]

When, however, this concentration of attention on "the one thing needful," namely, on our sinfulness before God, is accomplished before Jesus as the Christ, then a much more specific understanding of the relationship between confession/repentance and forgiveness/reconciliation comes to light. This specifically Christian understanding we find spelled out by Kierkegaard in part 3 of *Upbuilding Discourses in Various Spirits*, which is entitled "The Gospel of Sufferings" and is the only part that is specified as "Christian Discourses." In the second of these discourses (and in anticipation of no. 1 of *Practice in Christianity*), Kierkegaard is contemplating Jesus' words, "Come to me, all who labor and are

41. For the last two paragraphs, see *Postscript*, pp. 517–518; (KW 12.1:583–584); SV 10:249–250; (7:508–509).

42. *Upbuilding Discourses in Various Spirits*, pp. 178–179; (KW 15:122–123); SV 11:113–114; (8:216–217).

heavy laden, and I will give you rest. Take my yoke upon you, and learn from me; for I am gentle and lowly in heart, and you will find rest for your souls. For my yoke is beneficial, and my burden is light."[43]

Kierkegaard asks the question as to why this burden "that is specifically for Christians" is called "light" by Jesus. What is that burden? Obviously, the consciousness of sin is the heaviest of burdens. "But *the one who takes away the consciousness of sin and gives the consciousness of forgiveness instead* – he indeed takes away the heavy burden and gives the light one in its place." Then Kierkegaard asks the key question: "Why [is forgiveness] a burden, even if it is called light?" Why not pure joy and celebration? I am no longer borne down under the grievous burden of sin! I am like the prodigal son who came home and was welcomed by his father with joy and celebration. But Kierkegaard warns: "If someone will not understand that forgiveness is also a burden that must be carried, ... he is taking forgiveness in vain." Probably the older son never let the younger prodigal son forget that he had been forgiven, and perhaps the day came when the younger son could no longer stand the burden of this constant reminder, again rebelled and again fled his home, lost now beyond redemption. Exactly! says Kierkegaard. "Forgiveness, reconciliation with God, is a light burden to carry, and yet it is exactly like the light burden of meekness. For flesh and blood [common humanity] it is the heaviest of burdens, even heavier than the consciousness of sin, *because it is conducive to offense.* ... [T]he essentially Christian is of such a nature that it can be believed only in meekness" (emphasis added).[44]

Here is the heart of the Christian gospel. God comes to us in love and compassion to help us out of our sin and despair. He comes in lowliness in the common humanity of Jesus of Nazareth, because we must accept God's loving help and grace freely of our own will. And yet we are in the wrong. We must gladly accept forgiveness and reconciliation, as a gift, in meekness. "Forgiveness is not to be earned, ... not to be paid for" (previous note). We have no grounds for demanding or expecting it. We cannot even take the initiative. That is the nature of reconciliation with God. The willingness to offer, the giving, must come from God's side. God is willing to suffer in coming to us. God is willing even to suffer the

43. Mt 11:28–30. The Danish translation of the Greek is accurate in using the word *gavnlig* (beneficial) rather than the standard English word "easy." The Greek word χρηστός means useful, serviceable, beneficial. The RSV apparently just repeated "easy" from the King James because of its familiarity.

44. *Upbuilding Discourses in Various Spirits*, p. 44–45; (KW 15:246–247); SV 11:229–230; (8:331–332). The illustration of the prodigal son is mine, not Kierkegaard's.

waiting for our acceptance. But more God cannot, will not do – out of *love* for us. So in meekness we must gladly accept the gift of God's loving forgiveness, of God's acceptance of us, of God's welcoming us "back home." And yet in this moment, Kierkegaard insists, we may be offended.

Why? Because we must bear the light burden of admitting to ourselves and to God that we are not God, that we do not have life in ourselves, that our very life and being is a gift from God, and having misused this gift, we must once again accept the chance for a new life with the help and from the hands of our loving God. Forgiveness is a reciprocal relation: it must first be offered, but then it must also be accepted – it can be and may be refused. In human relations, it is sometimes very difficult for one party to bring him/herself to *offer* forgiveness, but is often even more difficult for the other party to *accept* – especially if it is offered with even a tinge of self-righteousness or resentment. It is one of Kierkegaard's profoundest insights and his persistent insistence that God's loving forgiveness (acceptance) of wayward human beings comes to us in all the delicate and sensitive indirection of the most humble of human beings in order to seek reconciliation in a way that does not bludgeon the tender human spirit with the (legitimate) claims of God's justice and righteousness – and yet in a way that those claims must finally be recognized and acknowledged by the human self in "meekness." John (the baptist) sent from prison to ask Jesus, "Are you the one who is to come, or shall we look for another?" And Jesus, with all gentleness and compassion, answered, "Go and tell John what you hear and see. … And blessed is the one who is not offended in me." (Mt 11:2–6) Jesus insisted that John "hear" and "see" for himself, that he appropriate the reality of God's presence for himself – even though he might be offended and refuse.

In *The Gospel of Sufferings*, Kierkegaard puts it this way. "The light-minded person wants to let everything be forgotten – he believes in vain. The heavy-minded person wants to let nothing be forgotten – he believes in vain. But the one who believes, believes that everything is forgotten but in such a way that he carries a light burden [namely:] … the recollection that it is forgiven him! … Eternal justice can and will forget in only one way, through forgiveness – but then the believer … must steadfastly recollect that it is forgiven him. … But *from* forgiveness a new life will spring in the believer, and as a consequence forgiveness cannot be forgotten. … Forgiveness through Christ is the gentle disciplinarian who does not have the heart to remind us of what has been forgotten but still reminds us of it to the extent of saying: Just remember that it is forgiven."[45]

This idea that in forgiveness of sin there is a blotting out or a "forgetting" of sin is a recurrent one in Kierkegaard's writings, and obviously it was very important to him, perhaps in his own personal struggle to deal with the memory of his father's sins (cursing God, fornication) and of his own (his youthful visit to a brothel, his broken engagement). But as usual, he takes his own personal experience as the phenomenological point of departure for contemplation of the general human condition. We find an early form of this idea in *Three Upbuilding Discourses* (of 1843), two of which are on the same theme, "Love Will Hide a Multitude of Sins" (1 Pet 4:7–12).[46]

These discourses, among the very first that Kierkegaard wrote, are very discursive and quite tentative in coming to any conclusions. Yet, they contain some fundamental insights that stay with him throughout the total authorship and that appear occasionally in his journals. The prime example is the anticipation of several of the main emphases that we find four years later (in *Works of Love*). He begins the first discourse with a paean in praise of love, drawing on Paul's poetic 1 Corinthians 13. He claims that when love is in one's inner being, the eye does not see or discover the act of sin in an other person, and the ear does not hear evil talk, because love "assigns ... a good meaning" to them. In fact, "when love lives in the heart, the eye has the power to love forth [*elske op*] the good in the impure, but this eye sees not the impure but the pure, which it loves and loves forth by loving it." Even "when sin resists it, then love ... never wearies of believing all things, hoping all things, enduring all things. When sin hardens itself against love, ... returns abuse and scorn and ridicule for kindness, then love does not repay abusive language with abusive language; then it blesses and does not curse."[47] In other words, to "hide" or "cover" sins means to ignore them

---

45. Idem.

46. In this case the Danish word *sjkule* (hide, conceal) is an interpretation of the Greek word καλυπτει which literally means to "cover." But in the Old Testament passages (Ps 32:1; Prov 10:12, 17:9), where forgiving sin is equated with covering it, the Hebrew word נבסה, means to cover in the sense of to conceal or to hide. So the Danish interpretation is correct. Note: this discourse was written three years before the one on The Gospel of Sufferings quoted above. And in an authorship that was completed in only ten years at the most and its major works within a seven-year period, a three-year distance is considerable.

47. *Eighteen Upbuilding Discourses*, kw 5:60–61, 63–64; sv 4:62, 65; (3:278–279, 281).

because love sees below and behind them, and discovers something good and pure to appeal to, something that love can love forth.

In the second discourse he gives this insight another depth or dimension. Kierkegaard appeals to the story of the sinful woman who invades the Pharisee's house and anoints Jesus' feet with oil, and her "tears of repentance became tears of adoration. She was forgiven her many sins, because she loved much" (Lk 7:36–50). But in the face of the Pharisee one could see nothing but "proud contempt" and "sanctimonious anger," because he was making "the judgment of the world; ... there was nothing to discover but a multitude of sins." Then Kierkegaard asks the obvious question: is not the Pharisee right? Does the wrong doer go totally free? "Is no judgment pronounced on a person from without? ... The world's judgment requires what belongs to the world." And we all know what the world demands: simple justice; that is, retribution, vengeance.

Kierkegaard replies: the God who is Love, the God who is present to us and with us in Jesus as the Christ, has a different justice and therefore a different judgment. "Love's judgment requires what belongs to love." Certainly, "the one who judges makes requirements, but the one who makes requirements *seeks* [something], and 'the one who hides a multitude of sins seeks *love*' (Prov 17:9); but the one who *finds* love hides a multitude of sins; the one who finds what one sought indeed conceals what one did not seek" (emphases added). Then Kierkegaard applies this principle to Jesus and the sinful woman. "*Love* discovered what the world concealed – the love in her; and since it had not been victorious in her, the Savior's love came to her assistance, ... and he made the love in her even more powerful to hide a multitude of sins, the love that was already there, because 'her many sins were forgiven her, because she loved so much.'"[48] In other words, God's "justice" is fulfilled, and its demands are satisfied, only in the accomplishment of God's eternal nature and God's eternal purpose with human beings, namely, in achieving the living relationship of love, of us humans with God and of us humans with each other.

As already noted, these ideas that emerge here in these early discourses in such embryonic form receive their definitive statement four years later in *Works of Love.* There we find another discourse with the same title, Love Hides a Multitude of Sins. It adds nothing much on this topic to what is

48. For the last two paragraphs see ibid., KW 5:75–77; SV 4:74–77; (3:293–295). Curiously, the RSV translates the verb כסה in Prov 17:9 as "forgives," but the Danish has it right with "hides."

274 Kierkegaard as Theologian

found in the earlier ones, except for a couple of very significant introductory pages. There Kierkegaard defines the character and role of love in the event of forgiveness in terms of his complicated but important concept of reduplication (*Fordoblelse*). We have used this passage in the section, "God as Reduplication" (chapter 2 above), but not in its application to the loving involved in forgiveness. In this regard, Kierkegaard says, "God is love, and when a person out of love forgets him/herself, how then would God forget her/him! No, while the one who loves forgets him/herself and thinks of the other person, God is thinking of the one who loves. ... There is one who is thinking of her/him, and that is why the one who loves receives what s/he gives. Note the reduplication here: the one who loves is or becomes what one does. One has or rather one acquires what one gives. ... In this way love is always redoubled in itself. This holds true also when it is said that love hides a multitude of sins."[49]

However, it is in the opening discourse of the second series in *Works of Love* that Kierkegaard develops most significantly one idea from the discourses of four years before. It is the idea that love has power to "love forth the good in the impure," and that Jesus as love did just that to the sinful woman. He as love "discovered what the world concealed – the love in her. ... [H]e made the love in her even more powerful to hide [forgive] a multitude of sins, the love that was already there" (notes 46 and 47 above).

Now, in a discourse entitled "Love Builds Up," Kierkegaard expands this idea to mean that love toward neighbor "presupposes that love is in the other person's heart, and by this very presupposition one builds up love in that person – from the ground up, provided, of course, that in love one indeed presupposes its presence in the ground." And one can assume this presence *not* because "one human being [can] implant love in another human being's heart." The presupposition of love being in another human being is based on the prior assumption that "it is God, the Creator, who must implant love in each human being, [God] who [as God] is Love." And it is precisely "in this way that one draws out the good, one loves forth [*opelseke*] love, one builds up. Love can and will be treated in only one way, by being loved forth; to love it forth is to build up. But to love it forth is indeed to presuppose that it is present in the ground." In these words Kierkegaard is implying another main theme of *Works of Love*, namely, that all true love involves a triadic relation among God who is love itself, myself who is called on to love, and my neighbor

49. *Works of Love*, p. 262; (KW 16:281–282); SV 12:270; (9:268–269).

whom I am to love. And he also implies another such theme, namely, that I truly love my neighbor by leading that person to love God.[50]

But, Kierkegaard asks, what if the other person is unlovable, is full of obvious faults and weaknesses, is buried under a multitude of sins? Before one can "build up," is it not necessary first to "tear down," to "remove," to "pull out" what is in the way of building up?[51] This view is certainly supported by the concept of justice held by "the world" and the Pharisee. But Jesus' (God's) methodology of forgiveness is just the opposite. Certainly, he senses that the woman already has a profound consciousness of her sinfulness, but she dares to come in repentance to Jesus (not to the Pharisees), because she is drawn by his aura of understanding and compassion; indeed, his love for the sinner intensifies her sense of failure. But first and primarily, his loving concern loves forth her sense of her own goodness and love; first and primarily, Jesus affirms and evokes her own God-given and hence eternal, indestructible dignity and worth as a self in the image of God.

So God's forgiveness/reconciliation comes not seeking judgment, destruction, and retribution but *first* encounters us offering affirmation and encouragement for the human spirit, loving forth the love in the heart that is presupposed, not denying but covering, hiding, forgetting the very real sin and failure present in every human being by overcoming and making inoperative that sin. And only *then* comes the new life; only then, with the echoes of forgiveness ringing in one's ears, does the sinner hear, "go in peace," "go and sin no more." Kierkegaard concludes, "Among all the relationships in the world, there is no other relationship in which there is such a like-for-like, in which the result so accurately corresponds to what was presupposed."[52] And in one of the briefest discourses in *Works of Love* (The Victory of the Conciliatory Spirit in Love, Which Wins the One Overcome), he makes his point with a very telling thesis. What is the greater victory over one's enemy: to annihilate the enemy or to transform the enemy into a friend? Well, there is no question if one of the combatants is "one who loves" and "has the task of maintaining himself in the good so that the evil would not get

50. Ibid., pp. 205–206; (KW 16:216–217); SV 12:209–210; (9:208–209). This concept has been explored more fully in *Kierkegaard as Humanist*, pp. 359–374, in the section entitled "Love Presupposes Love" (chapter 7), and there the relation of this concept to those of reduplication, love's triad, and the principle of like-for-like is spelled out. This section should be read as background for the present treatment.

51. Ibid., pp. 207–208; (KW 16:218–219); SV 12:212; (9:210).

52. Idem.

power over him." Such a one always "is fighting *conciliatingly* for the good to be victorious in the unloving person, ... struggling *to win the one overcome*. ... [T]he loving one is fighting on the side of the enemy for his benefit. ... To fight on the side of the good *against* the enemy – that is laudable and noble; but to fight *for* the enemy – ... this is loving, this is the conciliatory spirit in love!"[53] In other words, authentic repentance of sin together with authentic forgiveness of sin precisely comprise reconciliation, in the relationship of mutual love.

This whole complex conceptuality about the inner relationship (the *ordo*) between consciousness of sin and forgiveness/reconciliation stays with Kierkegaard and informs all the rest of his writings to his dying day. While writing *Sickness* and *Practice*, he made several entries in his journal on forgiveness. In one he says,

To believe in the forgiveness of sins is the decisive crisis whereby a human being becomes spirit. ... The forgiveness of sins is not a matter of something particular. ... [I]t is just the opposite – it pertains not so much to particulars as to the totality; it pertains to one's whole self. ... Anyone who has experienced and experiences what it is to believe in the forgiveness of sins has indeed become an other human-being. Everything is forgotten. ... One has become an eternity older, because one has now become spirit. All immediacy and its selfishness, its selfish attachment to the world and to oneself, have been lost. Now one is, humanly speaking, old, but eternally one is young.[54]

In another entry he says,

Just as the first impression of a true and deep love is the feeling of one's own unworthiness, in the same way the need for forgiveness of sins betokens that one loves God. But all by oneself no human-being can ever come to think that God loves him/her. ... This is the gospel, [this is] revelation. ... [In] like manner no human-being can come to know how great a sinner one is. ... Without the divine yardstick, no human-being is the great sinner (this one is – only before God). *Both parts correspond to one another.* ... The inwardness of sin-consciousness is precisely the passion of love. Truly the law makes one a sinner – but love makes one a far greater sinner. Truly the person who fears God and trembles feels oneself to be a sinner, but the one who truly loves [God], feels oneself to be an even greater sinner. (emphasis added)[55]

53. Ibid., p. 309; (ĸw 16:334–335); sv 12:320–321; (9:318–319).
54. *Journals*, 67; viii¹ a 673.
55. Ibid., 1216; viii¹ a 675.

And again: "The eternal consolation in the doctrine of the forgiveness of sins is this: You shall believe it. For when the anxious conscience begins with heavy thoughts, and it is as if they could never in all eternity be forgotten, then comes this: You shall forget. You *shall* stop thinking of your sin. ... You shall believe that your sins are forgiven." And a year before he dies, Kierkegaard comments, "To forgive sins is divine, not only in the sense that no one is able to do it except God, but also ... that no one can do it without God." Humans have a "disposition to detect sin, to find out something evil about a human being," and the only kind of forgiveness they know of is "a mutual repaying." But "it is Deity's joy to forgive sins; just as God is almighty in creating out of nothing, so [God] is almighty in uncreating something, because to forget, almightily to forget, is indeed to uncreate something."[56]

Thus concludes our extensive and diverse analysis of how repentance and forgiveness, how sin-consciousness and God's love, are related to each other. As we have just heard, Kierkegaard's constant thesis throughout has been: "both parts correspond to one another." We have also come to see that forgiveness of sin is not a mere declaration but essentially consists in the establishment of a living, working, continuing relationship that binds together the individual human spirit and God's spirit. Hence the mutual, corresponding repentance of sin and forgiveness of sin is an event, also a continuing relationship, that is properly called reconciliation. But how does reconciliation become not an accomplished state of being but a continuing event, an active life? We have heard Kierkegaard say several times that the result of repentance/forgiveness is a new self. So our analysis of the *ordo salutis* is not complete without seeing how repentance and forgiveness are involved in and with a way of living, in what Kierkegaard calls being "followers" or "imitators" (*Efterfølgere*) of Christ as our "model" (*Forbillede*: pattern, example, prototype).[57] And Kierkegaard makes this transition himself in *The Gospel of Sufferings*, where the very first discourse is on What Meaning and What Joy There Are in the Thought of Following Christ. So we are ready to turn to the third aspect of Kierkegaard's *ordo salutis*.

56. Ibid., 1217, IX A 177; 1224, XI² A 3.

57. On the problem of translation of these two terms, see *Upbuilding Discourses in Various Spirits*, KW 15, p. 414, note 23. For *Forbillede*, I prefer "model" or "pattern" to the Hongs' use of "prototype" because these words seem to carry better Kierkegaard's idea of Jesus' *demand* that his disciples follow and imitate him, and the idea that a certain initiative is expected and required from the disciple. "Prototype," for me, distances Jesus from us as an impersonal, abstract ideal. Incidentally, there is no significant occurrence of this concept in Kierkegaard's works that precede the *Upbuilding Discourses*.

3 The Imitation of Christ

Some readers of Kierkegaard (including the present author) may be made uneasy when they discover that the Hong translations of this discourse and of *Practice in Christianity* use "imitation" and "imitator" for *Efterføgelse* and *Efterfølger*, in place of "following" and "follower" as generally used by previous translators.[58] Imitation usually connotes a purely rote and external copying, whereas following Jesus is anything but an obvious and objective procedure – as Jesus' first disciples soon discovered. And as we will soon see, Kierkegaard insists that this following/ imitating of Jesus as the Christ is a profoundly inward spiritual event, involving arduous, ethical/religious struggle and striving as one enters and lives in the faith-relationship with God.

The discourse on Following Christ begins with a prayer to Christ: "you who yourself once walked on the earth and left footprints that we should follow [*følge*]." Then it addresses him: "our God and our savior, let your pattern stand very clearly before the eyes of the soul ... so that by resembling [*ligne*] you and by following [*følge*] you we may find the way surely to judgment, ... but may we also be brought by you to eternal blessedness with you in the life to come."[59] Kierkegaard then proceeds to give a general characterization of "the way" (*Veien*: road, path) that one gets involved with when one follows Jesus.

It is a pilgrim's way, filling one with a great sense of restlessness, because one is not yet there, indeed, does not get there. That is, it is a

58. As indicated in a note (referenced in note 55 above), the Hongs associate Kierkegaard's usage of "imitation" with that of Thomas à Kempis in his famous medieval book of meditations, *De imitatione Christi*. Kierkegaard owned the Latin version but does not refer to the book anywhere in his journals until after he bought a Danish translation that appeared in 1848 entitled, *Om Christi Efterfølgelse*. Then there are numerous (and favorable) references to and quotations from it in the journals of 1849, which would have been written after Kierkegaard had completed *Practice in Christianity*. Whether he had this book in mind when he wrote *Upbuilding Discourses in Various Spirits* and *Practice in Christianity*, and whether he had the sense of "imitation" in mind when he used the Danish word *efterfølge*, we do not know. The Danish word that specifically means to imitate is *efterligne*, and it is interesting that Kierkegaard uses it twice in *Practice* in ways that are exactly analogous to his use of *efterfølge* [pp. 38, 237; (KW 20:36, 244); SV 16:45, 227; (12:33, 223)]. So the Hongs's use of imitation may not be incorrect, but we have to be clear about precisely how Kierkegaard means it.

59. *Upbuilding Discourses in Various Spirits*, KW 15:217; SV 11:203; (8:305). The language of "leaving footprints that we should follow" will also make those uneasy who remember a little volume published many years ago entitled, *In His Steps* – a very superficial account of the glad and easy way in which Christians are to fulfill this idea of "following" Jesus.

pathway of faith, because the one who is being followed "is no longer visibly walking ahead," and hence one "cannot settle down at rest in this world." It is a pathway of hope, because the pilgrims are not yet "what they should be and ought to be, what they hope sometime to become when faith is laid aside and the pilgrim staff laid down."[60]

But this "task assigned to one who is to be someone's follower" is a spiritual task, a path that one "must learn to walk by oneself and to walk alone," that is, "to walk alone along the path that the teacher walked." Essentially the task consists in this: "to conform one's mind in likeness [*Lighed*] with the teacher's [mind]." And in this task "there is not ... a single human being who can choose for you or in the ultimate and decisive sense counsel you about the one and only important issue, counsel you decisively about your blessedness [salvation]." No help can "come from the outside and grasp your hand. ... [O]nly when you completely yield, completely give up your own will, and devote yourself with your inmost heart and mind – then help comes invisibly."[61]

What, then, is in the mind of the teacher? What is the actual content of the "way" one follows? Kierkegaard answers (with a typically loose quotation of Scripture): "this mind that was in Christ Jesus, he who thought it not robbery to be equal with God but humbled himself and became obedient unto death, even to death on the cross" (Phil 2:5ff.). In other words, "to *follow Christ* means to take up one's cross," and "to carry one's cross means to deny oneself." And Kierkegaard warns, "it is a *slow and difficult task* to deny oneself, a heavy cross to take up, ... and one that, according to the model's instructions, is to be carried unto death, so that the imitator [*Efterfølger*], even if he does not die on the cross, nevertheless resembles the model in dying 'with the cross on.' " Kierkegaard gives two qualifications that are requisite in carrying the cross of self-denial. First, it is not accomplished once and for all in some dramatic act, but is a continuous way of life that is engaged in daily. And it makes no difference what one's external circumstances are (king or beggar), "because self-denial is the inward-intensity [*Inderlighed*] to deny oneself." Secondly, it requires lowliness, humility, and meekness, as seen in the life of Jesus. He said, "learn from me, for I am meek and lowly of heart."[62]

This second requirement of meekness must be looked at more closely, and with this topic we move on to the second discourse in *The*

60. Ibid., KW 15:218–219; SV 11:203–205; (8:306–307).
61. Ibid., KW 15:220–221; SV 11:205–206; (8:308).
62. Ibid., KW 15:221–222, 240; SV 11:206–207, 223; (8:308–309, 326).

Gospel of Sufferings (in all of which Kierkegaard explores other aspects of
following Jesus). For meekness he gives the example of turning the
other cheek (Mt 5:39). Meekness is a basic attitude toward the world: to
be free of the world, of its ways, and its demands. "The meek person
who has the courage really to believe in the freedom of the spirit carries
the heavy burden lightly." Outwardly turning the other cheek is inwardly
to forgive your enemy. Indeed, "the meek person is so solicitous to forgive that it almost seems as if he were the one who needed forgiveness,
or that the meek person, who humbly knows how heaven's forgiveness
of him depends on his forgiveness, actually *needs* to forgive his enemy."
And on the side of the recipient of forgiveness, the same meekness is required. As we have heard already, "forgiveness is not to be earned, ...
cannot be paid for." So "here again meekness pertains to believing [*at
troe*], to carrying the light burden of forgiveness, to bearing the joy of
forgiveness. ... Forgiveness, reconciliation with God ... is exactly like the
light burden of meekness. ... [S]o the essentially Christian ... can be believed only in meekness." And from this reconciliation "a new life will
spring from the believer."[63]
So there is meekness on both sides of the event of forgiveness. On the
one hand, the Christ (and his follower, imitator) must humble himself
as the lowliest of human beings, and suffer, even to death on the cross,
in order for the love of God to come to and touch and embrace the human being lost in sin, despair, death. On the other hand, the lost human being must humble him/herself in meekness in acknowledgement
of one's sinfulness and in yielding to the loving offer of forgiveness and
thus become reconciled. But in a key passage (in the third discourse)
Kierkegaard interjects another term and concept in his explication of
this requirement of meekness, and thus in his characterization of The
Imitation of Christ. It is the term *obedience*.[64]

63. Ibid., KW 15:242, 245–247; SV 11:225–226, 228–230; (8:328, 330–332).
64. Kierkegaard becomes attracted to this idea of obedience very early on, and it remained a central concern throughout his life. It appears first in an early journal entry of
1839 where he expresses the conviction that it is God's will that he prepare for his theological examination, and he quotes 1 Samuel 15:22, "Obedience is dearer to God than the fat
of rams" (5385; II A 422). This verse becomes a kind of mantra for Kierkegaard. In 1842
it is quoted in *Either/Or* (2:248; (KW 4:244); SV 3:138; (2:127), and then appears in a published work once a year until *Point of View* in 1848, as well as in the journals of 1846 and
1848. There are significant comments on obedience in *Either/Or* and *Eighteen Upbuilding
Discourses,* and then (as we shall see below) in *Upbuilding Discourses in Various Spirits, Christian Discourses,* and the 1849 discourse on *The Lily of the Field and the Bird of the Air* (appended
to Lowrie's translation of *Christian Discourses*).

The theme of this discourse is, "that the school of sufferings educate for eternity." And we must remember that, in Kierkegaard's language, "eternity" for the human being is to live in the faith-relationship with God. So he reminds us that "the Lord Jesus Christ, *although he was Son, he learned obedience from what he suffered* (Heb 5:8)." And the instance of this learning that Kierkegaard chooses as especially revelatory is the spiritual struggle Jesus had in Gethsemane as he faced the possibility of his death: "If it is possible, Father, let this cup pass from me; yet not my will be done but yours" (a conflation of Mt 26:39 and Lk 22:42). What this event reveals is that obedience has two parts. First is the fact "that he said this," that is, "the praying question," seeking to decide "whether it is the Father's will, whether another way is possible." Secondly is the act that followed, "that he emptied the bitter cup" by dying voluntarily on the cross.[65]

Kierkegaard emphasizes that without the first part, his dying would not have been an act of authentic obedience. Obedience is not blind, not uninvolved or unquestioning, not automatic. Obedience involves an agonizing, inner, spiritual struggle to come to understanding and to decision. At the heart of authentic obedience to God is freedom. God-in-Christ will not have it any other way. This integral factor of obedience is what Anti-Climacus is pointing to when (in *Sickness*) he defines faith as: "in relating to itself and in willing to be itself, the self rests transparently in the power that established it"; and when (in *Practice*) he says that God-in-Christ draws us to himself (that is, into the faith relation) *first* by "helping [the self] truly to become itself," that is, "to draw the human being as a free being to himself, that is, through a choice."[66] On the same page (referred to in the previous paragraph) Kierkegaard makes the point that suffering "innocently" provides only the "opportunity [*Anledning*] to learn, ... but that does not mean that obedience is learned. ... Humanly viewed, the suffering itself is the first danger, but the second danger, even more terrible, is: failing to learn obedience."

Then he goes on to analyze the inner spiritual struggle through which one may learn obedience from innocent (that is, freely entered into) sufferings, what he calls "inwardness in suffering." Such a struggle en-

---

65. *Upbuilding Discourses in Various Spirits*, KW 15:250, 255; SV 11:233, 255; (8:336, 340).

66. It would seem that, in this analysis of obedience as having two parts, Kierkegaard must be aware of the fact that the root verb behind the Greek word for obedience in Heb 5:8, namely, ὑπακούω, refers to two different but reciprocal actions. It means "to listen" in the sense of "giving ear to, to listen to and answer," or colloquially, "to answer a knock at the door": there is a voice *and* my answer, a knock *and* my opening.

sues because "when a person suffers and will learn from what one suffers, *one simply [and] unceasingly comes to know something about oneself and about one's relationship to God; this is the sign that one is being educated [molded] for eternity.*" The first requirement for this learning (being molded or shaped) is what Kierkegaard has already spelled out in part 1 of the *Upbuilding Discourses* in the discourse on "purity of heart is to will one thing." There must be a concentration of one's "attention" so that one is "quiet" and "alone with God." In order to give this attention, there must be a "dying away from [*Afdøen*]" the world and the things of this world, whether one loves it or is "embittered by it." In this silence and solitude, one can then concentrate attention on "the one thing needful," because in "the school of sufferings … only one thing is learned: obedience." But *what* is learned? What does "obedience" mean? And even more difficult, *how* does it happen?[67]

Kierkegaard says the question of "what" can be easily answered. "[L]earning obedience in the school of sufferings" is simply "to let God be master, to let God rule in everything." There is really no other viable option because "what is all eternal truth except this: that God rules," and hence "what other correlation and harmony are possible between the temporal and the eternal than this – God rules and to let God rule."[68] So the central issue, the real secret, in obedience is not in the "what" but in the "how." At the heart of this self-conscious encounter with God is the crucial moment of uncertainty, of an either/or. In all of his discourses on the lilies and the birds, Kierkegaard stresses that we must learn from them the lesson of perfect obedience, and that along with this obedience comes God's gift of beauty, goodness, and fullness of life, that is, "eternal blessedness." But in his last discourse on that theme, he stresses that there is a critical difference between human beings and the lilies/birds. Unlike humans, they cannot be offended and thus fail to obey. "In nature everything obeys God unconditionally because there is no other will but [God's] in heaven or on earth." So the lilies and the birds exist merely in "their absolute obedience, which is happy innocence," and hence are spared "the tremendous danger in which the human-being exists simply by being human," namely, the "mortal strife" between "God and the world, good and evil" for control of the human being. In this situation, "the tremendous danger consists in the fact that the human-being is placed between these two tremen-

---

67. *Upbuilding Discourses in Various Spirits*, KW 15:257; SV 11:238–239; (8:341–342).
68. Idem.

dous powers and the choice is left to him/her," that is, "the human-being must either love or hate, [and] not to love is to hate."[69]

"How," then, is this conflict resolved? Does God's love irresistibly overwhelm the human heart? As we have spelled out several times before, it is precisely God's love, according to Kierkegaard, that deliberately leaves room for the human being to decide, to turn to God as a choice, because God's will is consistent with God's love, that is: God's will is that the human being, who is created in God's image, love God in return. And as God, without need or any finite restrictions, has freely loved the human being, so the human being can only love God *freely* – except, of course, the human creature *needs* to love and to obey God as "our Creator and sustainer, the One in whom we live and move and have our being, the One by whose grace we receive everything."[70] How then do these two unequal kinds of freedom come into reconciliation?

We assume that the human spirit (self) – profoundly and intensively self-conscious – is "before God" in the most personal and intensively subjective awareness and "attention" possible (which Christian faith maintains is uniquely possible through God's presence in Jesus as the Christ). We assume that the human being has come – in silence and solitude – to the conviction: before God, I can do nothing. We assume that the Voice of the Eternal (which one hears in the silence of self-negation) speaks in the accents of love, that is, affirms the infinite dignity and worth of the unique, individual self one is, and offers one the fullness of life (of course, with the implied, single alternative: death). We assume that in this crucial moment the human heart *either*, in weakness and defiance, can and may be offended; *or*, the human spirit is able "to *let* God rule." But how does the self "let" God rule?

"To let" is the simple, but infinitely complex, event in which lies the key to that reconciliation that "is indeed God's plan for the salvation of humankind." This is so because "in obedience the humble assent, the confident, strengthening yes of devotedness is heard." That is, "when you, disciplined by sufferings, have subjected yourself in perfect, unconditional obedience, then you have also discerned the presence of the eternal within you, then you have found the peace and rest of the eternal. ... To find rest is to be educated [formed] for the eternal." This is so

69. *The Lily of the Field and the Bird of the Air* (published with *Christian Discourses*, pp. 337, 345; SV 14:149, 156–157; (8:28, 36).

70. Ibid., p. 335; SV 14:147; (8:26). Louis Dupré also stresses this role of freedom in the human relationship to God (see his Chapter 3, sections 4 and 5).

because "there is only one way in which rest is to be found: to let God rule in everything." For Kierkegaard, then, "reconciliation" is the term to indicate the entire complex process/event from the initial sense of guilt-consciousness to the final "peace and rest of the eternal," with the critical turning point consisting in that assent, that yes, that subjecting of the human heart-of-hearts. And it must be emphasized that this assent, this yes of subjection, is not something we can take credit for and hence "rest" in dependence on our own efforts. In our sin-consciousness, in our repentance, in God's forgiveness and acceptance, we find rest only in the fact that it is "God who gives both to will and to do, gives the growth and the completion;" it is God who rules in all things – even, or especially, in leaving room in our heart-of-hearts for us to respond *freely* in our believing and loving God. In this relationship we come to see and to believe that there is only one option open to us: our humble, glad, wholehearted and *free* obedience.[71]

So are we not exaggerating the role of human freedom in this event and in this relationship? Erik Erikson once said that the whole subject of freedom is unimportant, that all it comes down to, at the very most, is merely our saying "yes" to what is inevitable and to what we cannot do anything about anyway. On the contrary, at the heart and core of Kierkegaard's whole conceptuality are two basic theses. First, by saying "yes" to all that I have become, and by saying "yes" to what I perceive to be the "one thing needful" in the next moment, I transform my entire being and existence by making both past and future to be *mine*: I choose my self absolutely – even though it is God who gives me my very being and existence, even though it is God who gives the possibility "both to will and to do." The actual willing and doing must be *mine*. Secondly, if I weakly refuse to say "yes," or if I defiantly say "no" to God's right to define the "one thing needful," and "no" to God's loving gracious offer of help, then I am doomed to a bitter and self-annihilating existence of mediocrity, triviality, and ultimate despair.[72] In one of his reflective journal entries in that reflective year of 1850, Kierkegaard puts it this way:

71. *Upbuilding Discourses in Various Spirits*, KW 15:258–259; SV 11:339–340; (8:342–343).

72. I have explicated these two theses of Kierkegaard in great detail in chapters 4, 5, and 6 of *Kierkegaard as Humanist*. In those chapters it becomes clear that the "willing and doing" involved in saying "yes" is infinitely complex when we analyze the various elements or factors that play a role in "willing," in what sense it is "caused," in what sense it is "free," but in no sense is it an arbitrary act of a pure and independent capacity called the "will." And in the next section on faith and love, we will see that it is not at all adequate to explain this "yes" simply by saying that faith is "a gift of God."

Christianity can say to a human-being: You shall choose the one thing needful, but in such a way that there must be no question of any choice. ... Consequently there is something in relation to which there must not be, and by definition there cannot be, any choice, and yet there is a choice. Consequently, the very fact that there is no *choice* expresses the tremendous passion or intensity with which one *chooses*. ... [F]reedom-of-choice is only freedom's form-determinant. ... Freedom's content is the decisive-factor for freedom to the extent that freedom's truth is precisely this: there must be no choice, provided there is yet a choice.[73]

In other words, I cannot choose to decide *what* is good and evil, but that I choose *either* one *or* the other is all-decisive as to whether I become the self that God has given to me. The determination of "the plan of salvation" and the nature of love/reconciliation is totally outside my choice, but that I choose it, that I say "yes" – on that hangs the fulfillment of the plan and accomplishment of love.

Many Christians would shudder at such a statement. It would seem to deny what is central in the entire Judeo-Christian description of the God who has come to us in the totality of the Biblical account: a flat denial of God's sovereignty. Kierkegaard does not see it that way. He contends, "The ultimate thing [*det Høieste*] that can be done for a being ... is to make it free. In order to do just that, omnipotence is required." He admits that "this seems strange," since omnipotence is almost always used (by human beings) to make others dependent and subservient. But true, divine omnipotence is seen precisely in its

qualification of being able to withdraw itself again in a manifestation of omnipotence in such a way that precisely for this reason that which originated through omnipotence can be independent. ... Only omnipotence can withdraw itself at the same time it gives itself away. ... God's omnipotence is therefore [God's] goodness. For goodness is to give [oneself] away completely, but in such a way that by omnipotently taking oneself back one makes the recipient independent. ... [Only] omnipotence can make [a being] independent, can bring forth from nothing something that has subsistence [*Bestaaen*] in itself through the continual withdrawing of omnipotence.

In this way omnipotence "can give without giving up the least of its power." Even though I am free in my God-given independence, I am

73. *Journals*, 1261; X² A 428.

free only within the scope set by my Creator, namely: free *for* love of my Creator and of my neighbor, not free *from* my creator and my neighbor. And if I try to be free from Creator and neighbor, then I become unfree, losing not only my independence but even my very being as a self. Only in this sense, "the One to whom I owe absolutely everything, although that One still absolutely controls everything, has in fact made me free." Thus omnipotence is able to create "the whole visible world" but also "the most fragile of all things – a being independent of that very omnipotence."[74] My freedom is fragile just because its operation and continuance must take the form of obedience, that is, the form of "humble assent," of saying "yes," of "subjecting myself" in "letting God rule in everything." That is, obedience consists in turning to God in solitude and silence, to listen for God to tell me what is "the one thing needful" in each concrete situation of life, and then to make room in my heart and mind so that God's spirit can enter in and inspire my spirit to act in self-denying love – and in this *way* "learn obedience" from whatever sufferings are required in the act of love.

This, then, is the answer (as formulated in the last several pages) to the question (posed at note 69 above): "how" is the "mortal strife" between "God and the world, good and evil" to be resolved? On the one hand, we have stressed the initiative (prevenience) of God's grace in providing the occasion or "opportunity" (at note 66) for us to "learn obedience," and thus, in Christ's "drawing" us to himself, "God gives both to will and to do, gives the growth and the completion" (note 71). Without God's initiative, there could be no consciousness of sin, confession and repentance, forgiveness and reconciliation, no new relationship of faith/love. On the other hand, we have asserted at every point that it is precisely God who, out of love, leaves room in our hearts and minds, indeed requires of us, to respond *freely* in our loving of God in return. And (as noted in note 72 above) this position will be re-explored in the next section of this chapter in the context of a discussion of the relationship between faith and love.

Some readers of Kierkegaard will find this description of the role played by factor of human freedom (the voluntary) in the faith relation to be overstated and over stressed (in both this current study and in its precursor, *Kierkegaard as Humanist*). For example, Lee Barrett has said that this description tends to "systematize" the relation of grace and

74. *Journals*, 1251; VII[1] A 181. This entry was made in late 1846, just as Kierkegaard was finishing *Upbuilding Discourses in Various Spirits* and just before he started *Works of Love*.

freedom in that it presents "the freedom theme as foundational for al-most everything in Kierkegaard's corpus." He argues that "while 'free-dom' certainly is a pivotal motif, at times Kierkegaard juxtaposes it to other concerns, including the efficacy of God's grace, which tend to minimize the centrality of the free response. It is not clear that Kierkeg-aard's treatment of 'faith' and 'freedom' can be systematized in an 'Arminian' direction; it is not clear that it can be systematized at all."[75]

One must agree that "the efficacy of God's grace" is the only human hope for delivery from the despair into which sin/failure has landed the human race. As Climacus puts it in *Fragments*, "inasmuch as the learner is in untruth but is that on his own, ... he might seem to be free. ... And yet he is indeed unfree and bound and exiled, because to be free from the truth is indeed to be exiled, and to be exiled on one's own is indeed to be bound." And the only way for one to be set free again is for the teacher who is God to come and to "give the condition and give the truth."[76] And of course Kierkegaard (Anti-Climacus) defines this condition as being made able to stand "before God" in the presence of Jesus as the Christ.

Nevertheless, (as we have noted before, at note 19 in chapter 3) it is precisely the ultimate Christian assertion of Anti-Climacus (in the very concluding section of *Sickness*) that God comes in Jesus as the Christ to deliver human beings from their "exile" in sin and despair, "but in this infinite love of [God's] merciful grace [God] nevertheless makes one condition: [God] cannot do otherwise." That is to say,"the possibility of offense [Christ] cannot take away. ... Christ cannot, 'love' cannot make this impossible."[77] It would seem, then, that this condition set by God's own omnipotent determination, namely, to leave room for the human person to accept God's "merciful grace" *or* to be offended, means that, for Kierkegaard, grace is resistible. Kierkegaard does not speculate about what might happen to such a person in some other "eternity;" he only can speak about what happens here and now when a person en-counters "eternity" before God in Jesus as the Christ.

75. These words are from a pre-publication review of this present volume, which Mr. Barrett graciously supplied to me, and are quoted with his permission. I should add that his general comments on the study are very favorable, and he says that this "slight tendency to over-systematize" is "perhaps [its] only flaw." (I only wish that were true!) I have acknowl-edged this tendency and commented on it at several points in *Kierkegaard as Humanist*.
76. *Fragments*, p. 19; (KW 7:15); SV 6:20; (4:185). In translating Kierkegaard's *udelukket*, I have used David Swenson's "exile" rather than the Hongs' "excluded," as more richly con-notative of the human condition.
77. *Sickness*, pp. 256–257; (KW 19:125–126); SV 15:174–175; (11:235–236).

This point brings us to the final and decisive characteristic of what it means to "follow" Jesus as the Christ: imitation of his "way" of *living*. And in making this point Kierkegaard clarifies what he means when he says that one really "learns obedience" only in "the school of sufferings" that "educates for eternity." Here is the clincher to the thesis that Jesus' *ordo salutis* is not sequential or linear but cyclical, in a spiral.[78] The follower comes into a profound sin-consciousness only in the encounter with God's love in forgiveness, and one only comes to believe in one's forgiveness by learning obedience, and finally one only learns obedience as one starts living the new life – *but* one can only start the new life if one has some intimations of one's need of help from God in and through one's sin-consciousness and forgiveness. In this spiral and constant repetition there is no set starting point and there is no completion or ending.

In the gospels according to Mark, Matthew, and Luke, it is impossible to determine how each disciple was first attracted to Jesus or how each decided to follow Jesus or when each, within this new relationship, reached a decisive belief and commitment. But long before the disciples had any clear idea of who Jesus was or what Jesus was about or had a firm commitment to it (and to him), Jesus sent the twelve (and later the seventy) out on their own, to proclaim the coming of the kingdom and to heal both bodies and minds, that is, the whole self (Mk 6:7ff.; Mt 10:5ff.; Lk 9:1ff.). And he warned them that they would be like sheep among wolves, that they would be arrested and flogged. They would learn by doing and from their doing. By following and imitating the *life* of Jesus, they would enter their "school of sufferings," and only there they would learn who Jesus was and what he meant by "the kingdom (rule) of God," only there they would be "educated for eternity."

Anti-Climacus finally comes to this point in the penultimate section of *Practice*. In the opening prayer to "Lord Jesus Christ," he says, "You yourself were the way and the life – and you have asked only for followers/imitators." So "wake us up, rescue us from the error of wanting to admire you instead of wanting to follow you and be like [*ligne*] you." Admirers turn the teacher into an "issue" and make "observations" about him. In this way they lose the sense of the teacher as a personal "I" and therefore the sense of their being the personal "you" who is being addressed. But when Jesus asked for followers, he made clear that he was not seeking admirers or "adherents of a teaching" but "imitators of a

---

78. See text above in this chapter at note 32 and following.

life." So he did not represent himself as a teacher who "only had a teaching to present" and who "could be satisfied with adherents who accepted the teaching." Rather, he spoke of himself simply as "the way and the truth and the life" (Jn 14:6), and "his whole life on earth, from first to last, was designed solely to be able to have imitators and designed to make admirers impossible."[79]

This emphasis on the idea that one comes to know the truth by doing or living the truth, rather than by intellectual comprehension of an abstract concept, is not unique to this stage of Kierkegaard's intellectual/ spiritual development. As we have noted in chapter 1 of this work (at notes 36 & 41), Kierkegaard made the same point in a journal entry during his third year at university (1834) by saying that "Christian dogmatics ... must grow out of Christ's activity." And at the end of his life (1854) he repeats this language and insists that "the Christian thesis" is this: "*Act* according to the commands and orders of Christ; *do* the Father's will – and you will become a believing-one" (emphasis added).[80] He makes the point also three years after *Practice* in *Judge for Yourself!* by saying that, to be savior of the world, Jesus "did not come into the world to bring a doctrine, he never lectured. ... His teaching was really his life, his existence. If someone wanted to be his follower, ... he said something like this: Venture a decisive act. ... One does not become a Christian by hearing something about Christianity, by reading something about it, by thinking about it. ... No, a *setting (situation)* is required – venture a decisive act; the proof does not precede but follows, in and with the imitation that follows Christ."[81]

Anti-Climacus, in *Practice*, does not spell out the specifics of "the way" that the follower lives in imitation of Christ, except in general terms. Of course, if one truly follows and imitates Jesus as the Christ, one will, like the model (pattern), live the life of lowliness and self-negation, and will hence offend the world and suffer the world's opposition, rejection, and persecution. So Anti-Climacus approves of the way Magister Kierkegaard, in *Works of Love*, has pointed out that Christian self-denial involves a "double-danger," involves not only the demand for inward, spiritual suffering that is required to love one's neighbor, but also the external suffering of rejection and persecution by the world. Anti-Climacus

79. *Practice*, pp. 227, 230–232; (KW 20:233, 236–238); SV 16:217, 220–221; (12:213, 216–217).

80. *Journals*, 412, 3023; I A 27, XI¹ A 339.

81. *Judge for Yourself!*, KW 21:191; SV 17:211–212; (12:459).

concludes that "the second danger ... is the decisive qualification" of Christian self-denial and suffering. "The way" is always the way of the cross, not merely in the sense of carrying the cross for the sake of others but of being nailed to the cross by the world. Hence in this world Christians know only the church militant, not the church triumphant. For this reason " 'fellowship' is a lower category than 'the single-individual' [*den Enkelte*]," and "the congregation really belongs only to eternity." So "this life" is meant to be only "a time of testing for each individual."[82]

As we have noted in the previous chapter,[83] this reversal of priorities between Kierkegaard's *Works of Love* and the two works by Anti-Climacus has much to do with the latter's definition of Christian suffering and with Kierkegaard's eventual dark and pessimistic views not only of the church but also of the world in general, of marriage and the having of children, and finally of even women themselves. The bearing of this bitter fruit can be seen already in a shift of attitude from the concluding section of *Practice* to a major emphasis (three years later) in *For Self-Examination*.

The conclusion of *Practice* is an extended prayer to "Lord Jesus Christ." Granted, in the opening paragraph one can hear at least a hint of Kierkegaard's own self-pity in his characterization of Christian suffering as that of being "forsaken" and "unappreciated" (*Miskjendelse*, literally "misunderstood"). He certainly thought of himself as a misunderstood genius, and this bitterness is partly what is projected into his late pessimism. However, the main body of the prayer is a remarkably tender and sympathetic plea for understanding and patient treatment by Christ/God toward all: toward "the little infant," toward the adult who has confirmed but broken one's baptismal vows, toward "those who in love have found each other" in "the most beautiful earthly meaning of this earthly life," toward "the husband" in "his important task" that can be derailed by "his busy activity or his toilsome labor," for "the wife" so that "while doing her loving tasks at home she may ... preserve her *collectedness* by feeling more drawn to you," for "the one who dying ... that it may have been the meaning of that person's life to be drawn to you." And he goes on to pray for "the happy and the fortunate, ... and for the sufferer," for "those who have need of conversion," for "those who are servants of the word" as well as for "lay

82. *Practice*, pp. 217–218; (KW 20:222–223); SV 16:207–208; (12:204–205). It is this sense of "testing" (*Prøvens*) that is meant in the title, *For Self-Examination*. The Danish word for "examination" is *Prøvelse*, and so the title means "for self-testing," an "exam" in the sense of taking a test in school, not in the sense of examining or analyzing the self.
83. See the section on "Omission of Relation to Neighbor as a Third."

Christians." So he says, "we pray for all," that Christ will "draw all to yourself."[84]

The whole tone and concern of this prayer is in total contrast with what we hear in *For Self-Examination*. The second section is entitled "Christ Is the Way," and the main point is to define in what sense the way is "narrow." In another treatment of this idea, Kierkegaard had stressed that "narrowness" means that I must tread the way alone, utterly by and for myself. But here the emphasis is on the "poverty and wretchedness" of the way, and finally on the fact that the way leads to one thing: death. Hence the daily lives of the original followers of Jesus "were marked by persecution." Their "daily agonizing sufferings" were made up of "all the opposition, scorn and ridicule and ribald laughter and bloody cruelty at the hands of the people." Their only comfort was their faith in "the Ascension of the Lord and Master." So in the third section, entitled "It Is the Spirit Who Gives Life," the main point is that the imitation of Christ leads to a "new life" only in this sense: "literally a new life – because, mark this well, death goes in between." And this "death" means one thing: "to die to the world and to oneself." That is, "you must die to every merely earthly hope, to every merely human confidence; you must die to your selfishness, or to the world, because it is only through your selfishness that the world has power over you."[85]

Interpreted in one way, of course, these words express the heart of the Christian way. That is to say, "purity of heart is to will one thing" (based on Jas 4:8, "purify your hearts, you double-minded"); "seek first the kingdom [rule] of God, and all things will be added to you;" so "lay not up for yourselves treasures on earth, where moth and rust consume, and thieves break through and steal, but lay up for yourselves treasures in heaven; for where your treasure is, there will your heart be also" (Mt 5:19–21); remember: "the things that are seen are transient, but the things that are unseen are eternal" (2 Cor 4:18). Indeed, Kierkegaard's words can be another way of saying that the Christian life is a life of obedience, of "letting God rule in all things." But here in *For Self-Examination* he applies these words in a totally negative and reductionist way. As his prime example, he refers to and brings forward the distinction he already made in *Works of Love* between a love (*Elskov*) that is preferential and concentrated on one or selected person(s), and, in contrast, a love

84. *Practice*, pp. 251–254; (KW 20:259–262); SV 16:239–242; (12:236–239).

85. *For Self-Examination* KW 21:61–64, 67, 69, 76–77; SV 17:101–102, 105–107, 114–115; (12:346–349, 351–353, 360–361).

(*Kjerlighed*) that is self-denying out of concern and compassion toward one's neighbor in need.[86]

In *Works of Love* he says that the latter type of love must penetrate, inform, and hence transform (not exclude) all forms of the first type (whether that of romance, friendship, or family).[87] But here (in *For Self-Examination*) the "death" that precedes the "new life" in Christ means the extinction of all forms of preferential love, because they are expressions of pure selfishness, of self-love. There is only one alternative: "Let go of this object!" In this "you have an example ... of what it is to die to. ... [P]ersonally to have to shatter one's fulfilled desire, personally to have to deprive oneself of the dearly desired one who is now one's own: that means to wound selfishness at the root. ... [B]efore the Spirit who gives life can come, you must first die to." Hence, "only when [*først naar*] you have died to the selfishness in you and thereby to the world so that you do not love the world or anything in the world, do not selfishly love a single human-being – only when you in love of God have learned to hate yourself, only then can there be talk of the love that is Christian."

And what did the first followers of Jesus experience for trying to live according to this ideal? Just what Jesus, their model, experienced. "They died, everything grew black around them ... when they had the dreadful experience that love is not loved, that it is hated, that it is mocked, that it is spat upon, that it is crucified in this world, ... while judging justice calmly washes its hands and while the voice of the people clamors for the robber." So, while they "swore eternal enmity to this unloving world," yet they "in conformity with their model, resolved to ... to endure all things, to be sacrificed in order to save this unloving world."[88] One wonders how total, unrelieved rejection can lead to salvation. Granted, unlike Kierkegaard's asseverations of his last few years, these words do not yet clearly condemn all sexuality, marriage, child-bearing and even women themselves as inimical to Christian faith and to be avoided. But the seeds are planted.

86. For references in this paragraph and the next, see ibid., KW 21:83–84, 78–79; SV 11:120, 115–116; (12:366, 362–363).

87. *Works of Love*, for example pp. 65, 73–74, 117, 141–142, 255; (KW 16:52, 61–62, 112, 131, 273); SV 12:56–57, 65–66, 112, 138–139, 262; (9:54–55, 64, 109, 135–136, 260–261). For my own analysis of and comments on this topic, see *Kierkegaard as Humanist*, pp. 345–350.

88. *For Self-Examination*, pp. 91–93, 99–101; (KW 21:78–79, 83–85); SV 17:91–93, 99–101; (12:362–363, 366–368).

What a far cry are these words and this mentality (of the Kierkegaard of 1851) from the thoughts and mind-set of the one who wrote in *Works of Love* (in 1847) about a love (*Kjerlighed*) that "presuppose[s] that love is present in the heart of the other human being," about a love that is able "to entice forth the good," to "love up love," in such a way that "that which comes forth exactly corresponds to what had been presupposed."[89] What has happened in Kierkegaard's mind even since the end of *Practice in Christianity* where he spoke of romantic love in marriage as "the most beautiful earthly meaning of this earthly life," and of the "important task" of being a husband and of the wife's "loving tasks at home?" He prays simply that these things will not interfere with the loving individuals' being "drawn to Christ." In other words, he hopes for the result of a both/and possibility rather than expecting inevitably the harsh either/or that characterizes his depiction of the Christian life increasingly from 1851 onward.

One is tempted to surmise that when Kierkegaard describes the life of the first disciples as being enveloped in darkness, as being mocked and spat upon (as he was mocked and spat upon in the streets of Copenhagen), that he is projecting upon them the mood of darkness, pessimism, and world-weariness that increasingly engulfed his own heart and mind during the last years of his life. Kierkegaard's picture of the life and spirit of the early Christian community hardly corresponds to that found in Acts of the Apostles, where, in spite of frankly noted sufferings of being reviled, beaten, imprisoned, and even executed, the overruling spirit of the early Christians is described as one of wonder and joy at the power of the gospel to be heard, to bring healing and hope into human lives, and to win increasing numbers to the faith. If one takes the Gospel According to Luke and Acts of the Apostles as a single book, one has a story that traces Jesus' lineage backward to Abraham, Issac, and Jacob, and thence back to Adam himself (Lk 3:23–38); and then in Acts the story of Jesus moves forward and outward until the spread of the Christian movement has penetrated to Rome itself, the center and ruler of the known world: that is, from the beginning of the world in the Garden of Eden to its climax in the Roman empire. And this theme is restated theologically in even more inclusive and expansive terms in the Pauline view of the cosmic Christ as being the clue and the key to God's plans for the entire universe (Eph 3:7–13; Phil 2:5–11; Col 1:15–20). Hardly a mood of pessimism, defeat, and world-weariness!

89. *Works of Love*, pp. 205–207; (KW 16:216–219); SV 12:209–212; (9:208–210).

So we come to an end of the first part of our analysis of Kierkegaard's depiction of how the uniquely Christian experience of the Eternal offers a "way" to the "truth" and the "life" that promises the possibility of "recovering my self," namely, in the event of forgiveness/reconciliation. Now we want to see if more light can be shed on this entire complex process by considering certain problematic aspects of it. As indicated in the outline at the beginning of this chapter, the first topic of consideration will be a very general one. In all the material considered thus far, Kierkegaard has repeatedly insisted that this lifelong process of forgiveness and reconciliation consists in entering into a new relationship with God that can be designated both as a relationship of faith and as a relationship of love. A transition to this topic can be found in Kierkegaard's treatment of obedience in the passage in the discourse on *The Gospel of Sufferings* that we have already looked at carefully above (at notes 63, 65, 69 above).

In one sentence Kierkegaard relates obedience to both love and faith. This sentence follows Kierkegaard's insistence that, indeed, there is the promise of forgiveness and reconciliation for "the person who is brokenhearted," but one cannot "rest in this thought" if one "does not first rest in obedience." How does one "rest in obedience?" Well, "faith and faith's obedience in sufferings love forth [*elsker ... op*] the growth [of the human spirit], because all faith's work aims at getting rid of egotism and selfishness in order that God can actually come in and in order then to let [God] rule in everything." In these words there are some subtle dynamics (in the interrelating of the key factors) that are difficult to unravel. But again the answer or key to the conundrum lies in the spiral interrelationship of the factors whereby one attains to higher (or deeper) levels through continuing cyclical movement. As Kierkegaard describes it, it works this way.

Obedience occurs within the faith-relationship between God and the human being. When that relationship finds expression in obedience, then "faith's obedience in sufferings *loves forth* the growth," that is, the fulfillment of the human spirit. How so? Well, the working (*Arbeid*) of faith, that is, the developing trust between God and the human spirit, "gets rid of egotism and selfishness" so that there is room for God truly to come in, and then I am able "to let God rule," that is, to obey. But in the very next sentence, Kierkegaard reverses the movement: the more suffering, the more selfishness is removed, and then the more obedience occurs "as the receptive soil in which the eternal can take root." So which is it: does God's deeper presence make obedience possible, or does obedience learned in sufferings make room for the eternal (God)?

Kierkegaard is saying that it works both ways, just because (as we have heard) God does not manifest sovereignty by overwhelming the human spirit but precisely by demanding and evoking and enabling its own voluntary participation in the event of reconciliation and spiritual fulfillment. So he immediately goes on to say (in this same passage) that the human spirit "cannot take [*tage*] the eternal" but "can only appropriate [*tilegne*] it." This means a reciprocal, even though not at all an equal, relation: the eternal (God) must be "willing to give it to you," but the price of our appropriation is obedience. "Then the appropriation is the inward-deepening [*Inderliggjørelsen*], ... and in obedience is rest."⁹⁰ But how does one enter this cycle? Is there a beginning point to appropriation? For the Christian it obviously lies in the strange and utterly ambiguous encounter with the lowly human being, Jesus, who speaks and acts with such authority that one's heart and mind is filled with wonder, and one is "drawn" to follow him. And somewhere in following the master, we enter the cycle and the process begins unconsciously, in the doing of the tasks that the master sets for us (as described above in the text following note 73).

This point about the complex interconnections among faith, love, and obedience is given another expression with a different conclusion in Kierkegaard's musings about the lilies and the birds (already referred to above at note 67 above). In *Christian Discourses* (of 1847–48) he says that "the fortress of faith is a world in itself. ... Cut off faith from all connection with the surrounding world: just so much the more impregnable it becomes, just so much the richer is its life. And along with faith in the fortress dwells obedience." Therefore, "the Christian is free from anxiety. ... That obedience is the way to this end [the Christian] has learned and learns from him who is the Way, from him who himself learned obedience, ... obedient in taking all upon himself, obedient in submitting to everything in life, obedient unto death." So "the life of the Christian is a hymn in honor of the Lord, because this life obeys God more willingly and with more blissful accord than do the spheres. ... For only by obedience can a human being praise God."⁹¹

But in his later discourse on the lilies and the birds (1849), he gives this theme a different twist. He stresses again that one comes into the presence of God only in "solemn silence," and this silence before God

---

90. *Upbuilding Discourses in Various Spirits*, KW 15:259; SV 11:240; (8:343). Obviously, Kierkegaard is here putting to use the concept of appropriation that he developed the precious year in *Postscript*. See the index to KW 12.1 for the appropriate passages.

91. *Christian Discourses*, pp. 89, 87; SV 13:86, 84–85; (10:89–90, 87–89).

brings with it a shattering sensation: "two contraries simultaneously touch one another so as to repel each other: ... either love or hate; ... either hold to [God] or despise [God]." Indeed, when you are totally alone with God in silence, this rule holds because "precisely there in the silence it is clear how close [*nær*] God is to you. ... God who never dies is closer to you, infinitely closer, than two lovers are to one another." And in this closeness, "what does God demand? ... [God] demands obedience, unconditional obedience. If you are not obedient in everything unconditionally, then you do not love [God] – then you do hate [God]." And "you can learn this unconditional obedience ... from the lilies and the birds." Then Kierkegaard makes this puzzling statement: "by being obedient oneself, one can learn obedience from oneself." And he repeats, "if you could become obedient like the lilies and the birds, then you also would be able to learn obedience from yourself."[92]

Of course, Kierkegaard says, we are not and cannot be obedient like the lilies and the birds, because we are not necessitated by nature to do what we do. But, he says, we can learn from the lilies and the birds to be obedient in this way. How and when, then, do we learn obedience from ourselves by being obedient? How else than did the first disciples! How else than by becoming, as Kierkegaard urges us to become, "contemporaries" of Jesus as the Christ! This means that, like the first disciples, drawn to Jesus in wonder and with puzzlement, we begin to do what Jesus urges us to do, to follow or imitate him – even before we truly understand what we are doing and before we can even dare call ourselves followers of his way, believing in and living his life. And from this initial and hesitant form of obedience, we learn from its *sufferings* what it means to be truly obedient from a pure and totally devoted heart. This cyclic spiraling way that leads into the mystery and wonder of faith and love has perhaps been best depicted in those entrancing words of Albert Schweitzer which we heard in chapter 1 above (at note 99): we "learn" the "ineffable mystery" when we "follow" the "unknown" Jesus by "obey[ing] him" in "the toils, the conflicts, the sufferings" that we "pass through in his fellowship."

Now we are ready to stand back from the infinite complexities of Kierkegaard's *ordo salutis* and to try to understand them better by looking at certain aspects or shapes of the whole. We call them "problematic" aspects, because Kierkegaard, who was deliberately and fiercely anti-systematic, never brings together in one place all his thoughts on

92. *The Lily of the Field and the Bird of the Air* (published in translation with *Christian Discourses*), pp. 334–336; SV 14:146–148; (11:24–27).

any one aspect. So our very attempt to do so is problematic in itself, as well as must be the results. Nevertheless, we will try.

PART TWO:
PROBLEMATIC ASPECTS OF KIERKEGAARD'S
ORDO SALUTIS

1 The Complementarity of Faith and Love

Faith and love are two basic concepts or categories that Kierkegaard explores throughout all his writings. The concepts are derived phenomenologically from two fundamental aspects of the God-human relationship as experienced in the Christian religion (although he sees analogues of both of them in Religiousness A). Kierkegaard discusses each of them separately for the most part (except in a few passages which we will look at below). Nevertheless, he uses them to describe a single reality, namely, the ultimate relationship between God and the human self, a relationship in which the self recovers and becomes itself, and in which God achieves an exquisite and significant expression of God's own essential being/nature. In this description, therefore, Kierkegaard is practicing the principle of complementarity; that is, in order to describe the single phenomenon of the relationship between God and the individual self, he must say two quite different things which together make up a whole that is not reducible to either one and is not adequately described or defined by either one.[93] The problem is that

93. This thesis was briefly noted in chapter 1 above (following note 98). The principle of complementarity has a long and ancient heritage. But it has come into prominence in the twentieth century because of its specific use by Niels Bohr in his development of his theory of quantum mechanics (or physics). I first became familiar with it in a doctoral dissertation presented to the faculty of the Graduate Theological Union (Berkeley, California) in October, 1975 (for which I was privileged to serve on the three-member advisory committee). The dissertation is entitled, *A Comparison of 'Complementarity' in Quantum Physics with Analogous Structures in Kierkegaard's Philosophical Writings, from a Jungian Point of View,* and its author is John L. Hitchcock. For those who may want to consult it, its library call-number (at the GTU Library) is: f BX 4827 K5H5. Before beginning his doctoral program at the GTU, Dr. Hitchcock had a doctoral degree in physics and had become involved in Jungian and Kierkegaardian studies while serving as a professor of physical sciences at California State University, San Francisco. There are many fascinating things about the interrelation of Kierkegaard's thought and twentieth century physics in this dissertation, including a detailed account of Niels Bohr's interest in Kierkegaard. And one of its main themes is the attempt to show how physics, psychology, and religion are interrelated so as to form one continuous truth or reality.

there is no single concept or term that captures both of the elements in this relationship, and therefore Kierkegaard must say both things. The prime example usually given is that of light. Light can be described as an electromagnetic wave or as a stream of minute particles (corpuscles), but it cannot be reduced to either one, and therefore there is no single definition or description of light.

We will not provide here a complete survey and summary of Kierkegaard's many and diverse treatments of these two concepts.[94] Rather, we will concentrate on a few aspects of their interrelationship.

The first primary example of Kierkegaard's attempt to analyze or depict the interrelationship of faith and love occurs in *Philosophical Fragments*. The way its first four chapters are related to each other poses an interesting problem. C. Stephen Evans observes that although chapter 3 may seem to be a digression, it actually is a reconsideration of the Socratic theme of chapter 1.[95] And although he says (as does Climacus) that chapter 4 resumes the "poem" of chapter 2, Evans also notes that it actually picks up with the problem that was posed at the end of chapter 3, namely, how "the understanding and the paradox happily encounter each other in the moment," and he notes that in chapter 4 that "happy passion" is finally given a name: faith.[96]

For our consideration of the relation of faith and love, an alternative perspective on the interrelation of these four chapters is proposed, namely, that the poetic treatment of the *love* relationship between king and maiden in chapter 2 is a deliberate interjection of a dialectical factor that is in sharp antithesis to Climacus's consideration of the *faith* relationship between the learner and the absolute paradox (as an alternative to the Socratic approach to truth) in chapters 1, 3, and 4. In other words, Climacus is suggesting that the entire traditional debate about the relation between faith and reason cannot be ultimately resolved, unless one simultaneously interprets that relation also in terms of the profoundly personal love relationship between God and the human self. And descriptions of both of these relationships must be stated in complementarity if one is to think and talk adequately about what

94. This has been done rather fully in *Kierkegaard as Humanist*, in which the reader should see the index entries under faith, and the entirety of chapter 7 on love.

95. In his *Passionate Reason*, pp. 58–59. This book is one of the clearest and most helpful interpretations of *Fragments* that I know. His limpid, direct, and deceptively simple style (which I envy) should not mislead the reader. There is a profound and subtle analysis going on below the surface, and close attention offers many rewarding insights.

96. Ibid., p. 96.

happens to human beings in existential encounter with Jesus as the Christ.

So Climacus (in *Fragments*) insists that the analogy or metaphor of the love relationship is inadequate by itself, not just because it is prone to be misidentified with a merely self-loving kind of romantic love, but because the relationship with God-in-time involves and requires a kind of knowledge or understanding that essentially qualifies the factor of authentic love. In other words, just as the God-relationship is impoverished if reduced to nothing but the problem of believing the absolute paradox, so also if reduced to a merely blind, irrational passion.[97] In other words, human freedom involves and requires not only a form of willing obedience but also of thoughtful agreement. The crucial human "yes" toward God, the giver and redeemer of human spirit, comes from both the heart (as ultimate commitment) and the mind. To paraphrase Kant, willing obedience is not "blind" but involves understanding, and thoughtful agreement is not "empty" but involves obedience in fact.[98] Neither in *Fragments* nor in *Postscript* does Climacus explore this dialectical relation between faith and love in any detail. For this we have to wait for Kierkegaard's second, consciously Christian authorship and a number of significant entries in his journals, wherein he brings to bear several other major concepts in order to clarify this dialectic of love and faith.[99]

97. Stephen Evans of course recognizes this interplay as is clear especially in his sections on "Can Reason Have Limits?" and "How Is Faith Acquired?" (see especially p. 109). And the entirety of his chapter 7 is a perceptive refutation of the charge of irrationalism against Kierkegaard, especially when taken along with much of chapters 5 and 6. But as we will shortly see, I have some reservations about his analysis of the relation of "Belief and the Will." Also note: I have short-circuited Climacus's playful presentation of his alternative position B (as a mere hypothesis) by frankly designating it as the Christian position. This assumption is clearly that of Climacus (Kierkegaard) also, as evidenced in the first few pages of his discussion of "The Issue in *Fragments*" in *Postscript* (KW 12.1:361ff.) And Evans calmly falls in with this assumption without comment, as he proceeds through his book, occasionally supplementing Climacus's limited perspective on Christian faith in *Fragments* with references to the works of Anti-Climacus.

98. Cf. Immanuel Kant, *Gesammelte Schriften* (Berlin: Druck und Verlag von Georg Reimer, 1911), vol. 4, *Kritik der reinen Vernunft* (1st ed.), p. 48 (i.e., in his Transcendental Logic, Introduction. Section I: Of Logic in General): "Gedanken ohne Inhalt sind leer, Anschauungen ohne Begriffe sind blind."

99. Climacus's use of the analogy or "metaphor" (*Billede*) of love on the last page of chapter 3 of *Fragments* (just before the appendix) hardly comprises an adequate exploration of this dialectic.

However, we do find in *Fragments* an initial intimation of a basic problem about the love relationship, a problem with which Kierkegaard continues to struggle throughout the rest of his days. Under the topic of "The Teacher's Goals and Motives," Evans immediately states this problem, as he begins his discussion of chapter 2 of *Fragments*. God, he says, "has no need of others" but does have "a need within himself to love the other." And this "assumption about the god's motives provides Climacus with a goal for the god's activities as a teacher as well," namely, "to 'win' the learner, to establish and maintain a loving relationship with him."[100] This relationship between God's inner "need" and God's "love of the other" requires further analysis for clarification of our larger problem of the relation between love and faith.

First of all, Climacus makes clear a fundamental assumption about the entire faith/love relationship between God and the human being: the divine and the human are two different, unequal orders of being, and *yet*, at the level of being free self-conscious spirit (selfhood, personhood), they are capable of an authentic unity in equality. On the one hand, God's priority and superior uniqueness is manifest in the fact that God is not moved by anything external. "God requires [*behøver*] no disciple, ... and no occasion can induce [God] in such a way that there is just as much in the occasion as in [God's] resolve." God's "resolve, which does not have an equal reciprocal relation to the occasion, must be from eternity, even though, fulfilled in time, it expressly becomes *the moment*. ... The moment emerges precisely in the relation of the eternal resolve to the unequal occasion."[101]

On the other hand, God is also not moved by some internal urge (*Trang*, desire, craving), "as if [the divine] itself could not endure silence but has to break out into speech." If, then, God is not moved by some factor external or internal, "[the divine] must move itself. ... But if it moves itself, not from desire [*Trang*], what is it that moves it other

100. C.S. Evans, *Passionate Reason*, p. 47.
101. Here Kierkegaard clearly is using his reflections on the nature of the "occasion" (*Anledning*) as developed in volume 1 of *Either/Or*. There he says, "[T]he occasion is generative in the negative sense, not the positive. A creation is a production out of nothing, but the occasion is the nothing that lets everything come forth." So "without the occasion nothing actually occurs, and yet the occasion has no part in what occurs. The occasion is ... the essential category of transition from the sphere of the idea to actuality. ... The occasion, then, is nothing in and for itself and is something only in relation to that which it occasions, and in relation to that it is actually nothing," and hence is not "ground or cause." [pp. 234, 236; (KW 3:236, 238); SV 2:218, 220; (1:210, 212)]

than love, because this [love] does not have satisfaction of desire [*Trang*] outside of itself but within itself." So

out of love God must be eternally resolved in this way [i.e., to become the moment], but just as love is the ground, so also must love be the goal, because it would indeed be a contradiction for God to have a ground of movement and a goal that do not correspond to this. The love, then, must be for the learner, and the goal must be to win her/him, for only in love is the different made equal, and only in equality or unity is there understanding [*Forstaaelse*].[102]

Climacus is saying, then, that love is not one faculty or quality among others in God but is the primary determinant of the total divine being. In his hypothesizing about his position B (in contrast to Socrates), it is not appropriate for him to say, "God *is* love," but that is what he obviously means. And when he says that God as love has the characteristic of being "resolved" (*Beslutning*) and that "from eternity," Climacus is asserting that God as love is self-moving, that love is not static but dynamic in and of itself. But if, in this sense, divine love has its "satisfaction of desire ... within itself," then how can Climacus also say that the eternal resolve of God's love actually is "fulfilled in time" and "expressly becomes *the moment*" when that peculiar external "occasion" called the human self is faced by "the most terrible decision" of freely responding to God's anxious question, "Do you really believe me?"? Furthermore, if this love-relationship is totally an expression of the omnipotent and eternal divine resolve so that "God's love ... must be not only an assisting love but also a procreative love, ... meaning the transition from 'not being' to 'being'," how can it *possibly* become an "unhappy love?"

This latter question is intensified when Climacus admits that contrary to the obvious expectation that "the divine must be able to make itself understood," actually it is "not so easy" *if* God "is not to annihilate that which is different." The question is further intensified, then, by the recognition that God's love must come in such a way that the learner (the "unequal occasion") "becomes nothing and yet is not annihilated, ... owes everything and yet becomes boldly confident, ... understands the truth but the truth makes him/her free, ... grasps the guilt of untruth

---

102. For the last two paragraphs, *Fragments*, pp. 30–31; (KW 7:24–25); SV 6:27–28; (4:193–194). The Hongs translate both *behøver* and *Trang* as "need," but in Danish there is a clear difference between *Behov* as some requirement or need imposed from without and *Trang* as an internal desire, urge, or craving. And in this context I believe that Kierkegaard is making that distinction.

and then again bold confidence triumphs in the truth." And Climacus intensifies this issue finally by repeatedly speaking of God's "sorrow" at this possibility of unhappy love and of God's "anxious-concern" (*Bekym-ring*) in awaiting the beloved's response. And Climacus concludes the poem/story with the enigmatic question: "if God gave no indication, how could it occur to a human-being that the blessed God could need [*behøve*] him?"[103]

The problem or question, then, that is posed by all of these comments on God's love by Climacus is this: does not love-itself (the eternal God) *need* an object that, in a very real sense, is external or over-against or face-to-face with it? Is not love-itself *compelled* or propelled by its very nature to go out of itself to an *other*? If our story (analogy) "must find a point of unity where love's understanding exists in truth, where God's anxious-concern has overcome its pain," and if "the king [God] ... does not want his own glorification but the girl's [learner's],"[104] then, for divine self-fulfillment, does not God *need* (require) that strange *human* kind of "being" that – in all its temporality, contingency, accidentality – is not *nothing* (like the empty occasion), but is spirit in God's own image and freely becomes "nothing" before God in order to receive the gift of new life?

One possible answer, suggested by Climacus in *Fragments*, is the attribution of "resolve" as integral to love, integral to the eternal being of God. This attribution signifies that God-as-love is free, is self-conscious, is open, that God-as-love *moves* and lives, is not static but dynamic, constantly in creative process out of the eternal being-in-and-for-itself. And the wonder (miracle) that we humans experience (in encounter with that God as present in Jesus as the Christ) is that somewhere along in that eternal process, God-as-love *chose* freely to share with or give to us God's likeness, to us who are members of that peculiar species called "human" (are there others?). And what we have been seeing in the last two chapters (of this text) is that that gift is indeed wondrous but also terrifying in its complications of possible fulfillment and of possible failure.

These issues in Climacus's provisional and even tentative exploration of the nature of God's eternal being as love were not seriously reconsid-

103. The references in the last two paragraphs are a pastiche of words, phrases, and sentences found on the following pages of *Fragments*: pp. 30–31, 37–38, 41–42, 37; (KW 7:25, 30–31, 33–34, 36); SV 6:27–28, 32–35, 37; (4:194, 198–203).
104. Ibid., 35–6; (KW 7:28–29); SV 6:30–31; (4:197).

ered by Kierkegaard until the relative peace and contentment of his life
was shattered by the *Corsair* affair and he was compelled to reconsider
everything, especially how and why the God of love would bring such
suffering into his life. Out of this crisis in his own spiritual life came his
second, Christian authorship. By the end of the first year of this crisis
(1846), he had completed his "Christian discourses" called *The Gospel of
Sufferings*, and then plunged immediately (in January 1847) into the
writing of his "Christian reflections [deliberations]" called *Works of Love*,
which were immediately followed by his *Christian Discourses* (almost completed by the end of 1847). In *Works of Love* he provides a wide-ranging,
diversified, and unsystematic exploration of the content and ramifications of the notion that "God is love-itself."[105] And as has been shown at
length in chapter 2 above (in the text between note 31 and note 57), in
the latter two works and a number of late journal entries, Kierkegaard
brings to his understanding and interpretation of God several major
concepts other than love: being-in-and-for-itself, infinite subjectivity, reduplication, and personhood.

All of these shed light on the nature of God as love. It would take another chapter by itself to make this application with any thoroughness,
but here a few points can be made briefly.

The key passage (as quoted at note 35, chapter 2) is in *Works of Love*,
where Kierkegaard says that "if the eternal is in a human-being, then this
eternal is reduplicated in [a person] in such a way that every instant it is
in [the person], it is in [the person] in a twofold way: in an outward direction and in an inward direction back into itself, but in such a way that
these [two] are one and the same; because otherwise there is no reduplication. The eternal is not merely in its qualities, rather is in its qualities
within itself [*in sig selv*]" (emphasis added). But what is significant for our
present subject and was not pointed out in chapter 2, Kierkegaard immediately applies this abstract point to love: "So also with love. ... At the
same moment it goes out of itself (the outward direction), it is in itself
(the inward direction); and at the same moment it is in itself, it goes out
of itself in such a way that this outward going and this returning, this returning and this outward going are simultaneously one and the same."
And (as quoted at note 34, chapter 2) within months Kierkegaard expanded this idea in *Christian Discourses* by saying, "There is only one who
totally knows himself, who in and for himself [*i og for sig selv*] knows what

105. For a fulsome analysis of this content and ramifications see *Kierkegaard as Humanist*,
the entirety of chapter 7.

he himself is: that is God."[106] So Kierkegaard interrelates his concepts of reduplication and being-in-and-for-itself in order to show how God as love-itself can "need" to manifest anxious-concern and self-sacrificial care for the creature-in-God's-image and *yet* be "moved" only by what is interior to God and God alone.

In other words, the fact that Love goes out of itself (in creating) but always returns into itself (in reconciling) is the very nature of God-as-love. So this self-reduplication of the Eternal (outward) is not contradictory to its Being-in-and-for-itself, nor is *being*-in-and-for-itself contradictory to self-reduplication. It is all one motion. Is, then, this movement automatic, inevitable, involuntary, necessary? Not for the God/Eternal who appears in Kierkegaard's Christian experience. As we have heard Climacus say, the movement of this Love does not derive from some inner compulsive desire or craving (*Trang*) so that Love-itself "has to break out" (*maatte udbryde*); rather, this movement is a matter of God's eternal "resolve."

And as we have seen extensively, Kierkegaard's late and more mature reflections about God elaborate this notion of God's "resolve" by insisting that all of God's movement or action is qualified by God's being as subjectivity and personhood (see chapter 2 above from note 36 to the end of the chapter). Both of these characteristics of God's being stress the fact that God's actions are the result of conscious reflection about alternatives that are in accord with God's eternal righteousness and are then the result of freely choosing to do the unique and concrete thing that the totality of God's being wills to do. And in relation to those particular and peculiar creatures, each of whom is also conscious, reflecting, choosing, unique spirit, this personal and conscious action of God must be caring and careful to affirm and to help the other one in becoming one's unique identity as spirit, and must do all that in such a way that does not "annihilate" the otherness and freedom of the other.

Therefore, in all the indirectness and anxiousness and uncertainty of such an action, God is clearly not automatic necessity, but is loving, concerned, sensitive Person, responding precisely to the unique particularity of each individual human being in each unique and particular situation. As we have heard Kierkegaard say, "[P]ersonhood is not a sum of propositions, nor is it something *immediately* accessible; personhood consists

---

106. *Works of Love,* p. 261; (KW 16:280); SV 12:269; (9:267); *Christian Discourses,* pp. 42–43; SV 13:43–44; (10:45). To correct the gender prejudice in the latter quotation would make the English too awkward.

of a curving inwardly into oneself, a *clausum* [enclosed place], an αδυτον [sanctuary], a μυστηριον [secret]; personhood consists of this 'in there,' ... the in-there to which oneself (as personhood) must be related believingly. Between personhood and personhood no other relationship is possible" (emphasis added).[107] So God-as-love is not compelled in its actions either from within or from without, but simply moves freely from out of divine being, always consistent with itself, and brings back into itself what it has done.[108]

Now we are ready to return to the point made at the beginning of this discussion of the complementarity involved in any description of the Christian relationship with God-in-time (with the God who comes to us in and with Jesus as the Christ), namely, the point that this relationship is equally one of love and faith, never one without the other. In other words, on the one hand, this relationship always entails a kind of personal, earnest, passionate, out-going commitment (love) that essentially qualifies the element of faith; on the other hand, this relationship always

107. *Journals*, 180; XI¹ A 237.

108. One is tempted at this point to push Kierkegaard to consider whether the God who so clearly finds it consistent with divine being to participate in and to relate with the temporal, finite, contingent process of human existence actually remains unchanged when all the infinitely diverse wonders of human individual creativity "return ... in an inward direction back into" divine being. Kierkegaard firmly rejects any notion of any change in God (see text in chapter 2 above from note 38 to note 39). He insists that "in [God's] being subjective there is no imperfection at all that should be taken away, nor is there anything lacking that should be added, as is the case of human subjectivity" (*Journals*, 4571; XI² A 97; see also 2570, 1449; XI² A 54, 133). One of his last discourses is entitled *God's Unchangingness*, written in 1851 but published by Kierkegaard (in memory of his father) in September 1855, two months before he died. The suggestion that God could change within God's own being would be labeled by Kierkegaard as pure speculation and totally without ground in the Christian revelation/experience of God in Christ. Yet, in a speculative mood but also in contemplation of some passages of the Bible, one might wonder if God has not learned something from the entirety of the human experiment. Certainly on Kierkegaard's own absolutistic terms of the demands and expectations of the divine Unconditional, one would have to conclude that the experiment has been a failure, even though in some late journal entries, he stresses the divine mercy and patience. And in chapter 2 above, I have raised the question of whether the ideal goal of individual human self-fulfillment has been worth the untold and even unimaginable sufferings of the myriad of human beings who have been ground down under the horrifying tortures of war, of class and caste and racial hatred, of slavery, of poverty, disease, hunger, homelessness and hopelessness caused by economic oppression of the powerless by the powerful – what Eliade has called "the horrors of history." The early legends of the Hebrew Bible do not hesitate to represent God as responding experimentally to one human failure after another. We will return to this theme in the next chapter.

entails a kind of knowing, understanding, and believing that essentially qualifies the element of love. And both of these seemingly contradictory elements are simultaneously present as a unity in the living active relationship, even though the conscious observation and description of the relationship can be done only sequentially in the separate and distinct languages and conceptualities of each element. This fact means that one does not first love and then believe, nor first believe and then love. Hence if one wants to describe this relationship, one must speak of "love's understanding" and "faith's passionate commitment," because there is no one term or concept that captures both elements.

Even in chapter 2 of *Fragments*, in his story/analogy of the king's love for the maiden, Climacus speaks repeatedly about love's need for "understanding" (*Forstaaelse*) between God and the human being. As we have heard (above at notes 97, 98), it is true that God is moved only by the eternal resolve within the divine love itself, and hence God does not require a disciple in order for God to understand God. But since God's goal is also love, the object of that love must be won in accord with the nature of love, namely, "the different [must be] made equal," because "only in equality or in unity is there understanding." But this "understanding" that love requires between two qualitatively different beings "is not so easy if [God] is not to annihilate that which is different," because only God understands the misunderstanding that is intrinsic to the relationship from the human side. And yet without this understanding, this love relationship is inevitably "unhappy" – to say the least. The only resolution to this unhappy love is "to find ... a point of unity where in truth is love's understanding."[109] (Kierkegaard could have quoted Jesus (Mt 22:37): "You shall love the Lord your God with all your heart, and with all your soul, and with all your mind [διανοια, thought, intellect].")

What is it, then, that must be understood by the beloved? In the midst of the love story (analogy) in chapter 2, Climacus puts it this way: the disciple must learn that s/he "is in untruth" and yet that God "does indeed love the learner." This double truth is "what makes understanding so difficult" and so precarious, namely, that in the God-relationship "one becomes nothing and yet is not annihilated; that one owes [God] everything and yet becomes boldly confident; that one understands the truth, but the truth makes one free; that one grasps the guilt of untruth, and then again bold confidence triumphs in the truth."[110]

109. *Fragments*, pp. 30–32, 35; (κw 7:24–26, 28); sv 6:27–28, 30; (4:193–194, 197).
110. Ibid., pp. 34, 38; (κw 7:28, 30–31); sv 6:30, 32; (4:196, 199).

In chapter 1 Climacus has established that the learner, as created by God, must have been in possession of "the condition for understanding the truth," and that the learner's present lack of the condition (and the truth) can only be the learner's "own fault." Furthermore, the learner is no longer free to return to the truth because s/he "is indeed unfree and bound and excluded, because to be free from the truth is indeed to be excluded, and to be excluded on one's own is indeed to be bound." In other words, the learner lacks "the condition" for grasping the truth, and only God coming as the teacher "gives the condition and gives the truth."[111] If this happens, then the learner becomes "a *new* person" through "conversion" and "repentance," but Climacus does not identify what that "condition" is.

In chapter 3 Climacus picks up the themes of the two previous chapters. At both the beginning and the end of the chapter (before the appendix), he compares "love's paradox" with "reason's paradox."[112] Love's paradox is this: self-love awakens the sense of "loving oneself in order to command loving the neighbor as oneself." Likewise, "reason's paradoxical passion ... wills the collision" with the unknown, and hence "without really understanding itself, wills its own downfall" – with this result: "reason's paradox reacts upon a human-being and upon one's self-knowledge in such a way that the one who believed to know oneself now

111. Ibid., pp. 18–19; (KW 7:15); SV 6:20; (4:184–5).

112. Ibid., pp. 39, 59; (KW 7:38–39, 47–48); SV 6:39–40, 47; (4:206, 215). Contrary to the Hongs's translation in KW, I think it important to distinguish between the meaning of *Forstand* (as "reason") and *Forstaaelse* (as "understanding"). In his 1962 revision of Swenson's translation, Howard Hong retained this distinction (including Swenson's capitalization of the word "reason"). It is clear (to me at least) that Kierkegaard is using *Forstand* in the sense of *Fornuft* (the Danish equivalent of the German *Vernunft*). In a philosophical note (from a year or so before writing *Fragments*), Kierkegaard anticipates his treatment (in *Fragments*) of the interrelation of faith, reason, and paradox, making the same point that "Christianity consists of paradox," and therefore "faith cannot be proved, demonstrated, comprehended" by "reason" (*Fornuft*) (*Journals*, 3073; IV C 29). In *Fragments* Climacus is arguing that in and with faith comes a kind of understanding (between God and the sinful human being) that is qualitatively different from that which is sought by unaided human reason. This point is blurred, if not lost, when the Hongs (in KW) translate *Forstand* as "understanding." For example, they translate the first sentence of the appendix to chapter 3 as: "If the paradox and the understanding [*Forstand*, that is, 'reason'] meet in the mutual understanding [*Forstaaelse*] of their difference, then the encounter is a happy one like [erotic] love's understanding [*Forstaaelse*], happy in the passion to which we as yet have given no name" (that is, "faith"). So the contrast is clearly between faith and reason, not between faith and understanding. Stephen Evans quotes the Hongs's translation but then proceeds to use "reason" throughout his chapter, "Reason and the Paradox."

no longer is sure whether ... one has in one's own being a gentler and diviner part." But this unknown is really God, and if reason, in its own self-confidence, attempts to "demonstrate the existence of God," it does not end up with "an existence [*Tilværelse*]" but only with "a conceptual definition [*Begrebs-Bestemmelse*]."[113]

In this comparison, then, Climacus is intimating that the "condition" that is required for the achievement of a happy relationship (or understanding) between God and the human being is not simply the passion of thought in and by itself (reason) but also the passion of self-denying love/trust toward God. In other words, God is not a concept in the human mind, nor is the human being simply a concept in the divine mind – that is, concepts that can be directly and fully grasped and comprehended by abstract, pure reason. Rather, Climacus explains (in chapters 3 and 4 of *Fragments*), the understanding that is required for this relationship between God and the human involves an essential paradox for reason as such. God is "unknown" in the sense of being "the absolutely different" which "reason cannot even think."[114] So "we seem to stand at a paradox." But "just to come to know that God is the different, the human-being needs God." And what do we learn about this difference from the God who becomes our teacher in the humble human being, Jesus? We learn that this difference "can have its basis not in that which the human-being owes to [i.e., derives from] God (for to that extent they are akin) but in that which one derives from oneself or in that which one has committed." So the difference is very simply "sin."[115]

Here as elsewhere, Kierkegaard is very clear that the human being learns about the true nature and depth of human failure/sin only from God, from being "before God" in Jesus as the Christ. But that does not exhaust the paradox. God indeed (according to the story in chapter 2) wished to become the Teacher, but "in order to be that, [God] chose [*vilde*] to be equal to the single individual [*den Enkelte*] in order that this one could *understand* [God]" (emphasis added). Now, this wish or resolve by God infinitely complicates the paradox. To convince human beings that they are failures, and that they are to blame for it, is not all that difficult. But to convince them that this act of judgment and condemnation is an act of love and is to be accepted humbly and with gladness –

113. Ibid., pp. 48–9; (KW 7:38–40); SV 6:39–40; (4:206–207).
114. Ibid., p. 55; (KW 7:45); SV 6:44; (4:212).
115. Ibid., pp. 58; (KW 7:46–47); SV 6:46; (4:214).

well, that involves an infinitely more complicated and subtle relationship. "So the paradox becomes even more frighteningly appalling," because "the same paradox possesses this doubleness by which it manifests itself as the absolute [paradox] – negatively by bringing into prominence the absolute difference of sin, positively by wishing to annul this absolute difference in absolute equality [*Lighed*]."[116]

So the "condition" that the teacher (God) imparts, that gives the "moment" of encounter absolute significance, is precisely this "doubleness" or complementarity of understanding *and* love, of love *and* understanding, and it is imparted in such a situation or relationship that the learner knows it is the truth. How does the learner know this? by the fact that the condition engages and is offered to the human being in such a way that it enables, encourages, and makes it possible for the learner to "appropriate" this double truth as her/his own, *freely*: "the situation of understanding – how frighteningly appalling, for it is less appalling to fall upon one's face while the mountains tremble at God's voice than to sit with [God] as equal [*Lige*], and yet God's anxious-concern is precisely to sit this way."[117] And even the omnipotent God is anxious (*bekymret*), because God faces the situation of "wanting to express the unity of love and then not to be understood," as God "anxiously asks, even ... the lowliest of persons, 'Do you really love me?'"[118]

So in the very next paragraph after the statement of the absolute (double) paradox, Climacus again draws the analogy between reason's paradox and love's paradox, namely, that they both have the inherent seed of a passion for their own destruction, or better, for their own transcendence. We must now look more carefully at these two paradoxes and their interrelationship.

(1) *Reason's Paradox.* Climacus says that, by itself and on its own terms, "reason cannot think, cannot understand" its being confronted by the paradox of the unknown. Reason resents, or is offended by, this relationship. Yet it has a "passion" to grasp and understand it. What, then, is the "happy passion" that makes it possible for reason and the absolute paradox "to be united in some third" and hence come to "an understanding with each other?" The name, Climacus comments, is not important, "if only I am happy." But this mutual understanding has one

116. Ibid., pp. 58–59; (KW 7:47); SV 6:46–47; (4:214).
117. Ibid., p. 43; (KW 7:34–35); SV 6:35–36; (4:202).
118. Ibid., pp. 40–41; (KW 7:32–33); SV 6:33–34; (4:200).

requirement: reason must "give itself up [*opgive*]" before the paradox, and the paradox must "give itself to [*hengive*]" reason (Kierkegaard loved this kind of play on words).[119] A few pages later (in chapter 4) Climacus finally does give this passion a name: faith. In his analysis and depiction of it, he picks up and uses the notion (mentioned above) that this passion is a "third," within which two distinct and very different entities are united in mutual understanding. In what sense is faith a "*third* something?" Well, Climacus says, when "reason steps aside" and when "the paradox gives itself," this double action by two different parties involves "a third, in which this occurs, because it does not occur by [or 'in'] the reason that is inactivated [*entlediget*], or by [or 'in'] the paradox that gives itself – consequently in something." This third something is, then, that "happy passion" which "we shall call *faith*."[120] In other words, faith is a *relationship* in which human thinking finds the different kind of "understanding" that is beyond its own purely rational capacities.

From this perspective, the exploration of all the complex issues about the nature of "coming into existence" (in "Interlude" between chapters 4 and 5) simply makes the point that this relationship is one of freedom and not necessity. So "faith is not a cognition [*Erkendelse*] but an act-of-freedom, an expression-of-willing." Or, "the conclusion of faith is no conclusion [*Slutning*] but a resolve [*Beslutning*]."[121] Hence, the word "faith" may be taken "in its direct and ordinary meaning as the relationship to the historical." But for the Christian it must be taken "in the wholly eminent sense" as applicable to "only one relationship," that is, to the relationship between the human self and God-in-time. The object of faith, then, "is not a question of the truth of it but of assenting to God's having come into existence, whereby God's eternal essence is inflected back into the dialectical determinants of coming-into-existence."[122] So "faith" in this eminent sense is not a believing in some concept for which one has rational evidence (logical or empirical). When faith, as the resolution of the paradox of human thinking, involves "freedom" and "willing" and

---

119. Ibid., pp. 59–60, 67; (KW 7:47–48, 54); SV 6:47, 52; (4:214–215, 220–221).
120. *Fragments*, p. 73; (KW 7:59); SV 6:56; (4:224). A fuller exposition of this passage in *Fragments* may be found in *Kierkegaard as Humanist*, pp. 307–308. Read pp. 298–309 for different meanings of "faith" in Kierkegaard's writings. Kierkegaard also applies the concept of a "third" to the synthesis of the temporal and the eternal in *The Concept of Angst*, p. 76; (KW 8:85); SV 6:173; (4:355).
121. *Fragments*, pp. 103–104; (KW 7:83–84); SV 6:76; (4:247). For fuller treatment, see *Kierkegaard as Humanist*, pp. 146–148, 181–189.
122. Ibid., pp. 108–109; (KW 7:87); SV 6:79–80; (4:250–1).

"resolve," we are encountered by a paradox that has taken on new qualities and content. In other words, the paradox of human thinking and understanding is resolved only by being related to another paradox that involves dimensions of human existence other than that of thinking and understanding.

(2) *Love's Paradox.* We have heard Climacus define this paradox as follows. All love is rooted and grounded in self-love, which is natural to every human being. Hence any "religion of love" presupposes that loving oneself is a given condition that awakens the paradoxical urge (inner command) to love one's neighbor as one loves oneself.[123] But we must turn to the writings of Kierkegaard's second authorship and to some late journal entries to find a further elaboration of this theme.

In *Works of Love* Kierkegaard's "Christian reflections" on the interrelationships of self-love, love of others, and love of God are complex and tend to run off in different directions,[124] but for our limited purposes here we can summarize the relevant points briefly. His general point is that the God who comes to encounter me in time (in Jesus as the Christ) does so not as an ultimate Idea but in the very personal terms of judgment of sin and the offer of forgiveness. As we have heard, the point to this coming of God is not God's own justification and glorification by forcing the human being to confess failure/sin and to humbly accept help. God's goal is to set me free from my enslavement to untruth in order that I may become that free and loving self that is my true nature and destiny. God seeks me to help me to be able to recover my (lost/failed) self. In this encounter, therefore, I come to know that "God is love," because I experience for myself that God affirms my infinite dignity and worth as one created in God's image for eternal life with God.

In *Works of Love* Kierkegaard couches this view in several very suggestive and enlightening languages. As already noted above,[125] first, and basic to everything else, "the one who loves presupposes that love is in the other human being's heart and by this very presupposition builds up love in the other one – from the ground up, provided, of course, that one lovingly presupposes its presence in the ground." Indeed, "to be loving is to assume, to presuppose that other humans are loving." And

123. Ibid., p. 48; (KW 7:39); SV 6:39–40; (4:206).
124. As noted before, I have explored these reflections at length in chapter 7 of *Kierkegaard as Humanist*. For our present discussion, I draw attention especially to the section entitled "Love Presupposes Love."
125. Under the topic of forgiveness (in this chapter). See text from note 45 to note 48.

"in this way one draws out the good, he loves forth [*opelske*] love." Indeed, "there is no other relationship in all the world in which there is such a like-for-like, in which that which comes forth so accurately corresponds to what was presupposed." And all this presupposing is on firm ground, because "it is God, the Creator, who must implant love in each human being, [God] who [as God] is Love."[126] The most important point in this whole conceptuality is this: in the *love* relationship (both between God and the human being and between two humans) there is a fundamental continuity, what Kierkegaard calls an essential and universal "kinship" or "likeness" or "equality." And this continuity of given *being* manifests itself also in the dynamics of *functional* interrelationship.

In a second language, Kierkegaard gives this notion of continuity a profound ontological formulation and grounding (which he feels free to do in these upbuilding discourses since he has announced in their title that they are also "reflections" or "deliberations"). As noted several times before, Kierkegaard draws a direct analogy between the dynamics of love and the essential dynamics of God's eternal being (i.e., being-in-and-for-itself and subjectivity), namely, the dynamics of reduplication.[127] Here in *Works of Love*, he notes that in contrast to the temporal, the eternal "has reduplication in itself," that is, "the eternal *is* not merely in its qualities, rather is in its qualities within itself. It does not merely *have* qualities, but *is* in itself as simultaneously [*idet*] it has qualities" (emphases added). Or as he puts it in a late journal entry, God "is infinite subjectivity," and God "relates objectively to [God's] own subjectivity, yet this is only a reduplication of [God's] subjectivity." In other words, this notion of reduplication infers a fundamental distinction or differentiation within the unity of the eternal being-in-and-for-itself.[128]

But in this passage in *Works*, Kierkegaard uses a terminology that adds another whole dimension to reduplication by perceiving the inferred distinction as involving a kind of *motion*. He says that "when the eternal is in a human-being, then this eternal is reduplicated [*fordobler ... sig*] in him/her in such a way that every moment it is in her/him, it is in him/her in a twofold way: in an outward direction and in an inward direction back into

126. *Works of Love*, quotations in order of appearance: pp. 206, 211, 206, 207, 205; (KW 16:216–217, 223, 217, 219, 216); SV 12:210, 216, 210, 212, 210; (9:208, 214, 208–209, 210, 208).

127. See the entire section in chapter 2 on God as Reduplication, and in this chapter 4, see text at notes 48–50 and 104.

128. *Works of Love*, p. 261; (KW 16:280); SV 12:269; (9:267); *Journals*, 4571; XI² A 97. On this notion of a distinction within the divine unity, see text in chapter 2 above from note 35 to note 40.

itself, but in such a way that these [two] are one and the same; because otherwise there is no reduplication." Then Kierkegaard comes to his main point: "so also with love." Hence, when love "goes out of itself (in the outward direction), simultaneously it is in itself (in the inward direction); and in the same moment it is in itself, it therewith goes out of itself, in such a way that this going outward and this returning, this returning and this going outward, are simultaneously the one and the same." In other words, love is the factor or dimension of being that accounts for that being's motion; and this is first true of divine being-in-and-for-itself, and then (derivitively) of human being-in-the-image-of-God.

Again it must be noted that in all this second language about reduplication itself, about the eternal as being in a human being, about the motions of outward/inward as being the same, about the movement of love outward/inward as being simultaneous, there is an emphasis on *continuity* in the God-human and the human-human relationships. But now we must note a third language that Kierkegaard uses, in the very same context, to describe the relationship and the movement of love. It incorporates a theme that is repeated constantly throughout *Works of Love*, but we will look at just a few instances of it.

In the very discourse where Kierkegaard develops the thesis that love presupposes (and hence is "continuous" with) love in the other, he injects a disruptive element that creates a crisis for the person who claims to love others. He says that there are human qualities (*Egenskab*) that "one has for oneself, even though one uses them against others or for others," a "being-for-itself" quality; for example, talent or wisdom. But "love is not a being-for-itself quality but a quality by which or in which you *are* for *others*" (emphasis added).[129] But when you are for *others*, this requires that you forget yourself, that you deny yourself. "Love does not seek its own." God is love, and Christ was love, and it is true that Christ came "to draw human beings to himself so that they might be like him and truly become his own," but "he sought his own by giving himself, ... in sacrificial giving of himself. ... Love is a giving of oneself; that it seeks

---

129. *Works of Love*, p. 211; (KW 16:223); SV 12:216; (9:214). An interesting sidelight on this definition of Christian love came to my attention recently in reading the book *Frauen* by Alison Owings, about German women who lived through the Nazi regime. One of them was a nurse who had a devoutly Christian mother who explained that she had to help Jews and Russian prisoners of war because "we are to love our neighbors" whoever they are. The nurse also attended Bible classes of Martin Niemoeller and once met Dietrich Bonhoeffer who told her, "To be a Christian really means nothing else than to be there for others" (*Frauen*, New Brunswick N.J.: Rutgers University Press, 1994, p. 312). Bonhoeffer had read Kierkegaard; did he perhaps know this passage from *Works of Love*?

love is again [love] and is the highest love. ... This is the way it is in the relationship between God and humanity."¹³⁰

Such love brings with it "a revolution, the most profound of all," namely, "the distinction between *mine* and *yours* completely disappears." Passionate preferential love and friendship cannot live with such a radical revolution, because they "are only enhanced and augmented self-love," which expects in return what it gives. "Only for self-denying love does the specification 'mine' disappear entirely." So "the merely human idea of self-denial" expects that you will at least be "esteemed and honored and loved as righteous and wise," whereas "the Christian idea of self-denial" knows that your love will not be acknowledged and that you may very well be "insulted and ridiculed."¹³¹ Granted, Kierkegaard goes on (in the very next discourse) to show how the self that sacrifices itself in this way receives itself back, that is, in one's relationship to God, who is always present as love-itself in every act of self-denying love of one human toward another. "At the moment that one saves the other, one saves oneself from death. But love never thinks of the latter, of saving itself." Yet "the one who in love forgets oneself, forgets one's suffering, in order to think about someone else's ... – truly, such a person is not forgotten. ... God in heaven, or love, is thinking about that person." So "note the reduplication here: the one who loves is or becomes what one does. One ... acquires what one gives."¹³² But this miracle happens only after and beyond the stark fact that all one knows for sure is the sacrifice and the suffering inherent in every act of self-forgetting, self-denying love for the other, wherein "love never thinks ... of saving itself." That one "acquires what one gives" is a matter of faith.

In other words, the mystery and the wonder and the miracle that lies at the heart of Jesus' own life, namely, death/resurrection, this mystery that is captured and encapsulated in Jesus' own words: "whoever seeks to gain one's life will lose it, but whoever loses one's life [in an act of love] will preserve it" (Lk 17:33; cf. Mk 8:35, Mt 10:39), the fact that I have heard and continue to hear this mystery proclaimed times without number – all this does not make the *act* of giving and losing my life in self-negation and self-forgetfulness (out of compassion for those in need, or out of the obedience of conscience to the law of love) automatic or easy or even possible. Indeed, this demand is the *impossible* for any human being *as such*,

---

130. Ibid., p. 247; (κw 16:264); sv 12:254; (9:252).
131. Ibid., pp. 248–249, 188; (κw 16:265–267, 194); sv 12:255–256, 188; (9:253–254, 185).
132. Ibid., p. 262; (κw 16:281); sv 12:270; (9:268).

that is, on one's own. And when the imperative comes, in a particular situation, to "love your neighbor as yourself," you have entered that "moment" of crisis when the eternal breaks into your time and place, and all that you know and all that you believe in your heart of hearts is put to the test, and powerful temptations of self-deception assail you. Will you yield to the presence and power of Love itself, and will you understand and believe the Truth that confronts you? You must choose.

(3) *The Paradox of Complementarity.* In this moment, love's paradox and reason's paradox meet. They qualify each other. They are two factors or two dimensions of a single relationship. The *continuity* of the ontological reality and the dynamic power of love, in the self's relationship with both God and neighbor, is matched by the *discontinuity* inherent in the faith-relationship of the self with God and in faith's obedience of the self toward one's neighbor. This contradiction or paradox lies at the heart of the complementarity of faith and love, of love and faith. There is no love relationship which is not ingrained with the instability of the faith relation: to believe or to be offended, to obey or to be defiant. Equally, the instability of faith is totally untenable, unbearable, and unlivable without the affirming, encouraging, enabling presence and power of love. These two seemingly contradictory and mutually exclusive factors must be present and must be qualifying each other simultaneously in the one relationship, if the self is to recover itself in renewed and fulfilled reconciliation with God, with neighbor, with self.

This paradox of complementarity remained a fascination for Kierkegaard throughout the rest of his life, and he made several clarifying formulations of it. We will look at a few of them. The first is found in one of his collections of *Christian Discourses* (Thoughts Which Wound from Behind), written shortly after *Works of Love.* The particular discourse is a meditation on a statement in a letter of Paul (Ro 8:28), and Kierkegaard uses (typically) his own reformulation of the Greek: "all things must work together for good – if we love God."[133] In any case, his point

133. Twice he uses the conventional translation of the Greek, "all things work together for good to them that love God." (We will not go into the complications raised by the RSV translation, "in everything God works for good with those who love him [God]," which inserts an extra "God" from several highly respected manuscripts, and probably better represents Paul's own theology). Also, Kierkegaard's emphasis on the personal element ("is it thus *for me?*") is hardly the concern of Paul who identifies these lovers of God with the "called" and the "predestined." Nevertheless, Kierkegaard is correct that God's working in and through all things for good is directed (in this case) toward those that love God.

is inherent in the text and is intriguing for our present topic: "if God is love, then it follows of itself that all things work together for good to them who love God; but from the fact that God is love it by no means follows that *you* believe that God is love, that you love [God]. If on the other hand, *you* do believe, it follows of itself that you must believe that all things work together for good to you, because this is entailed in [*ligger i*] what you believe about God." So "the question is whether [*I*] believe that God is love, because if [I] believe this, then all the rest follows of itself, without proof: from the proof nothing follows *for me*, from faith everything follows *for me*."[134]

The main point is that Kierkegaard both distinguishes between and yet links together loving and believing: "believing that God is love" cannot be separated from "loving [God]," or "believing that all things work together for good" cannot be separated from "believing that God is love" – each "is entailed" in the other. In other words, the relationship involved in "believing" includes or encloses the relationship of "loving," and the relationship involved in "being love" and "loving" includes or encloses the relationship of "believing." Neither one precedes the other; neither one is derived from or "proves" the other; each "entails" the other. So all the proud "proving" and "refuting" (referred to earlier in the same paragraph) does not accomplish anything "for me": from such "proof" (rational deduction or induction) "nothing follows *for me*; from faith [or 'believing'] everything follows *for me*."

This point is made even more clearly in several later journal entries (from the years 1849–1851).[135] Kierkegaard says that "Christianity is not to be defined as a faith [*en Tro*], which is somewhat like a 'doctrine' – but is a believing [*en Troen*]." In other words, faith is not a conceptual resolution to a conceptual problem but is a living relationship. So "Christianity is a believing and a very particular kind of existing [*Exis-*

134. *Christian Discourses*, pp. 199–200; SV 13:182–183; (10:192–193). The emphasis on "you" is made in the Danish my using the personal *Du*. In the latter quotation I have changed "he" to "I" to fit with Kierkegaard's emphasized "me."

135. The journals of these years are rife with comments on the writings and on major themes developed in them. It would seem that Kierkegaard knew that his authorship was completed, and in this lull before his open attack on Christendom, he seems to be reviewing (did he actually reread?) what he had written and wanting to clarify and even correct some points. The entries being used here are (in chronological order): 4454, X^1 A 134 (1849); 2423, A 489 (1849); 1880, X^3 A 454 (1850); 2434, X^3 A 749 (1851); 1154, XI^2 A 380 (1854–55). Instead of using notes in what follows, I will simply insert (in the text) the number of the Hongs's translation.

teren] corresponding to it, [namely], imitation [*Efterføgelse*]" (no. 1880). In other words, believing on the one hand and existing-in-imitation (in obedience) on the other hand are two corresponding and inseparable dimensions of this living relationship. And what Kierkegaard means by "imitation" here is precisely the relationship of love. He says, "No one can see faith [i.e. believing: *Troen*]. ... But faith shall be recognized [*kjendes*] in love [*Kjerlighed*], ... because from a Christian point of view love is love's-works." This love is not to be defined aesthetically as a "feeling" or "the erotic," because "Christ's love was not an intense feeling and a deep heart, etc.; rather it was the works of love, which is his life" (no. 2423).

So, Kierkegaard says, "Christianity is [both] a believing and an imitating," and you cannot really say that one comes before the other. It works both ways.

One can put faith [*Tro*] first and imitation second inasmuch as it is necessary that there exists for me in faith that which I shall imitate. [But] one can put imitation first and faith second inasmuch as it is necessary that, by some action [*Handling*] that is marked more or less by conformity to the Christian ethic (the unconditioned), I must thereby be in collision with the world, so that there is provided for me the situation and the situational tension, wherein for the first time there can be any talk about becoming a believing-person [*Troende*] (no. 1880).

Kierkegaard concludes that the fact that "believing corresponds to situation [of act or deed] proves the reciprocal [*reciproke*] relation between faith [*Tro*] and imitation." So faith, believing, understanding feeds on and grows from the relationship of imitation, that is, from love toward God-in-Christ (the model) and love toward neighbor – which always lands a person in a "situational tension." But equally, I can only imitate or reduplicate that which, to some degree, I already know and accept in my faith-understanding. Here again (as in the *ordo salutis*) there is the cyclic motion that becomes a spiral. The point of entrance into the dialectical complementarity of faith/love is not important and will vary with the individual. But what "is necessary" is the presence and operation of both factors in the single unitary relationship between God and the human self.

One complication in this summary treatment of the faith/love relationship by Kierkegaard is that he still assumes the triadic relationship of self-God-neighbor (as developed in *Works of Love*), as is evident in several other late journal entries.[136] In a "loose paper" entitled Faith (*Tro*), he again stresses that "faith is not a determinant in the sphere of the intellectual, but is an ethical determinant, [which] signifies the relationship of personhood between God and human-being. Therefore faith is demanded (as an expression of devotedness), [in the sense of] believing against reason [*Forstand*], believing although one cannot see (wholly a determinant of personhood, of the ethical)." What is demanded is "the *obedience* of faith," and in this way "faith is tested" (no. 1154).

And how does the test come? "Devotedness" (*Hengivenhed*) literally means the giving and sacrifice of oneself to or for an other, and this is precisely Kierkegaard's definition of Christian or spiritual "love." But love (at the core of Christian existence) moves in two directions: toward God and toward neighbor. And these two, while distinct and different, are inseparable. So, Kierkegaard says, "love to God and love to neighbor are like two doors, which open simultaneously, so that it is impossible to open one without opening the other, and impossible to shut the one without shutting the other" (no. 2434). Hence there is a complementarity of the two loves within the complementarity of love and faith. On the one hand, we have heard that there can be no talk of becoming a believer except in the concrete situation of human relationships where one attempts to imitate God's love in Christ. But on the other hand, we also hear (in another journal entry) that I cannot "proceed directly to be ethical" in imitating the paradoxical model (God-human), because "only through worship/adoration [*Tilbedelse*] can there be any talk about wanting to imitate," that is, only if "the model himself helps the one who is supposed to imitate him" (no. 4454). Or as Kierkegaard emphasizes repeatedly in *Works of Love*, a person cannot truly and properly love one's neighbor without God's presence as the "third party" in the relationship.[137]

136. Another complication that does not fit into the present discussion but becomes a major issue in the light of Kierkegaard's increasing insistence, during the last few years of his life, that Christian, spiritual love toward God and neighbor is antithetical to and actually *excludes* the merely "human" forms of love in family relationships, in friendship, and in preferential, passionate, romantic, sexual love between a man and a woman, and therefore also excludes marriage and the reproduction of children. This issue has been dealt with in chapter 7 of *Kierkegaard as Humanist* under the topic "Unconditional Love versus Preferential Love." But the issue could be further enlightened by considering it in the context of the principle of complementarity, which will be commented on further in the next chapter.

137. The point to Kierkegaard's insistence on the role of worship/adoration toward God has a significant implication about the meaning of the term "love." It assumes that there is an essential distinction between, on the one hand, God's love toward a human being (and my reduplication of that love toward another human being) and, on the other

Sylvia Walsh makes this point in a helpful and compelling way by relating Kierkegaard's language/thought about "imitation" of Jesus as prototype to his concept of grace.[138] She says (on p. 238),

The prototype represents the ideal to us, not as something we can directly or realistically expect to fulfill on our own but as that which we cannot fulfill. If Christ did not appear then in his other form as a savior, he would, as prototype, fall on us crushingly, requiring something we cannot become. Thus, as Kierkegaard sees it, Christ never appears simply as prototype but incorporates with this the grace whereby real imitation is made possible.

In other words, "the gift of grace does not mean that imitation is thereby dispensed with. ... The requirement of imitation is reintroduced after grace, but as an expression of gratitude rather than as a matter of law or works righteousness. ... Far from exempting [human beings] from striving, grace requires renewed earnestness in striving, which quickly leads once again to a need of grace."

So once again, we see that love of God and love of neighbor are distinctions within the one relationship of love, and each feeds upon and grows with the other. And just as my love of God must be complemented by my believing that God is love, so also my love of neighbor must be complemented by my believing in the equality (of dignity and worth) of every other person, and by my believing (presupposing) that love is already present (even though dormant) in every other person.

---

hand, a human being's love toward God. God's love toward me and my love toward neighbor is the outgoing, self-forgetting, sacrificial love that seeks to affirm and evoke every human being's equal dignity and worth. Obviously, no human being "loves" God in that sense. Rather, I love God in the sense that I have come to know, and to believe with all my heart and mind and strength, and with awe and wonder and fear and trembling, that there is an eternal dynamic at the heart of reality which has given me my being and my identity and which comes after me to demand that I fulfill and to help me fulfill that gift, and now I try to live my whole life "before God" in utter adoration and devotion and obedience. (On the essential distinction, see *Kierkegaard as Humanist*, p. 370). In other words, my love toward God is that "inward" and "returning" dynamic of God's own love that has "gone out" to me. And the analogue of this "returning" love in the human experience occurs when I forget and sacrifice my self out of love toward another human being ("lose my life") and then I experience that *God* remembers me and the "like-for-like" occurs in God's affirmation of *my* self ("find my life"). In other words, love gets what it gives.

138. This comes in a succinct but revealing three-page treatment of "Christ as Prototype" in *Living Poetically*, pp. 236–239. At the end of it she uses a series of late journal entries, mainly from the years 1849–51.

Now we must turn to the second problematic aspect of the *ordo salutis* on which this entire analysis of the dialectical complementarity of faith and love sheds some peculiar light.

2 *Freedom in the Faith/Love Relationship*

Earlier in this chapter we have already spelled out how the whole complex event of confession, forgiveness, and reconciliation focuses on the critical "moment" in which the human self freely says "yes" (or "no") when God lovingly offers new life to the human being in sin and despair.[139] But this whole issue of the nature of freedom gains another dimension when looked at within the dialectical complementarity of faith and love. We have indicated several times that whereas the love relationship carries a sense of continuity, the faith relationship is marked by discontinuity. Although the emergence of the faith relationship does not occur without the concomitance of the power of love, still the perceived presence of God's love (or of God as love-itself) does not compel or guarantee the transition of the human heart and mind into the relationship of faith. Kierkegaard's general way of indicating this discontinuity is by speaking of the need to choose, to act freely or voluntarily, to "leap." We have heard Climacus insist (in chapter 2 of *Fragments*) that the entire indirection of God's loving approach to the human being is out of concern that the beloved will respond in love *freely*, in a relationship of equality. And in *The Concept of Angst* Haufniensis insists just as strongly that both sin and faith are qualitative acts of freedom and introduces the concept of "leap" to interpret such an act. Then Climacus (in *Postscript*) picks up this concept and develops it into a major tool for interpreting the nature and role of freedom (as choice and decision) in the transition to faith.[140]

This application of the term "leap" disappears in the second (Christian) authorship, but Kierkegaard makes significant usage of it in journal

---

139. See the text above from note 65 to note 72. Also reread note 72 about the treatment of freedom and willing in *Kierkegaard as Humanist*.

140. The topic of freedom and the leap has been explored and exposited at great length throughout *Kierkegaard as Humanist*, and that material must be assumed at this point. For Kierkegaard's concept of the leap, see the index under that term, but see especially chapter 6 on The Leap as Freedom's Form. For another analysis of the essential and continuing role of freedom in the faith relationship with God (according to Kierkegaard), see Louis Dupré's very persuasive account in his chapter 3, sections 4 and 5. Throughout his book he also shows how Kierkegaard at the same time resists and avoids a semi-Pelagian conclusion.

entries throughout that period; so it is not absent from his mind in the least. And Anti-Climacus clearly assumes and depicts this role of freedom in his analysis and description of the continuing possibility of the self's taking offense instead of believing, not only when confronted with God in the figure of Jesus as the Christ, but even as a continuing dimension within the new faith-relationship itself. In *Sickness* the transition from the disrelationship of sin and despair to the relationship of "resting transparently in God" (faith) is described in terms of the complexities of "willing" in its battles with self-deception.[141] So let us reconsider the locus of this leap in the context of the perception of continuity/discontinuity in the complementarity of the love/faith relationship.

The issue has been joined in recent Kierkegaard interpretation, even though somewhat indirectly.[142] Some elements of that interpretation will be briefly used here, while avoiding a complete reconsideration of the nature of willing and its role in freedom. The issue is: how is the transition accomplished from the state of unbelief (sin/despair) to the relationship of faith? Stephen Evans identifies the "leap" of freedom as "an act of will," and assigns to it a decisive role in the acceptance of God's gift of faith. On the other hand, Jamie Ferreira sees faith as being attained by a leap that is strictly an act of the imagination, and she limits willing (in intentional decisions) to phases before and after the leap.

141. On this particular problem, see the entirety of chapter 8 in *Kierkegaard as Humanist*, which has as its subtitle, "The Leap of Love Is Indeterminate" (see the table of contents for specific topics). And in the present book on *Kierkegaard as Theologian*, see in chapter 2 the sections on "The Fall: Freedom and Guilt" and on "In Offense Despair Becomes Sin."

142. In what follows I will first make use of an indirect exchange among three interpreters: C. Stephen Evans, M. Jamie Ferreira, David J. Gouwens. Evans had published several articles on faith, reason, and willing before and during the writing of his book *Passionate Reason* in 1988–89. But the book was not published until 1992, and so Ferreira had read Evans' articles but had not read his book when she wrote her own book *Transforming Vision* in 1990 (published in 1991). Evans' book was already being processed for publication when he read Ferreira's book, and hence he could not include a consideration of Ferreira's critique. He did send some comments to Ferreira, suggesting that she had not properly understood his position, especially as developed in his book, but the present author has not seen those comments. Gouwens published a book on *Kierkegaard's Dialectic of the Imagination* in 1989 without reference to Evans' studies, but Ferreira does make several significant references to Gouwens' book. Such are the unavoidable vagaries of progress in the development of ideas. In what follows, I will supply references to these three sources by simply putting page numbers in the text.

Then I will respond to how the issue has been treated in two more recent works by David Gouwens (*Kierkegaard as Religious Thinker*, 1996) and by Edward F. Mooney (*Selves in Discord and Resolve*, 1996). Both refer frequently to Ferreira's book, but obviously not to each other.

Let us see (briefly) how they spell out these positions. The present author finds important contributions in both positions but also has some reservations about both.

First, it seems unlikely that Evans' position "could lead one to ... the false and unnecessary dichotomy between God's grace and our activity" (as Ferreira contends, 149). He clearly sees God's grace and human response as cooperative in the event of faith. And he stresses the importance of Climacus' insistence that the transformation of the human condition that takes place in this encounter between God and the "learner" centers on the learner's coming to the recognition and humble acceptance of one's sin and of one's need of the help of God for its resolution. But Evans slips into a confusion of language. He speaks both of "the leap of faith" and of "the leap of the will" (140, 141). Yet he repeatedly stresses that "faith is *not* produced by an act of will, but rather is a gift of God" (139). So the "act of will" occurs and is "necessary if the gift is to be received" (140).[143]

This confusion can be resolved if it is remembered that Climacus does not say that God gives *faith* but that God gives or brings "the condition" that makes faith possible, namely, the condition that God is present both as God and as a human being. So, Climacus says, faith is neither *in* the reason (of the learner) nor *in* the paradox (God), but faith is a

143. Ferreira (p. 148n18) also sees this dichotomy in Gouwens's book on imagination, whereas I would suggest a lack of clarity on the issue because he simply does not address the nature of the transition here under consideration. Gouwens says imagination functions in one's accepting the "gift" of "one's new being in Christ" (p. 248), and yet he asserts that to see God present in the servant form is beyond imagination on its own, because only "grace grants the condition that educates the imagination ... , allowing one to see in Christ the presence of the lowly God" (250–251). Likewise, in his earlier section on the function of imagination in the ethical sphere, Gouwens argues quite rightly that "the choice of a particular concrete self ... is always mediated through the imagination," even though the ethical ideal pictured concretely by the imagination remains an external goal that "I must strive for" (pp. 203–204). But he never seeks to clarify what this "striving" is and how it is different from the "mediation" of the imagination. He quotes Anti-Climacus's blunt assertion that to become one's self, one first requires imagination but that the second and decisive condition is "the will," and yet he never explores the concept of "will" (p. 205). He makes the important point that ethical freedom is enabled by imagination's "becoming part of the ethical person's disposition," and hence the ethical "is not only making choices" but also occurs through "developing long-term dispositions" (p. 208). But do dispositions then determine actions directly, without any element of deliberation or decision? Gouwens simply does not address the problems of self-deception and one's acting "irresponsibly." So, as Ferreira has noted (p. 5n21), his book simply does not attempt to examine the interrelationship among leap, paradox, will, and imagination.

"third" something (a passion, a relationship) in which the two "encounter each other happily in the moment."[144] Hence the phrase "leap of faith" makes no sense. Evans properly associates the "leap" with the human act of being "willing" to accept the judgment of sin and the offer of help (love) from God, that is, being willing to humble oneself in opening oneself to the transforming presence of God in Jesus as the Christ.[145] From this perspective it makes sense that Climacus, on the one hand, can say that "faith is not an act of will, because it is always the case that [*bestandig*] all human willing is efficacious only within the condition," and yet can also say that "faith is not a cognition [or recognition: *Erkjendelse*] but an act of freedom, an expression of willing."[146]

144. *Fragments*, pp. 77, 73; (KW 7:62, 59); SV 6:59, 56; (4:227, 224). In the second reference, the Hongs's translation reads "through" the reason and "through" the paradox, rather than "in"; that is, they take *ved* to mean efficient cause, whereas *ved* is a preposition strictly of location: at, by, near, on, in, through (as a medium). This meaning is clearly indicated by Climacus's twice using "*in* something."

145. Here it should be noted that Kierkegaard often uses the term "believe" or "believing" to mean this fundamental attitude of mind and heart, that is, to mean my singleminded and totally earnest willing-acceptance and affirmation of God's judgment of my failure and (nevertheless, simultaneously) of God's gracefulness in unwavering care and concern and encouragement toward me. This attitude is, then, not a belief *that* something is true (a doctrine or concept) but is a believing *in*, is a relationship of trust between my self and someone else (in this case, God). In this sense Kierkegaard says that, contrary to "modern philosophy" that asserts "*cogito ergo sum*, to think is to be," Christianity asserts "as you believe, so you are, to believe is to be" (*Sickness*, p. 224; [KW 19:93]; SV 15:146; [11:204]). In so far as this believing is willing and voluntary, not compelled by anything or anyone external to me, it is what Kierkegaard calls "sudden," a "decision," a "leap." And since this believing is *my* willing act (even though "within the condition" given by God, that is, within the relationship opened up and made possible by God), then this believing is a "leap." But the reciprocal relationship – *in* which this human, personal, individual act of believing occurs – is not a leap, is not sudden, is not a decision. That relationship, as with all interpersonal relationships, is arrived at only slowly, through a qualitative indirection, with great spiritual agony and struggle. So one could speak of "the leap of believing" but not of "the leap of faith" in Kierkegaard's definition of faith. Indeed, Kierkegaard never uses either phrase. If one sees faith as *merely* a problem of independent human understanding or conceptualization, then one would speak of "the leap of faith," but one would not be representing Kierkegaard's thinking on the subject.

146. *Fragments*, pp. 77, 103, (KW 7:62, 83); SV 6:59, 76; (4:227, 247). It is unfortunate that Evans was limited here to what Climacus has to say about will and willing, because it makes Evans's treatment sound as if he conceives of will as a special, independent faculty, whereas he has specifically rejected such a view. As noted before, I believe that Anti-Climacus has provided (in *Sickness*) a much more complex and sophisticated analysis of willing. For my explication of it, see *Kierkegaard as Humanist*, chapter 8, from note 17 to note 27; also see from note 44 through note 53 on the subject of willing and self-deception.

The position of Ferreira on the nature and role of both willing and the leap (in the transition to faith) is more complicated because she is not limited to *Fragments* but ranges through the entire Kierkegaardian corpus, including the journals. Also, she brings to bear on the issue a broad range of other sources, including literary and more popular forms of philosophical writings. There are many aspects of her position that are intriguing and are relevant to the present consideration of the complementarity of faith and love in Kierkegaard's thought, but we will concentrate on two of them: the role of imagination in the transition to faith, and locale of willing as intentional decisions.

Ferreira's basic thesis is that the "leap" in the transition is one of imagination rather than willing. That is to say, "the leap is a reconceptualization process" (151), "an imaginative, reorienting, transforming shift in perspective" (16), "an activity of imaginative revisioning" (111). Imagination is the capacity to project images of the self's possibilities, but more especially it holds in tension an awareness of the present self in contrast with one particular pattern or paradigm that provides the qualitative shift in perspective (152). But "this shift in perspective occurs only when a 'critical threshold' has been reached," that is, when "an imaginative crystallization, a decisive engagement" has indicated that there is "only one way" in which the self should move. This is the mode in which the "leap" occurs, "rather than [through] a selection among perceived alternatives" (109–110).

This view of the mode of transition to faith means that "the new seeing *is* the leap of understanding; ... it is the new seeing itself which is effectively the leap or the qualitative transition" (111). Therefore, "deliberate decision can be said to play a role in the acquisition of faith, ... but what occurs at the moment of acceptance is not a volition, but rather a shift of perspective, an engagement or surrender, which is the achievement of imagination" (125). The repercussions of this analysis of the transition are absolutely critical in the realm of ethical behavior.

Consciousness is the criterion or determinant even of will. In particular, the emphasis on consciousness of self is at the same time an emphasis on imagination because the self, in order to fulfill its "task" – namely, the subjective task "freely to become itself" – "reflects itself in the medium of imagination."[147] The ethical task is fulfilled, not through decision, but through reflection in the medium of

147. *Sickness*, p. 168; (KW 19:35); SV 15:93; (11:148).

imagination. ... Clearly, it is imaginative vision, rather than deliberate decision, which is here said to effect change. (82–83)

In fact, Ferreira says, what we often call "decision" is just this "vision": "the moment of transition is the point at which what has been an abstract possibility ... suddenly comes into focus for us, the point at which it is so real that it seems to be the only way to see it. ... [T]his point or 'critical threshold' is what in the description of faith is often called 'the decision'."

What then is the "role" that "deliberate decision ... can be said to play ... in the acquisition of faith," and when does it occur? Ferreira says that "deliberate decision can be said to be involved before, during, and after the transition to love," even though "the transition itself is more a matter of imaginative engagement than of 'will-power'" (125). Her description of the role of decision before and after the transition is quite straight forward, but (as we will see) that of decision "during" it is highly ambiguous. The "intentional decisions" that are "necessary" for the "realization of faith" are both "preliminary to" and "a response to the new seeing." The former include "disciplined inquiry" and "preliminary material ... registered and processed" in order "to put oneself in a place conducive to the shift in perspective" (111). The responsive decisions (that "play a subsequent role") include "a deliberate commitment to the non-deliberate imaginative engagement or surrender," a commitment that occurs "in part by choosing to *stifle* what militates against the commitment" – *or*, Ferreira notes, "choosing to *cultivate* what militates against the experienced surrender" (emphases added) (125).

Just what role, then, does decision play *during* the transition to faith? Ferreira notes that "deliberate choice can be used to stifle those things that would *prevent* the occurrence of the imaginative shift" (125) (but does not note the correlative: *or* "to *cultivate* those things" that stifle the shift in the first place). (emphases added) It would seem, then, that decision/choice is a factor in enabling the imaginative shift and therefore is a factor distinct from the shift itself. But this differentiation does not hold as Ferreira turns to explore the relation of "interest" to decision. She comes to the conclusion that "choice or decision cannot be understood apart from interest, but even more strongly, we could say that choice may just *be* the decisive engagement or attraction – the one that wins out by decisively engaging or attracting us – and thus be understood in terms of the activity of the imagination" (emphasis added). In fact, "choice ... just is becoming decisively interested." Hence "to say that will can be understood in terms of *letting* an attraction win out, of affirming or validating that particular attraction rather than another, is to say that its [i.e., will's] activity is one of *affirmation or active recognition* rather than a selection through 'will-power' from what are perceived as equally real alternatives" (emphasis not added) (126–27). In other words, choice or decision is not to be distinguished from the activity of imagination, because "recognition" is an element in the event of imagination.

Ferreira's general position is a major contribution to Kierkegaard interpretation. She has demonstrated that imagination (in her subtle and complex analysis of it) plays an integral role in the transition from unbelief (error) to faith, as that transition is understood by Kierkegaard. But it would seem that she has denigrated the role of willing in that transition, as understood by Kierkegaard. Three comments may serve to enlighten the latter thesis.

First, there is a fundamental ambiguity in Ferreira's characterization of willing because at times she identifies it with an independent faculty of pure will, in Kierkegaard's sense of *liberum arbitrium* – which he clearly and rigorously rejects. Other times she speaks of "intentional decisions," which, in the language and thought of contemporary philosophy of action, are anything but independent, arbitrary, capricious choices, or as she puts it, "momentary, separable acts of will which fill a gap" (111). As has been shown extensively in *Kierkegaard as Humanist*, this sophisticated concept of intentional decision and action has strong similarities to Kierkegaard's understanding of freedom.[148] Ferreira's depiction of the role of imagination needs to be brought into synthesis with Kierkegaard's understanding of freedom in the terms of intentional decision and action, because, as Sylvia Walsh says, "The function of imagination in the ethical-religious ... is better understood as depicting or portraying the ideal self rather than imaginatively contructing, making, or creating it. ... [T]his is how Kierkegaard understands the proper role of imagination in human existence."[149]

Secondly, Ferreira's position on imagination should also absorb Kierkegaard's complex analysis and definition of willing and its rela-

148. See all the entries under "philosophy of action" and "Davidson, Donald" in the index of *Kierkegaard as Humanist*.
149. Sylvia Walsh, *Living Poetically*, p. 206. Later she says, "To have Christianity only in the form of imagination is not to have it. ... Nevertheless, imagination plays an important role in bringing us to the point of reduplication in existence." However, she does not analyze that "point" and what else operates besides imagination.

tionship to self-deception, especially as developed in *Sickness*.[150] The role of willful self-deception needs to be acknowledged as one faces imagination's depiction of the "one thing needful," no matter how decisive that depiction's power of engagement and attraction might be. Ferreira's position is in danger of becoming a form of determinism that eliminates any real element of the voluntary in the encounter between God and the self. At times she seems to be taking the position assigned by Kierkegaard to Socrates, only instead of defining sin as ignorance, she would define sin as lack of imagination. And while Socrates would deny that a person knows what is right and still does what is wrong, Ferreira would deny that a person may be interestedly engaged by and attracted to imagination's depiction of the one good thing and yet not surrender to it. In both positions, Kierkegaard would say, "sin does not exist at all," and that the "determinant" that is lacking is "willing, defiance."[151]

In other words, Ferreira must take more seriously her admission that one may "deliberately choose to cultivate what militates against the experienced surrender" (i.e., after the fact of surrender), and see that one may deliberately (or self-deceptively) choose to "stifle" or refuse the surrender in the first place. *Not* "allowing one interest or attraction to win out" (among others) is precisely what Kierkegaard means by "defiance," and throughout his entire Christian writings (and journals) he insists that the "possibility of offense" remains constantly as the alternative to faith, and it is present before the transition to faith and then within faith itself. Hence "willing" is a much more complex phenomenon than either intentional decision or an imaginative shift in perspective. Without this assumption the substance of the encounter with the "absolute paradox" makes no sense in Kierkegaard's scheme of things, because that substance is no less than my coming to "see," and then having to deal with (respond to) the fact and the shapes of my essential failure (sin) and *simultaneously* to deal with (respond to), the presence of and the invitation to forgiveness and reconciliation. One needs more (but not less) than imagination when so encountered.

Why? The transition to the relationship of faith with God is qualitatively more than an imaginative shift in perspective, because that transition is not once and for all, not a completed and stable thing. By

---

150. Again, I refer to the extensive treatment of this material in chapter 8 of *Kierkegaard as Humanist*.

151. *Sickness*, p. 220; (KW 19:89–90); SV 15:142; (11:200–201).

definition, "faith" includes not just a shadow of doubt but essentially the shadowy, disturbing possibility of resentment and defiance. Hence the commitment of trust must be refreshed and renewed daily, hourly, every minute that I continue to *exist*, that is, continue to face without ceasing the spiritual struggle to become the infinite, eternal self I have been given by God in the midst of all the pressing limitations of my finitude and temporality. The discontinuity at the heart of "faith" requires the continuity of the presence of Love-Itself, affirming and luring forth the love that is in me and that defines my eternal self. Then in the face of all the trials and uncertainties of my finite and temporal existence, by the power of that mutuality of love I can day by day, minute by minute, believe and depend on the ultimate Reality: that All-Things-Are-Possible, and that "God works through all things for good."

Thirdly, then, we must pick up on Ferreira's very suggestive investigations of the elements of both continuity and discontinuity in the transition to faith and recast them (at least if we are to be faithful to Kierkegaard).[152] In her early section on "The Ladder and the Leap" (11–15), Ferreira obviously prefers the ladder as a metaphor of continuity for the qualitative transition from "earth" to "heaven" rather than the leap as a metaphor of volitional discontinuity. And she accepts Bonaventure's suggestion that imagination is the ladder. So her study is an attempt to show how Kierkegaard's notion of discontinuity can be included in the ladder. In her "Concluding Applications" (chapter 6) she returns to the theme of The Ladder of Imagination and its implications for the topic of discontinuity and continuity (150–54). She argues that the element of "incommensurability" that she has included in her "interpretation of the leap as a reconceptualization process" does "justice to the intention behind Kierkegaard's understanding of the leap" (151). She claims the nature of discerning a "pattern" as "paradigm" to be evidence for her conclusion. So, for her, Anti-Climacus's concept of imitation as choosing a pattern consists of a paradigmatic shift, and that includes an element of discontinuity because "the process of reaching a critical threshold [inherent in such shift] ... involves a conceptual leap" (152).

However, Ferreira fails to note (as has been done several times above) that in Anti-Climacus's analysis of how a human being (as self) is

152. On this topic, I suggest that it would be very helpful to make use of Gouwens' insightful use and development of Climacus' concept of the "simultaneity of factors", or what the Hongs' translate as "the contemporaneity [*Samtidighed*] of elements" (from *Postscript*, p. 307; [KW 12.1:343]; SV 10:46; [7:297]). See Gouwens' index for his frequent application of this notion (in his *Kierkegaard's Dialectic of the Imagination*).

"drawn" to this pattern set for us in Jesus as the Christ, he stresses that indeed "Christ ... wants to draw the human being to himself, but in order truly to draw him to himself he wants to draw the human being only as a free being to himself, that is, through a choice."[153] Ferreira argues that her view of the transition as an imaginative shift of perspective does not "preclude" that the shift is "free rather than compelled." And for support she refers to a passage in *The Concept of Angst*[154] in which, she claims, "this possibility is affirmed in terms of the relevance of 'an intermediate term' in passing from possibility to actuality – such a term can have a necessary bearing on the outcome without being thereby said to 'explain' or 'justify' it" (153 and 153n30).

But the term there discussed is "angst" as the psychological condition that precedes the "qualitative leap" of the act of sin. And although the leap of sin does not occur except within the condition of angst, it can hardly be said to have a "*necessary* bearing on the outcome*" (emphasis added). Kierkegaard specifically says that "angst is neither a category of necessity nor a category of freedom." It is a totally neutral condition that possesses the ambivalent quality of being both sympathetic and antipathetic toward its object. It is true that here Kierkegaard firmly rejects the notion that sin occurs as "an act of abstract *liberum arbitrium*," but he just as rigorously denies that "sin has come into the world by necessity." Hence the freedom in which sin occurs is the "entangled freedom" of a human being whose existence is composed of a synthesis of both finitude and infinitude.

In attempts (by those drawing on Kierkegaard) to analyze how the human being can achieve a transition from sin/untruth to faith/truth, Ferreira believes that "the metaphor of the 'leap' has caused the dimension of discontinuity to be ... overemphasized," and it should be balanced with ways in which Kierkegaard "includes the dimension of continuity in the transition" (153). Of key importance to her is "the 'continuity' embodied in the notion of a 'transfiguring' move," which is accomplished, of course, by imagination. So Ferreira's conclusive statement is that her "reading of Kierkegaardian transitions includes both emphases, and my suggestion is that an emphasis on imagination does more justice to the element of continuity than does a volitionalist account of the human activity of transition." And then she reduces the role of willing even further by pointing out that "imagination is more closely tied to an understanding of will in terms of appetite and attraction rather than in terms of

153. *Practice in Christianity*, p. 160; (KW 20:160); SV 16:155; (12:150).
154. *The Concept of Angst*, pp. 44–45; (KW 8:49); SV 6:142–143; (4:320).

volition" (154). In this way, she intensifies her earlier observation that "seeing choice or decision in terms of 'identification with' [a desire or thought] would both emphasize the role of imagination in human activity and preclude a radical separation or contrast between will and imagination" (128).[155]

Several comments are in order. Ferreira makes a crucial point (and supports it persuasively) in her insistence that willing and imagination are not "separated" in a proper reading of Kierkegaard. But it is too much to say that Kierkegaard rejects a significant "contrast" between the two. Emphasis on "the voluntary" (*det Frivillige*, i.e., freely-willing) runs throughout the second authorship, and he sums it up in a journal entry of 1850: "if the voluntary goes, Christianity is abolished. ... When the voluntary disappears, 'spiritual-trial' [*Anfægtelse*] disappears, and when spiritual trials disappear, Christianity disappears."[156] And Kierkegaard cannot possibly be read as "understanding will in terms of appetite." For him, to live in accord with one's appetites and what one finds attractive is to live at the non-human level of immediacy where the self has not yet become truly conscious.

We now turn briefly to two very recent works about Kierkegaard, by David Gouwens and Edward Mooney, which, in very different ways from Ferreira and from each other, also put significant stress on continuity within the self and between the self and others.[157]

---

155. She bases this comment on a passage in *Postscript* but in its unfortunately misleading Swenson/Lowrie translation [p. 302; (KW 12.1:339); SV 10:42; (7:293)]. The phrases "real action" and "internal decision" comprise a serious distortion of Kierkegaard's meaning. The passage actually reads: "Actuality is not the external [*udvortes*] action, but an internality [*Indvorteshed*] in which the individual annuls possibility and identifies with what-is-thought [*det Tænkte*] in order to exist in it. This is the action." So "the action" is not just an imaginative move to "identify with" what is found to be an attractive idea but really centers in the additional move of determination and choice to "*exist* in" what has been conceived or seen.

156. *Journals*, 4950; X³ A 43.

157. These two works are: David Gouwens' *Kierkegaard as Religious Thinker* (1996) and Edward Mooney's *Selves in Discord and Resolve* (1996). They both give considerable attention to Ferreira's book on imagination. But they appeared after the manuscript for this present book had been completed, and hence I was unable to give them detailed consideration throughout the present study. But I want at least to mention here what, concerning the issue at hand, deserves very close attention. Gouwens accomplishes in one volume what I have stretched out over two, and it is good to have both Kierkegaard's anthropological and theological perspectives contained within the covers of one book – as I originally planned to do. And generally I find Gouwens' distinction between and interpretation of these two perspectives compatible with what my own. Mooney's book is a collection of his essays, modified to make a more or less coherent whole, and they reflect much of Mooney's own particular philosophical interests. Page references will be included in the text.

It should first of all be noted that Gouwens preserves a dynamic dialectic between human passivity and activity (continuity and discontinuity) in the faith relationship with God (see 97–98, 100–01). So he reacts to Ferreira's proposal, that the transition to faith involves "various kinds of imaginative shifts and transitions," by saying, "Yet faith involves the will; it is not sheer receptivity (as in thinking of a person as a *passive* recipient of the 'condition' of grace)" (137). And he insists that although "divine creation and omnipotence are the very ground of freedom[,] [y]et human freedom is truly independent" (138).

His emphasis on the element of continuity comes not in the role of imagination in the transition to faith, but in quite another mode of limiting the role of freedom as decision, as "leap," namely, in his concept of "active virtue." He claims that "Kierkegaard's language of 'will' points not simply to a discrete act of willing (the 'leap'), but to 'activating resolution' and self-control. ... Kierkegaard is quite clear that resolution is not *momentary* decisiveness. Indeed, it is not a 'leap.' ... The will is spoken of as developing a disposition of resolution." Hence "the will ... is embedded in a fabric of developing emotional continuities, new desires, and active virtuous dispositions" (101–02). So he argues that "Kierkegaard stands in the broad tradition ... of ethics as virtue, the development of ongoing intentions, dispositions, judgments, and motivations that characterize a person over time" (94). (For his further explication of this theme, see "virtue" in his index.)

The present author agrees that Kierkegaard stresses the importance of the formation of "character" in the self in these terms. In fact, in *Kierkegaard as Humanist*, it is argued that Kierkegaard's concept of "the self's possibility" signifies an "essential gestalt of both inherited and acquired characteristics which, in their continuing, integrated, functional unity define who I *am* in potentiality and possibility," and the list of characteristics includes all of Gouwens' and more (see *KAH*, pp. 166–67). Yet, it is difficult to find evidence in Kierkegaard's writings for the concept of ethics as virtue (see the treatment of Kierkegaard's concept of virtue in *KAH*, pp. 319–23).

In the sphere of the ethical-religious, and especially in the sphere of the ethical-religious of Christian faith, Kierkegaard sees ethics as not having to do with the everyday, more or less habitual or instinctive actions of the self in relation to others. The Christian ethical-religious has to do with the self's encounter with situations that involve matters of infinite and absolute significance in the realm of the spirit. And the particular, unique concrete conditions of each situation demand the total concentration of the self's passionate, concerned attention as to what is the "one thing needful" here and now as "necessitated" by one's accumulated character as spirit/self, but also "needful" as determined by one's standing consciously and transparently "before God" as the Absolute source and criterion of all good. Making such a *decision*, and having the courage to enact that decision, is not at all simply a matter of "disposition." It is, in each and every instance, in each and every such "moment" of the eternal-invading-time, a matter of intense, agonizing "spiritual-trial" (*Anfægtelse*). The decision involves escaping every form of self-deception and coming to a willingness of the whole self to accept and to "obey" the vision of the one thing needful that has taken form in the presence of God who comes to us in Jesus as the Christ.

In this moment, when we draw upon all the potential strength of the accumulated spirit-formed character of our selfhood, we face each time a sharing in Jesus' sufferings in the Garden of Gethsemane: "if it be possible ... , *but* your will not mine be done." At this point lies the inescapable "possibility of offense" at the heart of Christian faith as it faces the demand of the absolute, and therefore faces the opposition and onslaught of all the demonic forces of "this world," because, as Haufniensis puts it, here at the heart of *Anfægtelse*, "renunciation within possibility is itself a coveting."[158] Even Jesus considered, and so coveted and desired, some way around the utter, devastating alienation and aloneness of the cross, but he never wavered in his willing determination to follow the leading of the Spirit to the bitter end.

Gouwens asserts that Christian obedience never becomes habitual, but his heavy emphasis on the role of Christ-formed dispositions in "imitating" the "pattern" of Jesus' life sometimes seems to suggest that we are relieved of the "spiritual trial" that occurs on each occasion we must choose to do the "one thing needful." So his correct and helpful stress on the decisive role of the self's character in ethical/religious action leaves open the question as to *how* "human freedom is truly independent."

Edward Mooney has even greater reservations about the character and importance of Kierkegaard's notion of the "leap" than does Gouwens.[159]

158. *Concept of Angst*, p. 98; (KW 8:109); SV 6:194; (4:378).

159. The quotations in this paragraph are from a very gracious and stimulating presentation and critique of *Kierkegaard as Humanist* that Mooney presented to the Kierkegaard Society at its meeting in New Orleans on November 23, 1996. His remarks were entitled, "Sounding the Religious-Humanistic Self," which he distributed at the meeting, and which I quote with his permission. The quotations in the next paragraph are from his intriguing collection of essays, *Selves in Discord and Resolve*, and I include page references in the text.

One of his major and very legitimate concerns is with what he calls, "the conundrum of activity-intertwined-with-passivity in stage or concept shifts" in Kierkegaard's writings. In such transitions, he feels that *Kierkegaard as Humanist* (see pages 401, 411, 414, 416, 418–19, 430–34, 437, 439–50) puts too strong an emphasis on the idea that "we turn our attention," and asks, "do we turn our attention or is our attention turned? ... Perhaps we must leave more space for 'receptivity.'" Likewise, he wonders "if we could not put even less stress on the idea" of "the leap," because "the idea of a leap of faith blocks us from the 'receptive' pole in the idea of faith. ... The proper – and impossible – expression would be 'we are leaped into faith.'"

Obviously, Mooney thinks more in terms of continuities than disconti-nuities. He explains this emphasis by his view that "since the self ... is it-self a complex multi-layered field of relationships, ... a self and life-sphere can be conceptually coordinated, placed in reciprocal, mutual defining relationship." So on the one hand, "the self can be sketched from the inside out" as Kierkegaard does in *Sickness*. But "life-stages, on the other hand, are typically sketched by Kierkegaardian pseudonyms from the outside in. The relevant vocabulary does not exclude the 'psy-chological'; but it is also interpersonal and social – even political." So his thesis is that "the ensemble we've called self" is approximately what Marx called "the ensemble of social relationships." The self "can be seen ... as two sides of a single coin;" indeed, "there's a membrane ... between an active self and a mobile social world," and "it's more porous or transpar-ent than Kierkegaardians have supposed." In fact, he has "skeptical doubts" about those who "speak of a Kierkegaardian self as choosing it-self, ... making an existential 'leap' at each moment of decision or change." Rather, Mooney says that he seeks to "sketch an alternative pic-ture of the links between self and stage, and the dynamics of sphere- or self-transformation, ... elaborating the idea of self and life-sphere as mu-tually defining authorities." (pp.94–95)

Mooney does not want us to have to make a choice between these in-side and outside approaches to understanding the self, but he obviously gives the greater weight to the latter. And many would want to "correct" Kierkegaard in his lack of emphasis on the social sources and formation of the self. But for those who see *Works of Love, The Sickness unto Death,* and *Practice in Christianity* as normative, Kierkegaard simply cannot be read as providing material for such a program. Nowhere does he sug-gest a "porous membrane" that interconnects the active self and mobile social world, *except* in his description of those who have given up the task of becoming a self and submitted their lives to the external demands of "success" or acceptability in a flat, materialistic, bourgeois society.

In these volumes we have heard Kierkegaard both as humanist and as Christian theologian insisting that *we* as individuals must turn and concentrate our attention on listening to God define the one thing needful and then must gladly accept God's indispensable help in following after one thing. As Martin Buber says in his *Eclipse of God* (p. 164), "The one who is not present perceives no presence." Kierkegaard's constant and recurring thesis is that no degree or subtlety of increased quantification produces a "new quality" or a qualitative change. Such a change or transition comes only from the inner spirit. As Kierkegaard analyzed the self from both the inside and the outside, he came to a mysterious break or breach (*brud*) that yields to no conceptual reduction that explains it away in terms of some kind of continuity. So he came early to the adamant conclusion that "the view that sees life's doubleness [*Duplicitæt*] or duality [*Dualisme*] is higher and deeper than that which seeks unity [*Eenhed*]."[160]

Nevertheless, we must heed Mooney's call[161] for some standard or methodology for evaluating the degree and process of shifts and changes in concepts and between "stages" or "spheres" in Kierkegaard's writings, because, as he says, "There can be differences in concepts without there being sharp and explicit lines of division, for not all concepts have sharp edges. Some just *resonate* a certain way, through certain strata." Yet we must remember that, for Kierkegaard, basic shifts and changes came not simply from reflective reconceptualization or new imaginative perspectives in and by themselves, but from biographical events (his father's death, the broken engagement with Regine, the *Corsair* affair) and their impact on his own *self* understanding. The new insights that come from the latter sphere usually appear "irrational" or inexplicable, even to oneself.

To summarize: we have been considering the dilemma concerning the relative force of discontinuity and continuity in the transition from unbelief to belief, and in the relation of human freedom and divine grace. To resolve this dilemma, what is being proposed in this present study is that the tension between (1) the discontinuity of willing vis-à-vis

---

160. *Journals*, 704; IV A 192 (entered in February of 1844 just before writing *Concept of Angst* and *Philosophical Fragments*). This statement is taken as the motif for chapter 2 of *Kierkegaard as Humanist*, p. 18.

161. In his remarks at the New Orleans meeting.

(2) the undeniable continuities of imagination, of the self's character, and of the self with its social environment, should be recast in the terms of the complementarity of (1) the discontinuity involved in the faith relationship (between God and the human self) vis-à-vis (2) the continuity involved in the love relationship (among the triad of God, self, and neighbor). In this view of things, imagination (as analyzed by Ferreira) plays an integral role in both relationships (of faith and love), because I cannot choose what I do not "see" and recognize (God's righteousness and my failure), and I cannot surrender to what I do not "know" (the peculiar unity-in-diversity of love between God and self, between self and self). Likewise, the self's "ongoing intentions, dispositions, judgments, and motivations" (as analyzed by Gouwens) are actively involved both in maintaining the faith relation with God and in exploring and expressing love in all relations with God and neighbor. Likewise, all of the self's complex interactions with its social environment (as analyzed by Mooney) inevitably set the stage and the limitations for our relationships with both God and fellow humans. Understood in their complementarity, faith and love interrelate as a distinct and continuing contrast between two irreducible dimensions of a single relationship. And yet, within this single relationship, the two cannot be separated, either temporally or functionally, because the two dimensions are always present simultaneously, and each one operates in such a way that it is always qualified and empowered by the other.

Lee Barrett makes the same point.[162] He argues that the perception of faith both as "gift" and as "task" does not comprise an intellectual dichotomy that requires a conceptual resolution, but consists in a irreducible tension in the passionate personal life of every existing human being. The two senses of gift and task are "complementary," the one finding expression in worship and gratitude toward God and the other in personal concern and responsibility toward self and neighbor. They "reciprocally influence each other" (280–81). Their integration "does not take place through the auspices of a theoretic framework, but through the sagacity of passionate existers" (281). In other words, the concepts of sin and grace, of faith and freedom, find their "constitutive ... meaning" in and through "their role in the formation of human lives" (279). And he

162. Lee Barrett's brief but very perceptive article on "The Paradox of Faith in Kierkegaard's *Philosophical Fragments*" was published in IKC on *Fragments* in 1994 but apparently was written in 1992; so he had read Evans' articles but not his book, while he had read Ferreira's book but makes no mention of Gouwens' book on imagination. Page references will be included in the text.

agrees that although Ferreira sees the concepts of "leap" and "passion" as "parallel and as mutually and substantively correcting or qualifying each other," yet her view of the role of imagination "ironically ... has a tendency to mediate away the tension between 'gift' and 'task' aspects of the transition to faith" (282n15).

We conclude, therefore, that in the faith relationship it must be acknowledged that all willing involves the working of the imagination and its "new seeing" of a more true and attractive and persuasive paradigm that "reveals" what I *am* and what I *may become*. Likewise, all willing emerges from and is shaped by the ongoing character of the inner heart of the self. Likewise, all willing is engaged in a reciprocal give and take with the self's total environment. On the other hand, it is equally the case that the vision of the imagination, the character of the potential self, and concrete possibilities set by the self's actual situation never reach their fruition, do not attain their goal and intention, except with that strange, complex, and sui generis event of the "leap" of voluntary and gladsome acquiescence (by the whole self as a self-determining entity) to the vision of the imagination, the promptings of the self's essential character, the challenges of one's environment. And in the love relationship it is clear that there can be no bonding in reconciliation without the presence of a passionate vision of Love-Itself as the ultimate universal dynamic that has gone out of itself to give me being, and that constantly works through all things to bring my being back into eternal harmony with Itself. And yet, on the other hand, at the heart of Kierkegaard's vision of Love-Itself lies the conviction that Love (as present in Jesus as the Christ) does not compel or force or necessitate this return of my being into that harmony; the return must be voluntary, must be by one affirmed as equal at this one point in one's relationship with the Eternal. And in this "moment" always lurks the shadow of "the possibility of offense."

If this conclusion is an accurate interpretation of Kierkegaard, then one must conclude that it is *Works of Love* that contains Kierkegaard's ultimate and truest representation of what is "Christian" (rather than *The Sickness unto Death* and *Practice in Christianity*).[163] There alone the thesis

---

163. On this point, I read *Works of Love* rather differently than does Louis Dupré. He does not see this work as part of the "second," essentially Christian authorship, because in it "Kierkegaard still tries to interpret Christianity as pure interiority (and thus only reiterates the conclusion of the *Postscript*)" (p. 163). So "*Works of Love* ... marks the end of the more passive ethics of interiority" (p. 173), whereas in *Training [Practice] in Christianity, For Self-Examination* and *Judge for Yourselves*, Kierkegaard "places increasing emphasis on the external realization of Christianity," and "continues this criticism of 'hidden,' that is, inactive,

is clearly developed and exposited that to choose to become oneself means: to learn to love oneself – not, of course, in the usual "human" sense of egocentrism and self-seeking, but in the form of accepting with joy, but also in fear and trembling, God's gift: to be something in oneself, and thus to share in God's creativity in the terms of one's own unique individual selfhood. And this self-love is achieved only by coming to know and to experience that God's love takes the form of self-denial and self-negation in order to help *an other* to exist in and to fulfill and to glory in this gift of selfhood from God. The only pathway to finding my self is through losing my self. And thus I find my own self through a way that (no matter how faintly) is an analogy of, an "imitation" of, a "reduplication" of, God's own creative being.

Thus we come to the consummation and the conclusion of, My Self: In Need of the Eternal.

Christianity" (p. 164). As I have shown extensively in chapter 7 of *Kierkegaard as Humanist* and specifically in chapter 3 above at 208ff., it is in *Works of Love* that Kierkegaard defines and stresses the *most* Christian involvement in "external realization" and in the most active ethics, namely, in love of neighbor. And it is spelled out (in chapter 3 above) that it is precisely the lack of this emphasis in the later works from *Practice* onward that leads Kierkegaard to overemphasize that kind of Christian suffering that comes from overt and specific attack on the unchristian character of church and society. Dupré gives a good, brief summary of love of neighbor (pp. 160–163) but insists on classifying it under the topic of "The Ethics of Interiority" (p. 156). He then goes on to argue that "Kierkegaard's later writings ... could be considered as prolegomena to a theory of Christian ethics," because they contain "a new insight into the ethics of faith. If faith demands works, it must be manifested externally" (p. 165). This seems to contradict an earlier statement that, in earlier writings, Kierkegaard rejects "renunciation of the temporal life" and "the ascetic attitude" that encourages a "complete detachment from ordinary life," whereas "in his later writings, he came more and more to the conclusion that this ascetic life represents not the exception, but the most adequate expression of Christianity." (p. 46) Dupré seems to ignore the fact that this "new ... ethics" (of Kierkegaard's late writings) is strictly negative, and that its point is not a program for the renovation of the structures of the external social/political life, but a call to a re-awakening of the ethics of love: individual to individual. He also seems to ignore the fact that this new "prolegomena to ... Christian ethics" did not end in hope for Kierkegaard, but in "the extremity of life-weariness [*livslede*, literally, 'loathing-of-life']" (*Journals*, 6969; x1² A 439). So, unlike this present volume, Dupré's book does not take seriously Kierkegaard's notions of God-as-love-itself and of this divine love's "reduplication" in the human being through the faith-relationship with God/Christ.

5

The Christian Community In History

We come to the conclusion of our long journey through the labyrinthine paths of Kierkegaard's exploration of the nature of the human being as self, as spirit.

SUMMARY

First (in a previous volume), we listened to Kierkegaard as humanist, defining the self as a twofold relation (of finitude and infinitude), which relates to itself and which has the task of becoming itself. We saw how this task involves every self in becoming self-conscious through the dialectic of the temporal and the eternal, and simultaneously through the dialectic of possibility and necessity. Within these dialectics the self comes to know itself as freedom, freedom defined formally as a leap, and freedom defined substantively as love. Altogether, these themes comprise Kierkegaard's profound understanding and incomparable vision of how every human being is called and is able to engage in "discovering my self."

Now (in this volume), we have listened to Kierkegaard as Christian theologian, exploring and expositing the many ways in which this entire humanist vision is recast and redefined when the individual self is brought under the impact of encounter with and living "before" God, that is, God as present to us in Jesus as the Christ. We saw how such a self centrally comes to know that being a self is a gift from God, a creation out of nothing, the gift of being something instead of nothing, the gift of the infinite and eternal possibility of becoming a self in the image of God and for life with God. We then turned to the major subject that could not be dealt with within the purely humanist consciousness of selfhood: the mystery of human failure to move directly toward the accomplishment of the God-given task of becoming self, a failure that dooms human existence to despair and is most profoundly understood as sin. Finally, we could try to plumb the wondrous depths of the particular "way" which the follower of Jesus as the Christ takes in recovering the self that is "lost" in sin: the way of the cyclic spiral through confession, forgiveness, and imitation. And we found at the core of this way the mystery of the complementarity of faith/love in the new life and relationship with God and neighbor.

KIERKEGAARD'S GENERAL VIEW OF SOCIALITY

In this entire study we have followed Kierkegaard's lead in limiting our consideration of the human self in its individuality, indeed, in its separateness and aloneness as it faces God and the God-given task of becoming its self. Does this mean, then, that Kierkegaard has no concern for and nothing to say about the corporate and communal dimensions and expressions of Christian faith and love? His whole conceptuality has long been taken to task and often derided and rejected as irrelevant because of his seemingly total concentration on what he called "my category," namely, the individual.

However, during the last twenty years there has been an increasing number of studies that undertake to demonstrate that this accusation is an erroneous misreading and serious distortion of what Kierkegaard actually was saying.[1] They have been primarily concerned with Kierkegaard's view of the role that the social and political spheres play in shaping the life of the individual, as well as in being the locale where the Christian life is lived out. And this topic was frequently mentioned in passing in *Kierkegaard as Humanist*.[2] But this larger issue is so complex,

---

1. A few evidences of this interest are (in chronological order): John W. Elrod's *Kierkegaard and Christendom* (1981); Bruce Kirmmse's article, "Psychology and Society: The Social Falsification of the Self in *The Sickness unto Death*" in *Kierkegaard's Truth: The Disclosure of the Self*; Merold Westphal's *Kierkegaard's Critique of Reason and Society* (1987); Bruce Kirmmse's *Kierkegaard in Golden Age Denmark* (1990); *Foundations of Kierkegaard's Vision of Community* (1992), edited by George B. Connell and C. Stephen Evans, especially part 3 on "Social and Political Thought". And I am privileged to have seen an article by Robert L. Perkins entitled, "Person and Polis in Kierkegaard's *Postscript*," in which he makes creative use of Plato to evoke some interesting aspects of Kierkegaard's thought (it will appear in the volume of the International Kierkegaard Commentary on *Postscript*). I am sure there are many other articles on the subject, of which I am not aware.

2. See the index under the entry "social/society: crowd, mass."

the relevant materials in Kierkegaard's writings are so dispersed, and background knowledge is so demanding that it lies quite beyond the scope of this present interpretation of Kierkegaard as theologian, as well as beyond the capacities of the present author (as of now). Merold West-phal has brought to it his considerable skills as philosopher, and Bruce Kirmmse has supplied to its consideration his excellence as historian. But the entire issue is still relatively new territory and remains to be ex-plored more broadly and more deeply. So the present chapter will limit itself to a consideration of Kierkegaard's view of the nature and possibil-ity of *Christian* community, with the hope that it will be a small contribu-tion to the study of the larger issue.

The problem posed for the task of defining Kierkegaard's view is clearly indicated by the usual negative interpretation. Mark C. Taylor puts it this way: while "Kierkegaard does not deny that there are social dimensions of selfhood," he does "reject Hegel's contention that authen-tic selfhood presupposes membership in spiritual community." So for Kierkegaard "the birth of spiritual individuality requires severing the um-bilical cord of sociality through the difficult labor of differentiating self and other. The one who undertakes this spiritual pilgrimage ever re-mains a lonely wayfarer."[3] Dozens of quotations can be marshaled from Kierkegaard's writings and journals to support such a view, but it is not what he really meant or wanted to say. To say what he meant will require some subtle analysis of diverse materials and will even include a critique of some of his statements as inconsistent with his fundamental under-standing of spirituality. But the struggle is worth the effort.

As introduction, it must be stressed that he strongly affirmed "the so-cial dimensions of selfhood." This point was stressed and illustrated in our earlier consideration of Kierkegaard's basic, humanistic view of the individual. That is to say, the human being is a synthesis of finitude and infinitude, and our finitude includes not just our bodies but our place-ment in the whole temporal/spatial order of family, society, nation, and world history.[4] But he argues that "the social is related essentially to the psychic-physical [*sjelelig-legemlige*] synthesis," and that "Aristotle says cor-rectly that 'the crowd' is an animal qualification."[5] And so his primary

3. Mark C. Taylor, *Journeys to Selfhood: Hegel & Kierkegaard*, pp. 179–180.

4. See entries under the item "social/society" in the index of *Kierkegaard as Humanist*. For a general statement, see pp. 102–103.

5. *Journals*, 43; X[4] A 226. The Hongs give a reference to Aristotle's *Politics*, 1278 c-d, 1281 c (para. 5), and note that Kierkegaard's reference is accurate but not representative of Aristotle's positive view of the state "as an organic unity expressive of man's nature."

concern is with the central struggle that the individual is engaged in to remain free of the tyranny of those social structures that seek to control, delimit, and determine not only what the individual does but even what one thinks and believes.

CHRISTIAN SPIRITUALITY AND COMMUNITY

When this issue is translated into the setting of the individual's struggle to exist and live "before God," and especially "before Christ," then the basic human relation between the individual and the social becomes the intensified problem of the relation of a Christian-as-spiritual to the community called "church" and finally becomes the even more intensified problem of how the individual *as Christian* lives as citizen in the social-economic-political community at large. Kierkegaard concentrates on the first problem, and so will we, with only a few comments on the latter problem.

First, it must be emphasized that Kierkegaard does not seek to reduce Christianity simply to individual terms and to deny its corporate and even institutional character; quite the opposite, as has been spelled out in chapter 1 above.[6] He is profoundly aware of his own indebtedness to the church in all its historical forms and to its variety of formulations of the Christian faith. As noted in chapter 1 above, he sees the church of his own day as apostate to the best of that tradition and feels profoundly that he is especially called, fitted, and educated (as an *extraordinaire*) to serve as God's "gadfly" and "corrective" to the church, hoping and expecting an "awakening" and "reform" within the church. And so, although he undoubtedly derived some of his emphasis on awakening and inwardness from the Herrnhut tradition of his father, he did not share its strict congregationalist and anti-establishment attitudes and hence derided this tendency in the Grundtvigian movement of his own day.[7] So (as we have heard) he never sided with the opposition that wants to get rid of "government", and in retrospect he viewed *Practice in Christianity* as "an attempt ideally to find a point-of-strength for an establishment" (see note 91 in chapter 1).

It would seem, however, that the most positive construction Kierkegaard can put on the church as a community with an established order is

---

6. See text (of chapter 1) from note 83 through note 94, and read notes 84, 85, 92.

7. For an account of the importance of this tradition for Kierkegaard, see Bruce Kirmmse's *Kierkegaard in Golden Age Denmark*, pp. 28–35. Kirmmse also tells us a lot about Grundtvig (see his index); see also our text above at note 94 in chapter 1.

that it serves to meet our purely human needs. So in *Practice*, he contends that this life is designed strictly as "a time of testing for each individual," and "'fellowship' [*Fælledsskab*] is a lower determinant than 'the individual' [*den Enkelte*]." The church is simply a collection of individuals who are "struggling in the spiritual and Christian sense." Hence what Christians call "the congregation" really "has no place in time but only in eternity, where it is, at rest, the gathering of all the individuals who endured in the struggle and passed the test."[8] And in a series of journal entries from 1848 to 1851, he insists that sociality in general and the church or congregation in particular are "concessions" to the "frailty" and "weakness" of humans who cannot "manage to be unconditionally the single individual" and who are not "able to endure being spirit."[9]

On the other hand, we find in *Works of Love* an intimation of another notion of "fellowship" at work in Kierkegaard's mind. This idea was dimly anticipated two years earlier in a discourse, "On the Occasion of a Confession." He starts off by saying that in confession, one is in a "closed room ... in stillness" where "there is no fellowship [*Fællesskab*] – each one is by oneself. ... [T]here is no invitation to community [*Samfund*] – each one is alone." But at the end of the discourse, he modifies this assertion. He exclaims, "Oh, in the stillness, what beautiful harmony [*Samdrægtighed*] with everyone! Oh, in this solitude, what beautiful fellowship [*Fællesskab*] with all!" And what is this harmony and fellowship? It lies in the fact that every human being has "the same essential task" as every other one. And even though "each one understands it a bit differently and in one's own way," yet they all are following "many roads leading to the one truth."[10]

This distinction is picked up in *Works of Love* where Kierkegaard repeatedly plays on the dialectic between what he calls "the universally-human" (*Almene-Menneskelige*) in which all humans have "equality" of dignity and worth, and what he calls the unique "distinctiveness" (*Eiendommelige*) of each individual. Both are true and of equal importance in understanding that essential human being that God has given us in God's own image. In one place, Kierkegaard refers to this universally-human as "fellowship with all human beings." In another long passage, he inveighs against the "fellowship" of romantic love and friendship as

8. *Practice*, p. 218; (KW 20:223); SV 16:208; (12:204–205).
9. *Journals*, 1377, IX A 315; 6705, X³ A 647; 1415, X³ A 658; 4341, X⁴ A 226.
10. *Three Discourses on Imagined Occasions*, KW 10:9, 38; SV 6:247, 271; (5:178, 201).

nothing but "enhanced and augmented self-love."[11] But in the very last discourse, which is on "The Work of Love Is Praising Love," he says that the one who knows that "God is love" can only praise love in the act of self-denial in order "to win [other] human beings to it, to make them properly aware of what is granted to every human being in the-offer-of-reconciliation [*Forligelighed*] – namely, the highest. ... [T]he one who praises love reconciles all ... in the fellowship [*Fællesskab*] of the highest."[12] And this statement recalls that early on in *Works* Kierkegaard noted that even though Christ chose very insignificant people as his apostles, "he did succeed in forming a band of eleven whose destiny was to stay together in a willingness to be ... persecuted ... , and whose destiny also was not simply to flatter each other but on the contrary mutually to help each other to humility before God." And in this way the disciples formed "a society [*Forening*] of love."[13]

Several comments (not Kierkegaard's) must be made on this "fellowship of the highest," this "society of love." First, the unity that is assumed in this fellowship is unseen, intangible, indirect, never directly manifested. It is not something that the members of this society hold in common *with each other*, but somehow they come to sense that each of them holds the same thing in common *with God*. How do they come to sense this and believe in it? Because they share in hearing the same words, singing the same songs, saying the same prayers, and finally (and necessarily) joining in doing the same acts of love – even though, as Kierkegaard says, "each one understands it a bit differently and in one's own way." So it has always been with those seekers who become followers of "the way" of Jesus, as we read (Acts 2:41–42): "those who received the word were baptized. ... And they devoted themselves to the teaching [*didache*] of the apostles and to fellowship [*koinonia*], to breaking of bread and to prayers. ... And all who believed were together and had all things in common [*koina*]." And Paul added to this list: "Let the word of Christ dwell in you richly, as you teach and admonish one another [no preacher here!] in all wisdom, and as you sing psalms and hymns and songs with thankfulness in your hearts to God" (Col 3:16; cf. Eph 5:19).

Here are the common "means of grace": the word, the breaking of bread (as Jesus said, "my body broken for you"), prayer, song, *and*

11. *Works of Love*, pp. 83, 247–251; (KW 16:73, 264–269); SV 12:76, 254–258; (9:74, 252–256).

12. Ibid., p. 335; (KW 16:365); SV 12:348; (9:346).

13. Ibid., p. 126; (KW 16:122); SV 12:121–122; (9:118).

344 Kierkegaard as Theologian

(necessarily) "sharing all things" with those in need. And somehow, through it all – not through just one or the other but all together – the mystery happens: *koinonia*.[14] So Christianity added a major word and concept to its language. And what was first applied primarily to sharing material things came to refer also to receiving the "bread and wine" as "a koinonia of the body and blood of Christ" (1 Cor 10:16), to receiving "the hand of koinonia" (Gal 2:9), to "koinonia for [*eis*] the Gospel" and "koinonia of Spirit [*pneumatos*]" (Phil 1:5, 2:1), to being "called to the koinonia of Jesus Christ our Lord" (1 Cor 1:9) and therefore to sharing in "the koinonia of [Christ's] sufferings" (Phil 3:10), and ultimately to being blessed with "the grace of the Lord Jesus Christ and the love of God and the koinonia of the Holy Spirit" (2 Cor 13:14).

It would seem that this vision of fellowship or commonality was what Kierkegaard had in mind when he spoke of that intangible and indirect "fellowship of the highest" and of a "society of love." But he refused to identify this society and fellowship with those notions of "congregation" and "established church" that were current in his day, since the congregation claimed to possess direct spiritual unity between and among its members, and the church establishment claimed to have direct divine authority in its own hands. The mystery and wonder, the fear and trembling, of being "before God" and of being possessed by Holy Spirit of God were lost. Kierkegaard spoke little and rarely about Holy Spirit because the claim of Christian "spirituality" of his day was not of being possessed by but of possessing Spirit in and by oneself, in and by the "congregation." Actually, his doctrine of Holy Spirit is camouflaged in his entire exposition of the faith/love union or relationship with God and of the life of obedience to God.

Kierkegaard makes this point in a comment on the definition of "church" in the Augsburg Confession, namely, the church is "the communion [*Samfund*] of saints where the word is rightly taught and the sacraments rightly administered." He says it is correct in its stress on word and sacraments but totally incorrect in its omission of any stress on the "existential" (*Existentielle*) element of "communion" (or "fellowship") with God. Without this dimension, word (as correct "doctrine") and sacrament rightly administered produce only a pagan religion.[15] This

14. The verb, κοινωνεω, means to be a partaker, to have a share in, to take part in; the noun, κοινωνια, means communion, fellowship, intercourse. But for first century Christians it was used more often to refer to the *act* of sharing to meet the very material needs as well as spiritual needs (see Rom 15:26, 29; 2 Cor 8:4. 9:13).

15. *Journals*, 600; x⁴ A 246.

pagan view, he says, actually sees the church as "due to the sociality [*det Sociale*] that belongs to human nature" and therefore "deduces the idea of church from human nature." On the contrary, "without wanting to deny the reality of the church or that Christianity affirms it," Kierkegaard insists that "Christianity is related to spirit," whereas "sociality [*det Sociale*] is related essentially to the psychic-physical synthesis" (literally, "the soulish-bodily synthesis").[16]

At this point (in this same journal entry of 1851), Kierkegaard manifests a basic confusion and loses his way (in the opinion of the present author). He immediately adds, "Christianity teaches that eternal life is simply not social [*socialt*]" (contradicting his insistence in *Practice* that "the congregation really belongs only to eternity" – note 8 above). And he compounds the problem by asserting, "community [*Samfund*, communion] cannot be deduced from 'spirit,' and the church exists precisely because we are not ... pure [*reent*] spirit. 'Congregation' is an accommodation, a concession [*Indulgents*] in consideration of how little we are [spirit] or able to endure being spirit."

The confusion is twofold. First, he seems to have forgotten that in *Works of Love* he had perceived and acknowledged the existence of a "fellowship of the highest" and a "society of love" which the original apostles formed (around Jesus) to "mutually help each other to humility before God." And he insisted that, in addition to word and sacrament, the church must stress the need for the "existential" element of spiritual "communion" or "community" (*Samfund*) in order to be the church. Secondly, Kierkegaard's own normative and ruling definition of "spirit" is: the self as a relation which relates to itself, wherein the basic "relation" is an indissoluble synthesis of infinitude *and* finitude, of the eternal *and* the temporal, of possibility *and* necessity. To become self or spirit does not mean to become *pure* infinite, eternal, possible *being*, as God is Being-in-and-for-itself. Indeed, there is no human *being*, as distinct from God and as individually distinct from each other, except within the dimensions of finitude and temporality. And Kierkegaard himself stresses that the individual's finitude includes one's connectedness with family, society, state, and universe, and that one's temporality includes one's own personal "history" set in the context of the process of world history. But the psychic-physical identity of the individual becomes authentic selfhood or spirit only when it freely turns to ("relates

16. Ibid., 4341; X⁴ A 226. Note that this entry is from the same time as the previous one, that is, the spring of 1851.

to") its dimensions of infinitude and eternity and unbounded possibility as definitive and determinative of its entire being and life.

So Kierkegaard's strong aversion to and critique of sociality in general and of Christian congregation and church in particular seems to be from other sources than from his own essential conceptuality. At the most general level are his own observations of how the individual's sense of uniqueness and one's commitment to ideals are ground down into conformity with external social demands and standards, or of how they are hidden inwardly behind a "locked door" for fear of social disapproval. Then, with the economic chaos and its attendant riots and revolutions throughout Europe in 1847 and 1848, Kierkegaard becomes convinced that henceforward tyranny will not be identified with the government (of pope, king, and nobility) but with "the public, the crowd, the rabble, public opinion."[17]

More specifically, on a very personal level, one might surmise that he had absorbed some of the anti-establishment and anti-clerical attitudes of the Herrnhut tradition from his father and from sitting in their meetings on Sunday evenings. And these attitudes would have been reinforced by his own bitter experience when the social and ecclesiastical leaders of Copenhagen sided with the street rabble in enjoying his discomfiture under the *Corsair* attacks. In fact, from the end of the first year of the *Corsair* affair and with the initiation of *Works of Love* (January 1847) onward, he became increasingly convinced that the church establishment had totally deserted the New Testament understanding of Christian faith, and that a radical critique was called for.[18] This became

---

17. Ibid., 4116, 4118; VIII[1] A 108, 123; see also 4167; X[2] A 52, where he notes that what he had foreseen at the conclusion of his "literary review of *Two Ages*" (in the section entitled "The Present Age") "was fulfilled two years later in 1848."

18. See Ibid., 5947, 5961; VII[1] A 169, 221. I believe that his reference (at the end of entry 5947) to "what constitutes my life" consists of his conviction from childhood onward that he was destined (in some undefined way) to be a martyr for the faith. And at this juncture of his life (end of 1847, beginning of 1848), the nature of that martyrdom became clear to him. Despairing of fulfilling his ideals of marriage and country pastorate, and having fulfilled (he thought) his ideal of authorship (with *Postscript*), he now has an intimation of realizing "something ... far greater." And in journal entry 5961 he declares it. The only church leader he has ever honored and respected has been Mynster, but now he is convinced that Mynster too "has now completely accommodated to [the established order]." So what "the present age" most needs is "an extraordinaire in the literary, social, and political situation," and he is convinced that there is no one "in the kingdom suitable to be that except me." Hence he will resume his authorship, and it can have only one result: "It is perfectly clear that I will be sacrificed."

obvious to him from sermons he heard and what he read in the religious publications, and it was finally and firmly confirmed by the fact that *Practice* was received by the clergy and bishops with embarrassed silence rather than creating the awakening he had hoped to stimulate.

The conclusion would seem to be, then, that the new authorship had a twofold aim. On the one hand, it would set forth as vivid a depiction as possible of the essential and absolute character of Christian faith and life. On the other hand, Kierkegaard hoped that this depiction would serve to startle the church with a profound sense of its apostasy and would produce a spiritual awakening of New Testament Christianity among members of the church. One of the by-products of this goal was that Kierkegaard deliberately avoided attempting a theological formulation of a positive concept of how the organized church and congregation could serve as the medium of the authentically Christian "fellowship of the highest" and "society of love." He did not want to tempt church members into one more compromise by diluting his message of the absolute Christian either/or: either the despair of sin, or the salvation of faith/love, on the part of each individual *qua* individual.

The closest Kierkegaard comes to such a theological formulation is found in a couple of journal entries from the autumn of 1848 (as he is completing *Practice in Christianity*). He begins by affirming in a positive way that no human being can sustain a moment-by-moment consciousness of being before God, in a living relationship with God. To be absolutely alone with God is "almost unendurable for a human being." In fact, it is presumptuous conceit for a human being to try to attain or even to assume that one is capable of such consciousness. This condition of human existence reflects the basic given that cannot be changed or even mitigated, namely, "the infinite difference of quality" that separates God and human-being (*Menneske*). In this light "we see that sociality is not the highest but is really a concession to human weakness." So when "the ideality of the God-relationship has become too strong for the single-individual [*Enkelte*]," and when "being literally alone ... is too frightfully strenuous," then "the real meaning of religious sociality [*Socialitet*] is to be found." God knows that "it is not good for the human being to be alone," and "hence the determinant of companionship [*Selskab*] must be [i.e., serve as] a middle term." This is possible because "God relates to the whole race," and "the fact of race (sociality) is then a middle term between God and the single-individual."[19]

19. Ibid., 1377; IX A 315.

A day or two later Kierkegaard must have re-read this entry and decided that he had gone too far in his "concession to human weakness." So in the very next entry[20], he places this middle term in a very negative perspective. He reasserts that "the God-relationship of individuality [*Enkelthedens*] (that every individual relates to God) is still sound and true. ... [T]o be human simply means ... that every single-individual is known *qua* individual by God and can know [God]. The task is to work oneself out of sociality [*Socialitet*] more and more, but genuinely and truly, to be able to maintain longer and longer having the thought of God-present-with-me."

What, then, is the role of "the middle term [of sociality] or of 'the other human'?" That term, Kierkegaard now says, comes into play only *temporarily* "when the God-relationship of the single-individual becomes sickly [*sygeligt*]" by "wanting to be or being a most uncommon individual" who does nothing but "sit and flirt with God." Or this sickness is that "spiritual-trial" which comes when "the deep underlying feeling of infinite unworthiness (basic to every true God-relationship) becomes overpowering" rather than a "greater joy in God," so that one feels oppressed, "anxious and afraid of ideality and oneself – and of God." Here Kierkegaard obviously has in mind everything he had written (that same year) about "the sickness unto death" that breeds defiance and despair.

But, he now says, "a person is not to give in; one is to fight against it, ... one *ought* to pray to [God], for otherwise it is hardly possible to force one's way through the spiritual trial. One is to remember that God is love, the God of patience and consolation. ... Remember that God at any moment has 100,000 possibilities for helping you, ... that this thing [God] has allotted to you is still at this very moment the best." What you need to do, then, is to "reflect upon God because you need God, because otherwise everything would collapse for you. Therefore you should pray most sincerely for help in always having work to do and then receive everything from [God's] hand." So "the task is directed toward being able to hold fast to the thought of God more and more for a longer time, ... to cling fast to [this task] within your work. There shall be no dreaming, because God is pure act [*Actuositet*]."

It would seem, then, that the only function of "the middle term of sociality" (as embodied in the "communion of saints") is to affirm to you that "God is love," and to encourage you to initiate your own "fight" against your disease of defiance and despair. And in this fight you must

20. Ibid., 2008; ix a 316.

not turn to your fellow saints for the help you need, but to God alone. In other words, in order to fulfill and to remain faithful to his own sense of unique calling and task under God (to be the gadfly and corrective to the church of his day, to be the extraordinaire to the concomitant culture and society), Kierkegaard refused to explore or to develop any formulation of a positive concept of Christian community.

Since it is beyond the scope of our present study, we are leaving aside the question as to why he also refused to formulate a positive view of social/political order, and whether there is, nevertheless, such an incipient, hidden view to be extricated from his many and diverse comments on that order. But we will try, briefly, to suggest a positive view of Christian community that is inherent in Kierkegaard's view of God and human-being, as that view is exemplified in the particular relationship that is opened up between God and human-being for those who become followers of the life (the "way") of Jesus as the Christ.

First, let us reemphasize what was noted above (on p. 338), that human-being as such, as created and intended by God, is integrally finite, temporal, and delimited by a kind of necessity, so that the human individual as spirit (self) is a *relation* of the finite and the infinite, of the temporal and the eternal, of necessity and possibility – of all three dialectics modifying and qualifying and empowering each other. And this process of the active and conscious interrelating of all three dialectics is described as "the relation relating to itself," which is "freedom." But now we must also add that in the act of the relation relating to itself, the relation simultaneously relates to an "other," namely, to the eternal as that very special Other which posited or gave the self its being and life. But we have noted before that at this point of his definition Anti-Climacus makes a grave omission.[21] The definitive "relation" of the human self is not just twofold: to self and to God, but is threefold, including also the relationship to neighbor.

It would appear that this omission is deliberate, because Kierkegaard continues to keep in mind this essential element of love toward neighbor, as is evident in journal entries throughout the 1850s. One could even surmise that Kierkegaard is deliberately suppressing this element, because he sees in it the grounds for a kind of "communal" relationship that can indeed "be deduced from 'spirit'" (see note 16 above). And in the year 1848, when he is mounting the first form of his attack on the

21. See above chapter 3, 208ff., entitled "Omission of Relation to Neighbor as a Third."

established order of the church (in *Practice in Christianity*), he does not want to encourage any form of dependence on "the communion of saints." What is being proposed here is that the threefold relationship of love means precisely that a *kind* of community is implicit in Kierkegaard's own basic conception of Christian "spirit." It would be formulated something like as follows.

When Kierkegaard says that "sociality is not the highest but is really a concession to human weakness" (note 19 above), he does not mean "weakness" in the sense of human failure. He specifies that he is referring to "the infinite difference of quality" that separates God and human-being, that is, to the permanent eternal *given* of human nature, which is the ground both of human identity and freedom and also of human dependence on God for life and blessedness. On this ground sociality serves as a "middle-term between God and the single individual [*den Enkelte*]." Two years earlier than this journal entry, and at the very beginning of the second ("Christian") authorship, he gives this concept a very positive twist (in another entry[22]). The entry is entitled, "The Dialectic of *Menighed* or *Samfund* Is as Follows." Both terms are those used specifically in Christian circles for the designation of their sense of community, the first referring usually to the "congregation" of disciples, the second having more the connotation of the spiritual bond of "communion" or "fellowship." Here Kierkegaard is using them as synonyms, each connoting the emphases of both.

The fact that he is analyzing what he calls the "dialectic" of this phenomenon indicates that he is after its fundamental structural character. It is also notable that he defines this bond of community as a "relation," in which "the unique-individuals [*de Enkeltheder*] relate to each other" – a clear anticipation of the language used in the definition of the synthesis that comprises the self (in the opening paragraph of *Sickness*).

He differentiates among three possible forms of this relationship of community. In the first, each individual is "lower than the relation." In the second, each individual is "equal under [*lige for*] the relation." In the third, each individual is "higher than the relation." And this third form is true of "the religiously highest form" of communal relation wherein "the particular individual relates first to God and then to the congregation [*Menighed*], but this primary relation is the highest, *only if* [*om*] one does not, however, neglect the second" (emphasis added). In other words, the individual's relation with God is what preserves the individual

22. *Journals*, 4110; VII[1] A 20.

qua individual within the congregational community, but this God-relationship does not exclude but actually requires the communal relation, because the dialectic of the "infinite difference of quality between God and human-being" requires a "third term" within which the two can be united in a positive way, that is, in a way that unites and yet does not erase the differentiation between the two. Or, as Kierkegaard puts it, "the task is not to move from the individual to the race [community] but from the individual through the race [community] in order to attain the individual." So he is implying what we have heard him say in a later journal entry (see at notes 19 and 22 above), that sociality serves, in a positive sense, as "the middle-term between God and the single individual."

This triad of God-congregation-self, however, anticipates another (and more fundamental) triad that Kierkegaard formulates a year later in *Works of Love*: self-God-neighbor, wherein God is the "middle-term," and the in-group of congregation is replaced by "neighbor" as the universal human. The triad of love is more fundamental in this respect: the Christian congregation is a third term (in the God-relation) that is occasioned by the self's weakness (need for help), whereas the neighbor is a third term (in the God-relation) that is occasioned by the self's strength (capacity for self-giving). The self is higher than the relation of community, whereas the relation of love-of-neighbor is "higher" than self in the sense that it defines and fulfills self. The self is always in danger of losing its identity in the communal relation, whereas the self finds its self in its self-giving in the relation to neighbor. *Love* (God) is the ultimate, absolute, final, eternal "third term" in which all things find their meaning and fulfillment, not as a static condition but as the dynamic of reduplication.[23]

Everything that was said in *Kierkegaard as Humanist* about love of neighbor and about God as love now receives a transforming accentuation when seen and known in the "pattern" or "model" of Jesus as the Christ, when taking the form of the relationship of confession and forgiveness, when informed by the Christian dialectic (complementarity) of the faith/love relationship, when ultimately enacted and embodied in "faith's obedience" that has the power to "love forth the growth, because all faith's work aims at getting rid of egotism and selfishness in order that God can actually come in and in order to let [God] rule in

23. Here I assume everything that is said about love in the sections entitled, "Love's Triad and Love Presupposes Love," in chapter 7 of *Kierkegaard as Humanist*.

everything."[24] And the ultimate form of obedience is the suffering involved in loving neighbor not as represented in fellow Christians, or in family, friends, and beloved-one, but in every other human being, particularly those who present themselves as enemy.

This triad of self-God-neighbor does not negate, invalidate, or eliminate the other one of self-congregation-God, but the imposition of the triad self-God-neighbor upon the triad self-congregation-God radically transforms the latter's function and therefore its orientation. In *Works of Love* Kierkegaard repeatedly inveighs against the self-selected group for its claim of knowing what love is (amongst its own members); he insists that such a group is nothing more than self-love writ large and so is one of love's worst forms. And in a number of journal entries he warns against the danger of the Christian congregation becoming a form of group-love. People will say, "Let a few of us get together in a group" because "this makes life easier and more comfortable."[25] So "by living in certain select circles one is able to live securely, aloof from the crowd."

But, Kierkegaard asks, "Did Christ live this way? ... Or is wanting to evade the fact that one is a human being just like all others anything else than abominable self-love?"[26] In defining "what a human being is," one must look to "the highest determinant, the God-humanbeing, who posits the quality 'human'." And then we see that "it is of utmost importance to him to exist for every human-being, unconditionally every human-being." In contrast, "the natural comfortable thing is to exist only for a particular circle that holds the same views as one's own; to exist for them signifies 'the togetherness' that provides life with earthly security." But "courage is to dare to will to exist for the whole range of one's contemporaries." To "dare to exist for others" requires that one "must be absolutely sure ... that s/he is human," and one comes to this assurance "most of all by the help of intimacy [*Medviden*] with God." For this reason the God-humanbeing did not belong to "the solidarity" of either rich or poor but to the "whole range" of humanity, to "unconditionally *every* human-being."[27] As Jesus said, "You have heard it said, 'You shall love your neighbor and hate your enemy.' But I say to you, Love your enemies and pray for those who persecute you. ... For if you love

24. *Upbuilding Discourses in Various Spirits*, кw 15:259; sv 11:240; (8:343). See the treatment of this passage in chapter 4 above, pp. 294–5.

25. *Journals*, 4186; x³ A 529.

26. Ibid., 4114; vii¹ A 212.

27. Ibid., 4183; x² A 643.

those who love you, what reward have you? Do not even the tax collectors do the same?" (Mt 5:43, 46; cf Lk 6:27–38, 32–36)

Then Kierkegaard draws upon a truly remarkable source for support of this position. He argues that "the social and communistic movements" of the year 1848 occasioned a radical "shift in the interpretation of Christianity." He declares that "the conflict about Christianity will no longer be doctrinal (this is the conflict between orthodoxy and heterodoxy)." The world at large has "consumed those masses of illusions" by which Christians protected themselves "so that the question remained simply one of Christianity as doctrine." From that year onward "the conflict ... will be about Christianity as an existence. The problem will become that of loving the 'neighbor'; attention will be directed to Christ's life, and Christianity will also become essentially accentuated in the direction of conformity with his life." In other words, the world is sick of doctrinal disputes. "The rebellion in the world shouts: We want to see action!"[28]

In other words (not Kierkegaard's), when the triad self-God-neighbor is superimposed upon the triad self-congregation-God, the transformation that takes place is this: the congregation as the "society of love" is turned outward instead of inward, outward toward "the whole range" of human beings. The "love" that unites the followers of Jesus is not their sense of "togetherness" with each other but their common participation in that "fellowship of the highest" wherein they are moved by "the love of God" to self-forgetfulness out of love and compassion for "unconditionally every human-being" who has lost the way and is alone and in despair in the darkness of this world. The congregation, the church as a whole, exists not for itself as an end in itself but for the whole of humanity, for all God's children. The church is not itself "the kingdom of God," the final repository of all those who find their way to God. Rather, it is one of the "lights" that God sets into the darkness of this world; it is a small piece of "leaven" that God puts here to transform the whole of this flat and stale life.

This point is made by Kierkegaard in the very passage where he speaks of "the fellowship of the highest." The members of this fellowship believe that "God is love," and hence every one "relates to God and truly loves [God]." He says, "This is *inwardly* the condition or mode in which praising love must be done," and it has its own "intrinsic reward" (emphasis added). However, as we have heard (note 12 above), praising

28. Ibid., 4185; x^3 A 346.

love has integrally another goal: "to win people to it" so that, through reconciliation, they may share in "the fellowship of the highest." Then in a sentence stressed, all by itself, Kierkegaard draws his conclusion: "*The work of praising love must be done **outwardly** in self-sacrificing unself-ishness.*"[29] In other words, the inward-outward movement of God's self-reduplication as the dynamic of *love* propels the members of that "fellowship of the highest" (that "society of love") *outward* toward the "whole range" of humanity as its members struggle in and with the darkness and chaos of existence in this world.

Of course, Kierkegaard assumes one other point. The congregation, the church, is made up strictly of *individuals* who are somewhere along the way of becoming forgiven by and reconciled with God. Each one, in silence and solitude, turns to listen to and to know the "voice" of God, to accept God's loving judgment and acceptance, and ultimately to bear the "sufferings" that come when one follows in the way of Jesus as the Christ. But Kierkegaard fails or refuses to follow the leading of one obvious question: if the "fellowship of the highest" transforms the very being and functioning of the very human and mundane organization called "church" and "congregation," does not this Christian "existence" also transform the life of the individual in every aspect and dimension of its dialectical unity of the finite and the infinite, of the temporal and the eternal, of the possible and the necessary? Such a view is certainly implicit in the concept of self as such a unity in *Sickness.*

In other words, Kierkegaardian scholarship's present interest in the possibilities of constructing a positive sociology and politics from his writings should be matched with a demonstration of possible grounds in Kierkegaard's essential conceptuality for a positive reformulation not only of an authentically Christian congregation and church, but also of friendship, sexuality, marriage, childbearing, and family – all of which Kierkegaard came late in life to brand as perversions of authentic humanity and contradictions of Christian "spirituality."

As with the former topic, the latter task is also beyond the scope of this present study. The issue has already been treated briefly in *Kierkegaard as Humanist* (pp. 74–76, 345–50), including evidence of a positive view in *Works of Love.* Also (as noted previously in note 138 of chapter 3 above), Sylvia Walsh has already provided some materials for one essential ground for the development of such a reformulation, namely, her

___

29. *Works of Love,* p. 335; (KW 16:365); SV 12: 348; (9:345–346).

insights into Kierkegaard's distinction between masculine and feminine, and they must be at least mentioned here. Briefly summarized (and limited to her materials in *Living Poetically*), her main ideas are as follows.

It must first be acknowledged, she says, that Kierkegaard's views of gender and sex are compromised "by the stereotyped and patriarchal view of women he and his pseudonyms shared with his age." Yet he transcends and even contradicts this view by affirming "a given structure of selfhood, of personal identity, that is the task of every human being," and that assumes "a wholeness of identity as a self in both males and females that includes both 'feminine' and 'masculine' modes of relating to themselves, to the divine, and to others" (257). Furthermore, Walsh affirms a certain legitimacy in Kierkegaard's gender distinction between the "substantive differences [that] may be observed in the ways woman and man are oriented toward themselves and falter on the pathway to selfhood by falling into despair." Essentially Kierkegaard "claims that woman's nature is characterized by devotedness [*Hengivenhed*] and givingness [*Hengivelse*]," while "man is more self-contained and intellectual" (what Walsh calls "the feminine mode" and the "masculine mode"). (258)

Walsh shows (both in her book and in her earlier article in *IKC*) how Kierkegaard's essential view of self and his characterizations of male and female often end in inconsistencies and contradictions. But her conclusion is more positive. She notes:

An important distinction that emerges in his analysis is that sexual identity and self-identity are not one and the same, although they are certainly interrelated and interdependent concepts. Those qualities that we naturally tend and/or are culturally conditioned to develop in order to establish our sexual identities as women or men may be characteristic of a particular sex but are not distinctive to either, nor are they sufficient in and of themselves to constitute the self, which requires a synthesis of factors established through a relation to the divine.

So what is called for is "a complementary wholeness of identity as a self toward which both women and men should strive." This wholeness requires both the "masculine mode" of individuality and self-consciousness and the "feminine mode" of self-giving and relatedness, and hence these modes point more to a need for "psychological androgyny" rather than expressing "essential gender differences between the sexes or of bisexuality in the makeup of the self" (261, 259).

Beyond such considerations, an attempt at a reformulation of Kierkegaard's (and our) view of preferential forms of love would also bring to bear the entire interpretation of sensuousness and sexuality in *The Concept of Angst,* including especially the somewhat enigmatic but provocative, intriguing conclusion of Haufniensis about the sexual:

Sensuousness is not sinfulness. ... The generic difference is posited in innocence, but ... not as such. ... Here, as everywhere, I must decline every mistaken conclusion, as if, for instance, the true task should now be to abstract from the sexual, i.e., in an outward sense to annihilate it. When the sexual is once posited as the extreme point of the synthesis, all abstraction is of no avail. The task, of course, is to win it deep within [*ind i*] the determinant of spirit. The realization of this is the victory of love [*Kjærlighed*] in a human being, in whom the spirit is so victorious that the sexual is forgotten [i.e., by itself, as the extreme point of the synthesis], and only recollected [i.e., engaged in] in forgetfulness [i.e., as expressing spirit]. When this has come about, sensuousness is transfigured [i.e., not annihilated] in spirit, and angst is driven out.[30]

Would not such a "spiritual" engagement in sexual relationship exemplify exactly Kierkegaard's insistence in *Works of Love* that for Christianity "a conflict between spirit and flesh is inconceivable," and that "the teaching about love for the neighbor was ... specifically intended ... for transforming sensuous-love and friendship." So Kierkegaard admonishes his reader, "in loving yourself, preserve love for neighbor; in sensuous-love and friendship, preserve love for neighbor."[31] In fact, if, on a broader scale of categories, we follow Kierkegaard's lead and apply his principle that God's essential act of self-reduplication is manifest in the nature of every love relationship, we come to some startling conclusions of our own.

We have heard (from Kierkegaard) that reduplication within God is a drawing of a distinction, and that this essential ontological characteristic is manifest in the outward direction of love in that God gives distinctive being to an other: to me and to every other human being. This gift is the ground of human courage "for the God-pleasing venture of humility and pride: *before God* to be oneself," so that the human being "in relation to God does not become nothing, even though [one] is taken from

---

30. *Concept of Angst,* pp. 71–72; (KW 8:80); SV 6:169; (4:349).

31. *Works of Love,* pp. 65, 117, 74; (KW 16:52, 112, 62); SV 12:57–58, 112, 65–66; (9:55, 109, 64).

nothing and is nothing but becomes a distinctive individuality."[32] Now, when the eternal indwells that creature created in God's own image, then this power of reduplication is reduplicated in the human self in the form of self-forgetting, self-negating love for neighbor.

When, then, this kind of love possesses and informs the whole dialectical being of a human self, it also moves (by its own inherent quality and intent) to be "preserved" in and thus to "transform" all forms of preferential love: for family, for friends, and for one's particular beloved, including the latter's sensuous (sexual) dimension. In this way, the infinite and finite, the eternal and the temporal, become "commensurable," even while there remains an "infinite qualitative difference" between them. And since the eternal Love-Itself chose, out of love and compassion, to enter the finite/temporal in a unique relationship of identification with a distinctive, individual human-being who was conceived in and born from the womb of Mary, then may not sexuality and child-bearing be "won over" to and in accord with the "spiritual" – contrary to Kierkegaard's hysterical accusation that "human egotism is concentrated in the sexual relationship, the propagation of the species, the giving of life," and that having children is simply the human way of claiming to be equal with God in the power of creating.[33] How often has the mother and father of a new-born child exclaimed in wonder and awe that they know that this infant is not really their own but is "a gift of God," temporarily in their care.

In other words, this possibility of spirituality within the life of a congregational "society of love," within the relationships of friendship and of sexually accented companionship, and of the family group that may ensue, is not just a logical conclusion from certain concepts of God and the human self. Rather, these possibilities must be considered as among those "all-things-are-possible" (that is, the very being of God) just because they are "given" as possibilities and do happen within the lives of those who have come *through* the devastating but transforming impact of confession and forgiveness and thereby have come *into* the faith/love relationship with God in Jesus as the Christ. And in this respect, one must raise a serious question about Kierkegaard's capacities to comment on these possibilities.

The question is: what personal experience did he have of these possibilities? He never consummated a relationship with his one and only

---

32. *Works of Love*, p. 253; (KW 16:271–272); SV 12:260–261; (9:259).
33. *Journals*, 2624; XI² A 154.

love, Regine. Even his single friendship with Emil Boesen was not that profound, as evidenced by the fact that his "letters reveal that he kept much from his only confidant." His relationships with members of his immediate family were usually ambiguous and strained. He had a love/hate relation even with his revered father, who had flooded him with love and attention but robbed him of his childhood and bequeathed on the youth/adult his own melancholy. From his letters we gather that his very human sense of concern and compassion went out not to brothers or sisters but to his crippled second-cousin, Hans Peter Kierkegaard, and to his mentally depressed sister-in-law, Henriette Kierkegaard.[34] His participation in the life of a Christian congregation came more and more to be limited to attendance of holy communion, where social relations were minimal, and Kierkegaard appreciated the fact that the priest could not confuse things with a sermon but had to stick to the language of the ritual. And, of course, he finally saw that his constant talk about seeking a country parish was an illusion, that he would make a poor pastor, just as he was clear that he "would be a bad husband and always will remain so."[35]

The critical point is this: one of Kierkegaard's most constant insights and most fundamental principles is that one *knows* only what one has experienced in the concrete "situation." Apart from such experience, all ideas and thoughts remain theoretical possibilities, and there is "an infinite difference ... between understanding something in possibility and understanding the same in actuality." In possibility "I remain essentially unchanged, ... and make use of my imagination; when it becomes actuality, then it is I who am changed. ... When it is a matter of understanding in possibility, I have to strain my imagination to the limit; when it is a matter of understanding the same thing in actuality, I am spared all exertion in regard to imagination."[36] Likewise, "*spirit* can be communicated only indirectly. ... The situation must be present. ... Here is the distinction between understanding in possibility (an understanding that is always a misunderstanding) and understanding in actuality. ... It is impossible to become spirit in 'possibility'."[37]

34. *Letters and Documents*, KW 25: xxiii, xxi, in the Hongs' Foreward.

35. Ibid., Letter 62, p. 120.

36. *Journals*, 3345, 3346; X² A 114, 202.

37. Ibid., 4326; X¹ A 417. For Kierkegaard's frequent reference to the "situation" see the index to the Hongs's *Journals and Papers*, or Cappelørn's index to *Papirer*. The word is the same in both languages.

On what grounds, then, can Kierkegaard, in the last few years of his life, pronounce so unequivocally his absolute denunciations of all sexual relations, marriage, and childbearing as violations of Christian faith and life, as being totally ruled out by God's demand that one love God alone, as deriving from women's instinctive drive and wily plotting to mislead and corrupt men? From what actuality in his own situational experience can he mock all clergy as interested only in financial security, and deride congregational life as nothing but a group form of self-love? These positions can hardly be interpreted simply as deliberate exaggerations in order to awaken the church to its apostasy and thus serve as a call to radical reform. And taken at face value, they can only produce ridicule or lead to the sense of "life-weariness" that had engulfed Kierkegaard himself when he wrote his last entry in his journal on September 25, 1855. And we have seen that they contradict his own essential conceptuality and theology as developed in his second, Christian authorship from *Upbuilding Discourses in Various Spirits* through *Practice in Christianity.*

So, to be faithful to Kierkegaard himself, and to rescue his authentic and powerful vision of how I may recover my self, it is proper and indeed urgent to call for the formulation of a Kierkegaardian view of "Christian community" as manifest in congregation life and in every form of preferential love. And every statement, every sentence, every word of such a formulation must ring and echo with Kierkegaard's warnings of the constant human temptation to allow these forms of spiritual love to drift and to transmogrify into destructive forms of demonic self-love.

CHRISTIAN COMMUNITY AND HISTORY

We come, now, to one final question about Kierkegaard's understanding of Christian community, namely, about its historical character. As in his attitude toward Christian congregation, Kierkegaard is also very critical of and indifferent to the notion of Christian "history." He had his earlier friend, Climacus, spell out his views, and what we find in the later journal entries on history adds nothing. In his second (Christian) authorship, Kierkegaard is almost totally silent about history, except for a few passages in *Practice in Christianity,* which also add nothing essential to Climacus' comments – except for one interesting item. He uses the intriguing phrase "sacred history" (*hellige Historie*) several times, and by it he means "Christ's life in abasement" here "on earth." This history is totally distinct from world or universal history and from the history of Christians. It is not "a development within the category of the human race" because it is "related to eternity." Therefore, for those who (in faith) "become contemporary ... with Christ's life on earth," this "sacred history stands alone by itself, outside history."[38]

The essential thesis of Climacus's view of history is made very simply in *Fragments* and then given numerous applications and illustrations in *Postscript*. But it should first be noted that the central thesis had already been stated in *Either/Or.* Judge William points out that "the spheres with which philosophy properly has to deal ... are logic, nature, and history. Here necessity rules." But history seems to contain an exception to this rule of necessity "because here, it is said, freedom prevails." But philosophy handles this objection easily by pointing out that "individual actions ... enter into the order of things that maintains the whole of existence." And "this higher order of things that digests, so to speak, the free actions and works them together in its eternal laws is necessity, and this necessity is the movement in world history." Hence "the external deed ... is assimilated into and transformed in the world-historical process."[39]

It is precisely this thesis that Climacus takes exception to in *Fragments*. He draws a basic distinction between the historical "in the more concrete sense" and the historical "in the stricter sense."[40] Concretely history is concerned with what is open to observation, wherein "immediate sensation and immediate cognition cannot deceive."[41] From this perspective, everything seems to happen of necessity. But if one looks at the same events more scrupulously (*strængere*), one sees a "more special" (*speciellere*), hidden dimension, due to history's being "dialectical with respect to time." Their "coming into existence can contain within itself [*i sig,* as such, intrinsically] a reduplication, that is, a possibility of a coming into existence within its own coming into existence." This inner event is the transition from possibility into actuality, that is, a "historical coming into existence ... by way of a relatively freely acting cause." The historical in this sense contains an essential element of "illusiveness" (*Svigagtighed*) that is not open to immediate sensation and cognition but requires that "passion that is the passionate sense for coming into existence, that is, wonder." Even though the past may be unchangeable

---

38. *Practice*, pp. 33, 68, 216, see also 36; (KW 20:30, 64, 221, see also 33); SV 16:40, 71, 207, see also 43; (12:28, 61, 203, see also 31).

39. *Either/Or*, 2:178; (KW 4:174); SV 3:163–164; (2:157–158).

40. *Fragments*, pp. 73, 94; (KW 7:59, 76); SV 6:56, 70; (4:225, 240).

41. Ibid., p. 100; (KW 7:81); SV 6:74; (KW 4:244).

in terms of its "thus and so," this is not true of its "how." The past of events involving human beings "belongs to freedom" in the same way as the future, because there is lodged in the past the same element of "uncertainty" as to "how" it came into existence.[42]

In *Postscript* Climacus develops this thesis in terms of his extensive exploration of the nature of human subjectivity, especially in his distinction between the "truth" arrived at through subjective reflection and the "truth" arrived at through objective reflection. From this perspective, throughout the whole length of *Postscript*, he constantly derides the attempt even (or especially) by Christians to "demonstrate" the truth of Christian faith by historical evidence. Indeed, objectively regarded, Christian history is not concerned with "the subjective truth, the truth of appropriation" by one who is "infinitely, personally, impassionedly interested in one's relation to the truth." This "interestedness ... fades away more and more" in the concerns of "the learned research scholar. ... The issue does not arise at all." And to many Christians the centuries-long success of Christianity seems to provided objective evidence for the truth of Christian faith and thus makes this personal involvement unnecessary.[43]

From this characterization of the historical in a genuinely human sense (in both *Fragments* and *Postscript*), Climacus comes to two conclusions. First, the historical that is "dialectical in respect to time" has only to do with the individual. Secondly, a sharp distinction must be drawn between the world-historical and the individual, because the historical "in the more concrete sense" can really become a scholarly discipline on its own only if it restricts itself to the history of the race, in which the individual is swallowed up as a mere example of the universal. The historical as concerned with the individual must include the ethical, and the ethical assumes the thesis that "every existing individuality has a possibility-relationship with God," which thesis is untrue when "viewed world-historically." When world history has deigned to think or speak of "God," it has been only in a "fantastical sense" as "the moving-spirit [*Sjelen*] in a process." The result is that "in the world-historical process God is metaphysically laced into a half-metaphysical, half-aesthetic-dramatic corset, which is immanence." But the individual's ethical possibility-relationship with

42. Ibid., pp. 90–96, 99; (KW 7:73–77, 80); SV 6:68–71, 73; (4:236–240, 243–244).
43. *Postscript*, pp. 24, 28, 45; (KW 12.1:21, 27, 46–47); SV 9:24, 27, 44; (7:11, 16, 34–35).

God is "God's freedom, which, if properly understood, will not in all eternity ... become immanence."[44]

So from the view of the world history of the race, the individual is of no consequence but exists only to contribute to the larger telos of the historical process; from the view of individual in the God-relationship, world history is of no consequence but exists only as the stage on which each individual is given time and place to discover and to enact the meaning of human existence. So Kierkegaard does not conclude with Winston Churchill that there is no such thing as history, only biography. Rather, he "does not deny the reality of the world-historical development, which ... has its time and place." But he contends that it is an illusion for humans who participate in it to claim the capacity to observe it as a whole and to explain it as a divine process which has its own telos quite apart from the individual participants. If "the generation or the race" is "the highest," then "how does one explain the divine squandering that uses the endless host of individuals of one generation after the other in order to set the world-historical development in motion? ... [H]ow horrible, tyrannically to squander myriads of human lives!" God is the "only spectator" who sees the whole because God is not immanent within but transcendent to the world-historical process. It is God who has composed the drama that is being played out, in which each "subject" seeks "eternal blessedness" within the ethical-religious relationship with God. Then, "if becoming subjective is the highest task assigned to a human-being, then everything turns out beautifully. ... There is no squandering, because ... the task of becoming subjective is indeed assigned to every human-being."[45]

Anti-Climacus agrees with this analysis. Toward the end of *Practice in Christianity*, he concludes, "If instead of humanly scrambling Christianity frivolously in with world history, one takes Christianity on its own terms, ... believes that Governance surely knew what it did, ... then everything is in order; then this life becomes a testing for each individual, and the Christian Church here in this world is always a striving [*stridende*] Church." But "to this striving corresponds 'the single-individual' [*den Enkelte*], that is, when it is striving in the spiritual and Christian sense, ... because spirit is precisely this, that everyone is a single-individual before God." Hence " 'fellowship' is a lower category than 'the single-individual'. ... And even if the single-individuals were in the

---

44. Ibid., pp. 138–141; (KW 12.1:154–157); SV 9:128–131; (7:127–129).
45. Ibid., pp. 141–142; (KW 12.1:158–159); SV 6:131–132; (7:130–131).

thousands and thus striving in community [*Forening*], Christianly understood each single-individual yet strives not only [*foruden*] in community with the others but also [*tillege*] within oneself."[46]

What Kierkegaard refuses to do is to explore further the nature of what Anti-Climacus here calls "striving in community" with other thousands of Christians, and he especially refuses to consider an inward *continuity* of that community in what elsewhere he calls "sacred history." He is as suspicious of "Christian history" as he is of "Christian community (congregation, church)." Yet, as we have seen in chapter 1 (text from note 86 to note 94), Kierkegaard had a high regard for and central loyalty to the established church, and he considered his life's work as an author to be God's calling to be the extraordinaire of his time, given the special task of reshaping all the basic conceptual definitions of Christian faith, in order to serve as a gadfly and corrective to the shape and life of the Christian community. He also read Augustine and other early church fathers assiduously. He was conversant with the developments of the church in the Middle Ages and was not nearly as critical of it as the Reformers (and so, surprisingly, some Roman Catholic theologians of today are favorably inclined to the study of Kierkegaard). He read with interest and appreciation a wide variety of Christian writers, from Augustine to Bernard of Clairvaux, from Thomas à Kempis to Luther, from Pascal to Schleiermacher.

Yet it must be remarked that he failed in his guiding devotion to what he called "New Testament Christianity" in the fact that he ignores Jesus' own sense of spiritual continuity with certain key emphases of the Jewish scripture, especially with some of the prophets. In the other direction, he also fails to take seriously Jesus' obvious anticipation of continuity with a community of disciples who would carry on after his death, as well as the commitment of these disciples to the formation of a human organization for the work of discipleship. He does not develop any major "conceptual definitions" that have to do with the spiritual unity, depth, and direction of this organization, such as we find in the gospel according to John and in the letters of Paul. Nor does he draw any historical implications for the historical impact of this organization from the eschatological and apocalyptic passages in the synoptic gospels. Unlike the views of more recent twentieth-century theologians, Kierkegaard's "sacred history" was strictly that of the individual spirit, rather than a kind of unity of mind and spirit that tied individuals together in spiri-

46. *Practice*, pp. 217–218; (20:223); sv 16:208–209; (12:204–205).

tual fellowship throughout the sweep of time from Abraham to Jacob to Moses to Isaiah to Jesus and on throughout the last two thousand years.

So in addition to the need for studies that explore the possibilities of a positive Kierkegaardian sociology and political theory, as well as of a positive construction on Christian community, there needs to be a serious consideration of a positive view of his concept of sacred history and its role in the process of world history. If Kierkegaard could lay down as a fundamental proposition of all his thought "that the way is the truth, that the truth is only in the becoming, in the process [*Proces*] of appropriation,"[47] then it behooves Kierkegaard interpretation to discover how *this* process involves concomitant processes in Christian community and Christian history. And if we take seriously Kierkegaard's fundamental thesis of the unity of the finite/infinite, of the temporal/eternal, of necessity/possibility within the *individual* existence of Christians, then it behooves us to explore how that unity is reflected within our given human unity as individuals with the social, political, and historical dimensions of existence – whether Kierkegaard did or not.

Only in this larger context of the historical process of the "becoming" and "appropriation" of the truth will there *perhaps* be found some answer to the nagging question of theodicy that Kierkegaard never adequately faced up to. He certainly thought of it. In a journal entry (from the fall of 1848, when he had completed *Sickness* and most of *Practice*) he says, "[T]here is something dreadful in the thought of these countless millions of human beings. ... One is reminded almost of other animal species with their teeming duplicated specimens in the millions, and of nature's almost horrifying wastefulness. And when one then reflects that every single human being is inherently constructed for [*lagt an til*] the highest religiously, and the religious is yet again the highest!"[48] One has to wonder how Kierkegaard's view of humanity and its religious destiny would have been affected if he had witnessed the terrors of twentieth-century history. The appalling horrors of the conditions into which most of humanity has fallen as a result of clear failures to curb and control certain human tendencies would seem to turn into a ludicrous joke all talk about that failure as just a difficult but unavoidable little phase in the process of the maturation of the human individual. Somewhere Samuel Beckett describes human existence as a quick drop from the womb into the pit, with but a glimpse of light on the way

47. *Postscript*, p. 72; (KW 12.1:78); SV 9:67; (7:59).
48. *Journals*, 2010; IX A 356.

down the chute – and he did not have to draw on the influence of his "profoundly religious" Protestant mother in order to be convinced that this is the dominant quality of life for most humans.

As one who has lived through most of the twentieth century (1918–), the present author absorbed as a youth the optimistic belief in unlimited human progress with which this century began. The Great War was fought to end all wars and to establish democracy as the universal ideal. But then came the shattering, numbing, bewildering experience of the Great Depression which seemed like it would never end. Soon reports crept out of the USSR of the massacre of millions of Stalin's political enemies and of uncooperative peasants. Fascism and Nazism arose in full view of the world and threatened to engulf Europe and the USSR. Hitler's *Mein Kampf* spelled out the mad philosophy of a super race, which led to the slaughter of millions of Jews, Slavs, gypsies, and homosexuals. World War II drew in the entire world, encouraged the expanding Japanese Empire to fantasies of dominance over the entire Pacific basin, caused the development of unimaginably destructive weapons, culminating in the dropping of the atomic bomb on Hiroshima for questionable political and military aims. The vision of a peaceful world through the United Nations organization quickly proved to be an illusion, as old empires disappeared and as even older simmering nationalisms and tribalisms came alive to tear asunder the fabric of human society on every continent of the earth and to foment ghastly and stupefying massacres in the division of India, in Ireland, in the Balkans, within the new nations of Africa, in Israel/Palestine, among and within the countries of the Near East, and now in the ethnic territories of old Russia and the former USSR. And hanging like a poisonous cloud of total destruction over all these lesser conflicts, the disturbance of the balance of nature by the needs of an ever-expanding human population threatens the annihilation of the whole human race.

Was all this in God's plan and intention when he created the first human beings and "let them slip, as it were, out of his hand?" Such a question led the author of a recent novel to have one of his characters say, "Me, I study history in small sections. Even so, it makes me think, if God's doing the best job He can, He picked the wrong profession."[49] Kierkegaard's idea of the role of failure as "an essential element in the whole production" of mature human selves may make sense in middle class suburbs of western society, but even for us who live there, the idea

49. Michael Malone, *Time's Witness* (New York: Washington Square Press, 1994), p. 61.

often grows hollow and meaningless, if not absurd, as we watch old film of the corpses in Hitler's concentration camps and in the killing fields of Pol Pot's Cambodia, or as we see pictures today, on nightly television, of the hundreds of recently slaughtered men, women, and children (each a human being, a unique individual self) in the warfare between two tribes in Rwanda. But even closer to home, in every major metropolitan area of every western nation, we can visit neighborhoods where poverty, crime, violence, and drugs have completely destroyed anything like normal family life and have deformed the human character of countless children and adults beyond any hope of a meaningful existence. And still closer are the facts of life in the homes of even the comfortable and the rich where increasing child and spousal abuse leads to thousands of cases of violent injury and personal degradation and to hundreds of deaths every year and to increasing rates of suicide among children.

We face the inevitable question: is the whole experiment that developed within that mutation called Homo sapiens really worth the sufferings that come in the apparently total failure to achieve human well-being by the majority of that species throughout its entire history? And this question is intensified by some of the things Kierkegaard says about despair in his allegedly Christian formulations of the restrictive requirements for the achievement of self-fulfillment. We are suggesting that his view (that the purpose of human existence is fulfilled simply in the testing of each individual) is woefully too restrictive. Within the Biblical vision of God and the universe, there are materials for the formulation of a philosophy or theology of history that sees purpose and telos in the frightful permutations of human existence and yet does so in a way that still affirms the ultimate dignity and worth of the individual above the race.

And in spite of these unfulfilled dimensions of Kierkegaard's thought that have been briefly outlined in this chapter, the present author wishes again to stress that for him Kierkegaard's vision and complex analysis of the human self – in both its infinite possibility and its unutterable degradation, and also in its beauty of recovery in the image of Jesus as the Christ – remains the most convincing and the most promising of any that has yet appeared on the horizon of human insight and wisdom, although, of course, as Climacus admits in *Fragments*, his "story" is a plagiarism.

CONCLUSION

In conclusion, it must be noted that, just as Kierkegaard insisted that our process of appropriation of Christian faith/love is never to be completed but is always in the process of becoming, so too will be our process of interpreting that multiplex phenomenon called "Kierkegaard." And we must constantly be grateful that there is a broad and diverse and exciting community of minds and spirits that are engaged in this process of interpretation. We who are privileged to be members of the philosophical/theological community of interpreters must never forget that we are but a small segment of a broader community that stretches into every discipline of the human mind, and that stretches even further into the untold and unknown numbers who are not "interpreters" at all but who are, each one alone, that favorite of Kierkegaard himself: "my reader." To all these different kinds of readers, these two volumes are offered as one possible perspective on, and one way of trying to interrelate, the diverse strands of Kierkegaard's complex and variegated writings. Here is not and could not be a system, because Kierkegaard denies the possibility of a system of "existence," and in his own writings and reflections, he remains faithful to that conviction to the end.

Postlude: A Backward Glance

Kierkegaard as Humanist ended with an Interlude, but *Kierkegaard as Theologian* is ending with a Postlude (not a postscript) that plays a new tune, raises a new question, that has not been sounded in either volume.

The need for this new theme arose after these two volumes had been completed and were being presented for review and discussion at a meeting of the Kierkegaard Society in New Orleans (November of 1996). Given this informal context, I will be more open and personal in the reflections that now follow.

I have already alluded to some of the thoughts presented there by Edward Mooney. But I have not taken the occasion to respond to those of another person who was at that meeting, and who holds a unique relationship to the production of these two volumes, namely the eminent Kierkegaardian scholar, Paul Sponheim. He was the very first person with whom I talked when these volumes were but a fuzzy, undefined idea and uncertain project in the fall of 1982 while we both were in residence at Cambridge University during Michaelmas term. He was kind enough to talk at length with me about the various outlines and approaches that were buzzing about in my mind. And he imparted a clarity and sense of direction and a spirit of encouragement that had a profound impact. We never talked or corresponded again as my writing proceeded over the following fourteen years until he was asked to be the presenter of *Kierkegaard as Theologian* in New Orleans, and to be an outside reader of the manuscript by McGill-Queen's University Press. It was his remarks (on both occasions) that suggested the topic for this Postlude.

He raises the following questions (although not in these words). In the subtitle of the second volume, is the notion of "recovering" my self really adequate for the radical event of Christian redemption, for what the apostle Paul spoke of when he said, "If anyone [is] in Christ, [that one is] a new creation" (2 Cor 5:17)? Does the language and concept of my self as a "failure" do justice to Kierkegaard's stress (in *Sickness*) on sin as defiance, or on sin as what might be called "clear-eyed evil?" Is not speaking of my self as in "need" of the eternal totally incongruous with the Christian experience of grace, with the utterly unpredictable, unexpectable, inexplicable, un-understandable coming of the eternal into time, especially in the form of the humblest, weakest, most vulnerable of human beings? Does not, then, the use of these terms – recovery, failure, need – signify that the approach of this volume to the entirety of Christian experience and theology is more anthropological than Christological? And is such an approach true to Kierkegaard's second, Christian authorship?

Sponheim very sensitively qualifies each of the questions with direct references to my actual development of themes in *KAT*. But I must confess that these questions shocked me awake and at first disturbed me, since I had not anticipated this kind of interpretation of these basic terms. On reflection, I have come to several (tentative) conclusions.

On a general level, human *failure, need* of God, and *recovery* of self must be seen and understood as *inclusive* terms or concepts that comprehend both Religiousness A and Religiousness B (and the latter in its presentations by both Climacus and Anti-Climacus). These terms and their inclusiveness are implied and assumed throughout both the first and second authorships – although in a bewildering variety of languages and at diverse levels of clarity and self-consciousness on Kierkegaard's part, and obviously in no systematic way.

Defiance "before God" and especially "before Christ" is the ultimate form of failure, that began in that most ambiguous state of innocence/guilt that emerges from angst. Acceptance of that "special" grace of God that comes in and with Jesus as the Christ is the ultimate form of need, that began in nothing but a vague sense of longing for the infinite/eternal immanent within every human being. The gift of a new self, reborn as a new creation out of the death of the old, is the ultimate form of recovery, that began as an agonized hope that the sense of undefined but infinite dignity and worth that is affirmed by the eternal within might be true. In these two volumes, I have tried to show that the pilgrimage from the first forms to the last forms is one that involves strange, various, difficult, dangerous, and agonizing discontinuities, and yet is also one that reveals wondrous, affirming, and rescuing continuities.[1]

But more specifically, the crucial point is this: unless we see and affirm – *on Kierkegaard's own terms* – this inclusiveness and continuity, then we are left with the position of accepting, literally and without qualification, all of Kierkegaard's statements (in Part Two of *Sickness*) of the *exclusive* uniqueness of Christian revelation of sin, of Christian possibility of forgiveness and faith-through-grace, of Christian new life of self in obedience and imitation of Christ the Prototype. And then the only possible conclusion would be: Part Two of *Sickness* cancels the validity of Part One as something that is accessible to general human nature, and in fact negates the entire conception of Religiousness A as developed by Johannes Climacus in both *Fragments* and *Postscript* – a conclusion that Van Harvey clearly asserted in the meeting in New Orleans.

If this conclusion is accepted as true, then I have no option but to put a stamp on the title page of every copy of *Kierkegaard as Humanist*, in bold red letters, reading as follows:

WARNING!

THIS ENTIRE VOLUME IS TO BE READ

AS NOTHING BUT

HOKUM – IRONY – A JOKE

But I do not accept this conclusion, because I hold to the principle enunciated by Climacus toward the end of *Postscript*, that

Religiousness A must first be present in the individual before there can be any consideration of becoming aware of the dialectical B. When the individual in the most decisive expression of existential pathos relates to an eternal blessedness, then there can be consideration of becoming aware of how the dialectical in the second place (*secundo loco*) thrusts one down into the pathos of the absurd. Thus it is evident how foolish it is if a person without pathos wants to relate to the essentially-Christian, because before there can be any question at all of

1. See the analysis of the variety of transitions in *Kierkegaard as Humanist*, first in the section of chapter 6 entitled "The Leap as Transition from Ethical to Religious." See also the index entries under "faith, and the leap" but adding pp. 298–309, 402–403; also index entries under "leap, in the transition." And in this volume I have repeatedly tried to show how the uniquely Christian experience of sin and reconciliation is both continuous and discontinuous with Religiousness A, and how the dangerous discontinuity of faith is matched by the wondrous continuity of love.

simply being in the situation where one *can* become aware of it, one must first of all exist in Religiousness A [emphasis added].[2]

And I believe that Kierkegaard also holds to this principle in the second (Christian) authorship. As I have pointed out before, when he (in May of 1855) said that he had "left behind me ... that view of Christianity" which he had developed in *Postscript,* he said that he had done so "in order to get *further* forward in the direction of discovering the Christianity of the New Testament" (emphasis added). In other words, what he develops in the second authorship is an intensification of what he had spelled out as Johannes Climacus, because "I do not find it silly for one to hold that view of Christianity." Indeed, a month earlier he lumps *Concluding Postscript* along with *Sickness unto Death* and *Practice in Christianity* as books that provide the "introductory knowledge" that is desirable for "the instant" (*Øieblikket*), that is, the moment of crisis and judgment that the established church faces if it will now see itself "before God" as revealed in New Testament terms.[3] Even as early as 1849 (after completion of *Sickness* and *Practice*), he says (in his journals) that "the Christian-religious is a unique sphere where the aesthetic relation reappears but paradoxically (as I have so often pointed out in *Concluding Postscript*)." So Christians are called not to admire Christ but to imitate him, with Christ's help of course.[4]

The point is that, if we use failure, need, and recovery as our inclusive terms, it is possible to show how these entry-level spiritual realities serve as the necessary ground for the occurrence of the peculiarly Christian consciousness-of-sin, grace, and new birth. But if we begin with the depiction and statement of the full-blown Christian realities of sin-consciousness, reconciliation by grace, and new life in Christ, it is difficult if not impossible to to take seriously the need to describe how they assume and require passage through the "existential pathos" of the universally human experiences of failure, of need of the eternal, and of the possibility of recovery of one's lost self – indeed, how they assume that that existential pathos *remains* an operative element within Christian faith/life.

And this point is not an "apologetic" one (defending the faith against attack from unbelievers) which falls away and loses its significance once

2. *Postscript,* pp. 494–495; (KW 12.1:556–557); SV 10:226; (7:486).

3. See Walter Lowrie's collection and translation of articles published by Kierkegaard in *Fatherland: Kierkegaard's Attack upon "Christendom" 1854–1855,* pp. 52, 40–41.

4. *Journals,* 4454, X¹ A 134; also cf. 4456, X² A 80 (1849).

one has entered faith. It is a substantive point concerning the ultimate correspondence and interdependence between the given universally-human and the particular realization of that humanity in its Christian configuration. Even Karl Barth, with his totally and rigorously Christological orientation, makes this point unequivocally. It sounds again and again throughout his four big volumes on the doctrine of creation.

In § 41 of his *Church Dogmatics* he develops his basic thesis of "The Creation as the External Ground of the Covenant." In § 42 ("The Yes of God the Creator") he says that "created being has, so to speak, its bright side" composed of a variety of things such as the sun shining, blossoms and fruit, pleasing shapes and sounds, purposeful order, intelligible elements that "enlighten the thoughts of the created mind, speak to the heart of the human-being, and correspond and accommodate to [the human's] will-for-life [*Lebenswillen*]." Of course, the justification of creation that comes from God alone "is not identical with this Yes" of God, but it "affirms" it and "encloses it within itself." Hence "a positive judgment concerning the creation [*das Seiende*] has its foundation and its rightful place. Also, recognition of its direct and immanent goodness is unquestionably demanded of the one whom the creator of existence [*Daseins*] confronts with Himself through His revelation."[5]

Then, in § 45 Barth asserts that the human being as created by God has a fundamental character in-and-for-itself, namely, "to exist for one's fellow-humanbeing," what Barth calls our *Mitmenschlichkeit.* Concerning this phenomenon he says,

What we have called this secret of humanity can be present and known in varying degrees of perfection or imperfection even where there can be no question of a direct revelation and knowledge of Jesus Christ. This reality of human nature and its recognition are not, therefore, restricted to the Christian community, to the 'children of light,' but, as we are told in Lk 16:8, the 'children of this world' may in this respect be wiser than the children of light, being more human, and knowing more about the truly-human [*das Menschliche*], than the often very inhuman and therefore foolish Christians.[6]

In other words, this approach to Christian theology through the concepts of failure, need, recovery, like Kierkegaard's original "anthropological contemplation" that eventually came to include the dimension

5. Karl Barth, CD 3–1:370–371; KD 3–1:424.
6. CD 3–2:276; KD 3–2:332.

of Religiousness A, does not mean for *me* that this present volume is more "anthropological" than "Christological." Like Kierkegaard, I do not believe that "Christology precedes soteriology," but neither do I maintain that "soteriology precedes Christology."[7] Rather, I have tried to show repeatedly that Kierkegaard rightly refuses to think in these terms, but describes the emergence of the Christian spiritual reality of the faith/love relation of an individual with God-in-Christ in terms of a circle or spiral (see index below). In other words, for Kierkegaard, it is impossible to formulate either a Christology or a soteriology "first." Hence, everything Kierkegaard has to say (as I interpret him in chapters 2, 3, and 4 above) about my self as a "gift," as a "failure," as in "need" of the eternal is Christological through and through.

I must admit that, in one critical case, I failed to abide by this principle of the basic correspondence and interdependence of Kierkegaard's anthropology and theology. After getting deep into the materials of chapter 3 concerning human failure, I became aware that I should have included some consideration of the nature of despair within the perspective of "Kierkegaard as humanist" – just as I had included the topic of love. At least to recognize this issue, I did include in chapter 3 above a significant section entitled "Despair as a New Category in the Authorship." There I address specifically the question of how much of the analysis of despair in *Sickness* is accessible to what Kierkegaard calls "the natural human-being," and whether his depiction of despair amounts to a denial of his pre-*Corsair* view of human nature and the validity of Religiousness A. I specify certain materials in *Sickness* that modify the apparent exclusivity of some of his language.

I also raise the issue (following note 119 in chapter 3) of what effect a real openness to conversation with the world's religions might have on some of Kierkegaard's views. And as an example (following note 192 in

7. See David Gouwens' discussion of this issue in "ontological" versus "epistemological" terms in *Kierkegaard as Religious Thinker*, pp. 144–146. I believe that it is dangerous if not catastrophic for the Christian community to claim that it can take an "ontological" position on this matter that for one single instant ignores the epistemological character of every belief and every formulation of that belief. As I point out in chapter 1 above (following note 99), Kierkegaard rejects the traditional distinction between the Person of Christ and the Work of Christ. And later I also show how Kierkegaard insists that we are *always* confronted by the ambiguity of the paradoxical presence of the divine in the most humble human form possible, and hence we should reject every tendency to assume a church triumphant (in opening section of chapter 4: "The Dialectic of the Human-Divine in Encounter with God"). Hence I think that Gouwens goes too far when he says that Kierkegaard's "othodox Christology begins with Christ's identity as Redeemer and Pattern" (pp. 144–145).

chapter 3), I suggest that the spirituality involved in being in despair "over oneself or of the eternal" is much more widespread in various cultural expressions and religions of the world than Kierkegaard ever realized. This correspondence or similarity of spirituality among the religions and philosophies of the world does not mean that they all mean the same thing and can be coalesced into a unified perspective and description. The nature of a Christian "sin consciousness" and the nature of a Christian understanding of love – as spelled out by Kierkegaard – have a uniqueness that can only be experienced through a particular piety or "practice" of confession, forgiveness, and reconciliation. They cannot be shared through a purely conceptual analysis and explication or by a comparison with corresponding elements in another religion, philosophy, or psychology.

However, these unique, particular elements of Christian faith *can* be and *are* shared with and learned by those who are strangers to this tradition. And the unique particularity of various forms of Eastern contemplation, meditation, yoga, etc. *can* be and *are* shared with and learned by many who are sincere and serious Christians. The results are always enrichment. How is this possible? As Karl Barth implies, there remains an inherent need and structure in universal human nature for the coming of the divine, eternal spirit, in spite of all human failure and degradation. But unlike Barth who brands *all* religions as idolatrous in comparison with Christian "revelation," Kierkegaard proposes a basic correspondence between a universal, human Religiousness A and the particularity of a Christian Religiousness B.

I for one maintain that that correspondence holds for Religiousness B as spelled out in his attempt "to get further forward in the direction of discovering the Christianity of the New Testament" in his second authorship. In all the writings from *Upbuilding Discourses in Various Spirits* to *Judge for Yourself!* there are very diverse perspectives on this issue of correspondence. And in these two volumes there has not been a concerted and thorough attempt to characterize and to interrelate this diversity. Whether these materials support or deny a fundamental correspondence between Kierkegaard as humanist and Kierkegaard as theologian needs to be further explored. So perhaps I am not through with Kierkegaard after all. One thing is clear to me: both humanist and theologian agree that in failure and despair, the human self has been deformed and is wandering in exile from the truth, but that the potentiality of selfhood, given by God, has not been annihilated. It needs be set free and recovered and set on the way toward its fulfillment – all with the help of God.

Bibliography

PRIMARY SOURCES

Danish

Søren Kierkegaards Papirer. First edition, edited by P.A. Heiberg and V. Kuhr. Copenhagen: Gyldendalske Boghandel, 1912.
- Second enlarged edition, 25 volumes or part-volumes, edited by Niels Thulstrup. Copenhagen: Gyldendal, 1968.
- Electronic Text of *Kierkegaards Papirer A*. Ten mg., edited by Alastair McKinnon. Montreal: Inter Editions, 1993.
Søren Kierkegaards Samlede Værker. First edition, 15 volumes, edited by A.B. Drachmann, J.L. Heiberg, and H.O. Lange. Copenhagen: Gyldendalske Boghandel, 1901 ff.
- Third edition, 20 volumes, edited by Peter P. Rohde. Copenhagen: Gyldendal, 1962.
- Electronic Text of 3rd edition of *Søren Kierkegaards Samlede Værker*. Sixteen mg., edited by Alastair McKinnon. Montreal: Inter Editions, 1988.
- Electronic Text of 3rd edition of *Søren Kierkegaards Samlede Værker*. Twelve mg., edited by Alastair McKinnon. Clayton, Georgia: InteLex Corporation, 1990.

English Translation of Søren Kierkegaards Papirer

Søren Kierkegaard's Journal and Papers. Seven volumes, edited and translated by Howard V. Hong and Edna H. Hong, assisted by Gregor Malantschuk. Bloomington: Indiana University Press, 1967–1978.

English Translations of Søren Kierkegaards Samlede Værker

THE SERIES *KIERKEGAARD'S WRITINGS*
Edited by Howard V. Hong and Edna H. Hong. Published in Princeton by Princeton Univerity Press. Translations are by Howard and Edna Hong unless otherwise noted. The series is incomplete as of date of publication of this book.

KW 1: *Early Polemical Writings*. Trans. by Julia Watkin. 1990.

KW 2: *The Concept of Irony*. 1989.

KW 3: *Either/Or,* Part I. 1987.

KW 4: *Either/Or,* Part II. 1987.

KW 5: *Eighteen Upbuilding Discourses*. 1990.

KW 6: *Fear and Trembling; Repetition*. 1983.

KW 7: *Philosophical Fragments; Johannes Climacus*. 1985.

KW 8: *The Concept of Anxiety*. Trans. by Reidar Thomte in collaboration with Albert B. Anderson. 1980.

KW 9: *Prefaces*. (not yet published)

KW 10: *Three Discourses on Imagined Occasions*. 1993.

KW 11: *Stages on Life's Way*. 1988.

KW 12: *Concluding Unscientific Postscript to Philosophical Fragments*. 1992.

KW 13: *The Corsair Affair*. 1982.

KW 14: *Two Ages: A Literary Review*. 1978.

KW 15: *Upbuilding Discourses in Various Spirits*. 1993.

KW 16: *Works of Love*. 1995.

KW 17: *Christian Discourses; The Crisis and a Crisis in the Life of an Actress* (not yet published).

KW 18: *Without Authority; The Lily of the Field and the Bird of the Air; Two Minor Ethical-Religious Essays; Three Discourses at the Communion on Fridays; An Upbuilding Discourse; Two Discourses at the Communion on Fridays*. (not yet published)

KW 19: *The Sickness unto Death*. 1980.

KW 20: *Practice in Christianity*. 1991.

KW 21: *For Self-Examination; Judge for Yourself!* 1990.

KW 22: *The Point of View: The Point of View for My Work as an Author; Armed Neutrality; On My Work as an Author*. (not yet published)

KW 23: *The Moment and Late Writings: Articles from* Fædrelandet; *The Moment; This Must be Said, So Let It Be Said; Christ's Judgment on Official Christianity; The Unchangeableness of God*. (not yet published)

KW 24: *The Book on Adler*. (not yet published)

KW 25: *Letters and Documents*. Trans. by Henrik Rosenmeier. 1978.

KW 26: *Cumulative Index*. (not yet published)

OTHER ENGLISH TRANSLATIONS
These were used in the writing of this book. They are listed in chronological order, as is roughly done in KW, but here the chronology followed is that of the actual composition of the works as worked out by Niels Jørgen Cappelørn and
Alastair McKinnon and published in *Kierkegaardiana* 9, 1974, pp. 133–146.

The Concept of Irony. Trans. by Lee M. Capel. Bloomington: Indiana University
Press, 1968; Second Printing, 1992.
Either/Or, Vol. 1. Trans. by David F. Swenson and Lillian Marvin Swenson with
revisions by Howard A. Johnson. Garden City, New York: Doubleday Anchor
Books, 1959.
Either/Or, Vol. 2. Trans. by Walter Lowrie with revisions by Howard A. Johnson.
Garden City, New York: Doubleday Anchor Books, 1959.
Fear and Trembling. Trans. by Walter Lowrie. Garden City, New York: Doubleday
Anchor Books, 1954.
Philosophical Fragments. Trans. by David F. Swenson. Princeton: Princeton Univer-
sity Press, 1942.
– Trans. by David F. Swenson, revised by Howard V. Hong. Princeton: Princeton
University Press, 1962.
The Concept of Dread. Trans. by Walter Lowrie. Princeton: Princeton University
Press, 1957.
*Thoughts on Crucial Situations in Human Life: Three Discourses on Imagined Occa-
sions.* Trans. by David F. Swenson. Minneapolis: Augsburg Publishing House,
1941.
Stages on Life's Way. Trans. by Walter Lowrie. New York: Schocken Books, 1967.
Concluding Unscientific Postscript. Trans. by David F. Swenson and Walter Lowrie.
Princeton: Princeton University Press, 1941, 1974.
The Present Age. Trans. by Alexander Dru. New York: Harper Torchbooks, 1962.
This is a translation of less than half of Kierkegaard's work entitled *Two Ages: A
Literary Review* (KW 14).
The Present Age and Two Minor Ethico-Religious Treatises. Trans. by Alexander Dru
and Walter Lowrie. London: Oxford University Press, 1949.
The following three books are translations of parts 1, 2, and 3 respectively of
Upbuilding Discourses in Various Spirits (KW 15):
Purity of Heart. Trans. by Douglas V. Steere. New York: Harper Torchbooks,
1938, 1948.
Consider the Lilies. Trans. by A.S. Aldworth and W.S. Ferrie. London: C.W. Daniel
Co., 1940.
Gospel of Sufferings. Trans. by A.S. Aldworth and W.S. Ferrie. Cambridge,
England: James Clarke and Co., 1955, 1982.

On Authority and Revelation: The Book on Adler. Trans. by Walter Lowrie. Princeton: Princeton University Press, 1955. (Not in *sv* but in *Papirer* VII², pp. 3–230.)

Works of Love. Trans. by Howard and Edna Hong. New York: Harper Torchbooks, 1962.

Of the Difference Between a Genius and an Apostle (with *The Present Age*, trans. by Alexander Dru. New York: Harper Torchbooks, 1962). This item is one of *Two Minor Ethical-Religious Essays* written in 1847. The other essay, *Has A Man the Right to Let Himself Be Put to Death for the Truth?*, trans. by Walter Lowrie, may be found in the British edition of Dru's *The Present Age*: London: Oxford University Press, 1940.

Christian Discourses. Trans. by Walter Lowrie. New York: Oxford University Press, 1961.

The Sickness unto Death (with *Fear and Trembling* as listed above). Trans. by Walter Lowrie. Garden City, New York: Doubleday Anchor Books, 1954. (Referenced in notes.)

– Trans. by Alastair Hannay. London: Penguin Books, 1989.

Training in Christianity. Trans. by Walter Lowrie. Princeton: Princeton University Press, 1944.

The Lilies of the Field and the Birds of the Air of 1849 (with *Christian Discourses* as listed above). Trans. by Walter Lowrie. New York: Oxford University Press, 1961.

Three Discourses at the Communion on Fridays: The High Priest – The Publican – The Sinner (with *Christian Discourses* as listed above). Trans. by Walter Lowrie. New York: Oxford University Press, 1961.

The Point of View for My Work as an Author and *My Work as an Author.* Trans. by Walter Lowrie. New York: Harper Torchbooks, 1962.

For Self-Examination. Trans. by Edna and Howard Hong. Minneapolis: Augsburg Publishing House, 1959.

Armed Neutrality and *An Open Letter.* Trans. by Howard and Edna Hong. New York: Simon and Schuster, 1968.

Kierkegaard's Attack upon Christendom. Trans. by Walter Lowrie. Boston: Beacon Press, 1959.

SELECTED SECONDARY SOURCES

Barrett, Lee C. "The Paradox of Faith in Kierkegaard's *Philosophical Fragments*," in *International Kierkegaard Commentary: Philosophical Fragments and Johannes Climacus*, Robert L. Perkins, editor. Macon, Georgia: Mercer University Press, 1994.

Cole, J. Preston. *The Problematic Self in Kierkegaard and Freud.* New Haven: Yale University Press, 1971.

Come, Arnold B. "Kierkegaard's Method: Does He Have One?", in *Kierkegaardiana*, Vol. XIV (1988), pp. 14–28.

– *Trendelenburg's Influence on Kierkegaard's Modal Categories.* Montreal: Inter Editions, 1991.

– *Kierkegaard as Humanist: Discovering My Self.* Montreal: McGill-Queen's University Press, 1995.

Dupré, Louis. *Kierkegaard as Theologian.* London: Sheed and Ward, 1964. Originally published as *Kierkegaard's Theologie,* Antwerp: De Standard, 1958.

Evans, C. Stephen. *Passionate Reason.* Bloomington: Indiana University Press, 1992.

Ferreira, M. Jamie. *Transforming Vision.* Oxford: Clarendon Press, 1991.

Gouwens, David J. *Kierkegaard's Dialectic of the Imagination.* New York: P. Lang, 1989.

– *Kierkegaard as Religious Thinker.* Cambridge: Cambridge University Press, 1996.

Hannay, Alastair. *Kierkegaard.* London: Routledge & Kegan Paul, 1982.

Heschel, Abraham. *A Passion for Truth.* Woodstock, Vermont: Jewish Lights Publishing, 1995.

Kirmmse, Bruce H. "Psychology and and Society: The Social Falsification of the Self in *The Sickness unto Death,*" in *Kierkegaard's Truth: The Disclosure of the Self,* Joseph H. Smith, editor. New Haven: Yale University Press, 1981.

– *Kierkegaard in Golden Age Denmark.* Bloomington: Indiana University Press, 1990.

Lowrie, Walter. *Kierkegaard.* London: Oxford University Press, 1938.

Mackey, Louis. *Kierkegaard: A Kind of Poet.* Philadelphia: University of Pennsylvania Press, 1971.

Malantschuk, Gregor. *Fra Individ til den Enkelte.* Copenhagen: C.A. Reitzels Boghandel, 1978.

McKinnon, Alastair. *Kierkegaard Indices.* Leiden: E.J. Brill, 1970–73.

Meissner, W.W. "Subjectivity in Psychoanalysis," in *Kierkegaard's Truth: The Disclosure of the Self,* Joseph H. Smith, editor. New Haven: Yale University Press, 1981.

Mooney, Edward F. *Selves in Discord and Resolve: Kierkegaard's Moral-Religious Psychology from* Either/Or *to* Sickness Unto Death. London: Routledge, 1996.

Rohde, H.P., ed. *Auktionsprotokol over Søren Kierkegaards Bogsamling* and *The Auctioneer's Sales Record of the Library of Søren Kierkegaard,* trans. by Helen Fogh. København: Det Kongelige Bibliotek, 1967.

Smith, Joseph H. ed. *Kierkegaard's Truth: The Disclosure of the Self.* New Haven: Yale University Press, 1981.

Sponheim, Paul. *Kierkegaard on Christ and Christian Coherence.* London: S.C.M. Press, 1968.

Taylor, Mark C. *Journeys to Selfhood: Hegel and Kierkegaard.* Berkeley: University of California Press, 1980.

Thompson, Josiah. *Kierkegaard.* London: Victor Gollancz, 1974.

Thulstrup, Niels. *Kierkegaard's Relation to Hegel.* Princeton: Princeton University Press, 1980. Trans. by George. L. Stengren of *Kierkegaards Forhold til Hegel.* Copenhagen: Gyldendal, 1967.

Walsh, Sylvia. "On 'Feminine' and 'Masculine' Forms of Despair," in *International Kierkegaard Commentary: The Sickness unto Death,* Robert L. Perkins, editor. Macon, Georgia: Mercer University Press, 1987.

– *Living Poetically: Kierkegaard's Existential Aesthetics.* University Park, PA.: The Pennsylvania State University Press, 1994.

Westphal, Merold. *Kierkegaard's Critique of Reason and Society.* Macon: Mercer University Press, 1987.

RELATED SOURCES

Barth, Karl. *Church Dogmatics* (12 part-volumes). Edinburgh: T. and T. Clark, 1936–1962; Vol. 1–1, 2nd edition, 1975. *Kirchliche Dogmatik* (12 part-volumes). Zürich: Evangelischer Verlag AG., 1955–1959.

– *Die Menschlichkeit Gottes.* Zürich: Evangelischer Verlag AG., 1956. Trans. by John Newton Thomas, *The Humanity of God.* Richmond: John Knox Press, 1960.

Bonhoeffer, Dietrich. *Schöpfung und Fall.* München: Chr. Kaiser Verlag, 1955. *Creation and Fall.* New York: Macmillan, 1959.

Buber, Martin. *Eclipse of God.* New York: Harper & Brothers, 1952.

Cobb, John B. *Christ in a Pluralistic Age.* Philadelphia: Westminster Press, 1975.

Come, Arnold B. *An Introduction to Barth's Dogmatics for Preachers.* Philadelphia: Westminster Press, 1963.

Dam, Poul. *Nikolaj Frederik Severin Grundtvig*; trans. by Reginald Spink. Copenhagen: Royal Danish Ministry of Foreign Affairs, Press and Cultural Relations Department, 1983.

Habermas, Jürgen. *Legitimation Crisis.* Boston: Beacon Press, 1975.

Reznor, Trent. *Nine Inch Nails,* as recorded by Nothing/TVT/Interscope Records. New York: Atlantic Recording Company, 1994.

Reist, Benjamin A. *Processive Revelation.* Louisville: Westminster/John Knox Press, 1992.

Rosenstock, Gershon G. *F. A. Trendelenburg: Forerunner of John Dewey.* Carbondale: Southern Illinois University Press, 1964.

Tillich, Paul. *Systematic Theology, Volume I.* Chicago: University of Chicago Press, 1951.

– *The Courage To Be.* New Haven: Yale University Press, 1952.

– *Biblical Revelation and the Quest for Ultimate Reality*. Chicago: University of Chicago Press, 1955.

Trendelenburg, Adolph. *Logische Untersuchungen*. 1st ed. Berlin: 1840; 3d ed. Leipzig: Verlag von S. Hirzel, 1870.

– *Geschichte der Kategorienlehre*. Berlin: 1846.

Whitehead, Alfred North. *Adventure of Ideas*. New York: Macmillan, 1937.

– *Process and Reality*, corrected edition by David Ray Griffin and Donald W. Shelburne. New York: The Free Press, Macmillan, 1979.

Wollheim, Richard. *Freud*. London: Fontana Press, 1973.

Index